The Novel and the Menagerie

Totality, Englishness, and Empire

KURT KOENIGSBERGER

The Ohio State University Press
Columbus

Copyright © 2007 by The Ohio State University.
All rights reserved.

Library of Congress Cataloging-in-Publication Data

Koenigsberger, Kurt.
 The novel and the menagerie : totality, Englishness, and empire / Kurt Koenigsberger.
   p. cm.
 Includes bibliographical references (p.) and index.
  ISBN 978-0-8142-1057-4 (cloth : alk. paper) — ISBN 978-0-8142-9136-8 (cd-rom) 1. English fiction—19th century—History and criticism. 2. English fiction—20th century—History and criticism. 3. National characteristics, English, in literature. 4. Identity (Philosophical concept) in literature. 5. Whole and parts (Philosophy) in literature. 6. Literature and society—Great Britain—History—19th century. 7. Literature and society—Great Britain—History—20th century. 8. Social institutions in literature. 9. Imperialism in literature. I. Title.
  PR878.3557K64 2007
  823'.809358--dc22
                                            2007000236

Paper (ISBN: 978-0-8142-5734-0)

Cover design by Dan O'Dair.
Type set in Minion.

For Aidan

Contents

	List of Illustrations	vii
	Preface	ix
	Acknowledgments	xv
INTRODUCTION	The Novel as Zoo: Animal Stories and English Style	1
CHAPTER 1	Picturing Britannia's Menagerie: The Aesthetics of the Imperial Whole	32
CHAPTER 2	Circuses in Cabinets: The Victorian Novelist as Beast Tamer	82
CHAPTER 3	Elephants in the Labyrinth of Empire: Arnold Bennett, Modernism, and the Menagerie	118
CHAPTER 4	Monsters on the Verandah of Realism: Virginia Woolf's Empire Exhibition	149
CHAPTER 5	The "Anglepoised" Novel after Empire: English Creatures and Postcolonial Exhibition	182
EPILOGUE	Small Islands, Frozen Arks	212
	Notes	219
	Bibliography	245
	Index	261

Illustrations

Figure 1	Queen Elizabeth II and Runga-Rung Elephant, *The Daily Telegraph*, 10 May 2002. *Photograph by Ian Jones/Telegraph Group Limited.*	2
Figure 2	"Mr. Punch's Celebration of Queen Victoria's Jubilee, 1886," *Punch's Almanack for 1886, Punch,* 7 December 1885. *Courtesy Kelvin Smith Library Retrospective Research Collections.*	3
Figure 3	"Punchius Imperator A.D. MDCCCLXXVII," *Punch's Almanack for 1877, Punch,* 14 December 1876. *Courtesy Kelvin Smith Library Retrospective Research Collections.*	8
Figure 4	Sir Edwin Landseer, *Isaac Van Amburgh and His Animals* (1839). *The Royal Collection © 2007 Her Majesty Queen Elizabeth II.*	41
Figure 5	Engraving (ca. 1860) after Sir Edwin Landseer, *Portrait of Mr. Van Amburgh as He Appeared with His Animals at the London Theatre, 1847. Author's collection.*	42
Figure 6	"Wombwell's Menagerie in the Great Quadrangle, Windsor Castle," *The Illustrated London News,* 6 November 1847. *Courtesy Kelvin Smith Library Retrospective Research Collections.*	44
Figure 7	"The Royal Visit to Wombwell's Menagerie," *The Illustrated London News,* 6 November 1847. *Courtesy Kelvin Smith Library Retrospective Research Collections.*	45
Figure 8	Burmese Imperial State Carriage, The Egyptian Hall, 1826. *Permission The British Library (Shelfmark Th.Cts.52).*	56
Figure 9	Map of the World, Colindian Exhibition, 1886. *Permission The British Library (Shelfmark Maps.183.q.1(13)).*	63
Figure 10	John Foley's "Asia," from the Albert Memorial (1872). *Photograph by Kevin Anderson.*	64

Figure 11 "Kaiser–I–Hind," *Punch,* 13 January 1877. *Courtesy Kelvin Smith Library Retrospective Research Collections.* 67

Figure 12 W. L. Champney, "The Blind Men and the Elephant," John Godfrey Saxe, *Clever Stories of Many Nations* (Boston: Ticknor and Fields, 1865). *Courtesy Kelvin Smith Library.* 69

Figure 13 John Lockwood Kipling, "A Peri on a Camel," *Man and Beast in India* (New York: Macmillan, 1892). 73

Figure 14 John Lockwood Kipling, "Krishna on an Elephant," *Man and Beast in India* (London: Macmillan, 1892). 74

Figure 15 "Kaniyajee and the Gopees," Fanny Parks, *Wanderings of a Pilgrim in Search of the Picturesque* (London: Pelham Richardson, 1850). *Permission The British Library (Shelfmark 10055.f.20).* 75

Figure 16 Composite Elephant (n.d.). *Permission Bodleian Library, University of Oxford (Shelfmark MS.Ouseley Add.171b. folio 9 verso).* 76

Figure 17 "Destruction of the Furious Elephant at Exeter Change" (1826). *Permission The British Library (Shelfmark Crach.1.tab.4.b.4/14).* 78

Figure 18 William Makepeace Thackeray, "An Elephant for Sale," illustration to Chapter XVII of *Vanity Fair* (1847–48). 85

Figure 19 "The New Lord Mayor's Show—1850," *The Illustrated London News,* 9 November 1850. *Courtesy Kelvin Smith Library Retrospective Research Collections.* 93

Figure 20 Ad for elephant performances at Astley's, December 1853. Permission The British Library (Shelfmark Playbill 173). 97

Figure 21 Ad for elephants and "Billy Button's Journey to Brentford," 12 January 1854. *Permission The British Library (Shelfmark Playbill 171).* 98

Figure 22 "The Gorgeous East" at Wembley, *The Graphic,* 23 August 1924. *Permission The British Library (Shelfmark NPL Graphic 24–9–1924 pg.282).* 162

Figure 23 Ad for the British Empire Exhibition, Wembley, *The Graphic,* 24 May 1924. *Permission The British Library (Shelfmark NPL Graphic 24–5–1924 pg.834).* 165

Figure 24 English creatures at the London Zoo, August 2005. *Photograph by Gareth Cattermole/Getty Images.* 213

Preface

The historian of the future will probably find one of the great movements of world-history in the forces which are at present making for new ideals of imperial unity throughout the British Empire.
—Programme, *The Festival of Empire and the Pageant of London* (1910)

Mr. Thomas Cook . . . made his countrymen understand what the world was like as a whole. . . . The charm found in Mr. Thomas Cook's narrative is the novelty of the whole.
—W. Fraser Rae, on the story of Thomas Cook and Son travel business (1891)

Britannia has a menagerie that reaches all over the world
She has some animals rich and rare, some treacherous creatures are caged up there.
—"Britannia's Menagerie," music hall standard (ca. 1900)

THE SUBJECT OF THIS BOOK is the imperial animal and its English stories, narratives that foreground the "ideals of imperial unity" and that depend upon a notion of the British Empire as a novel and sometimes charming "whole." The chapters that follow explore the form of the English institutions that collected exotic animals and the shape of the novel in England over the past two centuries. In these pages I trace the precipitous rise and long subsidence of the zoo, menagerie, circus, and colonial exhibition in England, all prime examples of a rich imperial culture of display. These popular ensembles fashioned and framed a range of narrative practices in relation to a prevailing idea of the empire as a comprehensive whole. In its tents, arenas, enclosures, and caravans, the zoological collection managed both alien beasts and their meanings as it advertised, described, and mounted a range of exotic displays that evoked and delineated a burgeoning empire. The menagerie's spaces of exhibition form the backdrop for my explorations of the novel as the distinctive form of English narrative. In particular I describe the novel's constellation around the notion of imperial totality in the nineteenth century, its emphasis upon detotalization of form and imperial frames of reference in the era of aesthetic modernism, and its nostalgia for formal holism and an abolished exotic at the end of the twentieth century. In each chapter, I have sought to open new channels for understanding the novel as part of an ongoing public discourse of imperial totality, and the menagerie as a site of genesis and management of English stories about the empire.

My title gestures toward a fundamental conjunction of the zoological collection and the English novel, but their relation is far from simple; indeed, much of chapter 1 is devoted to mapping the cultural topography of empire in which both institutions took root and flourished. Broadly speaking, though, my approach to the subject emphasizes two primary roles for the collection of zoological exotica. First, the menagerie appears as a cultural form homologous to the novel to the extent that both the novel and the menagerie share a sense of the empire as the preeminent expression of English spirit, but also as something that England's domestic cultures struggle to grasp in its total aspect. In this respect, the novel and the menagerie represent comparable imaginative responses to the empire as a dominant, shaping factor in English daily life. They share important aesthetic strategies and cultural logics, and consequently both the novel and the menagerie are illuminated when we read them *with* one another—the novel as a collection of everyday imaginative practices, and the menagerie as an institution generating and managing narratives of empire. Second, the menagerie mediates the novel's relation to empire and to Englishness. That is, as a popular and distinct site for the production and direction of narratives of empire, the collection of zoological exotica furnishes the novel with material and figures for its own forms and practices. The appearance of the zoo, the circus, a traveling collection of animals, or an individual beast—tiger, elephant, camel, or boa constrictor, for instance—in the novel invites us to read *through* the menagerie to the exotic landscape it evokes and imaginatively maps.

The aim of these pages is less to theorize the movement of the English novel since the Victorian era than to historicize and contextualize some key terms in its traditional theory and practice: "life," "perspective," and especially "totality" or "whole." Though the theory of the novel—especially the theory of the novel as a total object in its form and as a totalizing instrument in its aim—is usually understood to begin in earnest with Henry James's prefaces to his novels, narrative praxis in the nineteenth century implies a set of theoretical principles even when they are not codified in an apology, pamphlet, preface, or review. Indeed, the chief claim I advance here is that the novel, assumed by critics across two centuries to be the essential literary form of the nation, embodies an ongoing imaginative *and* theoretical work related to the imperial system. A correlative to this argument is that when the novel introduces zoological collections in its texts, or collects animals and their stories in its own right, the novel can be understood to explore one of its own key contexts and to engage in an important theoretical enterprise in relation to empire.

The most intense novelistic explorations of what Wilma George calls "zoogeography"[1] in English cultural life took place in the Victorian and modernist periods, and the readings of *The Novel and the Menagerie* are most deeply invested in texts produced in these years. The decades from 1840 to 1930 saw the second British empire spread across the globe and begin to be seriously challenged, both imaginatively and politically. In the realm of the novel, the Victorian years witnessed the consolidation of realist practices in relation to totality as a horizon of possibility. With the gathering front of twentieth-century aesthetic movements and impulses we call modernism, totality—more particularly, *imperial* totality—ceases to be the cynosure around which the novel's theoretical universe revolves. As the final chapter and epilogue suggest, however, the problems of geopolitical totality and of the forms of the novel and zoological exhibition remain significant ones at the beginning of the twenty-first century, long after the official end of empire.

The shift in the practical theorization of the novel in relation to imperial holism from realist totality to modernist detotalization might usefully be characterized in terms of Havelock Ellis's belated treatment of aesthetic decadence. In his 1922 preface to an English translation of J-K Huysmans's *A Rebours* (1889), Ellis characterizes "classic style" as that which subordinates and harmonizes diverse parts in relation to a whole, and under this definition the theory and practice of the realist novel moved increasingly in the direction of the "classic style" in the Victorian period.[2] By contrast, Ellis identifies "decadent style"—a term which he strips of all moral valences—as that which finds the whole overwhelmed by its parts. This formulation of decadence neatly captures both the experience of, for instance, reading James Joyce's *Ulysses* (also published in 1922) for the first time and the prevailing sense of the overwhelming demands (imaginative, economic, and political) the colonies made upon the mother country in the surrounding years. While "classic" and "decadent" remain freighted with moral and literary-historical connotations that make these terms unconducive to redeployment, Georges Bataille's distinction between "restricted" and "general" economies marks a similar distinction to that drawn by Ellis between systems that can be characterized by principles of holism, conservation, meaning, and integration on one hand, and those marked by loss, expenditure, and constant dissolution of limits on the other. Bataille's distinction remains relatively unencumbered by deep-rooted aesthetic or moral prejudices, and consequently in the following pages I deploy the coordinates of "restricted" and "general" economy to map the shift in English novelistic practice first over the course of the Victorian, Edwardian, and Georgian eras, and then from modernism to postmodernism. Bataille's terms also usefully translate into theoretical coordinates a set of aesthetic categories that recur across these pages—for instance, the picturesque which frames up or delineates complete views of empire, and the carnivalesque which confuses and breaches boundaries of domestic and exotic, English and imperial.

The chief contribution *The Novel and the Menagerie* seeks to make to the study of narrative is to historicize the notion of totality in the theory and practice of the English novel, not to offer anything like a beast-theory of Victorian, modernist, or postmodernist narrative *per se*. That is, while I contend that the relation of the English novels treated here to the collection of zoological exotica does important theoretical work in imagining and reconceiving the formal contours of the empire as a whole, it is not the case that all narratives in this period are assimilable to the genre. In exploring narrative praxis in the novel by reading totality along what Susan Stanford Friedman calls the "geopolitical axis" of modern cultural formation[3]—in particular, recuperating imperial zoogeography as a crucial context for English stories—I envision the novel not only as responding and contributing to the situation of colonialism but also as part of a large-scale movement, collective rather than individual, to imagine the form of the empire. Edward Said notes that "the British empire integrated and fused things within it, and . . . made the world one,"[4] but his formulations uncritically accept the invitation of the imperial discourses that promoted the empire's integration. For all the critical value of seeing global connectedness as an important consequence of integrative imperial cultural practices, criticism has yet to pause over the collective discourse of imperial totality itself, especially in its various English instantiations. To this extent, *The Novel and the Menagerie* seeks to resist the languages of individual "otherness." Instead, thinking the novel's relation to empire in the menagerie's terms discourages an atomistic Hegelian language of "otherness," replacing it with a rhetoric of shared and widespread cultural work. The discourses of imperial totality that underpinned common cultural practices like those of the menagerie and the novel appear primarily as social rather than psychological formations.

In concentrating on the national as a cardinal social formation, this book participates in recent discussions about Englishness to the extent that both the novel and the menagerie are institutions that put English identities and characters on display and seek overtly or implicitly to narrate their relation to empire. In "What Is a Nation?" (1883) Ernest Renan proposed the nation as "a large-scale solidarity" and "a daily plebiscite," outlining a notion of the nation that depends upon the ongoing imaginative work of its constituents.[5] The fact of empire clearly complicates this formulation: when the empire itself is conceived as both an extension of England *and* an integrated whole in its own right, how does Englishness appear when understood to form just a part of this whole? What distinguishes it from Britishness or from Anglo-Indianness? While recent books like Ian Baucom's *Out of Place* (1999) and Jed Esty's *A Shrinking Island* (2004) have broached such questions in the context of English writing in the twilight of empire, none has taken up the question of totality and the relation of parts to whole that both the menagerie and the novel require us to think.

Each of these robust narrative forms grapples in its own way with questions of Englishness as a part of empire and as a whole in itself. As the following pages demonstrate, the exhibition of zoological exotica represents an ongoing and immediate negotiation, delineation, and construction of Englishness and empire (what Homi Bhabha calls the "performative" aspect of national formation), while writing about the English circus, zoo, and menagerie describes an institutional history of the relationship of Englishness to empire (what Bhabha describes as the "pedagogical" aspect of nationhood).[6] Navigating the novel's interventions in the context of imperial exhibitionary cultures, and thinking them through the mediating channels of the menagerie, means that the novel and the menagerie each triangulate a key set of other terms. The novel finally enables us to see the way in which the menagerie's zoological narratives put into perspective relations of Englishness and empire, while the menagerie's collections draw into sharper focus the novel's means of negotiating the crucial questions of imperial and postimperial Englishness. This pair of triangulations appears rich, dynamic, and varied over the past century and a half, and claims the attention of the pages that follow.

Acknowledgments

I owe a great deal to my teachers and colleagues at Vanderbilt University who fostered this project along in its earliest stages, especially Mark Wollaeger, Jay Clayton, Mark Schoenfield, Vereen Bell, Simona Sawhney, J. David Macey, Jr., Tom Haddox, Dan Hipp, and Eliza R. L. McGraw. At Case Western Reserve University, the College of Arts and Sciences and the Baker-Nord Center for the Humanities provided crucial travel grants that enabled the completion of archival work. I am grateful to the Kelvin Smith Library at Case for assisting in my heavy use of its Retrospective Research Collections and for timely help preparing images.

Colleagues at Case Western Reserve who offered careful commentary and much-needed conversation on drafts of chapters include Brian Ballentine, Tim Beal, Tom Bishop, Darcy Brandel, Jonathan Sadowsky, Rob Spadoni, Gary Lee Stonum, Thrity Umrigar, Athena Vrettos, and Angela Woollacott. Their indulgence—and temperance—of my many scholarly flights of fancy has made Case an ideal environment in which to write such a book. Beyond Cleveland and its environs, I am grateful to Kevin Anderson, Melba Cuddy-Keane, David Damrosch, Tom Koenigsberger, Jennifer Nesbitt, Doug Payne, Jim Phelan, John Potter, Peter Rabinowitz, and John Shapcott for crucial suggestions, corrections, and challenges to the arguments on offer here. The expert advice of The Ohio State University Press's anonymous readers corralled a loose, baggy monster and made it much the fitter for show.

Three people deserve special thanks for the way they have fundamentally shaped not only this project but my orientation to it. Martha Woodmansee pushed me daily to think beyond the bounds of the traditional canons and methods of English studies. Chris Flint offered not just unwavering confidence in the project and its author, but also sound advice, good cheer, and the occasional address of a defunct London pub. I am most deeply indebted to Kim Emmons, kettle to my pot in so many ways. Her exceptional generosity and constant friendship have not only made this project far better but quite literally carried it across the finish line.

My family, near and far alike, deserve thanks for their support along the way. Kristin especially has suffered this project, and the academic menagerie in which it finds its place, with great patience. Her imagination and strength have kept things whole along the way. This book is dedicated to Aidan, an inspired addition to our collection. He is always up for a visit to the zoo and, like his dad, always wants to see the elephants first.

An earlier version of chapter 3 originally appeared in *Twentieth Century Literature* 49, no. 2 (Summer 2003) and is reprinted here by permission of *TCL*. Select passages in chapters 1 and 5 originally appeared under the title "Of Blind Men and Elephants: Globalization and the Image" in *Genre: Forms of Discourse and Culture* 36, nos. 3–4 (Fall/Winter 2003), a special issue on "Globalization and the Image" edited by Kurt Koenigsberger. Those passages are reprinted here by permission of *Genre* and the University of Oklahoma. A condensed version of a portion of chapter 4 is scheduled to appear in *Locating Woolf: The Politics of Space and Place*, ed. Michael Whitworth and Anna Snaith (London: Palgrave, 2007).

INTRODUCTION

The Novel as Zoo

Animal Stories and English Style

Imperial Entanglements

IN THE SPRING OF 2002, a remarkable spectacle in the London borough of Newham stirred the imagination of British print media and emerged as a highlight of Queen Elizabeth's royal Jubilee progress across Great Britain. As a 10 May article in *The Daily Telegraph* reported, "A giant mechanical elephant, a Bollywood band and a crowd of people of all races and creeds waving the Union flag ensured the Queen a unique welcome to East London yesterday" (fig. 1).[1] The Queen's Golden Jubilee and her national tour served as occasions for the collection and production of stories about England and Englishness, and the moment in Newham generated a narrative of its own. The *Times* of London foregrounded the Queen's encounter with "the kaleidoscopic ethnic mix of the East End of London," construing the "almost life-size tin elephant, electrically propelled on wheels" as an emblem of the changing face of the nation over the half-century of Elizabeth's reign.[2] "When she ascended the throne in 1952, Britain was an overwhelmingly white nation," the paper noted, but the fantastic figure of the elephant "underlined the largest social change of the Queen's reign" by indicating the extent to which the nation had become polychromatic. In telling such stories about the shifting composition of England, newspaper reports understood the brilliant elephant in Newham to signal not only Britain's postmillennial multiculturalism but also a fashionable global significance that the East Enders imparted to England's sovereign: because she was escorted by the motorized elephant, the *Times* observed, "the Queen arrived in style."

Figure 1. Queen Elizabeth II and Runga-Rung Elephant, *The Daily Telegraph*, 10 May 2002. *Photograph by Ian Jones/Telegraph Group Limited.*

Over the past two centuries displays of zoological exotica like the tin elephant in the East End have lent style and form to stories of daily life in England's familiar spaces, and to the novel in particular. The remarkable display in Newham appeared uncanny, not because it was in any way unsettling but because it was "in reality nothing new or alien, but something which is familiar and old-established in the mind and which has become alienated from it."[3] For Freud, the experience of the uncanny marks the disturbing entanglement of the alien and the "old-established," the homely and the outlandish. The fascinating conjunction of elephant and Queen in Newham likewise mingled the exotic with the familiar, the domestic with the alien, but it was not as unique as media like the *Daily Telegraph* might have wished. It in fact reprised a history of royal entanglements with exotic animals over a century before Elizabeth II's reign amidst an era of multiethnic "style" in England: before she acceded to the throne, Princess Victoria was a patron of the Surrey Zoological Gardens, which housed her favorite monkey, Jocko; as Queen, Victoria and her family regularly attended spectacles that capitalized upon the exhibition

Figure 2. "Mr. Punch's Celebration of Queen Victoria's Jubilee, 1886," *Punch's Almanack for 1886*, *Punch*, 7 December 1885. *Courtesy Kelvin Smith Library Retrospective Research Collections.*

of exotic beasts and people; in 1871 a parade of Sanger's Circus, complete with live animals, a costumed Britannia, and a Royal impersonator, fell in behind Victoria's State progress through London; and, as in *Punch*'s commemoration of Victoria's 1886 Jubilee, Victorian iconography regularly surrounded Victoria and Britannia with imperial animals (fig. 2). As it did for Queen Victoria and the Royal Family, everyday life for nineteenth-century publics encompassed the experience of zoological collections in displays ranging from Windsor Castle to the Crystal Palace, from Astley's Circus at Westminster Bridge to Wombwell's Menagerie in England's industrial provinces. Indeed, over the past two hundred years Englishness and expressions of its stylistic character—its ostensible coolness, reserve, and civility, for instance[4]—have accompanied exhibitions and narratives of empire. These stories and displays provide the historical backdrop for Britain's current "kaleidoscopic ethnic mix" and multicultural "style."

This book takes up the relations among these exhibitions and narratives as they find expression in the English novel, the content of which is, in Fredric Jameson's formulation, "daily life and existential experience in the metropolis"—not only in London, but in the mother country generally.[5] The following chapters map the formal and thematic concerns of the domestic English novel in terms of popular understandings of the way in which the British empire as a whole incorporates and informs Englishness. As a description of how the novel accommodates itself to shifting modes of representing a global empire, this book explores the way that exhibitions of zoological exotica have generated and mingled with a series of memorable narratives of England and Englishness. In this context, it is not surprising that the *Daily Telegraph*'s vision of Englishness as a "crowd of all races and creeds" should be occasioned by an elephant. For more than two centuries, the overlapping patterns of imperial display and domestic narrative have defined Englishness and its characteristic expressions in the novel. The newspaper accounts of the motorized elephant in East London are just the latest in a series of encounters between displays of exotic animals that make up a genre that I call the "imperial menagerie" and the stories that England tells itself about its character and place in the world.

Interest in the elephant at the 2002 celebration prompted Newham's ceremonial mayor Sukhdev Marway to credit the borough's carnivalesque demonstrations on behalf of the Queen to the fact that "many of our people came from other Commonwealth countries, so the monarchy means something to them."[6] This book takes as axiomatic a correlative observation: that England and its literature have been understood to "mean something" distinctive in the world to the extent that, for better or worse, English life has been bound up with the empire—"a crowd of all races and creeds," too—as a complex and comprehensive cultural whole. In *The Expansion of England* (1883), J. R. Seeley effectively argued this point when he asserted that "England owes its modern character and its peculiar greatness" to its early colonial expansion.[7] A century later Gauri Viswanathan detailed the ways in which the modern study of English literature first took shape, not in the British Isles but in nineteenth-century curricula in India; in her account, England's literature largely owes its modern forms of study and its peculiar canons to what Seeley calls "the English Empire."[8]

Unlike other nineteenth-century commentators, Seeley conceived the empire as a virtually static totality that was intrinsically opposed to dynamic narrative, concluding his survey of the "English Empire" with an unusual admission: "I have narrated nothing, told no thrilling stories, drawn no heroic portraits, I have kept always before you England as a great whole. In her story there is little that is dramatic."[9] While Seeley insists upon the distinction between showing and telling, exhibition and narration, displays of the "English Empire" in the nineteenth and twentieth centuries were written about in accounts that slip indiscriminately from description to narration.[10] What is more, over the course of the last two centuries, keeping before the English public the empire as "a great whole" entailed the telling of just the kind of stories Seeley disavows, in the registers of exhibitionary culture and of the novel alike. These chapters follow a number of such stories as they develop from exhibitions, while exploring menageries and novels for their understandings of the empire as a geographic and historical whole.

The idea of totality has been treated most intensively in the twentieth century by Marxian theorists. English popular and literary cultures across the last two centuries employed exhibitionary languages that represent far more supple and imaginative means of engaging ideas about the empire as a whole than those that rely upon the Hegelian categories of "self" and "other." Indeed, while English thinkers avoided theorizing totality in the abstract idioms of their Continental counterparts, English exhibitionary cultures figured it richly in their modes of display, in their treatment of exotic animals, and in writing about their relation to empire. The novel also aspired to totality both in its form (a complete aesthetic object) and in its reach (a comprehensive treatment of its world). At roughly the moment that J. R. Seeley opposed totality to narrative, Henry James asserted their homology: "a novel is a living thing . . . all one and continuous," an "organic whole," the "main care [of which] is to be typical, to be inclusive."[11] By the first decades of the twentieth century, novelists such as Arnold Bennett understood the British empire to model the novel's totalizing aspirations. And at the beginning of the twenty-first century, Amit Chaudhuri could be found proposing once more that "the novel's mode of representation, its aspiration, is totality; it presumes the existence of, and also the possibility of representing, a continuous fabric of human and social interrelationship." What is more, the totality in play in the novel, the fabric of the nation itself, for Chaudhuri is explicitly "imperial England"; it is the empire that makes "this idea of the nation, and the novel, . . . a transcontinental way of 'being.'"[12] Concurrently with these developments in the theory of the novel, large-scale Anglo-American exhibitions aimed to reveal "the new unity of the globe [and to make] possible its consumption as a single, though diverse, spectacle."[13] In these fundamental ways, totality played a central role in narratives in the novel and the imperial exhibition alike; the British empire supplied a rich and dramatic field and figure for this totality, even as novels and menageries took the empire as a whole as their problematic field of representation.

Traveling Culture, the Novel, and the Zoological Cabinet

The central questions this book raises deal with the ways in which the English represented to themselves a global imperial culture and their place within it, and how the novel as a privileged form of narrative engages such modes of representation in the work of authors ranging from William Makepeace Thackeray to Julian Barnes. My primary claims are that (1) both novels about English daily life and exhibitions featuring collections of exotic animals strive to relate Englishness to a larger imperial totality; and (2) evolving attitudes toward the imperial whole in these two fields of English cultural production—the novel and the menagerie—reveal important things about large-scale shifts in narrative practices between the nineteenth and twentieth centuries, especially the movement from realism to modernism. Michel de Certeau observes that in late capitalism "the novel . . . has become the zoo of everyday practices," and though one of my aims is to show that this process of "becoming" begins in nineteenth-century writing, the modern novel in England can be productively understood as just such a collection or exhibition of English practices in the midst of a culture of empire.[14]

But de Certeau's dictum ought also to be reversed. The English menagerie and its attendant exhibitionary institutions deserve to be read for the narratives they dramatize and disseminate: they tell the story of England's place in the world, recount the shape of the imperial past, and imagine potential futures for England and empire. In exploring the relations among the novel, the menagerie, and the empire conceived as a "great whole," I assume both that the English novel is a cultural form intimately engaged with everyday imaginative practice and that documents of England's exhibitionary cultures are not dead letters but dynamic narrative media. The English zoo, circus, long-run exhibition, and menagerie are of course not cultural institutions fixed over time but flexible forms with complex and evolving histories of their own: the imperial menagerie is more than a convenient transhistorical metaphor, as a number of recent studies demonstrate.[15] This book looks at the dynamics that such histories bring to the fore, in order to plot the imaginative transactions between the imperial menagerie and the novel, with a special emphasis on the complexly mediated flows from the menagerie toward the English novel and narratives of Englishness in general. While it is true that English literature itself sometimes directly informed exhibitionary cultures in the nineteenth century—spectacular renditions of work by Byron and Dickens appeared in early Victorian circus programs, for instance—in the twentieth century this direct relation weakened considerably, as the gap between the novel as "high" culture and the popular exhibition as "low" culture widened in the era of aesthetic modernism.

The interpretation offered in these pages of the relations among the novel, the menagerie, and print cultures in the nineteenth and twentieth centuries challenges, however, the perspective that treats the menagerie as divorced from high culture or has seen it merely as sociological content or context for narrative fiction. Instead, I argue, these relations are complex, deeply ingrained, and interdependent. Indeed, this book assumes with Peter Stallybrass and Allon White "that cultural categories of high and low, social and aesthetic . . . are never entirely separable."[16] It is not simply that imaginative literature in the form of the novel is "high" and the varieties of the menagerie are "low," but that literary approaches to the menagerie can themselves appear high or low, honoring the vulgarity and corporeality of the collection, or transmuting it. Such treatments constitute the novel itself as a variable genre defined by a contest of high and low. So, for instance, Arnold Bennett, Angela Carter, and Salman Rushdie emphasize the fleshiness of the animals on show in the menagerie, Virginia Woolf and Charles Dickens desubstantiate zoological exotica by emphasizing the beast's symbolic character, and Julian Barnes strips the menagerie of the exotic altogether.

Figure 3. "Punchius Imperator A.D. MDCCCLXXVII," *Punch's Almanack for 1877*, *Punch*, 14 December 1876. *Courtesy Kelvin Smith Library Retrospective Research Collections.*

The colonial or imperial character of the exotic is key to the collection of zoological exotica, as John Berger recognized decades ago: "in the 19th century, public zoos were an endorsement of modern colonial power. The capturing of the animals was a symbolic representation of the conquest of all distant and exotic lands."[17] With the fortunes of their empire rising throughout the nineteenth century and into the twentieth, the English sustained a robust traveling culture: not only did they set out to explore the reaches of the world and to claim distant spaces under imperial standards, but they also exhibited the artifacts and traces of these extremities at home, including specimens of exotic fauna.[18] In this period, domestic English institutions of imperial display grew rapidly: circuses such as Astley's assumed their contemporary national and international forms; the Regent's Park and Surrey Zoological Gardens opened to the general public; Wombwell's and Atkins' Menageries traveled across England to show their collections; and, beginning with Prince Albert's Great Exhibition of 1851, the colonial, imperial, and world exposition—displaying collections of animals in several forms and media—became a mainstay of London's tourist season. Even pageants staged in the distant spaces of the empire found domestic expression: in the case of the 1877 Imperial Assemblage in Delhi to crown Victoria Empress of India, the government and popular press commissioned paintings and photographs that captured ethnographic and zoological exotica for presentation at home (and which *Punch* lampooned with relish; see figure 3); and for Edward VII's and George V's coronation "Durbars" (1902–3 and 1911, respectively), film companies raced to get moving pictures of the procession of state elephants to London screens.

Such modes of display facilitated a distinctive brand of imaginative travel across global expanses and cultivated the sense in England that the empire was a coherent, integrated, and knowable whole. Novels of the period explicitly register this brand of imaginative travel: in E. M. Forster's *A Passage to India* (1924), Aziz arranges to convey the Western women from the railway terminus to the Marabar Caves across the Marabar Plain on an elephant. The elephant materializes "the East" not only for the English ladies but also for Aziz himself: "That an elephant should depend from so long and so slender a string [of personal connections] filled Aziz with content, and with humorous appreciation of the East."[19] And in a fanciful instance, Rebecca West's *Harriet Hume* (1929) suggests the spectacular proximity of organized modes of English travel such as Thomas Cook's package tour business to the zoological exotic when it indulges a fantasy of a "sight, so familiar to Londoners, of Thomas Cook and his sons riding down to Ludgate Circus in the howdahs of elephants, wearing Egyptian sun helmets, and commanding Maori attendants, on their way to enable others to enjoy the pleasures of foreign travel."[20] Though selective, oddly synthetic, and even misleading understandings might result from the encounters they facilitated, the oriental procession, zoo, menagerie, and circus nevertheless served as important imaginative channels through which domestic English subjects such as Thomas Cook's clientele apprehended India, and empire more generally, in the nineteenth century.

In surveying what she terms "the animal estate" in Victorian Britain, Harriet Ritvo sketches many of the imperial circuits and networks to which nineteenth-century zoos and menageries were bound, and Richard Altick catalogs a large number of popular nineteenth-century entertainments that included exotic animals, people, and artifacts.[21] Ritvo's and Altick's rich investigations document the menagerie's contributions to a cultural complex of exhibition in Britain that supplied essential material for the domestic imagination of empire. Yet the English novel has received only glancing attention in this context, though it too formed a part of this "exhibitionary complex": it served as an instrument of display in its own right, staging encounters in England's domestic spaces between the English and exotic animals and people, as part of a larger print culture that also witnessed a rapid growth in attention to natural history.[22]

Michel Foucault situates the rise of natural history as a discipline at the middle of the seventeenth century "in the gap that is now [around 1657] opened up between things and words," between the ontological facts of the animal and the narratives and diverse lore that accrued to it. This gap, according to Foucault, marks the shift from undifferentiated zoological spectacles in the early modern period ("the age of the theatre") to the precise, scientific catalogs and displays characteristic of modernity (the age "of the catalogue").[23] The forms of the imperial menagerie, however, hardly witnessed such a gap, so thoroughly sedimented were they with narrative, description, and spectacle. The imaginative domain of the menagerie was simultaneously theatrical and catalogic or descriptive, its things and its words complementary aspects of a larger exhibitionary apparatus rather than antagonists posed across a representational or epistemological gulf. Books, pamphlets, newspapers, playbills and promotional ephemera, and broadsheet poems and ballads commented upon and narrated the material forms of exhibition, while the latter depended on the work of print publications to advertise them and to provide the rich narrative frameworks upon which they capitalized. So ubiquitous were these collections of anecdotal curiosities that by the end of the nineteenth century, Hilaire Belloc published parodies in the form of *The Bad Child's Book of Beasts* (1897) and *More Beasts for Worse Children* (1898), which chiefly offered absurdly unreliable information about animals and described creative means of destroying them.

In general, contemporaneous writing about the menagerie—including the miscellany of natural history[24]—serves to complement material displays, as narration complements the menagerie's descriptive apparatus, and as the aesthetic presentation of animals complements the political and social facts of their spectacular exhibition in England. The most prominent of the institutions of the menagerie generated characteristically successful animal stories, and if the menagerie's function was to manage animals, print genres affiliated with the zoological collection sought to manage the stories generated by the menagerie. The spectacle of the menagerie and writing about it do not check narrative possibilities but rather, as Barbara Benedict writes of collections in general in the period, "[liberate] information for private, implied narratives."[25] Sometimes, indeed, nineteenth-century displays aimed to impel spectators' own accounts of their relation to the exotic, as when Astley's exhorted its patrons to "GO AND SEE THE MIRACLE! That you may say when you grow old, I have seen a Man DRIVE A LIVING LION HARNESSED TO A SPLENDID CHARIOT! ON THE OPEN STAGE Make his Bed on a Troop of CONQUERED BEASTS."[26] The menagerie crucially lends not just impetus ("go and see the miracle!") but form to such narratives, selecting, arranging (harnessing or making of them a "bed"), and coordinating (or "conquering") the animals, the conditions of their appearance, and—with the significant exception of the rogue or disobedient animal—their plot.

Other printed ephemera such as the domestic political satire exploited the idea of the "cabinet" as a collection of curiosities and a group of political figures. *The Zoological Cabinet; or, Menagerie of Living Characters* (1832) took as its setting the Zoological Gardens in emphasizing the total management of exotic beasts associated with imperial landscapes:

> The place recall'd associations
> Of those unthinking brutes' relations;
> Who, once unus'd to bear command,
> Now brought from every clime and land,
> And here collected, seem'd to me
> To live in civil polity.

> You here may meet with ev'ry creature,
> Of each complexion, and all feature;
> And ev'ry character and form;—
>
> ...
>
> Each animal of every kind;
> And here assembl'd,—sure were cause
> That there should be controuling laws,
> By which the whole should be subdu'd,
> Though while the tenants of the wood . . .²⁷

The satirical verse holds up the menagerie as a model that demonstrates the need for imperial management through "controuling laws," and in particular for the administration of imperial lands so that "the whole" shall be rendered a "civil polity." And we might understand genre itself as a kind of cabinet or set of "controuling laws" for zoological stories that complement displays of the zoo, circus, or Durbar.

The novel, too, as a kind of zoo of everyday practices, appears a similar sort of cabinet, subjecting "the whole" of English life to "controuling laws" of its own. Yet as a wholly invented genre, the novel as a totality in its own right seems to *supplement* rather than complement the unifying work of the menagerie and its narratives. In the novel's negotiation of the "associations" and "relations" of the English to "each animal of every kind," realist and modernist writers fashioned their own comprehensive views of English life which, in J. R. Seeley's explication, extended "indefinitely" into imperial space.²⁸ If the novel and other print genres differ in their relation to the zoological collection because the novel as a totalizing genre on its own terms supplements the display while other writing complements the imperial menagerie, nevertheless Victorian and twentieth-century novels, like the zoo, the imperial exposition, and the circus, engage the problem of Englishness in relation to the empire as a dominant whole.

The writing of William Makepeace Thackeray, Elizabeth Gaskell, Charles Dickens, Arnold Bennett, E. M. Forster, Virginia Woolf, George Orwell, Angela Carter, Salman Rushdie, and Julian Barnes intersects at numerous points the forms and conventions of English exhibition, not least those featuring exotic animals. In the work of each of these writers, the imperial menagerie and its traditions furnish material for, and pose obstacles to, the design, content, and logic of the novel. Within both the menagerie and the novel, the figure of the elephant holds a privileged place, and consequently it also holds a privileged place in the pages that follow: the elephant is the cornerstone of collections of zoological exotica, constitutes a figure for large and unwieldy wholes, and dominates the spectacles informing the work of English writers, as it does in Miss Matty's apprehension of India's alien spaces in Gaskell's *Cranford*. This is so both because historically elephants constituted the most spectacular and highly touted attraction in displays of zoos, menageries, circuses, museum collections, hunting trophies, and imperial exhibitions, and because figuratively the elephant has long been understood as a trope for an expansive and only indirectly apprehensible totality such as empire.[29] The elephant is a synecdoche both for the menagerie in which it plays its spectacular part and for the empire whose practices and institutions bring it before the English public. Consequently, in the English novel the figure of the elephant serves as an imaginative tracer in the imperial system, an exemplary instance of megafauna marking the historical and rhetorical flows of domestic narrative and imperial exhibition and highlighting their cross-currents.

English Stories and Imperial Amnesia

Given the long associations of the elephant with the most exotic aspects of the empire, it is no wonder that the *Times* in 2002 should find in the mechanical animal at Queen Elizabeth's anniversary celebrations a striking symbol of a multiethnic, postimperial nation. The elephant, the largest and most prominent of all the beasts in England's extensive cache of imperial tropes and emblems, had strong associations first with India and then with Africa, the most important imperial landscapes described by mid- and late Victorian exhibitionary maps of the world. In the twenty-first century, narratives of Englishness continue to employ the figure of the elephant and to be oriented by such imperial maps, if only because so much red has disappeared from models of the reconfigured globe. Whatever the claims for its unprecedented character, the exhibition of the mechanical elephant at Elizabeth's Jubilee responds to two widespread contemporary stories about Englishness from a global perspective. The first story—"familiar and old-established," to borrow Freud's words again—enshrines Englishness in its "most potent unifying symbol," the Queen, in reading the Jubilee as an event of both growing and consolidating global significance. On one hand, the worldwide interest of English-language media in the Queen's anniversary dramatized the resilient hold that a radiant Englishness maintains over the global imaginary. On the other hand, the parade through

Newham celebrated the continued power of the Commonwealth to compose a shared cultural framework around a core of English symbols and traditions, as, for instance, Mayor Sukhdev Marway suggests in asserting the Commonwealth's continued allegiance to the Queen.

Describing the spectacle as a celebration of "cultural diversity and social harmony," as Royal publications did, also defends against the incursion into everyday English life of a second, less sanguine tale of alienation from visions of sociopolitical and cultural integration.[30] While the primary story at Elizabeth's Jubilee celebrates England's geopolitical relevance—indeed, its continued visibility on the global stage—this second narrative focuses on England's increasingly marginal role in the world after decades of decolonization overseas and of political devolution in the British Isles themselves. It has been rehearsed since the 1970s in a welter of books and popular reports about England's ostensible identity crisis, and narratives of cultural predicament and decline continue to influence English cultural and political thought. As Tom Nairn and Bernard Porter have argued, England's identity and economic welfare were tightly bound up with its overseas holdings from the late nineteenth century.[31] The appearance of compromised economic and political authority in the twentieth century, they maintain, was inevitable as soon as "Greater Britain" embarked upon its large-scale program of decolonization following the Second World War.

This "breakup" has been one of the most remarkable developments in English political life over the last century, culminating in 1999 with the devolution of legislative power in the United Kingdom and the elections of national parliaments in Scotland and Wales. Anticipating these events in 1998, Jeremy Paxman wrote that "The disintegration of empire is at last hitting the British Isles: the first colonies will be the last to gain their independence."[32] Splenetic descriptions of English cultural disorientation, estrangement, and decline accompanied political devolution in the UK. Paxman, for instance, argued that without the concept of Great Britain, in which they had invested the balance of their cultural capital, "the English had no alternative identity to rescue them."[33] That is, while the other nations in Great Britain preserved their local traditions and cultures and therefore had them to rely upon, England had few significant institutions that were not already bound up with those of Britain and its empire. "It is a paradox," wrote Jonathan Miller in the same year, "that in this reconfiguration of Britain, it is the English themselves who are being left behind in the rush for devolution. Unlike the Scots, Welsh and Irish, who retain a strong sense of national pride and identity, the English are profoundly confused about what to do amid a disintegrating United Kingdom."[34] The display of the elephant at the Jubilee, one might suggest, is designed to cultivate a sense of English unity in diversity as a practical rejoinder to these theoretical diagnoses of confusion and fragmentation.

Given this fundamental division in accounts of the situation of Englishness, it is perhaps not surprising to find that the line of fracture between the competing national narratives framing the Jubilee cuts across England's literary topography as well as its political and popular cultural landscapes. Advocating a multiethnic, globally central Englishness, organs like the *Times Literary Supplement* continue to boast that English writers are "unequalled anywhere else, the US included," and that the nation's racial diversity and cultural richness fueled contemporary English literary production.[35] On the other hand, the melancholic, postimperial view has been exemplified by critics like Terry Eagleton, who remarked the eclipse of English literary prominence and dated its wane from the early decades of the twentieth century, attributing the decline to the fact that English writers could no longer grasp English life as a whole in an era of political and aesthetic modernism.[36] Such divergent perspectives are thrown into high relief as they bear upon Britain's most prominent literary award, the Man Booker Prize. Graham Huggan for one deplores England's stubborn insistence on its "arbitrational cultural role" in the world, a "mantle ... now assumed by the Booker and its panel of 'disinterested' (white male) judges [who] determine what carries 'intrinsic' literary value [and] confer legitimacy, from the 'center,' on the literature of the periphery."[37] In contrast, Elaine Showalter, endorsing "protective literary tariffs" for Britain, argues that there is no longer "a uniquely British novel, nor a recognizably British standard of excellence," only an endangered "British literary culture, a mixture of aesthetic, intellectual, commercial, social, and journalistic elements" threatened by proposals to extend Booker eligibility to American writers.[38] The very legibility and significance of the contemporary novel in England—does it represent the highest aspirations for writing in English, or is it an endangered species?—seem to depend upon correspondingly discrepant narratives of postimperial England's identity in the world.

On 22 October 2002, five and a half months after the mechanical elephant's ascent to media prominence at the Jubilee, Yann Martel's *Life of Pi* was awarded the 2002 Man Booker Prize. The novel that rejects the "story that won't surprise you" and concludes that "The story with animals is the better story"[39] found critics sympathetic to the surprising beasts at the center of the story. Roz Kaveney in the *Times Literary Supplement* praised the novel's "meditations on humanity's relationship with animals, as well as [the] profusion of lyrical passages about fur, feather, and flower" for the way they evoked "the unfamiliar or the barely imaginable."⁴⁰ And the novel featuring zoological exotica, if "the better story," also proved a popular story: "the triumph of *Life of Pi* has been hailed as ushering in a new era, in which the People's Booker reigns," declared the *TLS* in evaluating the implications of the 2002 award.⁴¹ Yet however "barely imaginable" the novel's story might have seemed, its discourse cultivated familiar forms of exoticism and revived the menagerie's tarnished aura of charm and cultural authority. At least one critic remarked the novel's unregenerate orientalist perspective—the indulgence in "lovingly lacquered 'Indianness'"⁴²—evident in statements such as "I am Hindu . . . because of elephants standing around to bless."⁴³ Martel's animal story celebrates the zoo and the circus from the very beginning, suggesting that "if an animal could choose with intelligence, it would opt for living in a zoo,"⁴⁴ and the narrative turns its teenage protagonist into a circus handler when he subjugates the large Bengal tiger with whom he shares a lifeboat. *Life of Pi* cultivates a sense of wonder, the unknown, and the exotic, and yet, as James Wood observes, this "magical story is made plausible, and vivid and dramatic, only by the careful application of conventional realist techniques." While "in essence, [the protagonist] recreates the atmosphere of the zoo" in the boat as he displays his mastery of the exotic beast, the narrative also demonstrates "that realism is narrative's great master, that it schools even its own truants."⁴⁵ In its subject matter Martel's novel, hailed as the first winner of the British "People's Booker," celebrates the zoo and circus as spaces of human mastery; in its method it champions realism's mastery of the alien and the exotic. These tendencies are fundamentally those established by the Victorian novel in England. Indeed, the *donée* of Martel's story echoes stock performances of the Victorian circus: Astley's playbill of 11 October 1844 promises the thirty-minute progress of "MR. CARTER The Celebrated LION KING, in an Open Boat, with his Large BRAZILIAN TIGER!" navigating the Thames from Vauxhall to Westminster Bridge.⁴⁶

That the supposed novelty of *Life of Pi*'s narrative performance was, like that of Elizabeth's encounter with the mechanical elephant, largely illusory highlights a third notable condition of Englishness diagnosed around the Millennium—what the *Economist* called an "imperial amnesia."⁴⁷ A vast "memory hole" appeared to have swallowed the empire in England's home spaces by the end of the twentieth century: "the great figures of British imperial history are now largely forgotten" by the public, and Britain's ministers under Tony Blair "do not regard themselves as the heirs to the

British empire." Martel's book, too, seems to suffer this sort of amnesia, though from a Commonwealth rather than an English perspective: aside from the frame narrative, which gestures vaguely to Indian "stories about the struggle to boot the British out,"[48] Pi Patel's story offers little sense of Britain's formative role in India's history, or of Englishness as bound up with the institutional history of the zoological garden from which the narrative is launched. In its geography, the story arcs across the Commonwealth, from India to Canada, with no awareness of Great Britain's articulating cultural presence. Indeed, only the Man Booker Prize grants *Life of Pi* even a slim English dimension: for all its traditional exoticism, and for its reliance upon the familiar paradigm of the "zoo story," this novel seems curiously unaware of what imperial culture has entailed upon it, both in its subject matter and in its narrative approach. Though Martel himself is Canadian, in Britain this brand of collective forgetting or strategic refusal made possible fresh imaginings of what it meant to be English in the new century, and functioned as the condition of possibility both for the journalistic fascination with the processions in Newham in 2002 and the British critics' praise of *Life of Pi*'s "evocation of the unfamiliar." When the Queen followed the elephant through the streets of London, imperial amnesia rendered the scene a "unique welcome" not just to Royalty, but to narratives of a globally vital Englishness—like Martel's novel, writing in England largely ignored the indebtedness of its twenty-first-century animal stories to older forms of imperial exhibition.

Monuments of Empire, Memorials of Completeness

In a climate in which England appeared to suffer from amnesia about the empire, then, the Queen's progress through Newham on the heels of a motorized elephant uncannily called up the specters of Victorian stories about England's political and cultural place in the world, and prompted newer narratives that sought to respond to—or mask—the "disappointment, even shame" of England's alleged "descent . . . to second-rank industrial nation" without the empire.[49] Simultaneously overlooked or forgotten by accounts in the *Times* and the *Daily Telegraph* proclaiming the novelty of the Queen's parade through East London is the fact that the elephant is just one of many exotic figures or emblems that pervade the English cultural landscape; the material traces of the imperial past, in which England was the centerpiece of an empire that was regularly described as an integrated and indissoluble whole, persist across twenty-first-century England and the contemporary London cityscape. Just as the motorized elephant and "the splendidly bearded and turbanned" figures in Newham enable the Queen to arrive "in style," remainders and reminders of the empire continue to lend the mother country a novel "style."[50] Despite the prevalence of official, white "imperial amnesia," black Britons themselves have recognized the persistent influence of imperial policies and rhetorics in contemporary English culture. That imperial institutions and monuments survive in England is apparent not least to writers who, like Salman Rushdie and Hanif Kureishi, have written about the long half-life of imperial attitudes and frames of reference in the political and cultural environment of postcolonial England.[51]

Remnants of zoological engagements with empire endure across England's physical and cultural landscapes in monuments and museums; in a smattering of zoos, circuses, and wildlife parks; and in libraries and bookshops. Like the divergent narratives of Englishness and English literary culture, the stories that these traces and artifacts themselves foster have varied in tenor over the years, conveying both airs of celebratory nostalgia and strains of alienation and disorientation. The opening chapter of Hugh Kenner's *A Sinking Island* (1988) resonates with both of these qualities as it dramatizes the way that narratives of Englishness, empire, and literary history become entangled and confused in the iconography of menageristic display. Kenner casts the year 1895 in the role of "the best of times," a halcyon period before the rise of international modernism, before the English language "had ceased to be simply the language they speak in England," and before the English literary establishment ceded its authority as the primary arbiter of literature in English.[52] In Kenner's formulation, Queen Victoria's "memorial to the prince she mourned" embodies this late Victorian stability in the form of "a large eclectic masterpiece, guarded by stone lions and bedecked with proud standing-marble denizens of empire, the whole especially intimidating when it loomed through a morning fog. The book its stone prince held was not the Bible casual viewers took it for, but the Catalogue of the Exhibition of 1851."[53] Kenner's reading of the Albert Memorial in South Kensington as a kind of fossilized version of England at the end of the nineteenth century is striking, with its emphasis on the monument guarded by England's own regal lions, embellished by representatives of its imperial holdings, shrouded in London's bituminous mists, and presided over by that great emblem of modernity, the catalogue of the Great Exhibition.

Yet in describing this "especially intimidating" whole, Kenner unwittingly conflates two Victorian monuments and mistakes the animals in England's imperial iconography, for there are no English lions flanking the Albert

Memorial, as there are at the foot of Nelson's Column in Trafalgar Square, but rather a camel, representing Africa; a bison, symbolizing the Americas; a bull, standing for Europe; and an elephant, signifying Asia.[54] The Trafalgar monument to Horatio Nelson, who died during the reign of George III, was erected in 1843, at the very beginning of the Victorian age and before the Prince Consort's 1851 Great Exhibition had been conceived; the monument in Kensington Gardens to Albert was not completed until 1875, well after the success of the 1862 International Exhibition, and shortly before Britain crowned Victoria Empress of India in 1877. The lions are early Victorian in conception; the bison, bull, camel, and elephant mark the transition from mid- to late Victorian England. The Trafalgar marker commemorates a national triumph in the Napoleonic Wars, while the South Kensington memorial appears a monument to an empire swelling to global proportions.

Kenner's conflation of early and late products of Victorian culture highlights the fact that Albert's *fin-de-siècle* tableau presents a view of the English Prince Regent in which he is surrounded not by Landseer's English lions but by allegorical avatars of alien spaces, which do not merely "bedeck" the monument as a kind of satellite ornament but rather provide the frame for the way England's Prince Consort is to be remembered. If the Albert Memorial's Prince appears to preside over Asia and the elephant, these latter two nevertheless signal his dependency upon them by appearing to "guard" him. Albert himself was equivocally English at best (only securing the full confidence and affection of the English people after his brilliant organization of the Great Exhibition), and the iconography of the monument suggests that the signs that guarantee his Englishness (and that bind up this "intimidating" whole) are extrinsic to the nation's own symbolism. As it did with regularity across the nineteenth and twentieth centuries, Englishness emerges into view here as a result of totalizing engagements with, and displays of, the world—and such displays were frequently of a zoological character.

While the Imperial Institute down the Exhibition Road in South Kensington is long gone, in the first decade of the twenty-first century the importance of empire to the institutions of Englishness remains in evidence in the petrified remnants of the Memorial's menagerie, recalling what Kenner characterizes as "the best of times," an era during which, Jeremy Paxman adds, "the English knew who they were."[55] That period was, however, less a time of unbridled exuberance, confidence, and stability than of remarkable and often troubled transition both for the empire as a whole and for England's modes of narrating its own identity in relation to that whole. In these years, even such a voluble supporter of empire as J. R. Seeley was compelled to acknowledge the "bewilderment our Indian Empire produces" in the English imagination,[56] while a revolution in the pastures of the aesthetic, especially in the domain of narrative, resulted in what Richard Ellmann calls an "English literature out of countenance."[57] As they preoccupied the English imagination in their own distinctive ways, the novel and the menagerie crafted reflections of, and formulated responses to, imperial desire and bewilderment.

In 1947, when the empire was embarking upon its first major postwar project of decolonization, George Orwell reflected upon the past century as a time of dramatic change in English daily life, observing that "not much more than a hundred years since the distinguishing mark of English life was its brutality. The common people . . . spent their time in an almost unending round of fighting, whoring, drunkenness, and bull-baiting."[58] The striking difference of modern life a century later led Orwell to ask, "What had these people in common with the gentle-mannered, undemonstrative, law-abiding English of to-day?"[59] One answer is that the "brutish," licentious English of the early nineteenth century had in common with a Churchillian England—"stoical, homely, quiet, disciplined, self-denying, kindly, honourable and dignified"—a burgeoning empire that gave definite form and style to modern English identity and to the novel alike.[60] Since the publication of Orwell's book, England has not been able to take for granted such a makeup; the second half of the twentieth century was a period in which the British empire, the United Kingdom, Great Britain, and English identity itself appeared at times to be falling into diminished and disoriented forms. A quarter-century before Orwell and the movement toward large-scale decolonization, in his 1920 "Notes on the English Character" E. M. Forster was already worrying that "the shrinkage of the globe" in the twentieth century as a result of increasing political and technical interconnection revealed that "the English character is incomplete."[61] Forster's perception of incompleteness represents a striking contrast to the connotations of the stone elephant prostrate at Prince Albert's feet, which serves as a reminder of an age in which the empire was once understood as a frame for, and an extension of, the solidity, integrity, and character of England itself.

This contrast between convictions of solidity and holism, on one hand, and perceptions of incompletion and fragmentariness, on the other, is crucial to the story of the novel's evolution alongside English exhibitionary cultures. Discourses of imperial holism played an important role both in the configurations of the zoological imagination and in modernism's discountenancing and reorientation of literary form,[62] with which Eagleton and Kenner associate the decline of England's preeminence in letters. Between Victoria's accession to the throne and the end of George V's reign, perceptions of England's centrality in a total global field ("Our Empire [which] in itself is a whole world") gradually and fitfully gave way to views that such a whole itself was a political and cultural impossibility in both exhibitionary and literary registers.[63] This historical trajectory follows an arc similar to that of conceptions of the English novel across these centuries: where Henry James asserted in 1888 that "it would take much more courage than I possess to intimate that the form of the novel as Dickens and Thackeray (for instance) saw it had any taint of incompleteness,"[64] Virginia Woolf later faulted her predecessors for fostering "so strange a feeling of incompleteness and dissatisfaction" in their novels.[65]

COOL BRITANNIA AND THE ECONOMY OF THE IMPERIAL HOUSEHOLD

"Completeness," whether in geopolitical or aesthetic arenas, implies boundedness, a sense of limits and expectations fully met. Writing about these fields renders the ideas of wholeness, comprehensiveness, and integrity in economic terms, and the promise of national and imperial integration rises into view in nineteenth- and twentieth-century narratives always under the threat of insufficiency or excess. The tension between totality and incompleteness or superfluity marks the cultural transactions of the novel and the menagerie in fundamental ways as they engage the relation of Englishness to empire. While the "exhibitionary complex" in England sought to exercise and bolster "the power to command and arrange things and bodies for public display,"[66] this disciplinary order was always vulnerable to the strange savageness of the exotic animal. The menagerie, as its derivation from the Middle French term for the administration of a home or farm suggests, is a site of management and of ordering the otherwise unruly economy of the imperial household (including alien bodies, practices, and stories), and the novel's forms of narration across the nineteenth century also became modes of managing imperial attitudes and energies. Not only in its purportedly savage and strange rhetorical place but also in its corporeal agency (animals were sometimes spectacularly violent in breaching the fourth wall of the display), the exhibited beast appeared to embody excess and to threaten the power to command and to arrange. Likewise, the English novel as a kind of zoological cabinet sought to arrange, present, and manage domestic and imperial narratives—though, crucially, however much it labored, it never quite contained the cultural energies it strove to bring within its compass.

In exhibitions, narratives, and analyses of the empire as a whole since the nineteenth century, a complex calculus of excess and restraint has frequently accompanied appraisals of the English character. In this period a prevailing sense emerges that early modern England was a culture beset by excess and brutality, a conviction eloquently expressed by Orwell, while Englishness in high modernity is characterized by coolness and reserve, the central position of Forster. For the latter writer, the English character can be described in terms that are explicitly economistic: whereas "the Oriental has behind him a tradition . . . of kingly munificence and splendour" and "feels his resources are endless," Forster observes that "John Bull feels his are finite" and indulges a fiscal and emotional restraint associated with "middle-class prudence."[67] In defining Englishness in terms of frugality and over against the "Oriental," Forster's account is typical of modern discourses of Englishness that emerge from nineteenth-century encounters with empire.

The contrasting tropical poles of English coolness and oriental warmth, of Western humanity and civility and Eastern savagery and bestiality, and of European restraint and African or Asian license define the rhetorical field for treatises, exhibitions, and novels about Englishness and empire. As in Forster's essay, the most consequential distinction in this field opposes excess to restraint. Sometimes this opposition defining Englishness appears historical, ancient national tendencies serving as a foil to the English character in modernity: while the eighteenth-century English public gave free rein to spectacular displays of licentiousness in Orwell's reading, the modern English appear reserved and restrained. At other times, Englishness rises into view against the backdrop of images of imperial exoticism: in Forster's essay modern English parsimony opposes Asiatic "munificence" and extravagant expenditure. As in these English novelists' notes on the national character, so also in spectacles and dramatizations of empire English reserve emerges as a dominant trope concomitantly with the projection of excess onto the alien, whether in the guise of the premodern past or the contemporary exotic. This tropical landscape of imperial excess and English prudence functions as the setting for the complex cultural transactions among domestic narrative and imperial imagination, the novel and the menagerie.

The disappearance of the overt markers of English excess such as bullbaiting from public life in the twentieth century leads Orwell to wonder,

"Where are [the brutish English] gone?"[68] John Lockwood Kipling entertained the notion that "brutal Britons" might have gone to India to teach animal cruelty, as drunkenness, to Indians.[69] But English popular excesses did not sail altogether for the colonies with imperial administrators and transported criminals. Rather, in the nineteenth century the bullbaiting English, along with their profligate behavior and their national literature, went to see the imperial menagerie in all its forms. As they bound themselves imaginatively to ideas of the empire as a whole, a domestic English public (including the Royal Family) indulged a passion for the zoo, the circus, the traveling exhibition, the London pantomime, the lavishly illustrated volume commemorating imperial assemblages, and the cinema boasting films of oriental spectacles. Exhibitionary engagements with the empire in the nineteenth century sought to regulate domestic English excesses in part by staging them in the imaginative arenas of the oriental and the imperial: they rendered excess spectacular in such a way that it could be disavowed as the province of the other. Likewise, literary realism as it was codified toward the end of the nineteenth century sought to order its material so as to contain unseemly emotion and to render the social whole in appropriate perspective. But such excesses remained domestic affairs—the novel and the menagerie are in the final instance *English* displays—and returned to haunt the symbolic registers of modernism. The inscription of violence in the writing of D. H. Lawrence, Wyndham Lewis, and James Joyce might, for instance, be read as responses to the failure of an imperial Englishness to articulate itself satisfactorily as an integrated and settled totality.[70]

Victorian discourses of realism and of imperial totality were often rendered (though, as we shall see, they did not always function) as symbolic economies in which meanings, energies, and materials were arranged under principles of conservation. This conception is visible in Seeley's assertion that the empire would not "infect us at home with Oriental notions or . . . [cost] us money or [hamper] our finances. It is self-supporting, and is held at arm's length in such a way that our destiny is not very closely entangled with its own."[71] The systemic form of the principle of conservation is the capitalism that matured simultaneously with imperial expansion and with the consolidation of principles of literary realism. Toward the end of the Victorian period, convictions of the English empire as an integrated whole, established and maintained by practices of careful conservation and management, yielded to an emerging suspicion that insufficiency, excess, and incalculability serve as the dominant imaginative principles for Englishness in its relations with empire.[72] By George V's reign, modernist narrative and prevailing discourses of imperial totality tended to assemble around figures of what Fredric Jameson calls a "generalized loss of meaning" that resulted in part from the increasingly untotalizable horizon of empire.[73] In other words, excess, rupture, and incongruity became prominent in the style and form of the modernist novel in England in an implicit acknowledgment of the increasing difficulty of conceiving domestic English experience in relation to a total world empire, especially one threatened with the open revolt of India and Ireland. After the dissolution of the empire, the signs of discontinuity and imperial crisis encoded in modernist forms find a rich afterlife in the overt thematics of postcolonial writing by Carter, Rushdie, and Barnes. In the postimperial novel, the legacy of modernist practices is visible in the refusal or failure of the exhibitionary impulse to order, as technologies of display are subordinated to the overflowing and unmanageable forces of postmodern irrationality. Bill Ashcroft finds such overflow a characteristic of writing after empire, proposing that "excess is usually present in post-colonial writing," even that "the post-colonial place is itself 'excess.'"[74]

For Ashcroft, the central figure for theorizing postcolonial excess is Georges Bataille, who distinguishes "restricted" from "general economy," emphasizing a fundamental difference between prevailing philosophical emphases upon restraint and excess. Bataille's concept of "general economy" appears as a notion of an untotalizable whole, one in which the permanent, formal closure of a Hegelian or Marxian ("classical") totality is impossible. In his conception, the notion of totality in any register—political, commercial, symbolic, or libidinal—always appears an economic configuration. Bataille distinguishes a conventional idea of restricted economy, in which material, energies, and forms are conserved within closed systems, from his own conception of the whole of social and cultural life as a complex structure governed by dynamics of loss, dissipation, excess, and the dissolution and reinscription of limits. He describes the former as a "restricted economy" and the latter as a "general economy." General economy as (anti-)totality is characterized by an excess that ensures that the totality appears whole only insofar as it is characterized by a constant loss of its wealth and profusion of energies, a loss that implies a continual dissolution of the limits that define it *as* a whole:

> When one considers the *totality* of productive wealth on the surface of the globe, it is evident that the products of this wealth can be employed for productive ends only insofar as the living organism that is economic mankind can increase its equipment. This is not entirely—neither always

nor indefinitely—possible. A surplus must be dissipated through deficit operations.[75]

This process of "dissipation" performs a kind of alchemy, in which wealth is figured in a range of symbolic registers that define broadly a society's cultural formations.

Bataille's "general economy" neatly captures the modern—as opposed to mid-Victorian—sense of the empire as untotalizable: throughout the nineteenth century, empire itself promised a productive and prodigious "increase in equipment" for Englishness, but when it began to run up against its political, economic, and cultural limits, "deficit operations"—imperial wars in South Africa and Europe, for instance—and discourses of dissipation, decadence, and decline tended to dominate. Even at the height of convictions that the empire did or could function as a smoothly integrated whole, extravagance in the form of zoological "spoils of empire"—hunting trophies, ivory, and menageries that teemed with imported specimens, for instance—marked the surpluses generated by imperialist activity. Like totality itself and the lines separating spectator from spectacle, England from empire, excess and restraint are largely dependent upon perception of limits and their observation or transgression. Hence the distinction between restricted and general economies is primarily an attitudinal one. And it is just such a shift in perceptions of and attitudes toward the imperial totality that describes the trajectory of English writing—in the novel and about the menagerie—from the Victorian to the modern period.

To the extent that each of the interrelated stories that preoccupy these pages—about the movement from restricted to general economy, about shifts in the perception of empire from totality to dissolution, and about the novel's affinities to the menagerie—turns upon the moment of aesthetic modernism, these accounts should be understood as complementing other narratives that describe the emergence and afterlives of modernism in England in relation to colonialism itself or to a material history bound up with the processes of imperialism.[76] Because the chapters to follow consider the novel as an exhibitionary instrument whose representational practices are entangled with the "zoo stories" of the imperial menagerie and its "exotic captives," they are in dialogue both with studies of animals and their iconography and with recent exhibition studies.[77] In concentrating on the interchange and complexly mediated flows between the novel and the menagerie, however, this project necessarily forgoes a comprehensive account of modernism's rise and of the novel's philosophical engagement with totality in the early twentieth century. It does not attempt a comprehensive history of imperial displays and international exhibitions and zoos, either, since a number of recent studies have ably and eloquently described these institutions. This book chiefly aims to trace previously unmapped lines of filiation between the novel and the menagerie, in narrative registers both high and low, and invites a rethinking of the aesthetic notion of totality in the nineteenth and twentieth centuries as informed by the politics of empire in general, and the zoological imagination in particular.

The novel's relations with the imperial menagerie are marked by flexibility and contingency, and however consistent and resilient certain of their practices seem to be, neither the English novel nor the English menagerie can be explained exclusively by reference to a totalizing imperial imagination. Against arguments that aesthetic modernism is an "*immediate* consequence" of or response to the imperial world system, I maintain that though they are certainly consequences of the imperial world system, modern forms of the novel respond in highly mediated ways to representations of this system.[78] The traffic and display of exotic animals constitute just one significant line of mediation, and as a domestic English institution the menagerie itself is bound to empire in no simple way—its forms of representation are dependent upon communication and transport technologies and upon class-based ideologies, for instance. E. M. Forster maintained a healthy skepticism about fiction's debts to historical imperialism, denying the power of the empire to determine the forms of fiction. "A mirror does not develop because an historical pageant passes in front of it," he wrote in 1927. "Empires fall . . . but to those people writing . . . it is the feel of the pen that matters most."[79] While it is surely the case that Queen Elizabeth's Royal progress and her Golden Jubilee more generally were unlikely to "develop" the novel in England, it is entirely appropriate to expect that the novel, a reflective narrative form, engaged more or less directly the cultural dynamics governing the Queen's sensational encounter with the steel elephant in Newham. Indeed, it may be that the selection of *Life of Pi* as the "People's Booker" in 2002 acknowledges that the novel taps the same narrative veins as the Jubilee festivities: the strange encounter of an Indian boy and a tiger in transit along the edges of the Commonwealth in important ways constitutes the mirror image of the Queen's convergence upon the elephant at the heart of the old empire. Forster acknowledged that "If human nature does alter [the novel] it will be because individuals manage to look at themselves in a new way."[80] Over the past two centuries the imperial menagerie has offered one such evolving way in which English subjects "managed to look at themselves" in relation to empire, and not only the ephemeral moments at the Jubilee but also the enduring traditions of the novel in England bear the mark of these reflections and refractions, these ways of seeing Englishness and empire.

THE PLAYBILL

The mature discourse of the novel and common narratives of the exhibition depend upon a stock of characters and spaces that sometimes overlap: showmen, performers, and exotic animals, on one hand, and the circus ring, the parade, and the scene of exhibition, on the other, constitute the materials out of which both are fashioned to differing extents. Yet the cultural transactions among the novel and the menagerie are fluid and complex and do not yield a descriptive model through which the menagerie could be understood to inform the novel, or the novel the menagerie, without a high degree of mediation. The development of the novel and the rise of the modern circus, menagerie, and zoo accompanied a series of other significant historical developments in the early part of the nineteenth century: the advent of modern orientalism, the shift away from an older mercantilist colonialism and toward a state-centered free-trade imperialism, Hegel's articulation of the possibility of a total History in the *Phenomenology*, the Romantic insistence upon formal and philosophical holism, and the advent of technologies of mass exhibition (the diorama, moving panorama, cyclorama, and scale model, for example). All took place at roughly the same historical moment at the beginning of the nineteenth century and yet there is no invariable, determinate relation among all of these phenomena. They are, however, assimilable—however complexly—under the structural dominant of imperialism, which in England requires thinking imperial totality and imperial difference simultaneously.[81]

The idea of the British empire as a whole, which England both formed a part of and was held apart from, performs the essential work of mediating the formal narrative concerns of the novel and the menagerie. These genres represent homologous forms of cultural production and representation that respond to the common cultural experience of an empire growing rapidly as an expansion of the English nation, Seeley's "English Empire." An undeniable factor in English sociocultural life, the burgeoning empire nevertheless exceeded the bounds of the readily known: in 1924 G. K. Chesterton looked on the empire with awe, concluding that "It seems to me that man has made things almost too great for his own imagination to measure."[82] Technologies, practices, and narratives of exhibition constitute imaginative responses to this difficulty, and though the form of the empire was frequently taken for granted, these exhibitionary approaches to the imperial whole were largely responsible for rendering it material—if still very much imaginary—for an English domestic audience.

The key constitutive factor for both the novel and the menagerie, and the one governing the narrative relations between the two, is the discursive presence of empire—not only as an imposing if sometimes oblique situation or theme in their narratives but also as a formal injunction to totalize. The discourse of totality, along with the rhetorical and aesthetic principles that rely upon it, informs English narratives and exhibitions in the nineteenth and twentieth centuries and defines the complex imaginative transactions among them. Conceived as a comprehensive whole, England's empire provides the novel and the menagerie with a shared sociopolitical backdrop for their stories, whether domestic or colonial: a setting, in the broadest sense. Even more, the formal relation to the empire as a totality defines the novel and the menagerie as homologous forms. The novel and the circus, zoo, and exhibition aspire to describe English experience in relation to an empire understood as a whole; or perhaps better to say, they *fashion* Englishness in relation to the empire as a whole—that is, they work actively to forge from their imaginative stock, especially exotic fauna, a distinctive unity for England and its scattered imperial holdings.

Novelists and menagerists alike took as their more or less explicit aims the presentation of a national culture, one that was never confined to its narrowly defined political borders but stretched to encompass first the British Isles and then a global empire. The menagerie rendered Englishness and empire through a popular rhetorical program spanning a range of strategies from allegory to naturalism: it arranged, presented, and told stories about the exotic animals in its collections in order to furnish the widest array of spectacles, to attract the broadest audience, and to draw the most comprehensive view of alien natural and cultural landscapes. The English novel responded to a parallel imperative: as a line of critics and novelists stretching from Henry James to Amit Chaudhuri contends, the chief charge of the novel is to totalize, to render life itself as a comprehensive whole—typically from the vantage of the novel's native soil, England. The menagerie's deliberate and public strategies of totalizing England's relation to empire provide both a substantive map and a popular vehicle to guide the novel's work of totalization, especially visible in those signal moments in which the novel introduces exotic beasts. In such episodes the relationship that the novel establishes with the menagerie depends less upon metaphor, in which the novel appears in the borrowed trappings of spectacle or exhibition, and more upon metonymy or synecdoche: both the novel and the menagerie are parts related to the imperial totality, and key components of an imperial exhibitionary culture vested with the responsibility to relate its stories.

There are, of course, important attitudinal differences between the novel and the menagerie, and even among forms of the menagerie. Collections of exotic beasts and people in the nineteenth and twentieth centuries chiefly indulged English curiosity about empire from the direction of novelty and spectacle, and they foregrounded the exotic, the extravagant, and the extraordinary in their displays and narratives. On the other hand, and especially in its domestic guise, the novel took as its starting point a presumption of verisimilitude, engaging English curiosity through a set of strategies that orient themselves in relation to a rhetoric that asserts the fundamental truthfulness of its narratives. Yet discourses of the menagerie also regularly asserted zoological collections' fidelity to the real, while the novel offered glimpses of the spectacular. The attitudinal differences between the novel and the menagerie begin to dissolve over the ground upon which they both work, the empire as a dominant whole that encompasses and informs Englishness. The notion of an imperial totality furnishes a central framework—though not the only one—for understanding the novel's cultural work and aesthetic form, and one that the history and the aesthetics of the menagerie begin to open to us.

Chapter 1 begins to explore this framework by turning to a discussion of the notion of totality as a central concern in popular conceptions of empire, the menagerie, and their aesthetic presentations. The chapter treats the menagerie as a site for the management and arrangement of narratives of the empire as a whole, a rich field governed by a pair of antithetical aesthetic impulses, toward the picturesque, on one hand, and the carnivalesque, on the other. The picturesque serves a narrative function both in the novel and the menagerie, and a cultural function in English national discourses, of delineating empire as a particular kind of whole; exotic animals in general, and the elephant in particular, serve as keynote figures for the imagination and narration of imperial totality. In the cases of both the menagerie and the novel, a series of aesthetic strategies (particularly in the domain of the visual) serve to articulate and manage conceptions of imperial totality, and militate against a countervailing tendency in imperial representation toward what Peter Stallybrass and Allon White term simply "transgression," and which the menagerie served in the mode of the carnivalesque.

The second chapter turns toward a series of mid-Victorian novels that engage imperial exhibitions, either in their subject matter as in the case of Gaskell's *Cranford,* or in their mode of presentation, as in the showmanship framing Thackeray's *Vanity Fair* (1848). The chapter concentrates on the stories of the Victorian circus in an extended reading of Dickens's *Hard Times* (1854) that explores the implications for a rapidly maturing realism of the novel's strategy of excluding non-English acts and beasts from its portrait of the circus. Chapter 3 investigates the maturation of realism and its encounter of limits: by contrast with Dickens's highly selective rendition of the circus, Arnold Bennett embraced the carnivalesque aspects of traveling exhibitions, too; yet the menagerie exposes the limitations of his totalizing realism. Bennett has long been understood as a novelist who documents the intimate textures of provincial life, but the provincial focus of much of Bennett's writing is crucially marked by material cultures of empire. Bennett's best-known novel, *The Old Wives' Tale* (1908), demonstrates the way in which the traveling menagerie of the 1860s disrupts the fixities of provincial life, and the narrative holds an elephant accountable for the death of mid-Victorian England.

Virginia Woolf announced her allegiance to a modernist emphasis on aesthetic innovation by repudiating the fiction of Bennett, particularly *The Old Wives' Tale,* and where chapter 3 argues that imperial culture intrudes violently upon the provincial English life narrated by Bennett, chapter 4 considers the ways in which Woolf encodes such intrusions as images of detotalization, in figures such as the decaying elephant or the circles that expand and dissolve throughout *Mrs. Dalloway* (1925). The rich emblem of the elephant across Woolf's fiction, particularly in *The Waves* (1931) and *The Years* (1937), furnishes an index of the extent to which Woolf's own narrative stylistics are predicated upon a loss that is intimately bound up with the question of imperial disorientation, alienation, and dissolution. At its center, this chapter treats Woolf's essay on the British Empire Exhibition of 1924, "Thunder at Wembley," in relation to her modernist manifestos "Mr. Bennett and Mrs. Brown" and "Character in Fiction," in which she challenges Edwardian notions of realism in both exhibitionary and novelistic practice.

In the wake of the modernism that Woolf's essays announce and her novels exemplify, and after the movements toward decolonization that her writing anticipates, the exhibitionary cultures of empire and the narrative practices they entail would seem obsolete. After all, traveling menageries are all but extinct, circuses have begun to divest themselves of animals, and zoological gardens find themselves fundamentally rethinking their purpose and practices. Chapter 5 suggests, however, that the novel in English continues to engage with the traditional rhetorics of exhibition, whether in the magical realism of Salman Rushdie's *Midnight's Children* (1981), in the feminism of Angela Carter's *Nights at the Circus* (1984), or in the poststructuralism underpinning Julian Barnes's ambivalent "condition of England" novel, *England, England* (1999). The celebrated arrival of the "postcolonial moment" does not obviate exhibitionary modes or the rhetoric of the imperial menagerie. Englishness and its "Anglepoised" counterparts still find themselves articulated in relation to notions of (post)imperial totality, if not through nostalgia for a lost empire, then through anxieties about the impact on England of new chapters in the history of globalization.

Chapter 1

Picturing Britannia's Menagerie

The Aesthetics of the Imperial Whole

BRITISH BEASTS:
MRS. BROWN AND HER NATIVE ELEPHANT

IN ARTHUR SKETCHLEY'S *Mrs. Brown at the International Exhibition and South Kensington* (1871), the comic protagonist Mrs. Brown visits the Albert Hall in South Kensington, where she observes Edwin Landseer's painting either of *Isaac Van Amburgh and His Animals* (1839) or *Portrait of Mr Van Amburgh as He Appeared with His Animals at the London Theatre* (1847). While she initially confuses only the South Kensington Exhibition with the erstwhile Royal Academy space in Trafalgar Square—"I thought they meant that there picter show as is now moved to Pickerdilly, and used to be where the King's Mews stood when I were a gal, and arter that the skelinton of the gigantic wail in a wooden box, close agin St. Martin's Church"[1]—Mrs. Brown goes on to collapse thoroughly all distinctions of location, mode, and medium in her reflections on

> the picter of Wan Ambug in the lions' den, as Queen Wictoria were that fond on as she went to see 'em fed, and 'as 'ad 'is picter painted at Drury Lane Theayter, as is why she were called the Lady of Lions, thro' of course the lion bein' the British beast.... [I]t shows a proper sperrit in Queen Wictoria not to be afraid of a lion, nor yet a unicorn neither for that matter, as some parties says isn't nothink but the rhinoceros, but no more like 'im than I am, as is a ugly brute, tho's a deal tamer than he did used to be in the Jewlogical Gardins, as in course 'ave got used to it, the same as Queen Wictoria to lions and unicorns thro' 'avin of 'em about 'er all 'er life.[2]

Mrs. Brown confuses Drury Lane with the theater of Royal display, the lion tamer's show with exhibitions in the zoo, heraldry with natural history, and imperial allegories with discourses of acclimatization. Despite the carnival-like absurdity of her claims, the menageristic strands she weaves so deftly together illustrate the great range of sites and figures devoted to zoological representations of Englishness in the nineteenth century, as well as their complex entanglement. Indeed, Mrs. Brown appears a carnivalesque figure precisely because she is not able to grasp the way in which beasts are framed *as* "picters" in these forms of menageristic representation—indeed, she misses the element of the picturesque entirely, and ultimately she betrays the "proper sperrit" of Englishness embodied by such eminent figures as Queen Victoria and Sir Edwin Landseer.

This chapter is dedicated to the proposition that, though Mrs. Brown gets Landseer's "picter" of the American beast tamer Isaac Van Amburgh wrong, she gets the imaginative dynamics right. For the English, as for Mrs. Brown, the exotic animal mediates the relation of English "proper sperrit" to the world. The administration of that line of mediation falls to the collection of zoological exotica, whether that management is physical as in the "Jew-logical Gardins," or aesthetic as in the "Drury Lane Theayter," Landseer's art, or indeed in the *Mrs. Brown* series of stories themselves. The menagerie's approach vacillates between picturesque strategies, assembling rough parts into a coherent whole as Landseer's "picter" does, and an indulgence of the carnivalesque, which suspends the dominant order, threatens the extant social whole with the disorder of parts and celebrates categorical confusion. Mrs. Brown's narratives characteristically offer carnivalesque confusions about exotic animals and about empire, in this instance ranging her associations around Landseer's picture of the beast tamer. But the more usual English strategy is to impose picturesque order on the carnivalesque objects of display, especially by managing the wild beast's range of potential stories. Because it stands as a neat figure for totality, on one hand, and is the most fleshly of the exotic beasts, on the other, the elephant in particular illustrates the tensions between the picturesque and the carnivalesque, and it offers an exemplary instance of the menagerie's physical and textual management of zoological exotica, and of the operations of Englishness in relation to the world.

From 1867 to 1882, Arthur Sketchley (the pseudonym of George Rose) published thirty-seven book-length popular narratives and character sketches centering on the figure of the cockney Mrs. Brown, a large woman with predilections for drink and frequent naps, and who harbors strong affections for the Queen and the Royal Family—and especially for wild beasts: "It's been as much as my life's worth to even illude to Noah's ark afore [Mr.] Brown, cos he'd fancy I were a-goin' to bring up animals."[3] The "Mrs. Brown" books range over a series of topics that deal with cultural novelties, controversial subjects such as home rule and women's rights, and high-profile cross-cultural contacts, especially as these were concentrated in well-known spectacles, collections, and events: exhibitions and their spaces (with volumes on Mrs. Brown at the International Exhibition, at the Crystal Palace in Sydenham, and at two Paris Exhibitions), the material objects of display (books on Mrs. Brown and Jumbo, and on her impressions of Cleopatra's Needle), and narratives of travel (the Prince's visit to India, King Cetewayo's journey to London, the Shah's visit to Britain, and Mrs. Brown's trip up the Nile). Each of these books engages in comic geopolitical analysis generously laden with domestic humor.

Mrs. Brown's geopolitical critiques typically associate the behavior of political figures and institutions with those of zoological exotica. In Sketchley's books, exhibitionary cultures tack between notions of the picturesque, the framing of the world around a "keynote" figure such as Jumbo, King Cetewayo, or the Prince in India, and the carnivalesque, the confusion and destabilization of categories that Peter Stallybrass and Allon White describe as a "radical hybridity" and associate with the fair in general, and its animal displays in particular.[4] When, for instance, Mrs. Brown learns that a dramatic performance of *The Lady of Lyons* is playing at the Crystal Palace, and that the city of Lyons is in France, she concludes, "'ow awful! Wot a place to live in, with them wild beasts all loose about the place, with nothink but raw meat to live on; not as ever I knowed as they lives in no cities, but thought they was all out in them wildernesses, like monkeys in a gen'ral way."[5] These confusions often have to do with the imaginative fluidity and indistinctness of the world beyond England's borders, and "in a gen'ral way" in the empire. For Mrs. Brown, Indians appear indistinguishable from West Indians or black Americans; the shah of Persia might be expected to ride either an elephant or a camel (but not the London Underground); and the spaces of Africa and India are suffused equally with savagery and bestial wildness. Mrs. Brown's repeated solecism mistaking "native helefant" for "native element" neatly encapsulates her way of thinking: she is most characteristically herself when imagining beasts beyond England's borders running wild, or gesturing toward zoological exotica behind glass in England. She rhetorically finds her "native helefant" when she moves imaginatively beyond her "native element."

The logic of the Mrs. Brown series of books both typifies *and* overturns the logic of English exhibitionary cultures in the nineteenth century. The English in general were most engaged by the empire as it found expression in the zoological idiom: the English non-"native helefant" emerges as a linguistic marker of what ought not to be properly a part of the English "native element" unless symbolically differentiated, carefully held apart. Mrs. Brown's difficulty in her books is that she often cannot clearly distinguish exotic helefants from English elements, and to this extent, the exhibitionary apparatus that brings the empire home to Mrs. Brown's England—Van Amburgh's wild animals, for example—seems imaginatively to run interference with the lesson in imperial holism dramatized in the exhibition. In the Mrs. Brown novels, the unity of the empire slips into a risible homogeneity, an undifferentiated totality marked as other "in a gen'ral way": as much as the exhibitionary institutions and figures of display in these novels frame and delineate views of the empire, the leisurely spectacle they present also encourages a casual, carnivalesque confusion of categories.

Mrs. Brown's simultaneous typicality and eccentricity reflect the aesthetic poles of the picturesque and the carnivalesque, which frame the space in which the menagerie also performs its work. On one hand, the menagerie's beasts help consolidate views of exotic elsewheres for a domestic English audience around a range of rough and varied zoological and ethnographic figures. On the other hand, the spectacular collocation of beasts can never be fully contained, either in their corporeal behavior or their elaboration in the popular imagination, thereby rendering the categories and pictures they underpin unstable, excessive, and confused. The following section discusses the menagerie as a model and imaginative space for England's "proper sperrit" to emerge in the process of symbolically managing imperial relations. The chapter then turns to the characteristic exhibitionary forms of the menagerie by which the menagerie's narratives are disciplined. The closing sections of the chapter consider the collection of exotic beasts in its physical and textual forms of management—and in relation to its dominant emblem the elephant—as a rich but ambivalent cultural site: while Peter Stallybrass and Allon White in their influential reading of zoological displays emphasize the carnivalesque, destabilizing aspect of the collection of exotica at the fair, the aesthetic practices and forms of the menagerie itself emphasize a carefully assembled total order. The exotic beast in the collection harbors the possibility of carnivalesque, even violent, behavior, but the defining characteristic of the menagerie is its coordination of these beasts as an integrated and differentiated totality.

Proper English Sperrit:
John Bull's Collection of Wonder Fauna

For all the work the elephant and its companions do for Mrs. Brown in her narratives, the common and distinguishing characteristic of the menagerie's protagonists across the past two centuries has been a practical uselessness in the context of a domestic economy. Disquisitions on acclimatization in the later nineteenth century cited as the most compelling reason for domesticating exotic beasts their ability to "len[d] variety and animation to the [English] scene . . . [and] to render a ride through [the English park] one continuous round of enjoyment, instead of leaving upon the mind that dreary sense of solitude and of wasted opportunity."[6] The best the exotic animal could offer England in the way of domestic usefulness was an ornamental presence in the landscape and the promise of "continuous" visual pleasure, a stark contrast to the instrumental utility of animals of the English stable, farm, or dale. "Like lilies of the field," Angela Carter observed of zoo animals a century later, "they are not bred for food or service. They have another function, they are there just to *be*, in the best conceived of all possible paternalist utopias."[7] An 1829 handbook to the Tower Menagerie—in whose cramped conditions an animal could do no more than just be—pointed out that even in India, "the purposes for which [elephants] are commonly employed are rather those of pomp, of luxury, and of ostentation, than of utility."[8] Consequently the Tower's own collection offered up such beasts to the English public not just as ostentatious exhibits in their own right, but also as conspicuous signs of an imported or expropriated oriental pomp, luxury, and excess. Indeed, the beast in the menagerie finds its chief application in directing the imagination to a scene beyond the bounds of the island itself, outside the native element, and in furnishing the English with testaments to the extravagance, strangeness, and diversity of imperial elsewheres via the "native helefant," rather than feeding, clothing, or transporting domestic subjects.

To the extent that the diverse forms of the menagerie in the nineteenth and twentieth centuries worked to establish novel means of shaping the beast's exotic associations and imperial applications, Michel Foucault is correct to discern in the intense interest in natural history "a new way of connecting things both to the eye and to discourse. A new way of making history."[9] The Victorians constituted the collection of exotic animals as what Eric Hobsbawm calls an "invented tradition," a way of making history to which Terence Ranger notes "the concept of Empire was central."[10] The developing activity of *collection* defines the menagerie as a frame for the display of exotic animals and for the narration of their extravagant stories; collecting indulges the ordering impulse fundamental to both the menagerie's assemblage of zoological artifacts and their ongoing maintenance. The labor of management—to which the etymology of *menagerie* pays tribute—involved procuring, feeding and watering (or stuffing and preserving), transporting, and keeping in good condition the exotic beast, but also—and crucially—managing its cultural significance, its conditions of display, and the range of narratives in which it is permitted to play a part. Unlike Hans Sloane's chaotic collections that made up the initial holdings of the British Museum, the successful menagerie in the nineteenth and twentieth centuries did more than present an accumulation of zoological stuff. It selected, combined, and arranged its materials for display, offering English audiences a clear, if varied, set of avenues through which to relate to the animals on display—and, indeed, to the imperial spaces toward which wild beasts point.

The essential way in which the zoological collection is managed is the ordering of parts in relation to a whole or, rather, the representation of a whole through the exhibition of its parts. In this fundamental way it participates in the nineteenth century's "exhibitionary complex," the hallmark of which was the increasingly public display of bodies and objects, presented in such a way that they could be grasped as part of a larger totality.[11] Though no collection of animals could ever be verifiably complete, the standard by which menagerists and zoological exhibitors invited their collections to be evaluated was that of their extensiveness, whether measured by the extravagant cost of procuring beasts, the novelty of species on display, the sheer number of specimens in a collection, or the satisfaction of the spectators' expectations in finding all of the requisite beasts in the collection. The emphasis on the comprehensiveness of the menagerie itself often found expression in gestures to the expansiveness of the global field upon which the collection drew. An account from the 1920s offers a description of such a gesture, in recalling a scene at Bostock and Wombwell's traveling menagerie from late in the nineteenth century:

> On a platform in connection with a magnificent front entrance, brilliantly lit, appeared four figures, gorgeously attired, who proclaimed the good news of the arrival ... of the Most Wonderful Show on Earth. One of them described with amazing fluency the wonders of the jungle and the desert, wild animals from the frozen North and the torrid South, lions and tigers, bears and antelopes, elephants, camels, jaguars and snakes. Sweeping his arm around, he declared that within these cages were specimens of all the wonder-fauna of the world.[12]

The sweep of the arm to indicate that "*all* the wonder-fauna of the world"—or at least the world that comprised British commercial and administrative holdings—is on show at Wombwell's is a hallmark of the menagerie's management of its imaginative material. The menagerie claims a reciprocal relationship to "the world," particularly the world defined by the circuits of English trade and administration: the extent of a collection *reflects* the world's expanse, even as the world's extensivity is largely *defined by* that which is encountered in the collection.

The rhetoric of the menagerie asserted the collection's essentially naturalistic relation to the world of the exotic, claiming that its specimens and descriptions were typical selections, representative pieces of the landscapes and cultures from which they were taken, and—in the case of the preserved specimens—eminently lifelike. In advertising "Van Amburgh's WONDERFUL COLOSSAL LIVING ELEPHANT," for example, Astley's Circus boasted as a mark of the exhibit's authenticity that the beast "appears in the veritable equipage of its native soil."[13] Yet at the same time the relation of the menagerie's collection to the expansiveness of the English empire has a fundamentally allegorical aspect, one totality standing in for the other. Astley's in particular offered patently jingoistic representations in which animals figured prominently: in June 1849 Astley's advertised "An Allegorical Representation of the Triumph of Great Britain" in the Sikh War, and in December 1854 promised an "Allegorical Temple" that comprised "BRITANNIA's MAGNIFICENT EMBLAMATIC [sic] CAR & GORGEOUS MOVING TABLEAU OF UNITY."[14] The aesthetic principles and practices of the menagerie spanned a spectrum from naturalism to allegory as it constituted itself as a whole spectacle, and represented the empire as a comparable whole, in which every element rendered testimony both to the power of the collection of which it was a part and to the wonder of the wider imperial world toward which the collection gestured.

To the extent that both naturalistic and allegorical figures *belong to* the totality they delineate, Samuel Taylor Coleridge's definition of the symbol in the "Lay Sermons" (1816) serves as an incisive description of the figurative power of the animals on display and their relation to an imperial whole. Coleridge distinguishes symbol from allegory on the basis that allegory is removed from the scene that it renders:

> Now an allegory is but a translation of abstract notions into a picture-language which is itself nothing but an abstraction from objects of the senses. . . . [O]n the other hand a symbol . . . always partakes of

the reality which it renders intelligible; and while it enunciates the whole, abides itself as a living part in that unity of which it is the representative.[15]

While Coleridge did not have in mind demotic forms and figures such as those on offer in the menagerie, this definition of the symbol aptly captures the authority of the exotic animal in the menagerie: it helps "enunciate the whole" of the empire, even as it "abides itself as a living part in that unity of which it is the representative." This dynamic holds true even for the rough allegories assembled in the circus, which under Coleridge's definitions look more like an array of symbols than like an abstraction from objects of the senses. The animals arranged in zoological allegories are never merely elements of an abstract visual lexicon but abiding reminders of both the total order of life on the planet and the specific imperial order that brings them into English spaces to be exhibited. Approaching the menagerie's beasts as living symbols in the Coleridgean sense enables a neat differentiation of narratives of the menagerie from other tales of animals, exotic or domestic. Beast fables passed down from Aesop or reproduced in early modern bestiaries that predate the modern menagerie, for instance, explicitly make use of zoological idioms to translate moral, philosophical, and political abstractions, while other animal stories that emerged alongside those of the menagerie—stories personifying horses or dogs, for instance—do not suggest that the animals enunciate a larger whole.

The two fundamental factors defining the zoological collection—the necessity for managing exotic beasts in all aspects, and for managing them particularly in relation to an imperial whole that they both offer the image of and essentially imagine—were widely acknowledged, even taken for granted, in the nineteenth century. By the end of the century, popular representations entangled the empire with the menagerie so fully that the menagerie was elided with the imperial whole that it modeled and upon which it drew. In a music-hall standard from around 1900 titled "Britannia's Menagerie," the collection becomes an explicit political allegory reflecting imperial relations and providing the form in which they can be understood:

> Britannia has a menagerie that reaches all over the world
> She has some animals rich and rare, some treacherous creatures are caged up there.
> The name of the keeper is old John Bull, a man with a smiling face,
> He certainly does know how to keep each animal in its place.[16]

The several hallmarks of the menagerie are evident in the opening lines of the song: the broad gesture toward the empire's global reach (it "reaches all over the world"), the claim for the collection's opulence and extensiveness (Britannia collects "animals rich and rare"), and the emphasis upon the collection's ordering imperative ("to keep each animal in its place"). Many presentations of the exotic beast in the collection of living animals invited audiences to imagine its potential "treachery"—"What ravages might we not expect from the prodigious strength of the elephant, combined with the fierceness and rapacity of the tiger?"[17]—and the chorus of "Britannia's Menagerie" emphasizes the violence of the animal in the collection precisely in order to illustrate the mastery of the menagerist:

> Let 'em growl, let 'em howl, and grind their teeth with rage;
> They may bite, snarl and fight, but they mustn't get out of their cage—
> For they know Johnnie Bull is their master, and he holds the key,
> They'll be treated all right if they only keep cool in Britannia's menagerie.

In such representations, the menagerie models successful forms of imperial management, even as the empire stands behind the menagerie's collections as the material context and imaginative setting for the exhibitions of zoological exotica. The menagerie and the empire become mutually reinforcing figures: the imperial world comes into view as that which renders up material exotica for and is amenable to the exhibition's illustration and management, while the menagerie figures its task as the representation of that exotica as typical of a larger imperial whole.

This is the British empire's special refinement of the logic of modernity, the "age of the world picture," described by Martin Heidegger: the modern world is characterized by its view that the world is available to it as a picture. Indeed, as Timothy Mitchell observes of France's counterparts to England's colonial and imperial exhibitions, "the effect of such spectacles was to set the world up as a picture."[18] The era of empire constitutes "what one might call, echoing a phrase from Heidegger, the age of the world exhibition, or rather, the age of the world-as-exhibition. *World exhibition* here refers not to an exhibition of the world, but to the world conceived and grasped as though it were an exhibition."[19] The notion that imperial exhibitionary cultures depended upon a fundamental understanding of the whole world as itself an exhibition can seem like circular logic, but at bottom menageristic displays sought in presenting their spectacles "to create a distance between oneself and the world, and thus to constitute it as something picture-like—as an object on

Figure 4. Sir Edwin Landseer, *Isaac Van Amburgh and His Animals* (1839). *The Royal Collection* © *2007 Her Majesty Queen Elizabeth II.*

exhibit."[20] It created this distance by managing the role of English spectators as much as it did those of the exotic creatures, fostering something like the decorum of Mrs. Brown's "proper sperrit." Landseer's 1839 painting *Isaac Van Amburgh and His Animals* (said to be one of Queen Victoria's favorites) offers a perspective from within the animals' enclosure, but it carefully sets the English spectators safely beyond the bars and introduces Van Amburgh himself—an exceptional case, and a brash American—as a kind of alibi for the painting's viewer, prompting meditation on the relation of exotica to English subjects with a carefully cultivated separation and distance (fig. 4). A later Landseer painting, *Portrait of Mr Van Amburgh as He Appeared with His Animals at the London Theatre* (1847), displays a totalizing command balanced by a distance between the English viewer and the management of the beasts themselves (fig. 5).

In a comparable way, the picture of the world presented in English monuments drawing on the menagerie's idioms (the Albert Memorial, for instance) appears, as Richard L. Stein notes, "a map that can function in reverse—leading us outward toward a colonial globe only to return again to the imperial context of modern urban life."[21] Even as the imaginative labor of the menagerie serves to render "picture-like" the empire and—as

Figure 5. Engraving (ca. 1860) after Sir Edwin Landseer, *Portrait of Mr. Van Amburgh as He Appeared with His Animals at the London Theatre, 1847*. Author's collection.

we shall see—enables the narration of the act of forging an imperial whole, the collection also works to assemble visions of the English character. The menagerie manages not just the exotic beast or the imperial relations that underpin the animal's exhibition but also discourses and images of Englishness. Because the menagerie's display put the domestic viewer in relation to England's elsewheres, Englishness was always implicated in and at stake at the exhibition. Sometimes visions of the domestic were explicitly staged for the audience, in other moments Englishness rose into view as a part of the exhibition's assemblage, and on other occasions still Englishness was held up in contradistinction to spectacle. If, as in its work in the Albert Memorial, the menagerie offered an imperial map in reverse, it served as much to define the contours of modern Englishness as it did to bound and define empire for a domestic English public.

Emblems of Englishness appear openly in the allegory of the circus, the Lord Mayor's Show, and the traveling menagerie. Such representations were far from peripheral to the symbolic work of the menagerie and to the ways in which English power figured itself. In the first half of the nineteenth century, the repertoire of Astley's Circus—which exhibited at Victoria's Coronation Fair—emphasized national representations as well as exotic figures, and personified Britannia and presented lions as the quintessences of Englishness. Likewise, at the end of the century, on 17 July 1899 Queen Victoria ordered "Lord" George Sanger's circus to Windsor Castle, and Sanger's procession customarily gave prominent place to the figure of Britannia, performed by Mrs. George Sanger, who appeared with a "living lion on the top [of her car] to typify the nation and its strength." Often in these processions, Sanger recalled, "[t]he Queen, too, was impersonated, in her crown and robes, surrounded by representatives of her dominions all in correct costume."[22] When Britannia went to Windsor, then, the circus likely saw Victoria gazing upon her own "impersonation": as the original of the performance, the English queen in effect found herself sitting for her "living picture"; as a spectator at the performance, Victoria was invited to envision her symbolic authority in terms of that typification or impersonation. In the same way that the menagerie both described and mapped the empire's far-flung dominions, so also it reflected and projected visions of Englishness, and in multiple registers.

The national character of menageristic display was not always staged so openly as on the occasion in which Victoria was rendered a spectator at her own impersonation; indeed, at times Englishness was naturalized, submerged in the setting for the menagerie's narratives. On the occasion of an 1847 visit of Wombwell's Menagerie to Windsor Castle, for instance, the daily papers devoted a good deal of space to describing the menagerie and the Royal Family's interaction with it. The *Pictorial Times* offered the visit a place of prominence, dedicating its entire back cover page to the exhibition, noting that "The Prince of Wales fed the elephant" and that "Her Majesty, wishing to see the large elephant Jammoonah fully caparisoned, with the 'Lion-queen' seated on its back in the howdah, Miss Chapman, by her Majesty's command, rode round the menagerie."[23] The *Illustrated London News* likewise featured engravings of the visit to Windsor; one features the "fully caparisoned" elephant toward the center of the picture (fig. 6), and another shows the Royal Family gazing upon tigers and lions, thus juxtaposing figures of the exotic and the national (fig. 7).

These scenes are significant not only because they illustrate the preeminence of Wombwell's Menagerie at midcentury and its proximity to the symbolic

Figure 6. "Wombwell's Menagerie in the Great Quadrangle, Windsor Castle," *The Illustrated London News*, 6 November 1847. *Courtesy Kelvin Smith Library Retrospective Research Collections.*

Figure 7. "The Royal Visit to Wombwell's Menagerie," *The Illustrated London News*, 6 November 1847. *Courtesy Kelvin Smith Library Retrospective Research Collections.*

heart of English power, but also because they assemble and consolidate symbols of nineteenth-century Englishness in the space of the expanding national popular print medium. Press accounts locate the menagerie at the seat of the English monarchy, Windsor Castle, and in *The Illustrated London News* the Royal Family appears in a classically domestic nuclear grouping with Albert beside Victoria and the four children ranged around them, a stark contrast to the scandal of George IV and Caroline earlier in the century. The *Pictorial Times* notes that the ensemble at the menagerie in Windsor included "the band of Mr. Wombwell, led by Mr. Tidswell, performing the national anthem." These emblems of English national culture clustered around the spectacles of exotic beasts, orientalized in full trappings and under the command of the British Lion Queen and the banner of Union. As in the "national" monument that would later commemorate Prince Albert's life, the signs of Englishness rise into visibility, in the Windsor Castle courtyard and in the popular press alike, in concert with the key coordinating figures of the menagerie.

Reports of the Royal Family's encounters with the menagerie were important to establishing a sense of a common Victorian culture, especially since the experience of the traveling menagerie was available to most English subjects in a way that many London-based displays of nationalism were not. In viewing the menagerie, even the poor provincial laborer could feel himself part of a powerful nation, and the traveling menagerie helped to establish the rural provinces as "the repository of the moral character of the nation," in Martin Wiener's phrase, as a symbolic response to the joint pressures of imperialism and industrialization.[24] What is more, Harriet Ritvo observes, "Few English citizens were likely ever to wield the kind of power represented by the animals' captivity, but since that power was exercised by their countrymen over nature or the human inhabitants of distant lands, all could take vicarious pleasure in the evidence of its magnitude."[25] English patronage of the menagerie, whether in its provincial or metropolitan forms, and more particularly English viewing practices at the circus, zoo, and menagerie, fostered a shared sense of imperial power across England, not just mapping empire and the emblems of Englishness but also promoting an imperial ambition at the level of spectatorial affect.

How to calculate this affect formed the subject of a letter from Lord Salisbury to the Indian Viceroy Robert First Earl of Lytton in November 1876. At the time, Lytton was preparing for the enormous Imperial Assemblage, or Durbar, at Delhi, during which Queen Victoria would be proclaimed Empress of India, the spectacular centerpiece of which was to be the procession of native elephants. Salisbury wrote from Rome with suggestions about the address the viceroy was to give on the occasion, and particularly to

> Ask you, as to the form of [the address], to remember that you have two audiences: one in India, oriental, fond of the warm colours of oratory, and pardoning exaggeration more easily than coldness; the other partly in India, mainly in England, frigid, captious, Quakerish, Philistine, only considering a composition faultless when it has been divested of all richness and all force.[26]

The characterization of the English as "frigid," "Quakerish," and hostile to "richness" is hardly what one would conclude from a consideration of the English preparations for the Durbar (the effect of the English orchestrations of events was frequently compared with that of an enormous circus[27]) or for that matter from a more general survey of Victorian and Edwardian cultural forms, in which spectacle played such an important role. Yet the sense of a "cool" Englishness in the nineteenth century seems to have been consolidated through a disavowal of precisely the kinds of excess the English continually put on display. It is not that the English audiences described by Salisbury were "frigid" by nature (whatever that would mean), but rather that the English temperament found its characteristic expression in the act of rhetorically "divest[ing] of all richness" the magnificent spectacles—including the menagerie's exotic exhibitions—for which it simultaneously indulged a predilection. In a very real sense, the "warmth" of Lytton's "oriental audience" and the "coldness" of his English audience "partly in India, mainly in England" are both components of *English* cultural tendencies, the latter dependent on the former. In disavowing as "oriental" the kinds of "exaggeration" and excess they continually put on display themselves—in, for instance, the circus to which the 1877 Durbar was unfavorably compared—the Victorians brought into focus the prevailing "sperrit" of Englishness that Salisbury notes: an Englishness characterized by reserve, propriety, and coolness, contingent upon but disavowing the most intimate involvement with extravagant spectacle.

In its most egregious form, the imperial spectacle helped to shore up a sense of "cool" Englishness by projecting domestic impulses and signs of "savagery" onto imperial peoples and spaces. J. A. Hobson described the extreme instances of this pattern in his 1901 discussions of jingoism:

> I have distinguished the spectatorial passion of Jingoism from the cruder craving for personal participation in bloodshed which seizes most savage peoples when the war-spirit is in the air. Jingoism is essentially a product of "civilized" communities, though deriving its necessary food from the survival of savage nature.[28]

While Hobson adheres to the prevailing conviction that the English are more civilized than the "savage peoples" of the world, he also recognizes that the "spectatorial passion" of the "civilized" English exists parasitically upon that savagery, and that the process of "civilization" therefore depends upon the perpetuation of savagery elsewhere than in England. Yet the very fact that this "spectatorial passion" was not admitted *as* a passion in middle-class discourse, and that in any case was coded as civilized, meant that such desires were given general license across England, particularly where the savage beast was on show. As Stallybrass and White observe, "the *exclusion* necessary to the formation of social identity at one level is simultaneously a *production* at the level of the Imaginary, and a production, what is more, of a complex hybrid fantasy emerging out of the very attempt to demarcate boundaries, to unite and purify the social collectivity."[29] The wild beast's savagery and cool

Englishness were both produced from the license the managerial strategies of the zoological collections indulged.

This license was granted on the understanding that spectatorial impulses were matched by a studied distance from the spectacles that sated their "cruder cravings." The novelist G. K. Chesterton implicitly hewed to Hobson's distinction between "spectatorial passions" and "cruder cravings" when he argued that the Empire Exhibition of 1924 evinced a refined precision in its representation of the empire because of the British imperialist's disinterested observation of, rather than close entanglement with, exotic spectacle: "Because [the imperialist] was a spectator, he was fascinated by foreign things *merely* as a spectacle; and is capable of reproducing them in an exhibition which is meant primarily to be a spectacle. This spectacular quality of the trophies of English travel seems always to have been a character of the English."[30] Chesterton's confidence that the spectator's fascination with the alien was a simple one, with the spectator clearly distinguishable from the "mere" spectacle that fascinates, represents the obverse of the anxiety that imperial fascination might collapse the distinction between England and empire, spectator and spectacle. And, of course, the most spectacular trophy for well over a century proved exotic megafauna—live, or presented as preserved specimens.

Indeed, English commentators worried over the proximity of spectacle to Englishness—and in the menagerie, of the exotic beast to the English viewer—in much the way that they worried over the impact of the Orient upon English identity. In 1883 Seeley sought to reassure his readers that

> though it may be called an Oriental Empire, it is much less dangerous to us than that description might seem to imply. It is not an Empire attached to England in the same way as the Roman Empire was attached to Rome; it will not drag us down, or infect us at home with oriental notions or methods of Government. . . . It is self-supporting, and is held at arm's length in such a way that our destiny is not very closely entangled with its own.[31]

The anxious need to contain imperial "infection," the concern to ensure the profitability of the "Oriental Empire," and the resolution to hold all the signs of this empire "at arm's length": these are hallmarks of Englishness itself, and emerge in a tension with Seeley's conception of empire as an organic "expansion of England." As England expands, a Little England would appear to close itself off from a Greater Britain so that "it is not an

Empire attached to England" in any intimate way. Yet given the depth of England's imaginative investments, it was impossible that England's destiny could be anything but "very closely entangled" with that of its empire, and it is not "oriental notions or methods of Government" that are held at arm's length. Rather, relegated beyond the *cordon sanitaire* of Englishness and spectatorship to the realm of the oriental are those aspects of nineteenth-century domestic culture that accompany the features Salisbury identifies with India: passion, excess, exaggeration, dissolute behavior, disloyalty, and perfidy. Englishness, in other words, is constituted as free of "Oriental infection" by holding at arm's length its own excesses, displacing England's own "warm" desires onto convenient avatars of oriental "notions and methods" such as Mrs. Brown's extravagant elephant, the rapacious tiger, or the treacherous serpent. The "proper [English] sperrit" Mrs. Brown lauds in the Queen does not, therefore, have primarily to do with a general attitude toward the alterity of the wild beast. Rather, it is the *impulse* to manage the exotic beast in the first instance, and the specificity of the forms of zoological management in the second, that define English propriety as an ongoing practice of constituting and ordering the imperial whole. These forms and practices, though long-standing, consolidated and proliferated in the nineteenth century.

AGAINST VULGAR ADMIRATION: MANAGING THE ANIMAL KINGDOM AT LARGE

The first permanent collection of exotic beasts managed in England was in its early days not a public one, but the animals exhibited within it already conveyed a sense of English relations to alien places. In the thirteenth century the first permanent, standing menagerie[32] was established by Henry III, who ordered houses built at the Tower of London for the animals given him as diplomatic tribute. The emperor of Germany sent Henry three leopards to realize in flesh the emblematic beasts on Henry's heraldic device. From Norway came a white bear, and the king of France offered the gift of an elephant, the first in England in the Common Era.[33] For many centuries, however, these animals were available only for the viewing of the Royal Family and its guests, and the first recorded menagerie established primarily for the English public seems to have been at Bartholomew Fair in 1708, where a diminutive collection boasted a monkey, a kind of ostrich, an opossum, and an eagle.[34] Small menageries accompanied the traveling fairs throughout the eighteenth century, but they were chiefly sideshow attractions that could not accommodate large and difficult-to-maintain exotic animals. The limited range of animals kept in the eighteenth-century menagerie is suggested by the advertisement circulated by one showman in 1795 who had procured an elephant: he alleged it was "the only animal of the kind seen in this kingdom for upwards of TWENTY YEARS."[35]

In the decade spanning the turn of the nineteenth century, however, two sorts of menagerie experienced tremendous growth and, like the Tower Menagerie, placed emphasis upon the beasts' connections with alien spaces and people. One type exhibited animals in cages in a single location. The most famous of this sort of menagerie was the Exeter 'Change Menagerie, founded by Gilbert Pidcock in the late eighteenth century and transferred first to S. Polito and then to Edward Cross in the second decade of the nineteenth century. By 1820 Cross had rendered his menagerie sufficiently prominent to publish a guide in which he described his aim as "to procure rare and extraordinary animals, from every region of the Globe, for the information and entertainment of my countrymen."[36] So successful was Cross in pursuing this goal of relating the world's exotic spaces to England that, according to Richard Altick, "'Exeter Change' had become virtually synonymous with 'menagerie' in the London vocabulary," despite the visibility of the Tower Menagerie's competing attractions, which by the seventeenth century had come to be available to a wider audience, including Londoners such as Samuel Pepys.[37]

The second type of popular menagerie traveled extensively in large caravans and exhibited throughout England, from London's Bartholomew Fair to provincial "wakes" festivals. The most successful of these menageries was directed by George Wombwell from 1805 until his death in 1850; a number of shorter-lived outfits such as Atkins' and Hilton's ran distant seconds to Wombwell. Wombwell's show remained successful throughout the century, growing so large that by the time of George Wombwell's death it had split into three touring units, managed by his wife, nephew, and niece, respectively. In 1889 another niece and her husband, E. H. Bostock, took over the company under the combined name "Bostock and Wombwell's Menagerie," and during the Bostocks' management, one of the units traveled to Continental Europe, South Africa, India, and Singapore for a six-year run. The last showing of Bostock and Wombwell's menagerie was in 1931, after which time the company disbanded and the animals were sold off.

In the first years of the nineteenth century, the proprietors of both types of menagerie—standing and traveling—relied heavily upon England's colonial connections for their collections. At points in their careers, Pidcock and Wombwell operated beast shops and served as intermediaries between domestic English consumers and ships returned from colonized spaces with animals: Wombwell, for instance, cultivated relationships with Thames pilots who discovered for him whether incoming East Indiamen had exotic animals, and thereby ensured that he would have the pick of the most desirable specimens.[38] Edward Cross's correspondence reveals contacts both deliberate and occasional to do with amateur traders at St. Catherine's Docks, gentlemen speculators in Kent, and snake traders from Bristol.[39] Wombwell, Edward Cross, and their colleagues strongly encouraged the overseas trade in exotic animals by paying handsomely for the beasts sent to England, and the animal dealers who followed in their wake—William Cross, W. and C. Jamrach, Carl Hagenbeck, J. D. Hamlyn, and G. B. Chapman[40]—began to coordinate the trade abroad to such an extent that, as Harriet Ritvo contends, they "became part of the boundary between the African or Asian wilds and the streets of urban Britain; they were agents of the process of imperialism rather than exhibitors or celebrants of its results."[41]

Early in the century these same imperial agents also became brokers for theaters, such as the Royal Covent Garden Theatre, and circuses, supplying live beasts for lavish performances of "Eastern" stories. While the theater's employment of exotic animals was not appreciable after the 1830s, the circus—the chief exemplum of which was Astley's Amphitheatre at Westminster Bridge—took root as a robust urban phenomenon in the 1820s and continued its growth into the later parts of the nineteenth century. Circus and pantomime performances such as those at Astley's tended to emphasize the role of exotic megafauna in tales of imperial conquest, rule, and pageantry, employing them in hippodramatic representations of imperial military campaigns with titles like "The BURMESE WAR Or, OUR VICTORIES IN THE EAST" (27 March 1826) and "AFFGHANISTAN [sic] WAR! Or, THE REVOLT OF CABUL; AND BRITISH TRIUMPHS IN INDIA" (20 May 1850). Astley's began in 1768 as an equestrian show that emphasized trick riding and military spectacles, but in the early nineteenth century it increasingly orientalized its military displays by the inclusion of zoological exotica, and later, as the largest fairs such as Bartholomew and Greenwich declined, it absorbed the kinds of sideshow spectacles that had proved their worth at the fairs. By the end of the nineteenth century the menagerie and the circus were no longer so easily distinguishable, as both circuses and menageries traveled, the largest of the circuses, such as "Lord" George Sanger's, relied heavily upon their zoological collections for their attractions, and Bostock and Wombwell's Menagerie mounted its own circus (1893).[42] Much of what one can say about the traveling menagerie at the end of the century applies to the traveling circus, and vice versa.

Though the lines distinguishing the menagerie and the circus gradually blurred over the course of the nineteenth century, the Tower Menagerie—a metropolitan attraction rivaling Exeter 'Change[43]—gave way definitively to the Zoological Gardens in Regent's Park, the first experiment in what came to constitute the third major type of the imperial menagerie. In 1826 Sir Stamford Raffles—colonial administrator and founder of Singapore—issued a prospectus for a zoological society whose "great objects" should be the acclimatization, or domestication, of alien species for the purposes of English husbandry and "the establishment of a general zoological collection . . . so as to afford a correct view of the animal kingdom at large, in as complete a series as may be practicable."[44] The emphasis on completeness, on apprehending the animal kingdom in its entirety, was nevertheless always in the context "of national priorities and national service," as Ritvo observes—that is, it was shaped with an eye toward the ongoing work of imperial expansion.[45] The Zoological Gardens that opened in 1828 continued—indeed, succeeded—the Tower Menagerie's imaginative work of marking the nation's relation to the world, and Royal beasts such as the collection of animals given to the Prince of Wales on his state visit to India in 1875–76 (including four elephants) made their way to Regent's Park rather than the Tower.[46] By contrast with the Tower, the specimens exhibited at the Zoo were made available to a wide public, first Zoological Society members and then the general spectator, in a more spacious, comprehensive, and carefully planned set of exhibitions than the Tower was able to offer.

In establishing itself as a scientific venture, the Zoological Society sought not only to distinguish the foreign from the domestic within its collections but also to differentiate formally its institutions from the popular menageries—for instance, rejecting the offer of expertise and practical assistance from Edward Cross of the Exeter 'Change outfit[47] and insisting that the animals on display should not be the objects "of vulgar admiration" and that the collection must not aspire to "the mere exhibition of animals" but should fulfill "some useful purpose."[48] A guide to the newly opened Zoological Gardens in Regent's Park, for instance, distinguished the Zoo's spaces from those of the popular collections, arguing that the animals "are here seen to much better advantage than when shut up in a menagerie, and enjoy the luxury of fresh air, instead of unwholesome respiration in a room or caravan"; this represents an "improvement . . . altogether in accordance with the liberality of the age and all the animals are in duty bound to join in a concert of gratitude for so salutary a reform."⁴⁹ Yet despite its efforts to distance itself from the circus and the menagerie, particularly its attempts to cultivate the patronage of the fashionable and cosmopolitan classes over against the provincial and "vulgar" factions held to patronize the traveling menagerie and the urban circus, the zoo in the end had a good deal in common with these other forms of the imperial menagerie. The Regent's Park Gardens depended largely upon the same stock of animals, the same animal dealers, and the same East Indiamen that the menageries did; and soon the Zoo was compelled to admit the public and its "vulgar admiration" to the gardens' proper, disciplined, and "correct view of the animal kingdom at large."⁵⁰

If the lines separating the scientific from the vulgar were inevitably blurred, nevertheless the more important lines were observed: from their inauguration the Society and its collections of zoological specimens, both live in the Zoo and preserved in its museum, emphatically marked out the difference of the domestic from the foreign and the exotic even as they invited the educated spectator to imagine a global kingdom of beasts. While Raffles's 1826 prospectus called for "Animals [to be] brought from every part of the globe,"⁵¹ the 1829 *Catalogue of the Animals Preserved in the Museum of the Zoological Society* points out that "British species are distinguished from the foreign by a black margin on the base of the stands."⁵² The black margin differentiating the domestic and the alien invited the scientific researchers whom Raffles and the Society conceived as its primary patrons to think global totality and English difference simultaneously.

While the Regent's Park Zoological Gardens initially aimed at exclusivity and scientificity, its slightly younger sibling, the Royal Zoological Gardens, Surrey—established in Walworth by Edward Cross from the remnants of his Exeter 'Change menagerie, perhaps partly to spite the Regent's Park Zoo for having slighted him—was founded "so that the advancement of zoological science will be associated with popular gratification."⁵³ The emphasis of Surrey was upon the gardens' broad appeal, built upon zoological curiosities: "it has charms alike for all ages and conditions of persons; for the old and the young; for the cursory observer of nature, and the profound explorer of its purposes and mysteries."⁵⁴ But materials promoting the Surrey Gardens also stressed the naturalism of the environment and the exoticism of the views created: "The quadrupeds and birds must surely rejoice at their removal from the murky dens of Exeter 'Change to so delightful a region as the present, even slightly as it assimilates with the luxuriance and vastness of their native forests and plains."⁵⁵ Amidst fetes for Princess Victoria, dahlia shows, and balloon ascents, the Surrey Gardens also insisted upon documenting the high-caste pedigrees of its elephants Radjepoor and Hadjepoor and foregrounding the authenticity of the giraffes' North African keepers Drees, Hali, Mahomed Hamet, and Hamet Saffi Canaana.[56] Surrey emphasized its Royal patronage and connections, advertising widely Edward Cross's attendance at Windsor upon the death of the Queen's favorite monkey Jocko in 1839, and the transfer of the Queen's ocelot from St. Catherine's Docks to the Surrey Gardens.[57] Surrey survived for almost three decades, but the charms of its fauna grew noticeably tired after the retirement of Cross in 1844.

The strategies of the Surrey Gardens' "aristocratic rival" in Regent's Park proved more durable: though it did not furnish military spectacles or allegorical pageants figuring Englishness in relation to empire, as did the circuses and popular menageries, nor did it shamelessly tout its Royal associations as Surrey did, nevertheless its purpose as "a new type of establishment intended to serve the entire nation"[58] nonetheless dramatized the relation of England to its exotic elsewheres. As the zoo grew to be understood as an institution expressing and reflecting national and urban ideals, its form was replicated across the island. As one paper expressed the wish, "We hope that Surrey and Middlesex will not be the only zoological counties, but that gardens will spring up, ultimately, in every corner of the kingdom."[59] And they did: zoos arose in Bristol (1835), Manchester (1836), and Leeds (1840), and later in Southport (1906) and Birmingham (1910).[60]

Indeed, from the vantage of the twenty-first century, the zoo appears the most robust and enduring institution deriving from the menageries, surviving in an era from which menageries have almost vanished altogether and in which circuses are steadily divesting themselves of megafauna. Already in the nineteenth century the zoo had imposed its form substantially upon the older popular menageries. The showman E. H. Bostock, never one to miss an opportunity, expanded his repertoire to include a zoo in Glasgow in 1897, complementing his circuses and his several traveling menageries.[61] And beyond its material manifestations the zoo became an especially powerful trope, sometimes even subsuming the menagerie, as when Wombwell's came to be described as a "zoo on wheels."[62] The zoo's emphasis upon natural history was a guarantee of its cultural respectability, and its success meant that the zoo's rationale furnished the standard by which even vulgar collections were measured: in 1872 the *Scotsman* lauded Wombwell's Menagerie for educating the nation in natural history, arguing that the Menagerie had "done more to familiarise the minds of the masses of our people with the denizens of the forest than all the books of natural history ever printed during its wandering existence."[63]

The Regent's Park Zoo's relatively circumscribed framework as a scientific institution meant that it tended not to embed its displays of zoological exotica within larger exhibitions of imperial culture, as other small- and large-scale exhibitions (and the Surrey Gardens) did in the nineteenth century. These latter displays constitute a fourth major institutional form assumed by the menagerie. Smaller shows, such as those staged in the Colosseum in Regent's Park, the Egyptian Hall in Piccadilly, Saville House in Leicester Square, and the Lord Mayor's Shows often incorporated live or preserved animals as embellishments, allegories, and illustrations of exotic elsewheres. The Lord Mayor's Show hired camels and elephants from circuses and processed them through the streets of London as dramatizations of London's preeminence as the administrative and cultural heart of the empire. In a more naturalistic vein, "The African Glen," exhibited at the Colosseum in the 1830s, promised "to bring before the eye of the spectator the leading features of those far-off regions" of Africa by combining preserved specimens of gazelle, antelope, hyena, anteater, and other species with dramatic pictures of wounded elephants and "Hottentots."[64] Dioramas at the Portland Gallery in Regent Street and the Asiatic Gallery in Portman Square illustrated "the interior of the most important as well as the most interesting province[s] of the British Empire" by highlighting distinctively attractive exotica such as camels and elephants.[65]

The exotic beasts in these displays served not only to convey a sense of the alien or the imperial but also to render an exhibition of the imperial complete or to make a display intelligible by analogy with the zoological. In 1826 a Burmese State Carriage, captured by the British army in 1824, was on show at the Egyptian Hall as an instance of "Eastern magnificence" and of barbaric "taste and refinement."[66] Yet the carriage for all its opulence and exoticism—carved, gilded, and encrusted with gems—was apparently not an exhibition sufficient in itself; rather, the exhibition handbook noted, "In order to convey some faint idea of the effect of the whole, representations of the White elephant have been added" (fig. 8).[67] The elephant was thereby rendered a necessary aesthetic property, rounding out the composition's display of "elegance" and "taste and refinement," as well as providing a spur to the geopolitical imagination. If the Rath conveyed a sense of the Burmese as "a people, almost *wholly unknown* to us, and imagined to be in a state of rudeness scarcely removed from barbarism,"[68] the elephant helped approximate "the effect of *the whole*" (emphasis added). In translating the anthropologically "wholly unknown" to an approximation of a known "whole," the exotic animal was a frequent rhetorical prop. In 1847,

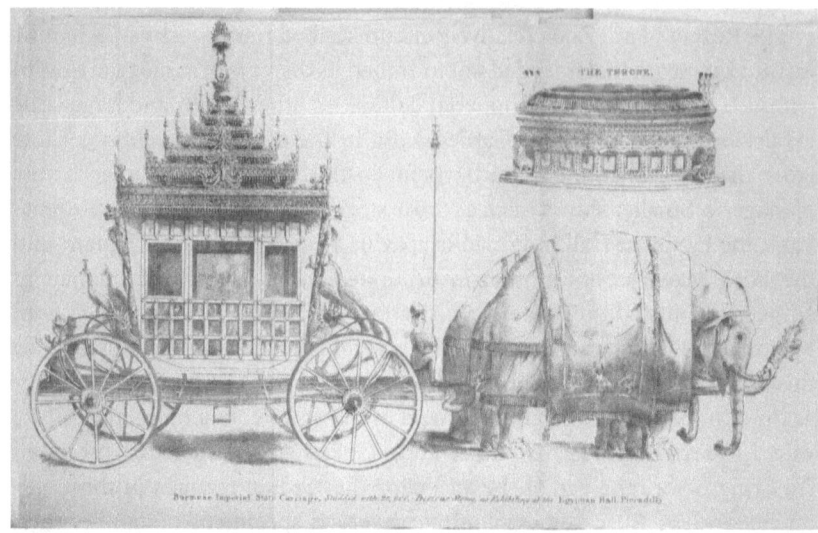

Figure 8. Burmese Imperial State Carriage, The Egyptian Hall, 1826. *Permission The British Library (Shelfmark Th.Cts.52).*

for instance, the Egyptian Hall offered a group of live African Bush People for public speculation, in order to "gratify . . . the man of science and the student in zoology." The Bush People were displayed alongside an exhibition of zoological curiosities: giraffe, lion, and zebra skins, bear's paws, African boar's tusk, and red-billed crane's head.[69] In its review the *Times* conflated the two portions of the exhibit, concluding that the Bush People were "mere animals in propensity, and worse than animals in appearance," while the *Morning Post* recorded that they "bear a marked resemblance to the baboon, ourang-outang, or chimpanzee."[70] Around 1850, at 6 Leicester Square, an exhibit of three African Bushmen was advertised as a display of "MEN MONKIES!" on the grounds that their conversation was "more like the gibbering of monkies than the language of men."[71] To the extent that the bestial rhetoric surrounding these exhibitions had an aesthetic component, it was one that conveyed a sense of the grotesqueness of the spectacle, rendering the novelty of the Bush People intelligible in the more familiar terms of the zoological curiosity—which, it was assumed, could be apprehended in a comprehensive way.

The "general long-period exhibition"[72]—as distinct from the shorter-run, smaller-scale displays in the Colosseum, the gallery, or the Egyptian Hall—similarly incorporated live, preserved, and artifactual zoological specimens as part of massive efforts to foster a "complete" and "exhaustive" sense of English holdings around the globe through the imaginative properties ascribed to the exotic animals.[73] In the displays at the Crystal Palace in Hyde Park in 1851 (the Great Exhibition of Works of Industry of All Nations), at the annual International Exhibitions in London (1871–74), in South Kensington in 1886 (the Colonial and Indian Exhibition), at Earls Court in 1895 (the Empire of India Exhibition), in the Great White City, Shepherd's Bush in 1908 (the Franco-British Exhibition), and at Wembley in 1924 and 1925 (the British Empire Exhibition), hunting trophies, collections of living animals, live-action pageants, and fixed dioramas all explicitly sought to illustrate imperial dynamics by incorporating zoological displays. The 1886 Colonial and Indian Exhibition, for instance, offered a constellation of exhibitionary exotica, in which the beast on show invited the spectator to imagine the stories of which it was a part and generated a series of complementary and supplementary narratives. The show featured an "Exhibition of Living Animals from the Colonies and India,"[74] taxidermic trophies dramatizing "Jungle Life" and "Elephant Hunting,"[75] any number of canvases depicting scenes of sport and natural history, and individual displays of native fauna in the colonial sections. The Queensland contingent, for instance, furnished a display of platypuses along with dramatizations of an eagle killing a wallaby and of a wild dog killing a kangaroo.[76] These were plainly among the most spectacular features of the exhibitions: in her contemplations on the International Exhibition of 1871, Arthur Sketchley's Mrs. Brown is struck particularly by the "stuffed beasts, a-gorin' and a-tearin' one another to bits"—in its savage substance evidence of the need to manage and contain the exotic, and in its taxidermic form a testimony to the masterful accomplishment of that goal.[77]

Comparable if varied dramatizations were openly on display at the 1908 Franco-British Exhibition at the Great White City, Shepherd's Bush. In the Indian Arena, three thousand spectators watched thrice-daily enactments of "Our Indian Empire," in which acrobats, tightrope walkers, and snake charmers performed, wrestlers ran races with animals, working elephants carried lumber, and—in addition to an impressive procession of fifty exotic animals—twelve elephants rode forty-foot flumes into a lake.[78] Even this 1908 collection of views of India appeared minuscule, however, compared to the performance of the Pageant of Empire at Wembley Stadium at the Empire Exhibition of 1924, which took three days to dramatize a unified narrative of the empire, drawing the many disparate narratives of the menagerie such as those on display in "Our Indian Empire" into a single master-narrative.

Hundreds of exotic beasts served as living illustrations of this lavish, unifying story:

> the future of the world is closely involved in what we make of the Empire. ... We thought, then, to put forward in music, poetry and movement, a spectacle, as striking as we might contrive it, of our wonderful story; to show in pageant the whole moving tale of our achievement; to light the torches of the future at the glowing heart of the past.[79]

In each of these large-scale exhibitions, and in a range of exhibits, spectacles, activities, and pageants, the mere appearance or description of the exotic animal was fashioned into a larger, more "wonderful" imperial story, as the comprehensive scene of exhibition opened onto still wider vistas of narrating "the whole moving tale" of imperial advance.

Even as the many forms of the menagerie shared a general strategy of rendering up the empire as an integrated but structured totality, they nevertheless challenged each other's representational authority and imaginative primacy. Critiques of competing forms of zoological display were formulated primarily on aesthetic bases and pointed up the relative strengths and weaknesses of the medium. Early in the century Edward Cross contrasted his Exeter 'Change Menagerie to illustrations of, writing about, and preserved specimens of zoological exotica, highlighting the extent to which differences among the kinds of zoological collection have essentially to do with form:

> The accounts of writers on the subject of Zoology, are generally too florid, or too dry, and often does imagination come in to decorate the former, or a barren supply of correct information compel the latter to be concise and unsatisfactory. One half of those writers never saw, probably, the animal, of which they treated, in a live state; plates or stuffed specimens affording them the only grounds of information, save an accompanying imperfect description.[80]

The implication is, of course, that the Royal Menagerie, Exeter 'Change, and Cross's own accounts alone could furnish the satisfactory blend of imagination and correct information that natural history writing and stuffed specimens could not manage, and to this extent Cross champions a particular aesthetic vision for the menagerie. Seventy-five years later, Rowland Ward, a self-proclaimed "practical and artistic taxidermist," promoted his collections as superior to the many written descriptions and narratives of animals offered in hunting, natural history, and travel volumes, on one hand, *and* to the living displays of the menagerie and the zoo, on the other:

> there are thousands of our fellow-countrymen who, had they the famous wishing-carpet of the Arabian Nights, would desire to be transported to those soul-stirring jungles of the East, where the lordly tiger disputes the sovereignty of the waste with the ponderous elephant.... But the written description leaves something yet to the imagination, and the caged animal conveys no idea whatever of the same creature in the untrammelled freedom of his natural existence. The flabby and tissueless tiger of the menagerie is by no means the same hard, muscular beast of the jungles.... No, you require something more than a caged beast or a written description to give you a just idea of what the king of beasts ... can be in his native forests; and the wishing-carpet of the East has been provided by Mr. Rowland Ward in the wonderfully lifelike Scenes in the Jungle.[81]

Unlike Cross, Ward does not worry over an excess of fancy or floridity (least of all in his own prose), but instead demands the proper conveyance of the imagination, a task for which he claims neither zoological description nor the collection of caged animals really has the carrying power. That both Cross and Ward offered descriptive guides to their work suggests, however, that neither the commercial aspect of their work nor the epistemological functions of their collections was ever seriously threatened by the simple existence of other media and forms of exhibition in the nineteenth century. The magic "wishing-carpet of the East," the instrument of representation that enables imaginative travel and sates imperial appetites, was sufficiently capacious to cover the diverse forms of zoological display, including written descriptions and narratives, and yet proved so evanescent that the many forms of the imperial menagerie proved necessary to conjure up the empire as a feature of daily life across Britain.

Picturesque Collections:
Delineating Empire, Framing the Carnival

The menagerie's management of the narratives in which its exotic animals participated and that they evoked relied upon a spectrum of strategies ranging from elaborate naturalism to fantastic symbolism. The central question of imperial representation confronted by the collection appears at once aesthetic and political: What is the relation of the zoological part to the imperial whole? In its aesthetic aspect, the circus and traveling menagerie crafted characteristic responses to this question in the form of "tableaus," "pictorial groupings," and "beautiful pictures" that arranged animals to form assemblages exemplary in their harmonious composition.[82] The Regent's Park Zoological Gardens, too, were "laid out with great taste" and "the zoological attractions," while not exhibited in the monumental idiom of the architecture elsewhere in Regent's Park, nevertheless were held to be "not a whit less picturesque."[83] The Surrey Gardens were said to "abound with what artists consider *bits* of the picturesque."[84] Closely related was the political answer: the Prince of Wales described the Empire Exhibition of 1924 as "a living picture of the history of the Empire and of its present structure."[85] For all that the menagerie foregrounds theatrical elements, the picturesque provides the most important aesthetic category for considering the management of zoological exotica in the nineteenth century, and carries with it political implications. In the era in which Astley's took root at Westminster Bridge at the end of the eighteenth century, William Gilpin defined the picturesque as that which "unit[es] in one whole a variety of parts; and these parts can only be obtained from rough objects"; Gilpin went on to offer the lion or wild boar as characteristic figures marking the picturesque.[86] Astley's, Wombwell's, and the other proprietors of zoos, circuses, and popular menageries sought to forge senses of unity from their exhibitions (even if many of their creatures were smooth-coated, the animals' wildness gave them a rough aspect), and sometimes, as in the case of zoo aesthetics, this comprehensiveness and variety was theorized in the terms of the picturesque itself.

A century after Gilpin, H. P. Robinson reiterated Gilpin's central definition of the picturesque, noting that "The province or function of unity is to combine and bring to a focus the secondary qualities, such as variety, contrast, symmetry, &c. It is equally opposed to scattered ideas, scattered lines, or scattered lights in a picture."[87] The cultivation of this picturesque "unity," according to Robinson, should be undertaken through "selection, arrangement, and combination . . . so as to produce an agreeable presentation of forms and tones, to tell the story which is to be elucidated, and to embody the spirit of what it is intended the picture shall represent or suggest."[88] The picturesque, in other words, described a mode of arrangement that not only exhibited a "suggestive" or descriptive spirit, did not just *illustrate* a story, but also helped *tell* a story. Toward these pictorial and narrative ends—and despite whatever "variety," "contrast," and "scattered ideas" it might also display and dramatize—the circus and the menagerie selected, arranged, and combined people and animals to compose "tableaus" and "beautiful pictures" that could be advertised to a public keen to see oriental spectacles and dramatizations of colonial campaigns. And though playbills and the menagerie's barkers often used illustrations to direct spectators' attention to their exhibitions, the governing unity the menagerie labored to compose was never purely self-referential: indeed, the picturesque composition of the zoological collection most frequently took as "the story which is to be elucidated" the forging of imperial unity itself—in the circus's dramatizations of military conquest, in the stories describing the captivity and transport of zoo animals, and in the menagerie's allegories that ended by assembling tableaus of imperial harmony.

In this respect, the menagerie's typical compositions and practices also had a political dimension, the picturesque defining the imperial itself. The empire exceeded any single person's ability to experience or comprehend in its entirety: between 1870 and 1914 alone, the empire claimed as its own an additional five million square miles.[89] This was a fact readily acknowledged: a writer early in the twentieth century noted that, though the British claimed to "bring the whole of India under their sole sway and sovereignty," nevertheless "No one man has ever seen, nor will ever see, the hundredth part" of even the Indian Empire.[90] This single piece of the imperial puzzle, India, was held by another author to be "like a wide sea, difficult to apprehend despite its pervasive influence on men's minds."[91] The exhibitionary complex represents a response to this dilemma, and in its exhibitions and tableaus the menagerie draws a boundary that defines the imperial as that which is amenable to menageristic display. Uvedale Price, Gilpin's contemporary, distinguished the picturesque from the sublime on the grounds that the picturesque imposed limits upon the overwhelming: "Infinity is one of the most efficient causes of the sublime; the boundless ocean, for that reason, inspires awful sensations: to give it picturesqueness you must destroy that cause of its sublimity; for it is on the shape and disposition of its boundaries that the picturesque in great measure must depend."[92] An important effect of the menagerie's work was the practical shaping of the cognitive boundaries of empire, stripping it of its infinite character and defining it as a singular totality: Britannia's menagerie allowed her to rule—that is, to give essential form to—the wide and sublime imperial seas.

Sometimes this work of bounding constituted a purely formal gesture, though striking, as in Astley's representation in 1825 of a "Grand Allegory. Neptune in his Car conceding the rule of the Seas to Britannia. Triumphal

Flags, inscribed with the Names of our Gallant Admirals. Europe, Asia, Africa & America lay their Offerings at the Feet of the British Lion."[93] Such representations hardly needed Seeley's reminder to "beware of putting England alone in the foreground and suffering what we call the English possessions to escape our view in the back ground [sic] of the picture."[94] But just as often the narratives and tableaus offered less figurative understandings of imperial holdings: Rowland Ward's zoological trophies at the 1886 and 1895 exhibitions, for instance, rendered India as the space in which the British sportsman would encounter the elephant and the tiger, and Arthur Sketchley's comic narrative *Mrs. Brown on the Prince's Visit to India* (ca. 1875) envisioned India as a place "with wild beasts at every pint, jest for all the world like the Zewlogical Gardins, without no cages nor bars to keep them wild hanimals in their places, as is apt to make too free, partikler the monkeys."[95] In Mrs. Brown's account, the zoo defines and delimits what she imagines about the Indian Empire, even as she laments the perceived lack of limits of the latter: "it must be that puzzlin' 'ow to walk [about in India], cos jest as you'er a-gettin' out of a tiger's way, slap you comes full butt on a lion, and preaps might set down on a serpint, as I can't abear the sight on myself, not even that case as is full on 'em at the Zewlogical Gardins, as is best in bottles filled up with sperrits."[96] The representations of the menagerie in both of these idioms—the allegorical and the naturalistic—constitute the basic stuff out of which zoological narratives are fashioned, defining an imperial landscape, its actors, and their relations. If the empire seemed to have "no cages nor bars" nor cases to keep things in their proper place, the collection and its display nevertheless furnished them symbolically.

Nineteenth-century writers employed the term "delineation" to catalog, describe, and advertise zoological collections and displays, as in the early *Delineation of Curious Foreign Beasts and Birds, in Their Natural Colours; Which are to be seen alive at The Great Room over Exeter Change and at The Lyceum, in the Strand* (1791) and *The Gardens and Menagerie of the Zoological Society Delineated* (1830–31).[97] Just as the catalog outlined and described the key features of the zoological display, so the menagerie furnished delineations of the empire, extending into global space the ethos of such circus performances as Astley's "Equestrian delineation of THE UNION OF NATIONS! OR, England, Ireland & Scotland."[98] Pressing the logic of such spectacles to its limit, one might say that the institutions of the menagerie thoroughly delimited and mapped the empire for a domestic English audience. This is graphically the case in maps of the empire produced for

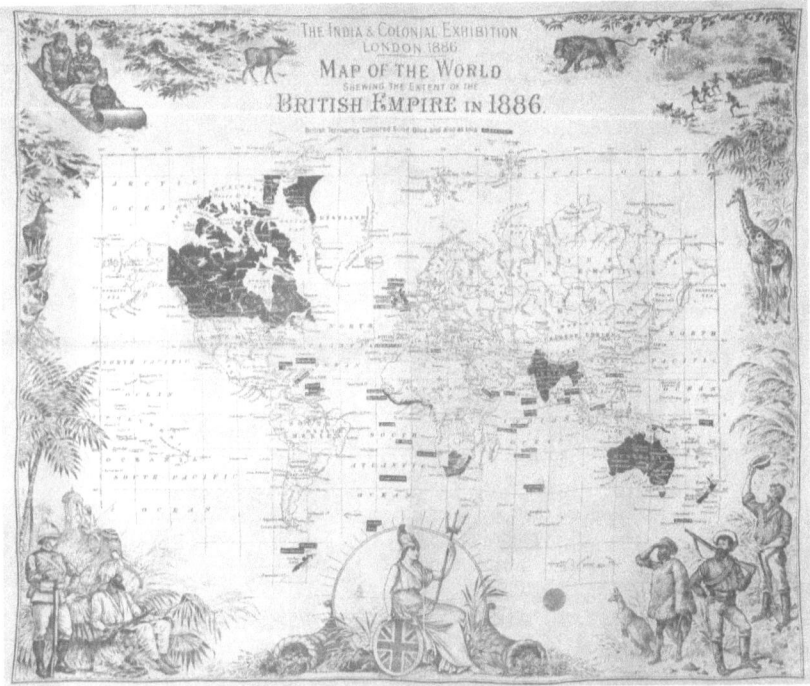

Figure 9. Map of the World, Colindian Exhibition, 1886. *Permission The British Library (Shelfmark Maps.183.q.1(13))*.

the 1886 Colindian Exhibition. There the representation of British holdings around the world is framed by the display of colonial administrators, sportsmen, exotic beasts, and native populations: the elk, lion, giraffe, kangaroo, and elephant define the outer limits of an empire that a radiant but firmly grounded Britannia rules from the center, the coordinating point for the world and a temperate, moderating middle (fig. 9).

So also with the Albert Memorial, which features signal animals around which Europe, Asia, Africa, and America are ordered: as Richard L. Stein notes, the monument "functions . . . *as* a map—not only filling but representing space, articulating the relations between places, picturing a world larger than itself."[99] The designer George Gilbert Scott originally conceived of these groups as "representing allegorically the quarters of the globe, with reference to the Great International Exhibitions which have done so much for art," and which serve as prime exempla of the Victorian desire to totalize the world (fig. 10).[100] The express purpose of the Memorial was to

Figure 10. John Foley's "Asia," from the Albert Memorial (1872). *Photograph by Kevin Anderson.*

become "monumental and national in character,"[101] even as it looked to the world to express that national character. The zoological sculptures recognize, therefore, both Englishness and its totalizing construction of its imperial elsewheres, in much the way that J. R. Seeley's lectures in *The Expansion of England* emphasize the English construction of India, acknowledging as "false" the impression that "presupposes India to have been a conscious political whole. The truth is that there was no India in the political, and scarcely in any other, sense" before England's cultural, political, and economic work in South Asia.[102] The monument to Albert maps and materializes for the English both the empire as a whole and England's relation to that whole.

And yet the animal of flesh in the living collection is not so easily contained as is the monumental beast of stone. John Berger observes that "In principle, each cage [in a zoo] is a frame round the animal inside it. Visitors visit the zoo to look at animals. They proceed from cage to cage, not unlike visitors in an art gallery who stop in front of one painting, and then move on to the next or the one after next. Yet in the zoo the view is always wrong."[103] The difficulty with the displayed animal as framed picture is that the animals are living their own lives, and nineteenth-century newspaper accounts abound with tales of animals declining to behave in accord with the picturesque, and refusing to "keep cool in Britannia's menagerie." Animals in collections frequently killed or mauled keepers and spectators, and when animals did not conform to the dictates of the menagerie's prescribed forms, when English spectators refused to abide by management's rules and abuse animals, or when the beast served symbolically to illustrate confusion and disorder—as for instance in Sketchley's *Mrs. Brown* stories—the carnivalesque element of the menagerie can be understood to emerge most clearly. Stallybrass and White emphasize that such "token transgressions" work against prevailing "model[s of] the double process of colonialism" that assured English viewers of both the essential assimilability of the exotic *and* its irremediable inferiority. Because the "critical divisions between spectator and spectacle ... were constantly renegotiated and unstable," they argue, the nineteenth-century exhibition consistently furnished regular "opportunity for symbolic acts of a self-consciously political kind."[104] Under this reading, the collection of exotica is always already carnivalesque, challenging frameworks that insist upon the beast's assimilability, inferiority, and reliable political symbolism.

Stallybrass and White take as their frame of reference, however, the social organization of the *fair* in the eighteenth century as it survived into the nineteenth, rather than the forms of aesthetic organization of the professional menagerie as it supplanted the fair in the nineteenth century. The menagerie, as we have seen, foregrounded its *management* of the collections in particular ways, the most important of which is the picturesque. The older forms of spectatorship and social organization affiliated with the carnival are precisely what the professional menagerie seeks to remake through its collections, emphasizing the "proper [English] sperrit" of the collection, with the approbation of Mrs. Brown and the Queen alike. For instance, while Wombwell's Menagerie began in an era of fairs and wakes, it soon became (like Astley's, Edward Cross and the Surrey Gardens, and eventually E. H. Bostock's circus) material practitioners of the history of imperialist capitalism, drawing upon the spoils of the East Indiamen and obviating the older forms of carnivalesque consumption—bear- and bullbaiting, cockfighting, wrestling and pugilism, and so on. What eighteenth-century conduct literature could not do in relation to the fair's displays, the nineteenth-century professional menagerie and zoo did with dazzling success; and in doing so, they also remade print genres surrounding the fair and popular entertainment to manage the narratives of the menagerie and thereby the conduct of the spectator. As much as the animal that is recalcitrant in behavior and unaccommodating in symbolism, the menagerie—rather than conduct literature—manages the spectator by its forms of display in the first instance and by its narratives in the second. That is, the professional deployment of notions of the picturesque—in the collection and in a growing print culture—increasingly contained and managed the carnivalesque aspects of popular entertainment by separating spectator from spectacle and delineating their roles and cultural locations. And the menagerie did so especially through its handling of the most spectacular of all megafauna, the elephant.

Seeing the Elephant: A "Keynote" Beast

Discourses of the picturesque in the nineteenth century called for painters and photographers to keep in the "foreground some object, or mass of objects, that will act as a keynote to keep the whole in harmony."[105] The figure of the elephant most often fills the function of "keynote" in the menagerie's varied compositions, forming the centerpiece for delineations of empire and exoticism, as in *Punch*'s framing of Victoria's coronation as Empress of India (fig. 11). Writing of the 1911 Delhi Durbar that crowned George V emperor and in which horses and motorcars largely replaced the spectacular elephant processions of the 1877 and 1902–3 coronation Durbars, Stanley Reed "lament[ed] the loss of picturesqueness in the disappearance of the elephant. The world can show no spectacle comparable to the procession of these noble beasts, painted to their eyes, clad in the gorgeous trappings of State."[106] The elephant was not only necessary to lend picturesqueness to the Durbar but also served as the linchpin of the circus's pictures. Garrard Tyrwhitt-Drake, the twentieth-century English circus proprietor, was more succinct in his mid-twentieth-century assessment: "a circus must have clowns, sweets, and elephants, and the greatest of these is elephants."[107] The presence of the elephant's keynote spectacle provided an important measure for gauging the success of the menagerie, pantomime, or circus throughout the nineteenth and twentieth centuries.

The spectacle of the elephant across the variants of the menagerie consistently took an orientalist cast, whether the animal's presentation was essentially static, with a caged animal available for casual viewing; dynamic, with an elephant as part of a scripted theatrical production; or interactive, with the elephant giving rides, shaking hands with its trunk, or waving handkerchiefs to ladies. The elephant was employed in performances representing North Africa, the Middle East, and India, and it became a kind

Figure 11. "Kaiser-I-Hind," *Punch*, 13 January 1877. *Courtesy Kelvin Smith Library Retrospective Research Collections.*

of synecdoche or stand-in for those exotic and difficult-to-imagine places: the choreography of the elephant's display combined with the common knowledge of its exotic origins made for unmistakably "Eastern" spectacles across England.[108] Though the lion had strong English resonances and the tiger was closely associated with India,[109] the elephant formed an ideal imperial beast, since it could be found across both Asia and Africa, it was richly ambivalent in its displays of both friendly and frenzied behavior, and it simultaneously coexisted with the tiger and lion and chased them down in hunts. The elephant's association with exotic spaces generally was a longstanding one, especially since trade in "the teeth of elephants," as Johnson's *Dictionary* (1755) calls ivory, was a conspicuous part of England's commerce with alien lands.[110] Early in the nineteenth century, the regularization of trade with the East Indies meant that live elephants could be efficiently transported to Britain and purchased at reasonable prices by menagerists and beast traders. In 1820 Wombwell's Menagerie offered the first acts staged exclusively for elephants, and by the end of the decade the London theaters began to mount oriental spectacles, such as the Adelphi's *The Elephant of Siam* in 1829, around the central presence of the elephant. These signal successes sparked a rage for performing elephants across England in the 1830s.[111]

The elephant maintained its preeminence in the circus ring, on the stage, and in the caravan long after the 1830s. Indeed, by midcentury the elephant came to form the central dramatic register of imperial totality in the zoological collection and served as the prime symbol (in Coleridge's sense) of both the zoological collection and the empire, conveying a sense of these larger wholes. As a necessary "keynote" or symbol for the exhibitionary display, the elephant no less than the exhibition in which it appeared helped to materialize and delineate the infinity of empire. One of the most enduring narratives of totality, John Godfrey Saxe's story of "The Blind Men and the Elephant," found a vogue in the mid-1860s, and in short order the tale formed a staple of American and British primers, children's books, and school songbooks. Saxe, an American poet, rendered into verse an Indian oral folktale about

> six men of Indostan
> To learning much inclined,
> Who went to see the Elephant
> (Though all of them were blind),
> That each by observation
> Might satisfy his mind.[112]

Intended as a "theologic" allegory about the inability to apprehend divinity directly,[113] Saxe's story describes the tendency to imagine the alien or unknown

Figure 12. W. L. Champney, "The Blind Men and the Elephant," John Godfrey Saxe, *Clever Stories of Many Nations* (Boston: Ticknor and Fields, 1865). *Courtesy Kelvin Smith Library.*

through the means of the known, and to approach the truth of the whole through the partiality of the familiar image. Because the elephant literally exceeds that which the blind men can individually grasp, they describe it in turns as a wall, a spear, a snake, a tree, a fan, and a rope—instruments rendered by W. L. Champney in the foreground of his illustration of Saxe's poem (fig. 12). The image of the known and the accessible enables the approach to the sublime, the abstract, or the total from a single perspective. In its "theologic" orientation and in its North American circulation, Saxe's story neatly exemplifies Coleridge's definition of allegory as that which translates abstraction into a picture language. When it was presented as an English school song, however, Saxe's note identifying the story's "theologic" moral was elided from the text: instead the verse appeared in the context of such imperial anthems as "The Empire Flag," "Coronation Day," and "God Save the King."[114] In the English rather than American context and with an imperial rather than "theologic" construction, the elephant forms a part of the whole it elucidates and consequently has more to say about a secular empire and its relation to the Eastern lands from which the fable emerged than it does about abstract demonstrations of religious disputation. In other words, the translation of the narrative from Saxe's New England setting to the English cultural environment also shifts the elephant in the fable from a simple allegory of divine unknowability to a rich symbol marking out imperial epistemologies.

The kernel of the story of the blind men and the elephant found its way into Anglo-American texts as a result of orientalist scholarship, and for an English narrative audience it is significant that all of the "disputants . . . in the wrong" are "men of Indostan," because "The Blind Men and the Elephant" appeared in the worried years following the widespread Indian rebellion against British rule in 1857. To the extent that reports of the "Mutiny" brought India into view of the English as an increasingly important though indistinct adjunct of English cultural and political life, the story of the blind men and the elephant illustrates a general anxiety about England's expansion into distant corners of the globe. Like the empire in the eyes of the English, the elephant in the narrative stands as an impressive whole whose enormity renders it impossible to grasp it in its total aspect. Yet elephants, unlike the empire as a whole, were available to the English public, both in Champney's illustration and in the menagerie's spaces of exhibition. Consequently, "The Blind Men and the Elephant" fashions the elephant as a figure elucidating this problem *and* implicitly proposes that the display of the elephant might constitute an effective way of solving it: in the menagerie one could both touch parts of the elephant *and* see the elephant in its total aspect. Harriet Ritvo notes that interactions with elephants frequently included taking rides, a practice that "encouraged visitors to think of them as temporary possessions or playthings," and hand-feeding the animals, "an act which symbolized both proprietorship and domination."[115] At the same time that the elephant symbolized the ungraspable extensivity of empire, it also imaginatively delimited it and demonstrated the promise that empire in its totality could be mastered by an English proprietary spirit.

By the early years of the nineteenth century, in fact, the human mastery of the elephant served as a robust analogy for the imperial mastery of the colony. In "The Irish Avatar" (1821), for instance, Byron compared colonial Ireland's subjection to England with "a bastinadoed elephant, / Kneeling to receive the paltry rider."[116] Yet as living symbols, elephants did not always kneel in obedience and in fact could display violently recalcitrant behavior: in May 1850 the *Times* reported on one of Wombwell's elephants that appeared as though it "would much rather break his caravan to pieces than draw it." This elephant smashed up the menagerie's wagons "like eggshells," threatened to liberate "animals perhaps even more prone to do mischief than the elephant," and provoked "the greatest alarm . . . amongst the observers."[117] When they were most alarming, rebelling rather than kneeling to their riders, pachyderms were most consistently identified with the colonized. When elephants revolt in the latter half of the century, they trouble the English imagination in a form of symbolic insurrection not easily laid to rest with the simple execution of the animal. In 1855, after two of Wombwell's performing elephants attacked a keeper, the *Times* paused over the volatile character of elephants: "We understand . . . that elephants are subject to sudden paroxysms of fury, in which they attack even those best known to them."[118] If the subjugation of the exotic animal in the menagerie conveyed a sense of English dominion in imperial spaces, the rebellion of such animals and their failure to be subdued provoked a general consternation, if not "the greatest alarm," about the potential instability of Britannia's menagerie.

As symbols, elephants constitute the center of the menagerie's pictures, suggest the possibility of empire's fundamental knowability, *and* install an uncertainty at the heart of both the menagerie's performances and the empire's management. Elephants, even when they kneel to receive their riders, harbor an unpredictable tendency to become entangled with savagery and to turn upon "even those best known to them." A "proper [English] sperrit," as Sketchley's Mrs. Brown conceives it, seeks to capture the elephant and render it picturesque, but the beast's living corporeality resists such formulaic reductions. Instead, it tends toward the carnivalesque, with significant representational implications, because the menagerie's animals were understood as symbols that abided as a part of that whole that they symbolized.

The sublime instability of the elephant is reflected in the phrase "see the elephant," which came into currency around the time of Saxe's publication of "The Blind Men and the Elephant" and at the point at which the phrase "see the lions"—to tour the leading features of London—began to disappear from common usage.[119] "Seeing the elephant" was a way to characterize an otherwise ineffable experience, especially a soldier's first experience in battle. It became in these circumstances a way to delimit an experience of sublimity that resisted the languages of realism and naturalism. "The other side of the coin," writes Robert A. Palmatier in explicating the phrase, "is *not* to see the elephant: i.e., either (1) to ignore *the elephant in the room* (something that is 'hidden in plain sight' or ignored because it is too frightening to think about), or (2) to arrive at a *description of an elephant* the way the blind men in the fable did."[120] As an integral part of the British economy, empire was always "hidden in plain sight" even in England's intimate home spaces; and, most literally, it was concentrated (if not exactly hidden) in plain sight in the arenas of exhibition. To risk a tautology, to "see the elephant" on show in the nineteenth century became quite literally a way to remedy "not seeing the elephant." That is, like the narrative of "The Blind Men and the Elephant" in the context of English imperial constructions, the elephant rendered concrete that which was always "hidden in plain sight"—the British Empire itself—even if it was viewed in the manner of the blind men, partially and in the distorting terms of the familiar.

Among the favorite ways of picturing the elephant at the height of imperial expansion was in the composite drawing or painting, scores of which were imported from India and reproduced from Indian originals. John Lockwood Kipling describes the composite as "a fantastic but very popular device [in which the artist] fill[s] up the outline of an animal with a jumble of various creatures."[121] Kipling dismisses them as "trivialities," arguing that they "scarcely bear description, and, like many more Oriental fancies, are safe from serious criticism."[122] Yet these "Oriental fancies" had a great success in England: Kipling himself includes three such images—of a camel, an elephant, and a horse—that overwhelm the very pages in which he dismisses them (figs. 13 and 14). Other nineteenth-century Anglo writers like Fanny Parks recorded and reproduced similar images among their Eastern travelogues, descriptions, and tales (fig. 15): what Kipling finds trivial Parks deems "clever" and of "much credit" to the artists.[123] Certainly these images are remarkable for the sense of dynamism they convey, suggesting a teeming animal life and purposive movement throughout the organic whole. Above all, they dramatize the way in which a number of incongruous elements can be gathered into a coherent totality: they select and combine elements carefully, and even if individual juxtapositions appear perverse rather than beautiful, sublime, or picturesque, nevertheless they still build toward an intelligible and picturesque whole, one that contains the carnivalesque elements of the beasts.

Picturing Britannia's Menagerie

A PERI ON A CAMEL

Figure 13. John Lockwood Kipling, "A Peri on a Camel," *Man and Beast in India* (New York: Macmillan, 1892).

The composite image of the elephant might be understood to constellate the fundamental dynamic of the elephant's relation to the menagerie and to the totalizing imperial aims of the zoological collection. Read solely as the "keynote" figure in the picture, the elephant frames the display of the other animals on show; it stands as a whole comprising other carefully ordered and managed wholes and parts; it forms a dynamic totality in a progress across the page or parchment; and from an English perspective (figure 16 is drawn from the holdings of the Bodleian Library) it invokes the exotic and (as for J. L. Kipling) constitutes an avatar of "Oriental fancies." Considered

KRISHNA ON AN ELEPHANT

Figure 14. John Lockwood Kipling, "Krishna on an Elephant," *Man and Beast in India* (London: Macmillan, 1892).

in relation to English zoological exhibitionary practices, it exemplifies the elephant's privileged place in the menagerie; it captures the menagerie's work to assemble coherent, sweeping views of the whole of the "wonder-fauna" of the world; its dynamism suggests the developing *activity* of managing both the traveling collection and an evolving empire in spectacle, scientific discourse, reportage, and popular narrative; and its gathering of other beasts within its corporeal limits conveys a sense of the total collection, and by extension the English Empire as an overarching whole, as composed of individual and subordinate wholes that maintain their own distinctive relations to the collection *in toto*.

Figure 15. "Kaniyajee and the Gopees," Fanny Parks, *Wanderings of a Pilgrim in Search of the Picturesque* (London: Pelham Richardson, 1850). Permission The British Library (Shelfmark 10055.f.20).

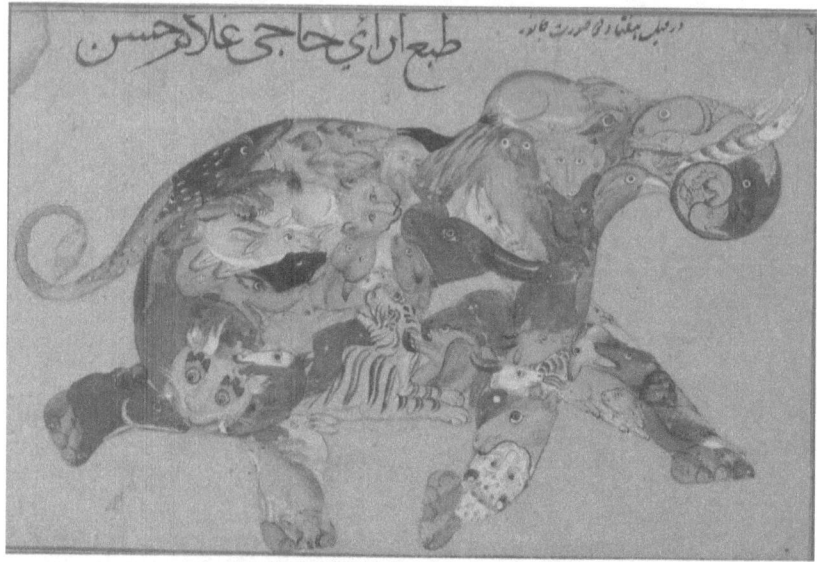

Figure 16. Composite Elephant (n.d.). *Permission Bodleian Library, University of Oxford (Shelfmark MS.Ouseley Add.171b. folio 9 verso).*

The elephant's special relation to the idea of totality, so richly illustrated in these composite images and in the tale of "The Blind Men and the Elephant," has proved remarkably durable, and what is more, this relation continues to be marked by associations with the exotic well after the formal ends of empire. For at least a century and a half the elephant has served not only as a "keynote" in exotic pictures shaped by exhibitionary institutions but also as a trope for totalities otherwise unrepresentable or inaccessible. When the body of the elephant is disrupted or disruptive, however, the totality is modified, threatened with a resurgence of the carnivalesque, and as a result it tends to generate rich, compensatory narratives that seek to come to terms with the disruption of the usual imaginative stream.

Dead Elephant Stories

The narrative genre of the disruptive elephant is a rich one: it includes the stories of the famed Chunee at Exeter 'Change, Wombwell's dead elephant at the fair, Jumbo at the zoo, and Rowland Ward's stuffed elephant fighting the tiger at the Colindian Exhibition, to say nothing of Wembley's Asian elephants pressing forward the "whole moving tale" of empire in 1924. The traveling and the fixed menageries generated a stock of tales repeated across the nineteenth century, especially those involving spectacular elephant deaths. Moments in which the menagerie's beasts became unmanageable and had to be put down, or in which they inconveniently died in the midst of exhibition, were always remarkable—that is, events that occasioned enthusiastic and repeated narration. Perhaps the most famous elephant story in the first part of the century involved Chunee, sent from Bengal, purchased by the Exeter 'Change menagerie in 1809, and first exhibited on stage in 1811 at Covent Garden. In 1826 Chunee began to smash his enclosure and Edward Cross concluded that he would have to be put down. As Richard Altick remarks, though, "to kill a berserk five-ton elephant in confined upstairs quarters, surrounded by agitated wild animals throwing themselves against the bars of their own cages, and in the midst of a great city, was not easy, and there was obviously no precedent for such an operation."[124] There was also no precedent for disposing of its carcass, which itself became a rank if highly lucrative spectacle, and a number of pamphlets and images emerged in the weeks following the elephant's death to render Chunee's life and final moments, supplementing the sensational newspaper accounts and anticipating the recollections of the episode published throughout the century (fig. 17).[125]

George Wombwell put into circulation a similarly spectacular and widely repeated anecdote about a dead elephant when, in racing to Bartholomew Fair from Newcastle one year to challenge his rival Atkins's Menagerie, his sole elephant died. When Atkins heard that Wombwell's elephant had died, according to Thomas Frost, he resolved

> to make capital of this, and placarded at once that he had "the only live elephant in the fair." Wombwell saw his chance, and had a huge canvas painted, bearing the words that within his show was to be seen "the only dead elephant in the fair." There never was a greater success; a live elephant was not a great rarity, but the chance of seeing a dead elephant came only once now and then. Atkins's was deserted; Wombwell's was crowded.[126]

The dead elephant at Exeter 'Change or in Wombwell's Menagerie, as much as the live elephant on stage in Covent Garden, was an unrivaled spectacle; it was also the raw material out of which some of the nineteenth century's most frequently repeated animal stories were fashioned.

Figure 17. "Destruction of the Furious Elephant at Exeter Change" (1826). *Permission The British Library (Shelfmark Crach.1.tab.4.b.4/14).*

The most famous resident of the Regent's Park Zoo in the nineteenth century, and the one giving rise to the most cherished—and outrageous—stories, was the elephant called Jumbo, who during his tenure at the zoo from 1865 to 1882 grew to be the largest animal in captivity, at "upwards of eleven feet."[127] Reportedly the first African elephant ever exhibited in England, Jumbo became a distinguished figure at the zoo, increasing "both in height and in the esteem of the British people": *Harper's Weekly* described the elephant as a kind of English "national pet."[128] As he approached sexual maturity, however, Jumbo began to behave violently, driving his tusks through iron plates and smashing up his reinforced enclosure.[129] The zoo's inability to accommodate the elephant resulted in the announced sale in January 1882 of Jumbo to the American circus proprietor P. T. Barnum for two thousand pounds and required his difficult relocation to the United States.

Jumbo anecdotes saturated print markets in Britain and the United States, partly as a result of Barnum's publicity, partly as a consequence of the genuine affection of the English for the zoo's elephant. The announcement that the national pet or, as one English paper dubbed Jumbo, "our amiable mascot" was to be removed to the United States sparked a national furor.[130] Letters to the editors of London newspapers protested his sale, schoolchildren and the more sentimental among adults sent in subscriptions to prevent Jumbo's removal, spectators flocked to the zoo to say farewell to Jumbo (attendance jumped by more than one thousand percent), and the popular press ran cartoons deploring the Yankee Barnum's theft of a national treasure. Although in previous years Queen Victoria had invited Barnum to exhibit Tom Thumb before her, to divert her with other portions of his show, and to play with her children, on the occasion of Jumbo's announced sale she became incensed by his ambitions.[131] Several accounts had the Queen telegraphing the Zoological Society to exhort it to cancel the agreement with Barnum at any cost to the State, and the Prince of Wales summoning the manager of the zoo to Marlborough House to urge the same point.[132]

The *New York Times* offered a facetious history of Jumbo's association with the Royal Family and the British state, targeting both the absurdly hyperbolic advertisements about Jumbo that Barnum was then circulating and suggesting the imperial dynamic that Jumbo, and by extension the collection of which he formed a part, exemplified. The paper suggested that

> from her earliest years her Majesty has been enthusiastically attached to *Jumbo*. There was a time when she was accustomed to keep *Jumbo* in the Windsor Castle Park, where she would often romp with him by the house, making him fetch and carry like a dog and rolling with him in innocent delight upon the turf.... After Lord Beaconsfield procured for his royal mistress the title of Empress of India, she became very fond of riding all around the back yard of Buckingham Palace in a *howdah* mounted on *Jumbo's* back, the Prime Minister sitting at the same time on the elephant's neck and acting as *mahout*.[133]

For all the patent absurdity of its imagined scenes, the American paper's story points up that Victoria's accession to the title "Empress of India" in January 1877 was an event that changed fundamentally the way England understood its relation to the world and to the exotic beast alike. In this view, if before her coronation in 1877 Victoria's affection for the elephant was domestic and innocent enough, after that event the elephant takes on unavoidable imperial associations, and it highlights culpable ambitions in both the Queen and in Disraeli, her "mahout"—ambitions that are far from in keeping with the expectation of English reserve and that edge toward the carnivalesque. The imminent removal of Jumbo from England, the American column suggests, will dispossess Victoria both of a sentimental favorite and of a currency symbolic of her empire. And this was not a view indigenous to the United States: Sketchley's Mrs. Brown entangles Jumbo with the Queen and her worries over matters imperial in *Mrs. Brown on Jumbo* (1882):

> [Jumbo's] a noble beast, and in course tho' Queen Wictorier is too much the lady to take a mean adwantage of any showman, and say as he shan't go, yet no doubt she'll give that Jewlogical Gardins a nasty one some day when they least espects it over Jumbo, as no doubt she'd 'ave went to 'ave said good-bye too, only 'ad 'er time that took up with Old Gladstin a-worretin' over Ireland, as put everythink else out of 'er 'ead for the time bein'.[134]

The expropriation of Jumbo finds Mrs. Brown, like Gladstone, worrying over the politics of empire, because it appeared he was "bein' sold like a negro black slave" without need, since with the proper attention in the London zoo, he would be perfectly manageable: "he'd obey anyone as he knowed was 'is real master, the same as Injier."[135]

In the most sustained and self-conscious meditation upon the elephant's relation to the imperial system, George Orwell made explicit the disruption of the settled notions of English administration to its imperial charges when the elephant's corporeality becomes more than an emblem of the exotic and imperial integrity in his essay-narrative "Shooting an Elephant," composed in the mid-1930s. Orwell's overt ambivalence ("I was stuck between my hatred of the empire I served and my rage against the evil-spirited little beasts who tried to make my job impossible") appears as a sign that "the British Empire is dying."[136] This ambivalence is exposed—and resolved in favor of anti-imperialism—as the narrator's desire "to drive a bayonet" into "the evil-spirited little beasts" is displaced by the necessity of making a bullet explode into the brains of a large beast, the elephant. In this sense, the elephant stands in as proxy both for the Burmese against whom the narrator's "rage" is more properly directed, and for Orwell's own ambivalence about the imperialist project. The shifting of the object of the narrative from "the evil-spirited little beasts" onto the elephant seems necessary to the production of the understanding at which Orwell arrives. "One day," Orwell writes, "something happened which . . . gave me a better glimpse than I had had before of the real nature of imperialism." That enlightening "glimpse" is of "an elephant [that] was ravaging the bazaar," and when the narrator is compelled by the protocol attendant upon his position to shoot the elephant, he is faced by his own ugly image as the agent of imperialism, an image emptied of all oriental romance: "I perceived in this moment that when the white man turns tyrant it is his own freedom that he destroys. He becomes a sort of hollow, posing dummy, the conventionalized figure of a sahib."[137] In its massive corporeality, the agency of the elephant makes visible for the narrator the structure of Western imperialism, in the end challenging the imperial administrator's sovereignty through the vicissitudes of its behavior.

Figures and tales of dead and disobedient elephants turn up in the novel, too, and the totalizing narrative's affiliations to the menagerie certainly include the wild beast as part of its content. Indeed, if the Mrs. Brown stories can be properly understood as novels, the animal is not only represented content but also constitutes part of the narrative discourse, while the beast's narrative management renders the novel a form both homologous and supplementary to the menagerie. What is more, both the novel and the menagerie negotiate competing desires to enframe zoological exotica and to indulge their tendencies to recalcitrance, balancing the picturesque and the carnivalesque in the midst of a developing culture of capitalism. If the model and primary referent for both the novel and the menagerie as totalizing forms is the empire as a contested but ultimately integrated whole, what happens to the belief in empire when exhibitionary styles—in the novel and the menagerie alike—change? Conversely, what happens to exhibitionary styles when belief in the regulative principle of imperial totality erodes? These are the questions to which I now turn, in order to explore the intersection of the novel and the menagerie across two centuries, in the writing of Thackeray, Gaskell, Dickens, Bennett, Woolf, Carter, Rushdie, and Barnes.

Chapter 2

Circuses in Cabinets

The Victorian Novelist as Beast Tamer

THE DOMESTIC SPACES IN WHICH wild beasts played out the imaginative repertoire of imperial England in the nineteenth century highlighted the convergence of the local and the global and enabled the national to define the imperial. They also helped dissolve traditional social boundaries and establish and refine bourgeois mores as the essence of Englishness. Narratives in the period capitalized upon such displays, offering them as arenas in which fancy could play, as salutary counterweights to the world of labor, and ultimately as spaces in which English cultural ideals could be explored and refined. In the middle of the century, and at the beginning of the "Golden Era" of circuses and menageries,[1] the work of William Makepeace Thackeray, Elizabeth Gaskell, and Charles Dickens exploited the narrative resources of the imperial menagerie, framing zoological exotica in a variety of forms and rendering collections of wild beasts as reflections of Englishness. These authors' speculations upon the menagerie vacillate in the ambivalent space between naturalism and allegory, as wild beasts figure empire in its totality and invoke a spectrum of associations these alien spaces sustain: gallantry, splendor, extravagance, excess, dissipation, waste, and savagery.

This chapter explores three prominent Victorian narratives that exploit the exotic animal on display. Of the novelists whose work is taken up here, Dickens relies most extensively upon the institution of the menagerie to craft a totalizing vision of England's relation to industrial modernity. The narrative discourse of *Hard Times* (1854) invokes the exotic with insistence, including allusions to the British in India, the *Arabian Nights,* simooms in desert lands, sultans, pigmies, savages, transportation and penal settlements, Turkish carpets, and Indian ale. Yet the story of the novel is resolutely domestic:

Dickens's novel reaffirms the imaginative boundaries between England and its imperial elsewheres and predicates a brand of domestic realism upon the containment of excesses and extravagances associated with the alien—including the signal exclusion of exotic beasts from the performances of Sleary's Circus. Dickens cast himself in the role of the famous American lion tamer when, in a letter to the zoological painter and sculptor Edwin Landseer, Dickens signed himself "otherwise Van Amburg."[2] In *Hard Times* Dickens's narrator comes to occupy the place of Isaac Van Amburgh, taming the wild beasts and turning them into profitable allegorical displays. In this novel, comprehending industrial society's relation to empire in holistic terms not only entails a symptomatic banishment of the exotic animal and the colonial excesses it represents from the English provinces, but also produces a selective realism that both demands the removal of the exotic animal from the disturbingly permeable space of the circus and depends upon its conscription into a profitable tropological service. Thackeray's *Vanity Fair* and Gaskell's *Cranford* anticipate elements of this service, however, and it is to them that I turn first.

Gallant Animals and Fancy Pictures: *Vanity Fair* and *Cranford*

Chapter 17 of William Makepeace Thackeray's *Vanity Fair* (1847–48) presents the auction house as a space like the zoo, the circus, or the menagerie in which the "gentle" and the "savage" mingle under the guise of "propriety," and in which diverse narratives as well as animals and things are gathered in collections:

> If there is any exhibition in all Vanity Fair which Satire and Sentiment can visit arm in arm together; where you light on the strangest contrasts laughable and tearful: where you may be gentle and pathetic, or savage and cynical with perfect propriety: it is at one of those public assemblies, a crowd of which are advertised every day in the last page of the "Times" newspaper.[3]

The auction house is a space of fictions and speculation, ultimately subordinate to profit. Because it both celebrates distinctiveness and renders it fungible, the goods and people who assemble in its rooms violate the usual boundaries separating the domestic and the imperial, the appropriate and the absurd, the pathetic and the laughable. The provisionality of the narratives animated by this space means that the auction can promise scenes even more remarkable than those afforded by Vauxhall's pleasure gardens, to which Amelia and Jos Sedley, George Osborne, Becky Sharp, and William Dobbin journey in chapter 6. In the whirl of advertised goods, even the most trivial of items gives rise to significant narrative adventures: one "minor object," described by the auctioneer as a "Portrait of a gentleman on an elephant," already physically framed as a picture (fig. 18), is nevertheless also contextualized by a pair of domestic narratives.[4] "'I wonder it aint come down with him,' said a professional wag, 'he's anyhow a precious big one;' at which (for the elephant-rider was represented as of a very stout figure) there was a general giggle in the room." The auctioneer dismisses the joke and in an attempt to assert control over the value of the piece goes on to describe the picture "as a work of art—the attitude of the gallant animal quite according to natur'; the gentleman in a nankeen jacket, his gun in his hand, is going to the chace; in the distance a banyhann-tree and a pagody, most likely resemblances of some interesting spot in our famous Eastern possessions."[5] Among the incongruous assemblages of the auction-house, the picture of the elephant gives rise to two narratives—one valued for the laughter it raises, the other for the price it puffs. How the Eastern scene is perceived is a matter of some consequence: the difference between the auctioneer's account of the picture and the wag's is visible in the portrait's final sale price—half a guinea, as compared with the auctioneer's estimate of five pounds.

In the auctioneer's "gentle" narrative of the portrait, which strives for authority in the auction house, the elephant and its rider are rendered a "gallant" instrument for imagining "our famous Eastern possessions." The scene pictured is "quite according to natur'" and the signs that guarantee the portrait's naturalism—and consequently its status as a "work of art"—are the Englishman's stock images of the East: elephant, nankeen jacket, gun, banyan tree, and pagoda. The auctioneer contends that the picture should command at least five pounds, chiefly because it conforms to English expectations of India as the realm of the "interesting," as the domain of the picturesque, and as the land of the "chace." Throughout *Vanity Fair* Jos Sedley himself capitalizes upon such images of India in the stories of tiger hunts he retails; he gets most mileage out of a spectacular yarn in which an enraged elephant dislodges Jos's mahout from his seat with its trunk.[6] Because in England they confirm this ostensibly naturalistic view of India, animal stories and tales of the hunt serve Jos as a means of passing in an English society in which he otherwise appears quite awkward and out of place: they first produce "an

Figure 18. William Makepeace Thackeray, "An Elephant for Sale," illustration to Chapter XVII of *Vanity Fair* (1847–48).

atmosphere of 'Oriental' comfort that attracts Becky";[7] and they later afford him the sense of social security or escape that Dobbin explicitly identifies at the end of the novel with India, to which he recommends Jos flee in order to elude Rebecca. Though his own "grasp on the realities of Indian life was fairly weak,"[8] Thackeray, like Jos, found a great deal of profit to be had from exotic tales. His contemporaries celebrated the domestic stories that he rendered satirical by dressing them in "Oriental disguises" as a distinctly English method of critique; the object of such fun they termed to have been "Thackerayized."[9] India and its beasts function for Thackeray, as they do for Jos, simultaneously as stimuli to credible and entertaining stories and as resources for escaping or criticizing English strictures and conventions.

At the conclusion of Thackeray's novel Jos reveals that the figure atop the elephant is his, and it becomes plain that the "cynical" comments of the "professional wag" are aimed at "Thackerayizing" Jos himself. The wag's joke, by contrast with the auctioneer's idealized constructions upon the portrait, exploits the enormity of both the elephant and the stout rider, whose excess threatens to overwhelm the beast. As a vehicle fitted for the "chace," the elephant is an overblown version of a noble courser, and yet Jos's stoutness threatens to collapse even that "gallant" beast. Over against the auctioneer's claims that the portrait is a naturalistic "work of art" describing "our famous Eastern possessions," the humorist suggests that the picture is merely ridiculous and outlandish, a grotesque display. In this alternative account of the portrait, the exotic beast does not appear as a "figur'" from nature but instead as an allegory of the incontinent and the perverse. Old Sedley fashions a similar joke from the image of the wild beast, invoking Edward Cross's Exeter 'Change menagerie as he calls for a carriage for his son: "'Order Mr. Jos's elephant, Sambo!' cried the father. 'Send to Exeter 'Change, Sambo;' but seeing Jos ready almost to cry with vexation, the old joker stopped his laughter."[10] George Osborne poses yet one more iteration of the joke during the Waterloo campaign: "as there is one well-known regiment of the army which travels with a goat heading the column, whilst another is led by a deer, George said with respect to his brother-in-law, that his regiment marched with an elephant."[11]

In this way, the elephant becomes the standard-bearer in the novel for jokes about Jos's "stoutness." What is more, elephants serve throughout *Vanity Fair* as markers of superfluity and social pretension, as for instance when one British regiment does march with an elephant: in Madras the narrator archly reports Lady O'Dowd "at the head of the regiment seated on a royal elephant, a noble sight. Mounted on that beast, she has been into action with tigers in the jungle: she has been received by native princes, who have welcomed her . . . into the recesses of their zenanas and offered her shawls and jewels which it went to her heart to refuse."[12] Though in most other locations Lady O'Dowd's actions would appear vulgar and overreaching, India functions like the auction house—a space in which shawls, jewels, and elephants are exhibited, contemplated, and sometimes declined. India likewise offers an exhibition, simultaneously genteel and savage, in which propriety is unusually capacious, even if it is primarily a site apprehended by analogy with domestic theater as it is for Becky Sharp, who in conceiving a future Indian existence for herself draws upon a knowledge of circus pantomime: for her, India means riding "upon an elephant to the sound of the march in Bluebeard, in order to pay a visit of ceremony to the Grand Mogul."[13]

For all the difference between the naturalistic and allegorical accounts of the portrait of Jos and the elephant, each version at the auction treats the elephant as a narrative prop that throws into relief English propriety. As Patrick Brantlinger notes, "significant though it is, India remained *background* for Thackeray in both biographical and fictional terms."[14] In the auctioneer's rhetoric, emphasizing the gallant figure of the elephant is an attempt to restore dignity and order to the English house that the portrait's graphic absurdity has unsettled—relegating Jos to the background of India, "an appropriate dumping ground for a man of Jos Sedley's nonexistent talents."[15] Indeed, when the exotic animal is the narrative property of the auction house wag, George Osborne, Old Sedley, and the narrator himself, it functions as the protagonist in a beast fable, highlighting what prevailing English sensibilities find grotesque, pretentious, or absurd. The elephant as a stock figure in *Vanity Fair* helps define the moral bounds of desirable forms of Englishness as it exposes Jos as "feeble and degrading," a "compound of silly vanity and selfishness," in the words of John Forster.[16] To this extent the elephants labor alongside the narrator, "the Manager of the Performance," in his effort to expose the folly of Vanity Fair to "the very best company in this empire."[17] Thackeray famously casts his narrator as a showman who manipulates his puppets to display their vanities. The exhibition in the auction house, the retailing of narratives of tiger hunting, and the staging of jokes about the elephantine are designed to expose and deflate vanity and pretension; to this extent the use Thackeray makes of India and its beasts is consistent with his larger exhibitionary aims. In making use of zoological exotica, Thackeray becomes not only the primary exhibitor but also, in a sense, the equivalent of the "professional wag" in the auction house, or of Old Sedley who calls upon Edward Cross's Exeter 'Change menagerie for the animal that will bear the burden of humiliating Jos.

The deft deployment of stock from the imperial menagerie—images of elephants and stories of tiger hunting—to "Thackerayize" Jos, Lady O'Dowd, and even Becky Sharp constitutes one of those "brief, decisive, yet always most discriminative touches" that Thackeray's contemporaries applauded.[18] Charlotte Brontë noted that Thackeray avoided any "meretricious ornament" that might "attract or fix a superficial glance,"[19] and exotic beasts function in the novel as more than decorative elements or satellite embellishments to be easily dismissed; they constitute an important if minor narrative thread in the fabric of a novel that represents itself as an exhibit at the fair. Yet the novel in which the elephant plays its part was itself faulted for failing to represent a total vision of English social life. Robert Stephen Rintoul noted that "Mr. Thackeray seems to have looked at life by bits rather than as a whole.... But something more than this is needed for a finished picture of human life.... [S]ketches of passing phases of society do not... suffice to form the materials of a fiction."[20] Elizabeth Rigby went so far as to argue that "It is not a novel, in the common acceptation of the word."[21] In the service of "Thackerayizing" domestic excess, vanity, and folly, the stories, images, and jokes that make use of tigers and elephants are intended as local demonstrations; they do not function explicitly to further a totalizing purpose. Thackeray's menagerie and his novel alike constitute incomplete performances or sketches, rather than perfectly framed and complete portraits: if his careful exploitation of zoological exotica reinforces the exhibitionary character of his narrative, it also reflects a broad narrative decision to play up partiality and incompleteness in a text that advertises itself as a "novel without a hero."

Five years after the last number of *Vanity Fair*, Elizabeth Gaskell offered a turn to the menagerie in chapter 12 of *Cranford* (1853) that explicitly renders the exotic beast a totalizing figure, as an elephant in Wombwell's Menagerie becomes a medium especially suited to the task of imagining India in provincial England. As a boy, Peter Jenkyns disgraces himself when, for a joke, he dresses as his sister Deborah and parades before all of Cranford in the front garden. As a consequence of this ill-conceived performance, Peter exiles himself from Cranford and England, and it is only many years later that "Peter had... been heard of in India, 'or that neighbourhood.'"[22] This information arrives in the town "in a year when Wombwell came to Cranford, [a year that was remembered] because [Peter's sister] Miss Matty had wanted to see an elephant in order that she might the better imagine Peter riding on one; and had seen a boa-constrictor too, which was more than she wished to imagine in her fancy pictures of Peter's locality."[23] Miss Matty is compelled "to imagine in her fancy pictures" an India that is inaccessible to her save through such artifacts as the occasional India-muslin gown that finds its way to Cranford or through people such as Signor and Signora Brunoni (otherwise known as Brown), who have been stationed with a regiment near Calcutta. Miss Matty's "fancy pictures" of India engage the elephant as a kind of avatar of that "locality," and the favorable comparison of the elephant to the boa constrictor illustrates how well suited the large beast is to the task of representing India. That this imaginative encounter should be remembered is itself unremarkable—the menagerie does not visit Cranford every year, and the arrival of such traveling performances constituted a "great to-do."[24]

It is a memorable occasion that provides such a powerful stimulus for "fancy pictures" and thereby closes the distance between India and places like Cranford in the bourgeois imagination.

Wombwell's elephant in Gaskell's novel serves as more than just a spur to Miss Matty's imagination, however. The singular appropriateness of the exhibited elephant to connote India obscures the process by which it performs this gesture; instead, the failure of the boa constrictor to signify "Peter's locality" clarifies the role the elephant plays in Miss Matty's mind and consequently in the novel. The boa constrictor, the narrator tells us, is "more than [Miss Matty] *wished* to imagine," and so it fails to satisfy her. The elephant, on the other hand, appears to reflect to Miss Matty precisely what she "had wanted to see," and so it reflects her own orientalist desires.[25] The elephant, like the impostor Signor Brunoni, appears as an oriental conjuror when it confronts the English desire for spectacle and confirms the belief in the illusion of the East. Indeed, the appearance of the exotically attired conjuror in Cranford immediately calls up the menagerie, for Brunoni's performance promises to be "such a piece of gaiety . . . as had not been seen or known of since Wombwell's lions came, when one of them ate a little child's arm."[26] Like the magician, the elephant (but not the snake) establishes the connection to the alien primarily because it furnishes what the English audience expects to see—not only because it is a spur to the imagination, but because it provides what the English have *already* imagined they want to see.

In both *Vanity Fair* and *Cranford,* values of Englishness rise into view against the background of the exotic menagerie, and are thereby bound to it: the disavowal of the spectacularly excessive represents the counterpart of the desire for the exotic. *Cranford*'s narrator exploits the menagerie to render Miss Matty a figure of fun, though unlike Jos's treatment at the hands of the Manager of the Performance, *Cranford*'s humor is tender, and it emphasizes not Miss Matty's moral culpability but the poverty of her cosmopolitan experience. Indeed, more than she resembles Jos Sedley she appears like the adolescent Becky Sharp who imagines India as a place where she could don "an infinity of shawls, turbans, and diamond necklaces," or ride on an elephant, and whom even Old Sedley is inclined to treat kindly.[27] Unlike Miss Rebecca's hyperbolic conviction that "*everything* must be good that comes from there,"[28] however, Miss Matty treats India as a whole that must be imagined with a careful selectivity. For Miss Matty, the elephant functions as a totalizing condensation of India, or that "locality," an instrumental role that the boa constrictor cannot quite perform despite sharing the elephant's synecdochic properties. Her partial treatment of the menagerie renders her an amusing figure, but the narrative treats her with a respect not afforded dissemblers like the Brunonis: her restrained taste in exotic animals testifies to an English integrity and good sense that more widely traveled but vulgar figures like the conjurors—or *Vanity Fair*'s Lady O'Dowd—do not necessarily share.

Boz, The "Zoological" Incognito

In a letter of 18 February 1854 to Elizabeth Gaskell, Charles Dickens noted that while not a Fellow of the Zoological Society—"I am not one of the Zoologicals"—he would write to Regent's Park for some details about the animals in the zoo that Gaskell required. He notes, too, that *were* he a "Zoological," he would "have been delighted to have had a hand in the introduction of a child to the lions and tigers"—recalling the misbehavior of Wombwell's lion Gaskell narrated in *Cranford*.[29] Because they were widely available to him, the zoo, menagerie, and circus served the metropolitan Dickens as an even richer imaginative resource than they did the provincial Miss Matty, and he had to take even more care in his principles of selection. In July 1847 Dickens visited Wombwell's Menagerie in Kent, where he observed Ellen Chapman ("The British Lion Queen") command lions, tigers, and leopards. Dickens was deeply impressed and wrote of it in separate letters over the course of two days, describing the way in which the "wild beasts (in cages) have come down here, and involved us in a whirl of dissipation"; he expressed his particular enthusiasm for Chapman by proposing to have her "painted by Landseer."[30] Early in his career, Dickens wrote explicitly about exotic animals in English popular culture—about, for instance, "travelling menageries, or to speak, more intelligibly, the 'Wild-beast shows,'" outside of which are "large highly-coloured representations of tigers tearing men's heads open, and a lion being burnt with red-hot irons to induce him to drop his victim";[31] about "beasts confined in dens ... behind their bars, [gazing] with eyes in which old forests gleamed" in the Tower Menagerie or the menagerie at Exeter 'Change;[32] about the "scenes in the circle" at Astley's Circus, which featured tricks by an elephant supplied by the Exeter 'Change menagerie, monkeys riding dogs, and other exotic "simulacre";[33] and about the "Zoological lion and his brethren at the fairs," who are exhibited alongside bears, monkeys, and elephants, but outside their native environment "under a tropical sun."[34]

The wild beasts of Astley's and Wombwell's were visible across London, whether in the Lord Mayor's Show, in the circus ring at Westminster Bridge, on the theater stage, or at Bartholomew and Greenwich Fairs. Elephants, lions, camels, and other zoological exotica formed an important part of popular English dramatic performances even before Dickens's birth (London theaters began hiring exotic beasts from pantomimes in 1811), and since Andrew Ducrow's management of Astley's during Dickens's adolescence, beasts of spectacular dimensions and provenance had come to headline pantomime and circus acts, especially since the "rage for elephant drama" in the 1830s.[35] During this period, the circus's "Golden Era," Astley's handbills announced Ducrow riding on an elephant, remarking that "the most intense Curiosity continues to be excited by the Nightly Appearance of that unwieldy but stately Beast, the LIVING ELEPHANT."[36] Throughout the 1830s and 1840s, traveling performances of "Mr. CARTER, THE LION KING . . . WITH THE WHOLE OF HIS NATIONAL MENAGERIE OF ACTING LIONS! TIGERS, LEOPARDS, And other Animals!" and of "Van AMBURGH's EXTRAORDINARY LIVING ELEPHANT" garnered top billing at Astley's.[37] Dickens knew this business well: in *Our Mutual Friend* (1865), he traced the specialized trade of Mr. Venus, whose traffic in preserved specimens finds him "down at the water-side, looking for parrots brought home by sailors, to buy for stuffing."[38] Dickens's journalistic endeavors, *Household Words* and *All the Year Round*, likewise collected, displayed, and narrativized zoological exotica, especially elephants.[39]

Dickens's writing countenanced processions of zoological exotica to the very end of his career. At the opening of *The Mystery of Edwin Drood* (1870), John Jasper's "scattered consciousness . . . fantastically piece[s] itself together" after an opium binge: "cymbals clash, and the Sultan goes by to his palace in a long procession. Ten thousand scimitars flash in the sunlight, and thrice ten thousand dancing-girls strew flowers. Then, follow white elephants caparisoned in countless gorgeous colours, and infinite in number and attendants."[40] The difficulty for Jasper (and for the narrator) is that this procession occurs against an English background, "where it cannot be." The incongruity—"How can the ancient English Cathedral tower be here!"— gives rise to "drowsy laughter," and the dissipation and the confusion of the scene are signaled by the confounding of the Asiatic and the English. Scenes of domestic dissipation are figured by the incursion of the sultan's campaign into England's most familiar spaces along with a zoological entourage.

Such metaphorical incursions are given force in Dickens's writing by the already established synecdochic associations of exotica. The commercial interests of importers like *Our Mutual Friend*'s John Rokesmith and his "China house" with its "wholesale vision of tea, rice, odd-smelling silks, carved boxes, and tight-eyed people"[41] extended, for instance, to "ELEPHANTS. WHOLE-

SALE AND RETAIL," as an article in *Household Words* expressed the matter. This article traces the associations and "circumstances which have been instrumental in bringing about the voyage of [the elephant] Bibi Sahibeh and her infant daughter to England," and it marks out a trade route extending from the capture of the elephants by "A party of a dozen Hindoo hunters" in provincial India to the pachyderms' arrival "at this time in the Zoological Gardens of the Regent's Park."[42] Since the English could not persuade elephants to reproduce in captivity,[43] every elephant that appeared in Britain traversed a similar path as did Bibi Sahibeh and her daughter. The elephant therefore made visible to the English the linkages across the circuits of trade to "The grandeur and state pomp of the mightiest Oriental kings, the enormity of whose magnificence sometimes reads like a fabulous wonder," and which "seems almost inseparable" from the figure of the elephant.[44]

Though *Edwin Drood*'s narrator denies the possibility, such processions were a part of the domestic English streetscape in the nineteenth century, and Dickens wrote memorably about one such procession through the streets of London. His essay on the 1850 Lord Mayor's Show deliberately foregrounded the kind of confusion with which Jasper grapples when it appeared in *Household Words* on 30 November 1850, under the title "Mr. Booley's View of the Last Lord Mayor's Show." Dickens frames his meditation on zoological allegory by telling us that a certain "Mr. Booley[,] having been much excited by the accounts in the newspapers, informing the public that the eminent Mr. Batty, of Astley's Amphitheatre, Westminster Bridge Road, Lambeth, would invent, arrange, and marshal the Procession on Lord Mayor's Day, took occasion to announce . . . that he intended to be present at that great national spectacle."[45] One of these newspaper accounts, in the *Illustrated London News*, describes the Order of Procession as a kind of intercontinental *pax britannica*, beginning with "PEACE / Having in her train / EUROPE, ASIA, AFRICA, and AMERICA" figured by the "Horse of Europe," the "Camel of Asia," the "Elephant of Africa," and the "Two Deer of America." The procession concluded with "A CAR, / drawn by Six Cream-coloured Horses, three abreast, containing / FOUR SAILORS, / BRITANNIA, / and / HAPPINESS" (fig. 19).[46] Dickens's essay undertakes a critique of this outward-looking tableau as a culpable display, an irresponsible extravagance when so much domestic work remains to be done. This point is made through that figure of fun, Mr. Booley.

Mr. Booley's reading of the parade is decidedly idiosyncratic, as Dickens signals at the outset by noting that "Those who have any acquaintance with Mr. Booley, will be prepared to learn that the real intent and meaning of the [Show's display of] Allegory has been entirely missed, except by his sagacious

Figure 19. "The New Lord Mayor's Show—1850," *The Illustrated London News*, 9 November 1850. *Courtesy Kelvin Smith Library Retrospective Research Collections.*

and original mind."[47] As Daniel Hack observes, "Mr. Booley's 'mistake' consists in determinedly reading the exotica on display in terms of the most local and material of considerations, rather than as referring back to or embodying their ostensible places of origin."[48] At stake for Dickens's Mr. Booley is the status of the English nation in relation to this spectacle: while generally understood as a crude allegory with the nation at the head of and subordinating an empire, the procession appears to Mr. Booley as a complex display with a domestic origin and application—it is "an Allegory, devised by the ingenious Mr. Batty, in conjunction with the Lord Mayor, as a kind of practical riddle for all beholders to make guesses at."[49] In understanding it in this way, he perverts the logic of Thackeray and Gaskell's zoological narratives: where Gaskell's Miss Matty and Thackeray's auctioneer treat the exotic animal as an avatar of the exotic, allegorical because synecdochic, the approach of Mr. Booley involves reading the Lord Mayor's allegory without the synecdochic element—as a narrative like that of the "professional wag," intended to "Thackerayize" domestic English excesses and insufficiencies.

But Dickens's joke is partly on Mr. Booley as well: instead of accounting for the *form* of the encounter with the menagerie as defining the contours of acceptable Englishness, Mr. Booley short-circuits this logic and turns the exotic beast itself into a figure for Englishness. Upon his arrival at the Lord Mayor's Show, Mr. Booley observes "the Elephant of Africa" on its allegorical progress and proposes that the beast's "capacity of intellectual development under proper training, his strength and docility, his industry, his many noble qualities, his patience and attachment under gentle treatment, and his blind resentment when provoked too far by ill-usage, rendered him, besides, a touching symbol of the great English people." Rather than discovering in the elephant an emblem of the extent of the world rendered subordinate to Britannia and her people's "happiness" by its navy, Mr. Booley identifies the elephant as a symbol of the English themselves. In the Elephant of Africa, Mr. Booley therefore discovers not an exotic testament to the far-flung reaches of empire but rather a domestic sign; and in reading the intentionality behind the elephant, Mr. Booley discovers that "In parading an animal so well known for its aversion to carrion, and its liking for clean provender, the City of London, pleasantly but pointedly, avowed its determination to seek out and confiscate all improper human food exposed for sale within its liberties."[50]

Mr. Booley's reading of Astley's allegory becomes even more perverse when he comes to ponder "the two negroes by whom [the elephant] was led." Rather than perceiving them as part of an imperial tableau, Mr. Booley believes they have "reference to certain estimable, but pig-headed members of the Civic Parliament, who learn no wisdom from experience and instruction; and in humorous reference to whom, Mr. Batty and the Lord Mayor suggested the impossibility of ever washing the Blackamoor white."[51] The "negroes" become, therefore, an allegory of a kind of domestic savagery, and the persistence of such characters in the Civic Parliament and across England (indeed, England itself in the figure of the elephant is led by such savagery) is nearly a matter for despair.

Hack argues that "since Mr. Booley's interpretive ingenuity serves . . . to correct for the government's failings, its very extravagance functions as an index of those failings: his distance from a proper understanding of the parade corresponds to the authorities' distance from a proper understanding of their responsibilities."[52] I wish to emphasize first the fact that for Dickens the *form* of Astley's zoological displays is crucial to defining its relation to Englishness; and second, the way in which Dickens's essay makes its critical reformatory point by pairing Mr. Booley's interpretive "extravagance" with the extravagance of the exotica exhibited at Astley's. The very perversity of Mr. Booley's reading—and the power of Dickens's domestic critique—overshadows the dominant reading of the allegory of the Lord Mayor's Show, so that it becomes difficult for the elephant's extravagance in the London streets to function only as an emblem of Africa or as subordinate to Britannia when Mr. Booley has figured it as an indictment of English squalor. Equally an imperial beast and a symbol of the English people, the elephant's associations are destabilized by Mr. Booley; and Mr. Booley's disquisition likewise remakes the "negroes" not as Britons of African descent but as performers—or parliamentarians—in blackface. In this way, Mr. Booley becomes a kind of rhetorical Van Amburgh: his account domesticates the exotic Elephant of Africa and its "pig-headed" entourage, erases their strangeness by the strength of its misreading, and through its interpretive "extravagance" impels them toward a useful role in Dickens's journalistic efforts toward sanitary reform. At the same time, the patent absurdity of Mr. Booley's reading strategies—particularly when surveying an animal that appeared in Victorian England only as a consequence of imperial trade—renders Booley himself a kind of innocuous clown, such as might be found in Astley's hippodramatic performances on most any night.

Wise Elephants and the Thultan of the Indieth

It is plain that Dickens had an intimate knowledge of wild beasts and the institutions that brought them to England's shores, housed them, displayed them, and even stuffed them. An anonymous contributor to Dickens's *All the Year Round* maintained that he "labour[ed] under the painful conviction that the British public demands elephants in an account of Ceylon," but it is equally true that since the "rage for elephants" on stage in the 1830s, the British public was liable to think of "the East" in any fictional encounter with elephants. Sometimes Astley's capitalized upon this conjunction, as it did from December 1853 to February 1854, when it gave top billing to a performance of "The Wise Elephants of the East." Popular accounts of Dickens's composition of *Hard Times* have the author conducting intensive research, and perhaps even seeing the "Wise Elephants" at Astley's. An American acquaintance claimed that Dickens "arranged with the master of Astley's circus to spend many hours behind the scenes with the riders and among the horses," a fact that seems unlikely but testifies to his reputation as an informed chronicler of the circus in *Hard Times*.[53] To be sure, Dickens wrote to Mark Lemon, editor of *Punch*, to inquire about "any slang terms among the tumblers and Circus-people, that you can call to mind. . . .—I want them in my new story,"[54] and in their edition of *Hard Times* George Ford and Sylvère Monod describe Dickens touring circuses with Lemon in February, a detail repeated by Kate Flint in her editorial notes.[55]

If in fact Dickens did visit Astley's between December 1853 and February 1854, he would have seen as the chief act "an entirely Original Grand Hippo-Dramatic Chinese Spectacle, in 3 Acts, written expressly to introduce those 'Wonder of Wonders,' Mr. WILLIAM COOKE's TRAINED ELEPHANTS."[56] "The object of this Drama," which was widely advertised and praised in the London papers, "is to lay before the British Public in the most Interesting form, the Interior of China." Against this Chinese display Astley's gave second billing to "Billy Button's Journey to Brentford; or, Harlequin and the Ladies' Favourite," the hippodramatic spectacle that Sissy Jupe's father is reported in *Hard Times* to have performed under the title of "The Tailor's Journey to Brentford" (figs. 20 and 21). Also advertised in this period was "THE WILD INDIAN of the PRAIRIE," and *Hard Times* mentions Mr. E.W.B. Childers's popularity as performer of "the Wild Huntsman of the North American Prairies."[57] Astley's show was the largest and most influential circus outfit in the first half of the nineteenth century and so was widely credited as the model for Sleary's circus; certainly a number of figures from Astley's served as prototypes for characters and roles in *Hard Times*.[58]

Given that Dickens knew the zoo, menagerie, and fair so well and might have visited the circus in February 1854, it is quite curious that zoological exotica like the sensationally popular "Wise Elephants of the East" should

Figure 20. Ad for elephant performances at Astley's, December 1853. *Permission The British Library (Shelfmark Playbill 173).*

be excluded from Dickens's portrait of Sleary's Circus. Paul Schlicke offers several reasons why this might be so: first, that Sleary's was a small traveling outfit and could not afford to maintain wild beasts; second, that Dickens

Figure 21. Ad for elephants and "Billy Button's Journey to Brentford," 12 January 1854. *Permission The British Library (Shelfmark Playbill 171).*

disliked dangerous acts; and third, that Dickens avoided the contemporary, commercial aspect of the circus, preferring a nostalgic, idealized version from a period before exotic animals were center stage.[59] Yet prominent circus managers insisted that "Any circus that is a circus ought to have an elephant,"[60] and in expressing affection for the Greenwich Fair and for Ellen Chapman, Dickens had no difficulty overlooking the danger of the performances they staged. What is more, Sleary emphasizes his circus as a commercial endeavor when he requests "bespeaks," and in another moment in the novel a manager of the circus is described as making his fortune; as a matter of fact "the circus had always been commercialised."[61]

There is one curious exception to the rule that the circus in *Hard Times* avoids exotic acts, and this exception exposes a telling seam in the novel. An elephant makes an appearance in the novel and is narrativized in order to cure excess by excess. The closing pages of *Hard Times* present a scene in which Sissy Jupe, conscripted into the Gradgrind family after being abandoned by her circus-performer father, revisits Sleary's Circus and the friends among whom she grew up. During this scene of reunion, the circus proprietor Sleary enumerates the many changes experienced by the circus folk Sissy knew as a child. Among these performers is "Emma Gordon, my dear, ath wath a'motht a mother to you." Sleary narrates her history thus:

> Well! Emma, thee lotht her huthband. He wath throw'd a heavy back-fall off a Elephant in a thort of a Pagoda thing ath the Thultan of the Indieth, and he never got the better of it; and thee married a thecond time—married a Cheethemonger ath fell in love with her from the front—and he'th a Overseer and makin' a fortun.[62]

Sleary's story of Emma Gordon is significant—and funny—for the contrasts it introduces: Emma's first marriage ends when her circus-performer husband, in the exotic character of the Sultan of the Indies, tumbles from an elephant; her second marriage begins when a cheesemonger, in the prosaic role as an audience member, becomes enamored of her. There is a kind of balance in this contrast as well, a balance that underscores the allegorical significance of Sleary's Circus in contradistinction to the commercial world embodied by Bounderby and Gradgrind: if Emma's first marriage to the exotic "Sultan" occurs within the confines of the circus, her second marriage to the prosaic cheesemonger occurs outside the circus ring. Yet Sleary presents Emma Gordon's second marriage as somehow more satisfactory than the first; there is something gratifying in Emma symbolically wedding the fanciful circus performance to the world of workaday "fortun."

Emma Gordon's marriage to the cheesemonger is precisely the sort of union Dickens wishes to effect in *Hard Times*, reconciling the play of imagination characteristic of the circus with the profitable commerce that keeps

Coketown's laborers employed. At the opening of chapter 10, for example, the narrator asserts, "I entertain a weak idea that the English people are as hard-worked as any people upon whom the sun shines. I acknowledge to this ridiculous idiosyncrasy, as a reason why I would give them a little more play."[63] Her marriage takes on a special symbolic importance, since Dickens's "story as it progresses demonstrates the marginality of the circus and its irrelevance to the Coketown workers' troubles," and wedding Emma to the cheesemonger brings the circus back into the purview of the commercial world.[64] Yet the case of Emma Gordon demonstrates that there is a cost incurred as a precondition of this marriage of serious work and fanciful play: it requires first that the "Sultan of the Indies" be toppled from his elephant. The ignoble demise of Emma's first husband represents a curious loose thread in Dickens's narrative, a thread that when unraveled reveals just what must be divorced before imagination can marry labor.

A Rogue Elephant and a Fall for Extravagance

That the elephant is not to be found at Sleary's Circus suggests several possibilities when we consider Emma Gordon's first marriage. The first possibility is that Dickens has forgotten himself: Sleary's is strictly a horse-riding circus, but the attraction of an anecdote about a sultan being dumped from an elephant's howdah proves irresistible to Dickens, and he has unwittingly introduced another element of the Victorian circus into Sleary's Circus. In this case, Dickens would be rather like Sissy Jupe, whose "fancy" is inconsistent with the practices of the schoolroom that figures as "the Nation" in the novel, and whose attention is consequently distracted by the purely ornamental.[65] Publication in parts meant Dickens was able to indulge fewer satellite narratives and embellishments. John Butt and Kathleen Tillotson found remarkable the strict economy of detail that publication in weekly numbers imposed upon Dickens: "The difficulty of the space is CRUSHING," he wrote to John Forster in February 1854.[66] Under such restrictions on space in the shortest of Dickens's novels, the story of the "Sultan" and his homicidal elephant seems an extravagance that potentially compromises the ability of the novel to represent a whole, knowable world.

A second possible reading would bring Dickens in line with Gradgrindian "Fact" but also expose the satellite nature of Sleary's Circus—it would expose it as being outside the main line of traveling outfits and make it difficult to generalize the case for fancy and imagination it is supposed to instantiate. In this reading, Sleary's Horse-riding might be understood to exclude exotic animals because it cannot afford them; but Dickens seeks to acknowledge the larger circus world of which it is a part, and which does foreground exotic acts like "Wise Elephants of the East." If Emma's first husband belonged to another, larger circus company that offered performances of exotic animals in addition to hippodramatic attractions, Dickens might be seen to offer the sultan's intrusion into the narrative as a guarantee that Sleary knows the circus world. If Dickens can be seen to be strictly factual in this account, nevertheless the extravagance of the Sultan of the Indies on his elephant exposes the poverty—both material and imaginative—of Sleary's Circus and hence compromises the symbolic force of its agency in *Hard Times.*

In his editing of the memoirs of the circus clown Joseph Grimaldi (1838), Dickens insisted he had been "altering its form throughout, and making such other alterations as . . . would improve the narration of the facts, without any departure from the facts."[67] The intrusion of the elephant in the embedded narrative at the end of *Hard Times* does not exactly threaten a "departure from the facts," but it does open the question of how Dickens's selectivity in presenting the facts of the circus seeks to totalize. Though a small narrative detail, this micronarrative—like Thackeray's "minor object" of the elephant up at auction—opens up larger questions about Dickens's treatment of the circus because it establishes a place for the exotic beast in the circus world that is then vacated. Given that Dickens drew on Astley's performances of 1853–54 for his portrait of Sleary's Circus, the separation of the spectacle of Eastern elephants from such hippodramatic performances as the "Journey to Brentford" represents, like the disappearance of the clown, one of the most notable "gaps and vacancies" that Helen Stoddart notes characterize the circus in *Hard Times.*[68] In Dickens's *All the Year Round,* a piece titled "The Elephant at Home" informed readers that "an elephant separated from its herd . . . becomes solitary, and more or less vicious. . . . [R]ogue elephants haunt and destroy."[69] The "Sultan's" rogue circus elephant, separated from the exotica that permeate Dickens's discussions of the imperial menagerie elsewhere, haunts the narrative of *Hard Times,* a strange anomaly that courts both "Fact" and "Fancy" but without exactly wedding them.

It is a significant anomaly because, as F. R. Leavis has famously argued, the novel's "symbolic intention emerges out of metaphor and the vivid evocation of the concrete."[70] The "concrete" in *Hard Times* rests in large part with the circus that harbors a rogue elephant as well as real horses, a contrast to the "graminiverous" and "quadrupedal" abstractions of M'Choakumchild's schoolroom.[71] From the fanciful circus, Sissy Jupe enters the banal commercial world: Leavis argues that "Sissy's symbolic significance is bound up with that of Sleary's Horse-riding where human kindness is very insistently associated with vitality," in opposition to Bitzer's sterile, mechanistic, and finally inhumane embrace of Gradgrindism, which asserts that "the whole duty of man" is "to buy . . . for as little as he could possibly give, and sell . . . for as much as he could possibly get."[72] Dickens's solution to the problem of a fact-driven practice of political economy—the kind of "aggressive economic individualism" exemplified by factory owners such as Bounderby in Dickens's novel—is to temper it with a strong dose of the circus.[73] This set of symbolic oppositions produces a dialectical resolution in the deathbed discovery of Mrs. Gradgrind that "there is something—not an Ology at all—that your father has missed, or forgotten" and in Gradgrind's own implicit acquiescence, amidst the generous and compassionate cast of the circus, to Sleary's assertion that "People mutht be amuthed. They can't be alwayth a learning, nor yet they can't be alwayth a working, they an't made for it."[74]

I contend that Dickens has no place for the performing elephant or other exotic animal acts in Sleary's Circus because they suggest a precarious and threatening extravagance associated with the Eastern and the colonial, as Dickens hints in his arch reference in 1848 to the "whirl of dissipation" into which the wild beasts drew him at Wombwell's. Dickens well knew the symbolic dynamics exotic beasts evoke, and the introduction of the rogue circus elephant in *Hard Times* follows close upon Elizabeth Gaskell's representation of Wombwell's Menagerie in *Cranford*, which finished its run in *Household Words* just eleven months before Dickens's narrative began. In his letter to Gaskell in February 1854, Dickens's allusion to Wombwell's lion devouring the child's arm demonstrates his close attention to such details. Like Gaskell's Miss Matty, Dickens associates the performing elephant with the colonial, but with native savagery rather than with the Company governance of Peter. In Dickens's novel, the "Sultan of the Indies" on his elephant is, like John Jasper's dream of the sultan's procession before the English cathedral, an incongruity—and, what is more, it symbolizes a threat to the happy resolution of a tension between "hard work" and "more play," the struggle of "the Circus against Coketown" (in Raymond Williams's formulation), for the pair signifies a kind of energy that cannot be satisfactorily reconciled to Coketown's domestic economy.[75] If one of the points of *Hard Times* is that Josiah Bounderby and Stephen Blackpool should be able to secure divorces from wives who are liable to excessive behavior—Stephen's wife to an excess of drink and Louisa to an excess of passion, at least from Bounderby's perspective—then in the case of Emma Gordon, Dickens can be seen to effect just such a divorce. Dickens extricates Emma from her marriage to the "Sultan of the Indies" by staging a scene of Eastern violence in which excess purges itself, the elephant dispatching the sultan, leaving Emma—like Sissy Jupe a symbol of vitality and imagination—free to marry into the world of fact represented by the cheesemonger.

Coketown's Empire

The concise narrative of Emma Gordon's first husband introduces a problematic narrative thread into Dickens's novel by inserting a circus elephant into a story about a circus that features only domestic animals (horses and dogs), a thread that exposes the curious absence of exotic beasts from the representation of Sleary's Circus in the novel. Despite this elision, *Hard Times* is surprisingly flush with elephants and serpents, but their role in the novel has been displaced from the story of the novel onto its tropology—its discourse—and if the circus is meant to represent the concrete against Gradgrind's abstract "Fact," it is curious that the elephant is abstract fancy. In 1857 Robert Brough, an occasional contributor to *Household Words*, published a parody of *Hard Times* that makes much of Dickens's symbolical elephants. Brough justifies his parody by observing "the striking want of poetical justice in the usually-received termination of this otherwise excellent story, wherein none of the good people were made happy, and the wicked were most inadequately punished," and he claims to rewrite the ending of the novel "on more orthodox principles."[76] Brough's complaint, in short, is that Dickens's concern to make a point about political economy has caused him to violate the conventions of a poetical economy. Particularly troublesome for readers attuned to narrative convention is the fate of Bounderby, who escapes the novel merely humiliated rather than punished. Brough rewrites the ending of the novel to emphasize an elephantine violence visited upon Bounderby, who tries to escape from a mob after Sleary divulges that Bounderby has murdered Signor Jupe:

> [Bounderby's] melancholy-mad elephants were at work. They were always at work—day and night. I shouldn't like to be a melancholy-mad elephant, to be always at work—night and day. Should you? Not that I don't now and then sit up all night myself. But on those occasions I am not melancholy. By no means. Nor in the elephantine line. Quite the contrary. Mr Bounderby entered the engine room.... The melancholy mad elephants occupied a good deal of room.... It required the greatest precaution, on the part of Mr Bounderby, to step over the foaming

> cylinders, exhausted receivers, cranks, levers, and what not, to reach the desired window in safety. . . . Bounderby fell back. Into what? Into the clutches of the melancholy-mad elephants. The fly-wheel caught him. Whirr! Burr! Whiz! Fiz! Round and round he went! He was a self-made man, but he had not made himself of sufficiently strong materials to resist the influence of the melancholy-mad elephants.[77]

Brough's parody exploits an important repetition in Dickens's novel, a repetition that almost comes to seem a stylistic tic, in order to render more "orthodox" the poetical economy of Dickens's novel. Five times Dickens describes the steam engines of Coketown as "melancholy-mad elephants" and the town's emissions as "serpents of smoke," and Brough redeploys the first figure to fulfill a narrative expectation that excess will be cured by excess: Bounderby's own exploited elephants churn Bounderby into a pulpy, historical fact, reversing the logic of the joke in which Jos Sedley's corpulence crushes the elephant.

Brough's narrator offers a personal disavowal of the elephant that echoes Dickens's banishment of the elephant from Sleary's Circus: "I shouldn't like to be a melancholy-mad elephant." In this statement of repudiation, Brough also suggests a relationship between the recurring image of Coketown's machinery and the argument Dickens makes about a fact-based political economy. Clearly one of Dickens's points is Stephen Blackpool's—that "reg'latin [people] as if they was figures in a soom, or machines" is misguided for, as Sleary says, "they an't made for it";[78] but Brough's statement reduces Dickens's economic thinking to a self-evident statement. Though Brough, like Dickens in the narrative of Emma Gordon's husband, constructs a scene in which excess expunges excess in order to establish a poetical or political economy founded on more "orthodox principles," Brough's parody—like Dickens's Mr. Booley—treats the elephants as a regular element in the English landscape.[79]

Gradgrind distinguishes the world of fact from the world of representation and insists that the two ought to be in accord.[80] In introducing elephants into Coketown, whether under the aegis of the circus or to describe steam engines—that is, at the level of narrative content, or story (what Gradgrind calls "fact"), or the level of style, or discourse ("representation")—Dickens's narrator invokes colonial spaces, just as surely when James Harthouse flees to Egypt or young Tom Gradgrind is sent "many thousands of miles away" to "North or South America, or any distant part of the world."[81] These exotic spaces—which are frequently interchangeable for Dickens's narrator, as "any distant part of the world" suggests[82]—play an important role in establishing the dialectical rapprochement between work and fancy that Dickens seeks to achieve in *Hard Times*, serving as repositories for excessive energies that are irreconcilable with labor or with play. Harthouse's failure to be compatible with Bounderby's commercial world, which is upheld by the labor of Stephen Blackpool and his class, or with Sleary's world of fancy is signaled by the fact that he "got bored everywhere"—as a cavalry officer, as a *flâneur* in Jerusalem, and as a leisured yachtsman.[83] After being rebuked by Sissy Jupe for his attempted seduction of Louisa, Harthouse discovers that he resembles nothing so much as "a Great Pyramid of failure"—a metaphor that takes on a curious reality to him:

> The Great Pyramid put it into his head to go up the Nile. He took a pen upon the instant, and wrote the following note (in appropriate hieroglyphics) to his brother:
>
> Dear Jack,—All up at Coketown. Bored out of the place, and going in for Camels.
>
> Affectionately, JEM[84]

Harthouse's boredom, which is impervious to work and amusement alike, can be assuaged only by "going in for Camels" (though significantly *not* at Sleary's Circus), and Dickens dispatches him to Egypt, never to be mentioned again in the novel.

A similar cure is prescribed for young Tom Gradgrind, whom Bitzer with good reason describes as "a dissipated, extravagant idler" and whose tendency toward excess is only exacerbated by the unrelieved boredom of Harthouse.[85] The emphasis of Tom's father upon pragmatism and "fact" fosters a grossly impractical backlash in Tom that results in the theft of money from Bounderby's bank—a patent violation of commercial "political economy." Rather than face the prospect of punishment, young Tom Gradgrind is sent off to "distant parts of the world." Somewhere vaguely in the tropics where he later dies of a fever, Tom is cured of his resentment and excess: Louisa's "lonely brother, many thousands of miles away, writ[es], on paper blotted with tears, that her words had too soon come true, and that all the treasures in the world would be cheaply bartered for a sight of her dear face."[86] Like the elephant that tumbles the extravagant "Sultan of the Indies" from its back, the dissipations of Harthouse and of the junior Tom Gradgrind would themselves seem to be punished, or at least tempered, by banishment to exotic elsewheres.

Yet Dickens is anxious that the exotic and the colonial do not yield back any traces of these excesses to England itself. For Dickens's political economy to work profitably, excess must move from England to those "distant parts of the world" that effectively function as purgatorial extensions of Great Britain and that are embodied in the imaginative world of the circus by exotic animals, but all evidence of these extravagant purgatories must be effaced from England itself. Like public displays of capital and sexuality in Dickens, which Jeff Nunokawa argues take "the eastern route" to extinction, the banished excesses of the English must not find their way back to England.[87] Instead, what remains is employed in order to, as it were, "Thackerayize" domestic excesses: lest we be taken in like outsiders who "made [Bounderby] out to be the Royal arms, the Union-Jack, Magna Charta, John Bull, Habeas Corpus, the Bill of Rights, An Englishman's house is his castle, Church and State, and God save the Queen, all put together," the narrator renders him "like an oriental dancer" beating "his tambourine on his head."[88] Dickens harshly condemned the Chinese display at the Great Exhibition of 1851 because it exemplified an extravagant culture that "came to a dead stop, Heaven knows how many hundred years ago" and Chinese "Stoppage" compares highly unfavorably with English "Progress."[89] Dickens complained equally about the appearance of a Chinese junk in the London docks near Blackwall, objecting that the junk represented nothing so much as the sad product of a "waste and desert of time" in China.[90] It is perhaps no surprise, therefore, that "The Wise Elephants of the East: Or, The Magic Gong" should be elided from a narrative intended to apply to England in general. For Dickens, "any part of the world" that is not England[91] may serve as a kind of adjunctive space to England (he certainly had no objection to the English presence in China, only the Chinese presence in England), a safety valve that will receive England's dangerous surpluses of energy and peoples. Yet in return, these spaces should yield back to England only profit, without any traces of the waste, profligacy, and excess that colonial spaces represent in the Victorian imagination generally and in Dickens's imagination particularly.

Making the Betht of the Circus: A Politico-Economic Place

In this sense, Dickens's fictional practice anticipates later Victorian conceptions of empire as a repository for Britain's surpluses. Daniel Bivona identifies J. A. Hobson's *Imperialism: A Study* (1902) as "an important event in the contest of ideologies for, in that book for the first time, British imperial appetites are analysed from the standpoint of an economy of the supplement."[92] In particular, Bivona argues

> To Hobson, Britain's excess—whether people or capital—is not innocent, for it actually threatens the foundation of a society built on inequality and privilege. This "dangerous supplement" must be "invested" safely overseas. Although seemingly exterior to Britain's economic system, the colonies are rather essential to it, essential by virtue of constituting a field for the deployment of the home country's otherwise destabilizing surplus. This investment of the surplus on the margins of its economic sphere is precisely what enables the system to function as well as it does at home.[93]

Dickens often seemed critical of this rapidly developing system: in *Bleak House*'s view of Mrs. Jellyby or in Mr. Booley's perspective on the Lord Mayor's Show, for example, looking beyond the bounds of the island nation—"telescopic philanthropy," Dickens calls it in the former text—comes at the expense of domestic progress. Yet as the 1850s moved forward he revised that position, to the point at which it is possible to argue that "Dickens uses imperialism to 'solve' the 'social problem.'"[94]

Hobson identifies as the cornerstone of Rhodes's thought an aphorism that uncannily echoes Dickens's conceptions in *Hard Times*, particularly those allegorized in the tale of Emma Gordon's marriage to the cheesemonger with a "fortun": "'To combine the commercial with the imaginative' was the aim which Mr. Rhodes ascribed to himself as the key of his policy."[95] Yet, as Hobson notes, "It may safely be asserted that, wherever 'the commercial' is combined with 'the imaginative' in any shape or sort, the latter is exploited by the former."[96] The combination of work and play in *Hard Times*, no less than in Rhodes's Cape Colony, suffers from such an exploitation. Even in the capsule narrative of Emma Gordon, the ascendancy of the commercial over the imaginative is visible: though the fanciful world of the circus marries the world of the cheesemonger's trade in the second wedding of Emma Gordon, the upshot of the story is that the cheesemonger has become an overseer of the circus, exploiting it to make his "fortun." More generally in *Hard Times*, Dickens has no real objection to "the commercial" per se, but rather to the personal practices of mill owners such as Bounderby.[97] As he wrote to Charles Knight at the end of the year, "My satire is against those who see figures and averages, and nothing else—the representatives of the wickedest and most enormous vice of this time—the men who, through long years to come, will do more to damage the real useful truths of political economy, than I could do (if I tried) in my whole life."[98] Dickens is committed to envisioning the circus in *Hard Times* in terms consonant with the exhortation of Sleary early in the novel:

> ["]People mutht be amuthed, Thquire, thomehow," continued Sleary, rendered more pursy than ever, by so much talking; "they can't be alwayth a working, nor yet they can't be alwayth a learning. Make the betht of uth; not the wurtht. I've got my living out of the horthe-riding all my life, I know; but I conthider that I lay down the philothophy of the thubject when I thay to you, Thquire, make the betht of uth: not the wurtht!"[99]

In short, in making the best of the circus, not the worst, Dickens has confined his attention to those aspects of the circus most compatible with the commercial values held by his bourgeois readers. F. R. Leavis imagines an objection to Dickens's ostensibly realistic representation of the circus that might follow these lines: "[Though] there would have been some athletic skill and perhaps some bodily grace among the people of a Victorian travelling circus, [nevertheless there would also have been] so much squalor, grossness and vulgarity that we must find Dickens's symbolism sentimentally false."[100] Leavis's answer to this objection is that the bits of the circus that Dickens does present are not demonstrably false and serve his symbolic purpose admirably. Likewise, Schlicke argues that Dickens "did not misrepresent, but offered a plausible, if incomplete" view of the circus.[101] Yet like Miss Matty's carefully confected pictures of Wombwell's Menagerie in *Cranford*, Dickens's selectivity in presenting the circus to a middle-class reading audience is important to considerations of the novel's form and key to understanding the totalizing politics of the fancy it seeks to marry to industry.

Dickens's omission of a certain "squalor, grossness and vulgarity" from his picture of the circus is of a piece with his elision of wild beasts: as representatives of a kind of excess, wild beasts—sometimes those "sluggish quadrupeds," the lions,[102] sometimes the elephant—and vulgar or dissipated behavior are incompatible with the "betht" values of the circus with which Dickens wishes to render more humane a certain kind of capitalistic "political economy." So long as circus values do not threaten the commercial order, but only temper those of its practices that threaten to "damage the real useful truths of political economy," Dickens finds them amenable to realistic narration—the alignment of Gradgrindian "Fact" and "representation."[103] Though the circus offered a "spectacular realism . . . dependent on elaboration, expense, luxury, and, it claimed, accuracy of painstakingly researched detail," Dickens strips this circus realism of much of its overt spectacle as of its overt squalor.[104] Those values that outrage or threaten middle-class sensibilities and the commercial order that underpins them must be excluded from the narrative focus, or divorced from its moral center as are both Signor Jupe and Stephen Blackpool's wife. Thomas Gradgrind prescribes the maintenance of collections of "shells and minerals and things" for his children, in order that their time might be spent profitably. As Mrs. Gradgrind points out, however, "no young people . . . keep circuses in cabinets"; if one cannot contain the imaginative energies that the circus represents within morally or fiscally profitable concerns as one might a mineral, then Mrs. Gradgrind's question naturally follows: "What can you possibly want to know of circuses then?"[105] In excluding aspects of the circus that are not morally profitable from his depiction, Dickens implies that the answer to Mrs. Gradgrind's question must be "Nothing," suggesting that Boz may be of Gradgrind's party without knowing it, certainly without acknowledging it. And though he may successfully defend Dickens's representation of the circus against those who claim it generally violates the tenets of realism, in his defense Leavis nevertheless seems to demonstrate Dickens's political desire to "keep circuses in cabinets," to circumscribe the imaginative play of the circus within the limits of bourgeois industry. Like Miss Matty's "fancy pictures," Dickens's prescription for what English "fancy" should entail includes chiefly a confirmation of restrained, middle-class wishes—no more than he "desires to see."

The selection of circus life that Dickens chooses to represent through Sleary's Circus is especially significant, since in *Hard Times* the circus serves as a space bridging the industrial provinces and "any part of the world," as it occupies a "neutral ground . . . which was neither town nor country."[106] When Sissy advises young Tom Gradgrind about how he might effect his escape from Coketown and from the law, she represents Sleary's Circus as a kind of underground railroad, a conduit from the English mainland to the safety of the sea:

> "[Tom] was in a tremble before I whispered to him, and he started and trembled more then, and said, 'Where can I go? I have very little money, and I don't know who will hide me!' I thought of father's old circus. I have

not forgotten where Mr. Sleary goes at this time of year, and I read of him in a paper only the other day. I told him to hurry there, and tell his name, and ask Mr. Sleary to hide him till I came. 'I'll get to him before the morning,' he said. And I saw him shrink away among the people."

"Thank Heaven!" exclaimed his father. "He may be got abroad yet."[107]

The sense of young Tom as a fugitive slave is heightened by the means of his sequestration: as Sleary says to Louisa, "Your brother ith one o' them black thervanth."[108] Dickens points out that Tom's blackface manifests a "disgraceful grotesqueness" and that his disguise makes him tantamount to a zoological specimen: "his hands, with the black partly worn away inside, looking like the hands of a monkey."[109] The exotic animal once again appears in analogical form, rather than as part of the "Fact" of the narrative of the circus. Tom is safe so long as he inhabits his "grimly, detestably, ridiculously shameful" disguise, but Gradgrind Senior despairs of this costume: "'But look at him,' groaned Mr. Gradgrind."[110] The circus occupies a privileged position in English society, wherein a "black thervant" can remain surprisingly invisible as long as he might wish. As a conduit to "any distant part of the world," however, the circus must turn Tom Gradgrind over to the quotidian world of English transport.[111] Reentering the world of coaches and trains means turning Tom white again, and this is effected through an agent of Stephen Blackpool's wife's alcoholic excesses: "I've never met with nothing but beer ath'll ever clean a comic blackamoor," says Sleary. In vacating the liminal space of the circus, excess washes away excess, as "Mr. Sleary rapidly brought beer, and washed him white again."[112]

Tom Gradgrind as a blackamoor is washed white in preparation for transportation to parts of the world in which it is probable that he will encounter people with dark skin, as well as camels or monkeys. This far-off space should represent new life for Tom, and yet we are told that as a "comic blackamoor," Tom's white eyes are "the only parts of his face that showed any life or expression, the pigment upon it was so thick."[113] Facing the prospect of black skin signifies just the opposite of life for Tom. In the privileged space of the circus, he may be hidden from the English penal system and its technologies of surveillance under the guise of "disgraceful" and "grotesque" black skin, but to be liberated into a new life, he must be made white again. If for Dickens the circus serves as a sort of intermediary space between industrial England and its distant colonial lands, his narrator is nevertheless anxious that the circus not be confused with those alien parts of the world—it, like Heaven, should be "a politico-economical place, [or] we had no business there."[114] Washing young Tom Gradgrind white before sending him away ensures that we do not mistake him for a real "blackamoor," for which Sleary's Circus—unlike circuses and menageries in fact—seems to hold no real place. As a conduit abroad, the circus is useful for its alien associations (for these are what conceal Tom), but it must be able to renounce these associations as illusory when confronted by the exigencies of the bourgeois world: Tom must only look *like* a comic blackamoor, a monkey, or a bushman.

Dickens's Smoke Serpents and Melancholy-Mad Elephants

The displacement of the elephant from the story of the novel—that is, from the "Fact" of Sleary's Circus—into the discourse of its "representation" should be read in the context of the circus's ambivalent place in English culture. The repeated representation of Coketown's steam engines as "melancholy-mad elephants" bound to the labor of commercial enterprise is an effort to conscript a figure of excessive and potentially violent behavior (such as the "Sultan of the Indies" experiences) into a profitable service within the novel. (In "Some Particulars Concerning a Lion," Dickens notes his "great respect for lions in the abstract."[115]) The context of the first mention of the steam engines demonstrates just how the displacement of the elephant from content to form turns it from an emblem of excess into a figure of profit. At the beginning of chapter 5, the narrator describes Coketown as "a triumph of fact; it had no greater taint of fancy in it than Mrs. Gradgrind herself."[116] Coketown

> was a town of red brick, or of brick that would have been red if the smoke and ashes had allowed it; but as matters stood it was a town of unnatural red and black like the painted face of a savage. It was a town of machinery and tall chimneys, out of which interminable serpents of smoke trailed themselves for ever and ever, and never got uncoiled. It had a black canal in it, and a river that ran purple with ill-smelling dye, and vast piles of building full of windows where there was a rattling and a trembling all day long, and where the piston of the steam-engine worked monotonously up and down like the head of an elephant in a state of melancholy madness.[117]

The laborious elephants are rendered within the larger portrait of Coketown as a savage, and they appear alongside "interminable serpents of smoke," first as metaphors and in some instances as capitalized allegories: we have only to recall *Cranford*, in which Miss Matty visits Wombwell's Menagerie and is impressed by the elephant and the boa constrictor as figures for the reaches of India, to understand that Coketown is imagined as just such a place as that to which Tom Gradgrind will escape.

What are we to make of this picture of Coketown as a painted savage? Just seven months before beginning *Hard Times*, Dickens had published his intemperate opinion of "The Noble Savage" in *Household Words* (11 June 1853). Noting the many "eccentricities" of the savage—"he is . . . cruel, false, thievish, murderous; addicted more or less to grease, entrails, and beastly customs; a wild animal with the questionable gift of boasting; a conceited, tiresome, bloodthirsty, monotonous humbug"—Dickens concludes that the savage is so "wicked" that he "might tempt the Society of Friends to . . . exterminate the whole kraal."[118] The "literary gentleman" among the savages "has the appearance of having come express on his hind legs from the Zoological Gardens" and broadcasts his paeans "incontinently."[119] If the savage is the beastly, so also the beastly is the savage: Dickens's conclusion is that "I call a savage a something highly desirable to be civilised off the face of the earth," and "that if we have anything to learn from the Noble Savage, it is what to avoid."[120] Turning his attention onto the English people themselves, he asserts, "It is my opinion that if we retained in us anything of the noble savage, we could not get rid of it too soon," a determination that bears directly on the theme of *Hard Times*.[121] The savage as represented in *Household Words* is repeatedly described as a painted beast, as a dangerous animal that might have come directly from the zoo; Coketown as a savage, too, is described as a painted monstrosity, and is associated five times with, and allegorized once by, the serpent and the elephant.

As a consequence of this opinion, Dickens's point in casting Coketown as a painted savage seems plain: as a "triumph of fact" without a "taint of fancy," Coketown—in its savage aspect—should be "civilised off the face of the earth."[122] Civilizing Coketown, as we have seen, means affirming Sleary's Circus as an anodyne to the excesses of fact and demands that a balance be struck between commercial and imaginative interests, between Bounderby and Sleary. A curious reversal emerges from Dickens's figuration of Coketown's fact-driven industry as savage and his implicit prescription for its civilization, a reversal that follows upon the displacement of the elephant from the circus onto the mills. In its movement from the represented content to the means of representation in the novel, the elephant, like Tom in the guise of the blackamoor or the monkey, is not only exiled from the circus but also comes to characterize the problem that the circus is designed to solve. It is not just that "Dickens collapses the boundary with which he separates the circus from the economic realities of industrial Britain," as Helen Stoddart argues;[123] the melancholy-mad elephants, as characteristic symbols of Coketown's domestic savagery, must be civilized by the agency of the English circus. The elephant as a symbol of excess serves as an avatar of all that must be civilized in Coketown, not—as Paul Schlicke has it—as a "reminder that, forbidden healthy outlet, people's need for entertainment will surface in wildly distorted form."[124] The melancholy-mad elephants are, as Robert Brough's parody highlights, the property of the narrator, not of the people of Coketown and, most remarkably, not of Sleary or his circus: though Dickens advocates the combination of fact and fancy in poetry or the circus, in practice he observes the Gradgrindian distinction between Fact and representation. In moving from the realm of story to that of discourse, the elephant is domesticated, like Mr. Booley's view of Astley's allegory, or Van Amburgh's lions, becoming a profitable figure within the symbolic economy Dickens establishes.

In two early essays the young Boz explored the madness of elephants and the means of their destruction. In "Gin-Shops," Dickens observes that "the disease to which elephants and dogs are especially liable [... is ...] to run stark, staring, raving mad, periodically," and promises that "If an elephant run mad, we are all ready for him—kill or cure—pills or bullets—calomel in conserve of roses, or lead in a musket-barrel."[125] In the first version of "Scotland Yard" he lamented the necessary demise of the famous elephant Chunee at Exeter 'Change under the weight of its madness:

> The death of the elephant was a great shock to us; we knew him well; and, having enjoyed the honour of his intimate acquaintance for some years, felt grieved—deeply grieved—that in a paroxysm of insanity he should have so far forgotten all his estimable and companionable qualities as to exhibit a sanguinary desire to scrunch his faithful valet, and pulverize even Mrs. Cross herself, who for a long period had evinced towards him that pure and touching attachment which woman alone can feel. This was a sad blow to us.[126]

Though the elephant was sometimes also associated with melancholia in Dickens's periodicals, as in one article in *Household Words* describing a "sad and demure" elephant that the Surrey Zoological Gardens sold to Batty's Circus,[127] nineteenth-century writing more often returned to scenes of the elephant's insanity. Dickens excised his description of the Exeter 'Change elephant from "Scotland Yard" in reprinting it in the collection of *Sketches by Boz* (though Dickens claimed not to have "remodel[ed] or expunge[d], beyond a few words and phrases here and there"[128]), but other authors in his periodicals rehearsed the famous story of Chunee, who in 1826 became "seized with raging mania, and threatened to anticipate the after-fate of the building [in which it was housed] by tearing it violently down there and then. ... The building shook with his furious onslaughts upon the beams that held it together, and with the vibrations of his own and his fellow-captives' roars. ... [A] few more beams splintered in twain, more crashing of floors, more lions and tigers mixed together by the snapping of partition bars" before the "elephantine maniac" was executed by a firing squad.[129]

In casting the elephants in *Hard Times* as a metaphor—at the level of discourse, as part of the novel's style—rather than presenting them within the context of Sleary's Circus, Dickens contains their excess even as he turns them to his profit: unlike Chunee at the Exeter 'Change, the melancholy-mad elephants are not free to shake down the architecture of the novel but rather are fixed laboring within Dickens's symbolic economy, just as the steam engines they represent are perpetually laboring for Bounderby. Though Sleary's Circus profitably serves as a conduit through which English excess may pass to "any distant part of the world," the elephant as a conduit for the return of such excesses must be suppressed by canceling its agency at the level of represented content and raising it into the novel's symbolic register. The single exception to this cancellation of the elephant at the level of represented content occurs in the narrative of Emma Gordon, a narrative that itself demonstrates the purgation of excess by Eastern magnificence. If, as I have argued, Dickens is of Gradgrind's party in his desire to "keep circuses in cabinets" and for the circus to be "regulated and governed," he also advocates Sissy Jupe's position. He obviously opposes Gradgrind's argument that "you are not to have, in any object of use or ornament, what would be a contradiction in fact. ... you don't find that foreign birds and butterflies come and perch upon your crockery; you cannot be permitted to paint foreign birds and butterflies upon your crockery. ... This is taste."[130] He does so, however, by inverting this perspective: by offering snakes, elephants, monkeys, and camels as properties of fancy and representation, not of actuality or fact, he affirms the salutary desire of Sissy Jupe for that which contradicts fact. Dickens's narrator pretends we *do not* see them as fact so they can be rendered all the more attractive as representations.

The elephant's displacement from content onto form is a move symptomatic of what Katherine Kearns calls the "tropology of realism in *Hard Times*," in which "'realism' is, in every case [in *Hard Times*], an epistemologically suspect, politically driven notion."[131] The schools inspector in M'Choakumchild's classroom, "ready to fight all England" for his principles, observes that "What is called Taste, is only another name for Fact,"[132] and the logical extension of this is, of course, that the form in which Fact is presented constitutes Taste: this is substantively the point made by Leavis and Schlicke about Sleary's Circus—that the portion of the circus Dickens chooses to represent indeed conforms to the strictures of realism. Yet the cancellation of the zoological exotica from the "limited reality" presented in *Hard Times* should be understood as entailing a political dimension—a dimension of "Taste"—as well, for if Sleary's Circus models the sort of human relationships that will revitalize English industrial relations, the divorces of the "Sultan of the Indies" from Emma Gordon and the elephant from the circus take on a wider a significance. Dickens intended the conclusions of his novel to be generalized across England: in a letter to Peter Cunningham on 11 March 1854, Dickens warned him against "localiz[ing] . . . a story which has a direct purpose in reference to the working people all over England."[133] Although, as Catherine Gallagher remarks, "the book seems suffused with a fear of making connections in a world where relationships are almost without exception destructive,"[134] the novel wants to totalize: Stephen Blackpool warns against the social fragmentation that Bounderby's brand of political economy will produce, in which "they will be as one, and yo will be as anoother, wi' a black unpassable world betwixt yo," and the circus's values of generosity, community, and fancy appear as the bridge between these worlds, or the stuff binding English "lives in the aggregate."[135] If generalizing the circus generates a vision of holism against the social atomization represented by the pursuit of "National Prosperity"[136] in the rest of the novel, it is nevertheless a vision of the whole from which the excess and "melancholy madness" of the elephant—as well as the painted savage, the blackamoor, the monkey, the camel, and the serpent—must be excluded or recuperated outside the bounds of realism.

Hard Times' Economy of the Imperial Household

Hard Times was conceived as a whole, unlike *Vanity Fair*, which offered a series of exhibitions or sketches, and *Cranford*, which began as serial stories before reaching the length of a novel. *Hard Times*' holistic fabric is woven upon a narrative frame that shuttles between the circus and Coketown, and if the warp of the weave is imagination, the woof is profitable industry. The figure of the elephant—and the colonial excess it stands for—is bound up in this fabric precariously. Dickens's "direct purpose" in representing relations "all over England" takes an economic cast, as we have seen, whereby imagination should be wedded to commercial profit, as in Emma Gordon's marriage to the cheesemonger and overseer. Indeed, the occasion for Dickens's own fanciful imaginings was the precipitous decline in the readership for *Household Words*: the publication of *Hard Times* was designed to, and did, raise the sales figures for the magazine. The profitable economic holism of Dickens's novel as we have seen is predicated upon the banishment of England's excesses to the margins of empire, whence they are permitted to return only in profitable form. The exile of the profligates Tom Gradgrind and James Harthouse forms a direct parallel to the banishment of the elephant from the circus; the return of such alienated surpluses, like the sublation of the elephant into the novel's tropes, is subject to the test of profitability.

In this way, the totality of circulated energies in *Hard Times* across England and its empire assumes the form of what Georges Bataille describes as a "restricted economy."[137] The novel's conclusion makes this clear: the moral profit to be had from the novel is that the English people need "to beautify their lives of machinery and reality with those imaginative graces and delights, without which . . . the plainest national prosperity figures can show, will be the Writing on the Wall."[138] In *Hard Times* Dickens turns *Dombey and Son*'s formula into a prescription to be followed "all over England": it creates England itself as "a form of estate that is sheltered from various forces that threaten private property, and this construction requires a strategy of containment and catharsis which takes the 'orient' as its scapegoat."[139] Such a sheltered totality is conceived in terms that are "accustomed to seeing the development of productive forces as the ideal end of [economic] activity," and which demand that any surplus be reinvested into the mechanisms of production.[140] In his conceptions at the level of political economy, Dickens is, I have argued, anxious to keep the imperial circus in cabinets, as it were, to harness what Daniel Bivona calls the colonial "economy of the supplement" to profitable English ends: when cloaked in the guise of the imperial menagerie, fancy should appear to contradict fact, and the procession of the exotic should raise the incredulous question that opens *Edwin Drood*, "How can that be here!" The rogue elephant appears as a guarantee of the real, but it must be reported offstage, as it were.

In conceiving England and its relation to empire as an integrated totality, a totality that operates under "restricted economic" conditions, the Dickens who keeps circuses in cabinets and trains a host of wild beasts to perform tropically in *Hard Times* might well have earned the right to sign his letters "otherwise

Wan Amburg." For Dickens, comprehending England's relation to empire in holistic terms depended upon a symptomatic banishment of the elephant and the excess it represents from the English provinces, just as his selective realism relies upon displacing the figure of the elephant from the represented content to a profitable tropological service. What might the implication be for a totalistic vision of empire—and for literary realism that increasingly sought to align the worlds of "fact" and "representation"—if the exiled elephant who overthrows the Sultan of the Indies returns to center stage in the traveling circus or menagerie? The next chapter investigates an elephant who, like Chunee at the Exeter 'Change, seeks to shake down the imperial household, throwing mid-Victorian England "a heavy backfall," as Sleary says, and disrupting the coherence of the selective allegiance to Fact that Dickens's novel works so hard to consolidate in the name of good Taste, improving narration, and beautifying England's literary and social machinery.

Chapter 3

Elephants in the Labyrinth of Empire

Arnold Bennett, Modernism, and the Menagerie

Poetry's Birth and the Death of an Elephant

While Charles Dickens approached the spectacle of the circus in highly circumspect and selective ways, a half century later Arnold Bennett looked back to the mid-Victorian years to embrace a comprehensive range of popular culture, celebrating "the wortht" as well as "the betht" in public displays. In the intervening years the New Imperialism pushed the limits of Greater Britain ever outward, seeking particularly to incorporate African spaces; small menageries, circuses, and exhibitions gave way to zoological display as big business; and the domestic English novel came to be balanced by the rise of imperial adventure fiction and the imperial gothic, both of which as a matter of course connect imperial exotica encountered at the margins of empire back to their familiar displays in the mother country.[1] Such displays also resulted in the most dramatic development of the century related to zoology. The theories of Charles Darwin, who in 1831 described the Zoological Gardens as "what I liked most in all London"[2] and donated the specimens from the *Beagle* voyage to the Zoological Society in January 1837, lent themselves to a popular notion of an "evolutionary tree." This "tree of life"[3] promised not only to account for zoological taxonomies in the present but also to extend them back in history and to subject humankind to the totalizing mechanisms of evolution by natural selection.

In the end, though, Arnold Bennett's fiction for the most part remained resolutely within the British Isles and attended to the textures of provincial English life, rather than imperial adventures or global voyages. Indeed, his fiction seems largely to ignore not only Darwinian science but also such contemporary productions as his friend H. G. Wells's *Island of Doctor Moreau* (1896). Instead, in his turn toward cultures of imperial display, Bennett renders excess at popular exhibitions in the service of a reserved and civil English culture. In "The Elixir of Youth" (1907), a story completed as Bennett was preparing to write *The Old Wives' Tale* (1908), Bennett's narrator describes a scene of the holiday "wakes" celebration in provincial Staffordshire, a carnivalesque occasion that resembles "not our modern rectified festival, but the wild and naïve orgy of seventy years ago," during the reign of George IV.[4] The Bursley wakes exemplifies the "squalor, grossness and vulgarity" that Leavis finds missing from Dickens's portrait of Sleary's Circus: it features bear- and bullbaiting, cockfighting, and bare-fisted pugilism, while the town "yield[s] itself with savage abandonment to all the frenzies of license."[5] This "savagery"—an "uncontrolled exuberance of revelry"[6]—sharply contrasts both the compassionate civility of Sleary's Circus in *Hard Times* and the restraint of the twentieth-century wakes, a "modern rectified festival" epitomized by a tamer brand of amusements such as "photographic studios and . . . cocoanut shies."[7]

Bennett's story is concerned with the bringing to account—indeed, the rendering poetic—of the "grossness" of the nineteenth-century wakes, demonstrating how this carnivalesque "orgy" was brought to heel. In a booth near the ramshackle old brick Town Hall ("not the present stone structure with its gold angel," the narrator notes[8]), a mountebank who calls himself "The Inca of Peru" sells his elixir. The Inca of Peru renders himself a splendid attraction, "dressed in black velveteens, with a brilliant scarf round his neck," and this exotic appearance ensures that he is "thoroughly inured to the public gaze." At the same time, however, he announces his discovery of the elixir "while exploring the ruins of the most ancient civilisation of the world": exotic though he may be, he nevertheless holds himself apart from this ruinous culture.[9] From the carefully cultivated middle ground of appealing strangeness, the Inca advertises the salutary properties of his elixir as Black Jack, a violent criminal, passes by in a constable's wagon. The Inca drums up business by offering a free glass of the magical red fluid to the criminal, who is to be hanged for kicking his "sweetheart" to death. Later in the evening, the criminal's new beloved, a fourteen-year-old girl, comes to the Inca in his tent to spend all her savings on a draught of the elixir in order to stay young for her beau, believing that he cannot possibly be hanged since he has drunk the elixir. As she leaves, "Simultaneously there was a rush and a roar from the Cock yard close by. The raging bull, dragging its ropes, and followed by a crowd of alarmed pursuers, dashed out. The girl was plain in the moonlight. Many others were abroad, but the bull seemed to see nothing but her, and, lowering his huge head, he charged with shut eyes and flung her over the Inca's booth."[10] This gruesome occurrence represents the climax of the constituent events of the story.

To this point Bennett's tale seems as sordid and "gross" a spectacle as the wakes he represents, but the narrative's conclusion draws all this grossness into abrupt but precise perspective:

> "Thou's gotten thy wish: thou'rt young for ever!" the Inca of Peru, made a poet for an instant by this disaster, murmured to himself as he bent with the curious crowd over the corpse.
>
> Black Jack was hanged.
>
> Many years after all this Bursley built itself a new Town Hall (with a spire, and a gold angel on the top in the act of crowning the bailiwick with a gold crown), and began to think about getting up in the world.[11]

The narrative discourse distills from the tragedy of the young girl a kind of poetry that takes as its correlatives the execution of justice and the rise of Bursley in the world—a civilizing progress crowned by the angel of history. The Inca's poetic pronouncement marks a kind of public catharsis, in which excess is purged by means of its own extravagance: the girl's naïve and irresponsible purchase of the elixir, on the one hand, and the baited bull's violence, on the other, enable the moment of poetry—and, the narrator suggests, higher cultural aspiration. The exoticism of the colorfully attired "Inca" catalyzes the scene, drawing out this cathartic dynamic without affecting the strange and "ancient civilization" he claims in part to represent.

The civility of provincial Englishness—its ability to "get up in the world"—depends upon both the alien and the excessive, though in Bennett's tale this is not primarily a material dependency but an imaginative one. While the sublimation (or "rectification") of the carnival's "savage license" remains incomplete (for the Inca is "made a poet" only for a moment, and it is only "many years after all this" that Bursley crowns its achievement by erecting the gold angel), the transformation of cultural coarseness sketched in "The Elixir of Youth" constitutes a significant theme in Bennett's oeuvre. Rendering the excessive poetic is one of the ways that Bennett distinguished the broad, cosmopolitan compass of his writing from the intemperate partiality of Victorian fiction. For Bennett, "getting up in the world" of the novel meant finding a perspective from which to totalize, to render meaningful as part of a cultural whole, such apparently superfluous provincial energies.

And yet despite his deep sympathies for things Continental and mild contempt for narrowly English cultural and political views, Bennett and his work came to be regarded as essentially provincial over the course of the twentieth century. This characterization put him at odds with high modernism and its cosmopolitan exponents, even when they became committed to a certain insularity of their own. In the years following Bennett's death in 1931, prominent modernists such as Virginia Woolf and T. S. Eliot embarked upon a "demetropolitanization of English literature,"[12] but by that point Woolf had declared Bennett's literary conventions the equivalent of "ruin" and "death," the effect of his novels "chill" and "distant," and his methods outmoded from "on or about December 1910."[13] Since those pronouncements, Bennett's writing has come to seem peripheral to twentieth-century canons that value formal experimentation and innovation over finely honed realism and writerly discipline. In such a critical climate, Bennett's best-known novel, *The Old Wives' Tale* (1908), will appear to confirm his place on the margins of modernism: the text narrates personal and cultural histories of industrial Staffordshire (the "Five Towns" now comprising Stoke-on-Trent), and its adherence to conventions of realism and its regional subject matter reinforce Bennett's reputation as a novelist of provincial imagination. The conclusion drawn by even a critic as sympathetic to Bennett as St. John Ervine exemplifies the prevailing view: "the farther Bennett gets away from his native Five Towns, the poorer his invention becomes."[14]

Against the grain of these characterizations, this chapter argues that *The Old Wives' Tale* imaginatively maps provincialism's relation to the cosmopolitan. Yet an irruption of the imperial exotic in the novel complicates this relationship and suggests a series of conclusions about the fate of Edwardian realism. Bennett's theories of realism, discussed below as the horizon toward which his novels tend, are broadly cosmopolitan in the Arnoldian sense, because they aim to see life disinterestedly and in its totality. At the level of content, however, Bennett's most memorable writing takes up local instances of English life, from the inhabitants of the Five Towns to the residents of London's Clerkenwell in *Riceyman Steps* (1923). *The Old Wives' Tale* might therefore be described as a cosmopolitan narrative in its realist method but a provincial one in the local focus of its subject matter. The plot of the novel traces the separate narratives of the Baines sisters: Constance lives out her life in one house in the Five Towns, while Sophia elopes to Paris, where she remains for four decades before returning to Staffordshire in her old age. The novel's unusually broad temporal scope—it encompasses a span of years from the 1860s to the first decade of the twentieth century—compensates for the narrowness of the sisters' lives, and in the course of fulfilling its realist mandate the novel situates their experiences within the larger social whole, first the local English community and then high modernity generally. As a result of these strategies, *The Old Wives' Tale* approaches the provincial as an integral part of the total fabric of modern life.

At the center of the novel, Sophia, her wayward husband, and their Parisian friend Chirac travel from Paris to Auxerre, a cathedral town populated by "heavy-witted provincials,"[15] to view the guillotining of a famous criminal. In broken English, Chirac explains to Sophia, who is "aghast" at the prospect of a public decapitation, precisely where the allure of the guillotine lies:

> "As psychological experience," replied Chirac, pronouncing the *p* of the adjective, "it will be very *intéressant* . . . To observe oneself in such circumstances . . ." He smiled enthusiastically.
>
> She thought how strange even nice Frenchmen were. Imagine going to an execution in order to observe yourself![16]

Sophia's incredulous reaction to the "strange" Chirac's observation betrays her own naïveté and provinciality, but it is also characteristically English, instancing the English desire to hold "at arm's length" such spectacles, to recall Sir John Seeley's phrase. Sophia's surprise at a scene of self-reflection is also typically English according to Bennett. In his most important and comprehensive essay in narrative theory, *The Author's Craft* (1913), Bennett writes that "French lamp-posts are part of what we [English] call the 'interesting character' of a French street. We say of a French street that it is 'full of character.' As if an English street was not! Such is blindness—to be cured by travel and the exercise of the logical faculty."[17] If Englishness typically entails a disengagement of spectator from spectacle, it also masks its own specificity with a curious kind of unselfconsciousness. Sophia's elopement to Paris with Gerald Scales represents just such an attempt to "cure" by the experience of travel what she feels to be a characteristically narrow English perspective on the world. Yet the cosmopolitan allure of France has drawn Sophia away from another scene of execution in the heart of England, a scene that Sophia refuses to witness because of its taint of provinciality. This other scene offers an allegorical moment of reflection on Englishness and its relation to empire, a moment that haunts the remainder of the narrative and informs the very structure of the novel: an elephant revolts in the town square, is executed, and then decomposes on the town playground.

The elephant's behavior reprises the role of the bull in "The Elixir of Youth," and its demise recalls the spectacular blood and gore of Chunee's execution and subsequent decay at the Exeter 'Change menagerie. The scene is "very *intéressant*" for considerations of realism, though not "as psychological experience," in Chirac's phrase, but rather in terms of a Victorian empire that understands itself to comprise a coherent totality. The scene of the elephant's execution offers both reflections of Englishness and a glimpse of an emergent modernist narrative practice. Wombwell's Menagerie consequently plays a crucial role in *The Old Wives' Tale* because it punctures both the cosmopolitan aims of Bennett's realism and the insularity of the novel's provincial protagonists. The intrusion of the imperial upon the domestic English landscape of *The Old Wives' Tale*—particularly in the emblematic figure of the elephant run amok—complicates notions such as Matthew Arnold's that the provincial appears antipodal to a metropolitan center and that it evinces a partiality of vision by contrast to cosmopolitanism's totalizing perspective.[18] Like the elephant that the blind men in the fable describe in so many incompatible ways, the elephant in Bennett's novel suggests the impossibility of the totalizing vision in which Edwardian realism places so much confidence. At the same time, the elephant as an avatar of the exotic colonizes Staffordshire's traditional way of life. Objective realism as an ideally cosmopolitan practice thus becomes entangled with provincial Englishness through the exhibitionary machinery of empire.

The Old Wives' Tale explores this machinery at the site that Wyndham Lewis sought to demolish in *Blast 1* (1914), the Victorian provincial town. Claiming a dynamic and cosmopolitan London as the seat of British modernism and disavowing all marks of the provincial, Lewis "blasts" the "years 1837 to 1900" and declares that "LONDON IS NOT A PROVINCIAL TOWN. We will allow Wonder Zoos. But we do not want the GLOOMY VICTORIAN CIRCUS in Piccadilly Circus. IT IS PICCADILLY'S CIRCUS! NOT MEANT FOR MENAGERIES trundling out of Sixties DICKENSIAN CLOWNS."[19] Bennett's novel, however, demonstrates the ways in which the menagerie of the 1860s itself disrupts the provincial, and the narrative goes so far as to imply that the elephant has killed off "mid-Victorian England." Unlike the Inca and the bull in "The Elixir of Youth," who jointly produce (however accidentally) a sense of cultural aspiration, the elephant menaces English civility at its center. Indeed, the elephant's symbolic violence prefigures Lewis's "blasting" and "the sound of breaking and falling, crashing and destruction" in which Woolf hears the note of the modern: it announces the need for fresh aesthetic forms to convey the irremediable partiality of English experience in the global environment of empire.[20]

Dreams of the Impossible East and Visible Proofs of Empire

Arnold Bennett's fiction is usually discussed in terms of the manifold expressions of class anxiety that figure prominently in his novels and in his life. Samuel Hynes, for instance, characterizes the disagreement between Woolf and Bennett in the exchange of essays that provoked "Mr. Bennett and Mrs. Brown" as one chiefly about class difference.[21] Bennett encourages such readings when, for instance, he concludes in his review of Woolf's *A Room of One's Own* (1929) that "She is the queen of the highbrows; and I am a lowbrow."[22] Though Bennett wrote frequently about London in his novels, it is chiefly as a chronicler of English provincial life that Bennett is recognized. John Wain maintains that Bennett "knew that all great writers have understood a provincial life.... And obviously, even in a society that goes in for enormous capital cities, the majority of lives are lived away from the capital."[23] But even if Bennett concentrated his attention on provincial English experience rather than on life in the colonies, the Englishness about which he wrote came into focus in the nineteenth century in relation to empire. The very notion of English "provinciality" is owed to an incipient lexicon of colonialism. Samuel Johnson's *Dictionary* (1755) offers as a definition of "provincial": "3. Not of the mother country." As John Lucas notes, a person accused of provinciality in this conception "is, at least metaphorically, 'not of the mother country'; he is banished."[24] The application of this term to the internal extreme reaches of England in the nineteenth century suggests that a cartography of empire, in which spaces "not of the mother country" are "provincial," has been mapped onto "the mother country" itself.

Even by early twentieth-century standards, though, Bennett himself was hardly "provincial" in any simple sense. He left the Potteries for London early in his life, moved to Paris in 1903 when he was thirty-six, lived in France during the portion of his writing career in which his reputation was largely established, and died a well-recognized figure in the London social scene. In his personal and professional life, Bennett moved from provincial Staffordshire to London, then to France, and back to London, and he became a world traveler with a tour of Algeria in 1903 and a lecture tour that crossed the United States in 1911. The shape of his career looks, in fact, a good deal like that of the "cosmopolitan" modernists who later repudiated him, and though Virginia Woolf attacked Bennett's fictional practice relentlessly, the two authors circulated in overlapping social circles—both were to be found, for instance, in the company of T. S. Eliot, at Lady Ottoline Morrell's salons, and occasionally at dinner together. Bennett, in fact, anticipated the modernists by cultivating his life and literary productions with a preference for the cosmopolitan. A year before *Blast*'s "Manifesto" declared that "No great ENGLISH Art need be ashamed to share some glory with France,"[25] Bennett wrote that he found himself "liking and comprehending the French more and more, and feeling more and more at home among them, until now I do believe I have a kind of double mentality—one English and the other French."[26] *The Old Wives' Tale* is a product of this cosmopolitan "double mentality," having been written in Avon-Fontainebleu in the French countryside about the lives of English women both in provincial England and in Paris. David Trotter locates Bennett's writing as a whole—not just *The Old Wives' Tale*—beyond national boundaries altogether, in a style "that was not available to Bennett in either the 'French' or the 'English' traditions."[27]

Missing from Bennett's and Trotter's cosmopolitan formulae, however, is the realm of British experience about which Bennett's contemporary Leonard Woolf exercised himself through much of his career. In *Imperialism and Civilization* (1928), Woolf declares, "When we have all been dead for several hundred years, the historian of that time will probably consider this movement of nineteenth-century imperialism and the reaction against it as the most important facts in our area."[28] Contrary to received wisdom, Bennett's fiction, even that which treats the provincial Five Towns, is far from oblivious to the fact that domestic English life is bound up with imperial space. Because this space was not apprehended directly by Bennett or by the domestic figures whose lives he narrates—neither Bennett nor his characters made E. M. Forster's passage to India, for instance—Bennett's fiction engages empire primarily in figurative terms rather than in its subject matter. Though less explicit than the pointed interventions of contemporaries such as Leonard Woolf, Goldsworthy Lowes Dickinson, or J. A. Hobson, Bennett nevertheless engaged with the culture of imperialism even in his earliest professional writing. From 1897 to 1899 Bennett edited the penny-weekly magazine *Woman,* and as editor he regularly wrote columns on household management and reported on fashionable parties, in addition to contributing reviews of novels, travel journals, the theater, and even pantomimes. In these columns he demonstrates an awareness of empire and its "most important facts" as they affect domestic English life. In the midst of characteristically domestic feature articles, significant traces of the material "facts" of empire can be found. In the second issue under his editorship, for example, Bennett placed an article on "English Girls transplanted to India," and two weeks later he introduced a feature on "Miss Mary Kingsley's trip to

West Africa."[29] Though such articles certainly indicate the appeal that narratives promising exotic descriptions held for a domestic English audience, Bennett's publication primarily offers testimony about the extent to which cultures of imperialism saturated English domestic experience at the end of the century.

As the festivities surrounding Queen Victoria's Diamond Jubilee unfolded in June and July 1897, Bennett and *Woman* reported on the most striking events of the summer's celebrations. On 14 July 1897 *Woman* related that "The State Ball at Buckingham Palace on Thursday was an affair not without dulness—a dulness, however, which was relieved by the presence of many Indian Princes and of a fire in the second floor in the Palace." Amidst a general exhaustion about post-Jubilee entertainments, the "Indian Princes" appear as thrilling as a conflagration in the palace, provoking an excitement that echoes the enthusiasm of the previous week's report. A leading piece likely written by Bennett himself on 7 July 1897 reported on "The Garden-Party at Buckingham Palace":

> The constant *va et vient* of Royalties, the groups of gorgeously attired Indian princes, the great ecclesiastics of East and West, the crowds of beautiful and beautifully-dressed women, the palace servants in their bright liveries shining with gold, and the visible living proofs of Empire and a power in the persons of foreign envoys and Colonial representatives, made a never-to-be-forgotten scene.[30]

On the unique occasion of the Queen's last Jubilee the empire in its entirety reveals itself symbolically at Buckingham Palace to Bennett and the staff of *Woman*. The stuff of fantasy—Indian princes, Eastern ecclesiastics, and colonial representatives—appears in flesh as the "visible living proofs of Empire," as though the empire in its vastness and distance needed a testament in the domestic space of Buck House. For Bennett's *Woman*, the garden party serves as "a never-to-be-forgotten scene," and it is indeed worth remembering this convergence of West and East, "beautiful [English] women" and colonial representatives, *Woman* and empire, when we read Bennett's novels about the English provinces under Victoria, whose reign can be said to have achieved symbolic culmination in the Diamond Jubilee. Bennett in the end seems not to have forgotten the hypnotic, almost hallucinatory allure of such an exotic scene in England as he wrote novels such as *Clayhanger* (1910), and later in his life he took particular pride in owning a house at 75 Cadogan Square, London, that had once belonged to a viceroy of India.[31]

Such exoticism initially seems utterly alien to *The Old Wives' Tale*, however, which simultaneously identifies the English nation with its provinces and emphasizes the novel's narrative allegiance to realism by invoking the typicality of Staffordshire, the county that "has everything that England has."[32] The Baineses, the novel's protagonists, exist at the heart of the "central labyrinth of England," while the narrator claims that the Five Towns community more generally is "England in little, lost in the midst of England, unsung by searchers of the extreme."[33] The narrator stresses "its representative features and traits," and the novel's opening pages announce both that the narrative in good realist fashion will typify a set of extradiegetic historical relations and circumstances, and that it considers the English provinces as a synecdoche for the nation as a whole. Bennett's novel claims to present characteristic instances of the local—"England in little"—and to distinguish England's "central labyrinth" from its "extreme" others, wherever they might be situated. The narrator's exposition in *The Old Wives' Tale* in this respect conforms to Bennett's conception of the realist novel as an instrument that presents cultural particularities by treating them as expressions of a whole way of life.

It is a mark of the novel's broad, objective narrativity that while the narrator enumerates the story's representative features, the characters themselves have little sense of their typicality. The sisters and their family have no conception that their lives in industrial Staffordshire run congruent to the "calm and characteristic stream of middle England," and only later, after Sophia's migrations to London and then Paris, are they able to measure the degree to which Sophia's itinerant impulses diverge from Constance's insular tendencies as the "stay-at-home sister."[34] By contrast with the capacious narrative voice, the characters to the very end perceive their own marginality when judged by the centers of national life; considered in the light of the latter, the industrial district "might almost as well be in the middle of the Sahara."[35] So alien does London appear to the Five Towns that for its inhabitants to contemplate the metropolis is tantamount to "dream[ing] of the impossible East."[36] The sense that they lead an "uncolored" peripheral existence appears as the negative image of the impression cultivated in metropolitan centers of the "impossible" but brilliant margins of empire.[37] From the perspective of the provinces, the metropole appears as exotic as the empire itself seems from London. Meanwhile, Bennett's novels themselves offer views that take in all of these perspectives, rendering each a part of a total vision of modern life.

Spectacular Shows and Realism's All-Red Routes

In the chapter of *The Old Wives' Tale* crucial to its division into domestic and Continental stories, Sophia and her future lover disparage the local, thinking that by doing so they manifest a broadness of outlook. The annual carnivalesque holiday called the "wakes" serves as the backdrop to a flirtatious exchange between Sophia and the traveling salesman:

> "I see it's your wakes here," said he.
> He was polite to the wakes; but now, with the least inflection in the world, he put the wakes at its proper level in the scheme of things as a local unimportance! She adored him for this; she was athirst for sympathy in the task of scorning everything local.[38]

The novel exposes this disdain for the local as itself a kind of provincialism; as we shall see, wakes celebrations, a typical feature of popular culture in the North of England, attracted "traveling cultures" of their own, including menageries featuring exotic people and animals. Yet even in the context of the novel the wakes is more than a "local unimportance": Sophia's encounter with her lover during the holiday motivates her flight from the Five Towns. This departure does not, however, render a verdict on the justness of the lover's "inflection," upon which turns the difference between a respect for the local and a scorn for it as provincial, and the wakes' "proper level in the scheme of things" remains a central problem in the novel.

Sophia's peregrinations take her from the Staffordshire Potteries to an "impossibly" alien London and eventually to a shockingly cosmopolitan Paris. To her they figure as an escape from the provincialism of Bursley, but they are also a form of exile to which she consigns herself for having allowed her invalid father to die on her watch. At the moment when Sophia scorns the local and exchanges glances with the alluring traveler, John Baines lies paralyzed in his bed at the heart of the "central labyrinth of England." In the interval during which Sophia meets the salesman, "Mr. Baines had wakened up, and, being restless, had slid out partially from his bed and died of asphyxia. After having been unceasingly watched for fourteen years, he had, with an invalid's natural perverseness, taken advantage of Sophia's brief dereliction to expire."[39] Soon after her father's death, Sophia elopes with the commercial traveler and the novel splits into the separate narratives of Constance and Sophia. Yet Sophia is not the only member of the family to flirt dangerously with the exotic at this crucial juncture. While she is left to watch

John Baines, the rest of the family visits an elephant belonging to Wombwell's Menagerie that has gone mad and been shot by the town's rifle corps. John Baines's death appears as much a consequence of an enthusiasm for the exotic corpse of the elephant as it is of Sophia's refusal to attend sufficiently to local matters, whether the wakes or John Baines.

Despite Sophia's scorn, the wakes affects her, and *The Old Wives' Tale* sketches the local determination of Sophia's cosmopolitan adventure. The novel also maps the way in which a larger traveling culture shapes the local: both the salesman and the menagerie's elephant are agents of an increasingly mobile capitalism that disrupts the fixities of mid-Victorian provincial life—those certainties of English culture signaled by John Baines's place as patriarch at the center of England. The novel's map goes beyond mere snapshots of local color to represent a whole complex of social relations, encompassing both provincial life and its others—metropolitan, cosmopolitan, and imperial. In *The Author's Craft*, Bennett lays out such mapping projects as the primary task for English novelists. "[A]ll physical phenomena are interrelated," Bennett asserts, and so

> there is nothing which does not bear on everything else. The whole spectacular and sensual show—what the eye sees, the ear hears, the nose scents, the tongue tastes and the skin touches—is a cause or an effect of human conduct.... Hence he who would beyond all others see life for himself—I naturally mean the novelist and playwright—ought to embrace all phenomena in his curiosity. Being finite, he cannot. Of course he cannot! But he can, by obtaining a broad notion of the whole, determine with some accuracy the position and relative importance of the particular series of phenomena to which his instinct draws him.[40]

In coordinating the "particular" through the perspective of "the whole," Bennett's theory embodies a broadly cosmopolitan ethos ("a detached individual view of the global," in Bruce Robbins's characterization).[41] The (male) writer occupies the position of a spectator at a "spectacular and sensual show," a spectacle from which he must distill a "broad notion of the whole" before he turns to local "phenomena." When Sophia perceives her lover justly to place "the wakes at its proper level in the scheme of things," she imagines him as just such an author with a totalizing command—but this is a serious misreading, she discovers, since his estimations are frequently wrong-headed and even offensive (he soon reveals himself to be a cad).

By contrast with these faulty and immoderate readings—both Sophia's and her lover's—in Bennett's view a genuinely cosmopolitan outlook on life's "whole spectacular show" tempers such scorn and sentimentality with reserve and restraint. In a letter to George Sturt on 4 October 1902, Bennett admonishes his friend for "looking for something which you will never get in my fiction, or in any first-rate modern fiction—the Dickens and Thackeray grossness. I 'let myself go' to the full but this does not mean that I shout and weep all over the place."[42] In the spirit of the "modern," according to Bennett, the sentimental "grossness" of older strains of fiction must be reined in. The emotional reserve and distance characteristic of Bennett's fiction emerges from a coordinating perspective that orders "phenomena" according to their "position and relative importance" rather than their affective functions. From the realist's vantage as a reserved and detached observer, the proper coordination of perspective—what Sophia and her lover seem to get wrong—allows the material practices of a culture to illuminate the character of the people.

In the modern novel, "Every street is a mirror, an illustration, an exposition, an explanation, of the human beings who live in it. Nothing in it is to be neglected. Everything in it is valuable, if the perspective is maintained."[43] Framed in this way, the function of the novel becomes a specular one, replicating the external world within its covers. But while Stendhal in *Le Rouge et le Noir* (1830) compares the novel to a mirror moving along the road, Bennett distributes the reflective functions of modern narrative across typical material details—"the street," for example, with all its sights and scents—reserving for the text itself the broader task of presenting these reflections to a total effect.[44] Even more, the novel not only delivers a sense of the totality of represented content in its assemblage of these reflections—building to the "broad notion of the whole"—but also offers up its very form as a model of inclusive totality:

> [The novel] has conquered enormous territories even since [Zola's] *Germinal*. Within the last fifteen years it has gained. Were it to adopt the hue of the British Empire, the entire map of the universe would soon be coloured red. . . . It is, and will be for some time to come, the form to which the artist with the most inclusive vision instinctively turns, because it is the most inclusive form.[45]

Bennett's "whole spectacular show" as represented content finds its appropriate form in the realist novel, which is at least imperious if not imperial in its scope and which harbors aspirations that run congruent to those of the empire—to paint an expansive whole in a universal hue. While the primary figures of a novel such as *The Old Wives' Tale* cannot themselves bring into view—or even be fully conscious of—this "entire map of the universe," the heterodiegetic narrator's "perspective" should be expected to encompass it so long as the author's "inclusive vision" holds.

"Maintaining perspective" for Bennett means relating distinct phenomena causally (locating them as "a cause or effect of human conduct") and coordinating them—determining "position and relative importance"—according to what Georg Lukács calls a "hierarchy of significance": binding the "typical" and broadly representative to the particular and to the human "individual," to which Bennett argues, "all human observing does finally come if there is any right reason in it."[46] Material practices and artifacts serve as illustrations, expositions, and explanations of the local and the individual within a larger context: every street serves to reflect the inhabitants who make it. In the case of the section of *The Old Wives' Tale* that engenders distinct Continental and provincial story lines, the wakes and the exhibition of Wombwell's elephant are foregrounded as key material practices that furnish signs both of the relation of the translocal to the provincial and of the significance of the larger imperial whole to which the novel's form corresponds in Bennett's theory.

Wombwell's at the Wakes

What is the "proper level" of the wakes "in the scheme of things," then, if Sophia and her lover are wrong to judge it merely an "unimportance"? Ernest Warrillow has argued that, "like Dickens, Bennett was not only a novelist but a historian of great distinction,"[47] and the revolt of Wombwell's disobedient elephant at the Bursley wakes occurs at the intersection of two historical strands in the English cultural fabric: the embourgeoisement or "taming" of domestic excesses by a traveling culture of exhibition and the concomitant penetration of imperial spectacle into everyday life in England. The center of the wakes spectacle is the elephant, which—having knelt on a man inside a festival tent, wandered outside, put another man in his mouth, and wounded a third with its tusk—is forced to its knees "by means of stakes, pulleys and ropes" and then shot dead by six men from the town's rifle corps in a spirit of martial intoxication.[48] The dead elephant, "by the help of his two [elephant] companions, was got on to a railway lorry and disappeared into the night." The next day, however, the elephant's massive corpse reappears on the town's playground, "pending the decision of the Chief Bailiff and the

Medical Officer as to his burial. And everybody had to visit the corpse. No social exclusiveness could withstand the seduction of that dead elephant. Pilgrims travelled from all [around] to see him."[49] The brilliantly seductive corpse, the narrator explains, appears to such great effect on

> the morning of the third day of Bursley Wakes; not the modern finicking and respectable, but an orgiastic carnival, gross in all its manifestations of joy. The whole centre of the town was given over to the furious pleasures of the people. Most of the Square was occupied by Wombwell's Menagerie, in a vast oblong tent, whose raging beasts roared and growled day and night.[50]

For the Victorians, as for the middle classes in earlier centuries, such "furious pleasures" posed a problem because, as Georges Bataille points out, excess sorts poorly with bourgeois emphases upon economy, reserve, and continence, in personal behavior as in commerce. The wakes represented a particularly egregious instance of "grossness": though it originated as a devotional occasion in which a parish honored the saint after whom its church was named, by 1781 William Hutton noted that "now the devotional part is forgot, the church is deserted, and the festivity turned into riot, drunkenness and mischief."[51] In *The Old Wives' Tale* the obsolete devotional aspect of the wakes, in which lights were carried to the church and a vigil kept through the eve of the saint's day, holds no interest for Bennett or his characters. They are, rather, engaged by Bursley's "orgiastic carnival, gross in all its manifestations of joy."

Bennett observes the difference of the wakes-time celebrations of around 1864 from the "modern finicking and respectable" wakes of the early twentieth century and notes that, as in his repudiation of Dickens and Thackeray, the modern has expunged the grossness and excess from the holiday. The "furious pleasures" at the wakes included the drunkenness and riot mentioned by Hutton and were marked by the liberal exercise of sexual license and a spirited indulgence in blood sports—dog- and cockfighting, pugilism, and bear- and bullbaiting, for instance. As late as 1906, when Bennett was preparing to write *The Old Wives' Tale*, one author recalled bearbaiting on the very site where the elephant in the novel is supposed to have run amok.[52]

In *The Old Wives' Tale*, the Baineses' defiant exhibition of mourning goods in the windows of their drapery shop and their refusal to allow their servant out of the house represent not just statements of mid-Victorian moral censure of the wakes (in which a bourgeois display of solemnity is designed to counter the wakes' carnivalesque exhibitions) but also an index of the degree to which such holidays threw class norms into relief. Like the Baineses in the 1860s, John Ward had hard words for the manifold "abuses" of the wakes in the 1840s, pointing out that "they only operate as incentives to excess and licentiousness,"[53] and during the Industrial Revolution wakes were especially criticized by the bourgeoisie for the unreserved expenditure of the working classes at holiday time:

> People celebrated to the limit of their means, and beyond that if they could. Generosity and indulgence prevailed over thrift. In 1831 the Oldham diarist, Edwin Butterworth, complained that people were "fond of drinking themselves into the midst of distress, for the sole purpose of supporting the disgraceful, useless wake."[54]

This notion of the people's expenditure "to the limit of their means, and beyond" at wakes time, along with the excesses those expenditures engendered, formed long-standing targets of criticism. The manifest failure of the earliest forms of these attempts to curtail the wakes activity and the persistence of disgraceful license and orgiastic frenzies at wakes time spawned a kind of conduct literature full of exhortations to abandon the more "dissipated" pleasures of the wakes.[55]

Yet though the wakes continued until at least 1960 in the historical town of Burslem, by 1891 Alfred Burton was describing the most objectionable activities of wakes-time celebrations in the past tense: "Formerly these sports were of a more brutal character, and the wakes without a bait of some kind was considered a farce."[56] In 1908 Arnold Bennett could note the "modern finicking and respectable" tone, and just as the novelist sought to purge mainstream English fiction of the "grossness" characterizing the Victorian novel, the "shouting and weeping all over the place," so also the wakes about which he wrote were being purged of their many excesses in the second half of the nineteenth century, largely by commercial "devices for abstracting money from the pocket," such as rides, games, panoramas, "illuminated models," "living skeletons," and other exhibitions of curiosities.[57] Indeed, Bennett expected that his novels of careful observation would attain a similar success as popular entertainments: anticipating strong sales of *The Old Wives' Tale*, he announced to his wife that "We shall soon be rich."[58] In the late nineteenth century a burgeoning commercial culture in both arenas, the fair and the novel, channeled much of the excess that marked earlier forms into activities characterized especially by observation and spectatorship.

The newly commercial forms of the wakes directed the desire for riot and mischief that characterized the festival's earlier expressions toward entertainments that promised to display, rather than foster participation in, monstrosity, excess, and brutality. A chief strategy in this shift from participatory to staged violence and excess was to disengage the spectator from spectacle, relegating the world of tableau to a space behind the *cordon sanitaire* of the exhibit and preserving the realm of the viewer from its taint of unrestrained "grossness." The more vicious kinds of pugilism and other blood sports disappeared from fairs by the end of the century, and the displays that replaced them frequently offered dramatic imperial spectacles in their place. The menagerie in particular harbored these exhibitions, and newspapers treated them as suitable matter for viewing by middle-class audiences:

> George Oak and William Oscar, two Zulu chiefs, formerly with Barnum's Show, and now with Wombwell's, had a terrible fight at Scarborough last night. While in the dressing tent they fell upon each other like tigers, biting, kicking, and scratching most viciously. Oscar had pieces of his flesh bitten out of his lips and hands, and Oak had three fingers flayed. Oak did not cease his savagery until his opponent lay unconscious, when he was dragged out of the tent. The affair created intense excitement among the crowd near the show.[59]

As spectatorial titillation, this display of "savagery" does not implicate "the crowd near the show" in the violence, and spectators and journalists alike are able to achieve—as Bennett's narrative theory demands authors establish as well—their own distanced perspectives on a "spectacular and sensual show." Though the fight between Wombwell's tigerlike "Zulu chiefs" is ostensibly spontaneous, at other times such exotic displays clearly were scripted. One nineteenth-century advertisement for a menagerie promises "the most Bold, grand and Daring Human Display, ever presented," namely,

> A WHOLE CARAVAN OF
> WILD ANIMALS,
> LET LOOSE AT THE SAME TIME
> UPON THE INDIAN SLAVE.
> Who will gradually subdue, and playfully exhibit his remarkable skill
> in ELEGANTLY GROUPING THIS MATCHLESS ZOOLOGICAL
> COLLECTION.[60]

In the spectacular ordering of the collection in the "Indian Slave's" performance, the caravan show not only exhibits exoticism and stages wildness but also models a totalizing command: the slave's "skill in ELEGANTLY GROUPING" the exhibit resembles Bennett's emphasis upon the writer's craft in determining "position and relative importance" of phenomena in the novel's "spectacular and sensual show." The gradual subdual of excess that marks the historical progress of festivals such as the wakes thus came to be staged in the realm of the exotic, and it is characteristic of these exhibitions to displace the violence and frenzy for which the fairs were once indicted onto avatars of oriental and exotic spaces: "Zulu chiefs," "Indian slaves," tigers, or elephants. The pageant of the provincial fair, rendered respectable in part through the exotic performances in the menageries, exonerates the English patrons of active complicity in scenes of profligacy and excess they witness by framing them as imperial exhibitions.

As Wombwell's Menagerie became attached to these local festivities, the bearbaiting and blood sports of the lower-class holiday gave way to the staged "savagery" and "fierceness" of the exhibited animals. Wombwell's Menagerie, the traveling outfit, was so well known at wakes that a ballad in broadsheet form was presented to George Wombwell in 1838, remarking that "while many are the methods which, to rise in life, men take, / Yours' was—to never be asleep when others '*kept a* WAKE!'"[61] The success of Wombwell's traveling shows meant that they gradually consolidated a circuit of the local in the nineteenth century, establishing a uniform culture of popular exhibitions across the nation's many individual fairs and wakes. Bennett's narrator notes that "no social exclusiveness could withstand" the elephant in the menagerie: in spite of Sophia's scorn of it as a mark of the local, "the dazzling social success of the elephant . . . cannot imaginably be overestimated." The dazzle of Wombwell's on the translocal circuit resulted from both the exoticism and the danger of wild animals at the menageries. While exhibitors frequently assured their patrons of the safety of their exhibits, citing, for example, the "mild and tractable" disposition of the elephant, they also traded upon the potential for violence in their promotions: "What ravages might we not expect from the prodigious strength of the elephant combined with the fierceness and rapacity of the tiger?"[62] As is the case with the elephant in Bennett's novel, such "ravages" indeed occurred, claiming the lives even of family members of the menagerists, as in one instance in which an elephant attacked George Wombwell's nephew, running its tusks through his body and beating him to death with its trunk.[63]

The Old Wives' Tale places the elephant at the center of its display as a mark of imperial alterity (though also preserving, as a palimpsest, the signs of "orgiastic frenzy" that mark was to have expunged). On one hand, then, what still appears to the Baineses as a suspect, potentially riotous holiday is gradually rendered bourgeois and made tame by the commercial exhibitions and performances of Wombwell's Menagerie. On the other hand, the local wakes are deeply scored with the traces of imperialism, "savagery" in general and the elephant in particular. The presence of the elephant in Bursley situates the narrow provinciality of the Potteries, typically English, within the larger totality of British economic and cultural imperialism, and begins to consolidate by means of Wombwell's commercial omnipresence across England a sense of a shared British imperial culture. In the contexts of such cultures of exhibition and Bennett's own quasi-imperial aspirations for the form of the novel, the narrative of provincial Bursley in *The Old Wives' Tale* takes on some of the shading of the British Empire, however "uncolored" the latter might appear to be in the provinces. Wombwell's show itself serves as an analogue to Bennett's theory of the exhibitionary function of the novel, which gives us a perspective on "the whole spectacular and sensual show" but without the indulgence in excess affect characteristic of Dickens's and Thackeray's popular fiction.

Stoke-on-Ganges: Short-Circuiting Empire

There is no historical account of an elephant visiting the kind of mischief described in *The Old Wives' Tale* upon a wakes celebration in the Five Towns. In fabricating the account of the elephant's revolt, Bennett emphasizes two of the most disturbing problems presented by the elephant on display: its potential for unprovoked violence and its massive corporeality.[64] Likely working from an 1872 incident in which a Wombwell's elephant crushed a boy who had abused it and from an 1898 report of another Wombwell elephant dying in the Five Towns, Bennett associates these troubling aspects of the elephant's character with imperial alterity.[65] The novel makes a point of noting that the elephant's attendant is Indian, though all archival evidence suggests that Wombwell's keepers were English, and the "raging beasts" of the menagerie appear alongside "the atrocities . . . of the Fiji Islands" in the novel.[66] That Bennett draws attention to the elephant's disobedience, the keeper's Indianness, and the wakes' pervasive exoticism points to savagery (even cannibalism) and colonial rebellion: just as the English excesses at wakes are curbed by being projected into an ostensibly alien arena, the unruly elephant's violence is likewise restrained—in its case by means of "stakes, ropes, and pulleys."

But the difficulty of putting down a colonial rebellion, such as the great Indian "Mutiny" of 1857 (seven years before the fictional episode) or the Jamaican rebellion quashed by Governor Eyre (just a year after the episode), finds expression in the novel in the additional problems first of containing the elephant's violence and then of cleaning up after its suppression. The elephant turns up repeatedly in the chapter after it seems to have been put down, appearing massively on the playground after it had apparently "disappeared into the night." If the elephant's violence resonates with overtones of colonial rebellion, its destruction—also an innovation of Bennett's—bears the hallmarks of a colonial execution:

> His head was whitewashed, and six men of the Rifle Corps were engaged to shoot him at a distance of five yards, while constables kept the crowd off with truncheons. He died instantly, rolling over with a soft thud. The crowd cheered, and intoxicated by their importance, the Volunteers fired three more volleys into the carcase [sic], and were then borne off as heroes to different inns.[67]

The death of the elephant before the press of the crowd anticipates Orwell's "Shooting an Elephant," in which the overwhelming demand of the Burmese crowd renders Orwell powerless to do anything but shoot the elephant that has trampled a "coolie." In Lower Burma in the twentieth century, shooting an elephant is cause for reflection on the impact of colonialism on Western consciousness. In provincial Bursley in the age of Victoria, by contrast, shooting an elephant is cause for the Volunteers to be "intoxicated by their importance," a turn of phrase that anticipates the evocation of London in another of Bennett's novels, as a place in which "the sense of Empire was in the very air, like an intoxication."[68] The intoxication of a quasi-imperial triumph in Bursley provides occasion for English self-aggrandizement, a chance to be "borne off as heroes to different inns" after a plain demonstration of overkill.

If this "intoxication" blinds the Volunteers to everything but their own importance, the novel nevertheless echoes Bennett's theory of realistic observation, since "every street is a mirror," and above all the execution of the elephant on the streets of Bursley reveals the Englishness of the Volunteers' "intoxication," spun from the airy stuff of imperial fantasy. In his novel *Clayhanger*, Bennett aims to show how "savage" such intoxication can be, especially when English crowds are not restrained by bourgeois mores or bobbies' batons. On the site at which the elephant revolts at the wakes in the earlier novel, Edwin Clayhanger watches Bursley's celebration of the Centenary of the Sunday Schools. Bennett's description of the local setting—though "every town in England had the same sight to show at that hour"[69]—itself echoes descriptions of colonized masses at imperial pageants:

> The whole Square was now suddenly revealed as a swarming mass of heads, out of which rose banners and pennons that were cruder in tint even than the frocks and hats of the little girls and the dresses and bonnets of their teachers; the men, too, by their neckties, scarves, and rosettes, added colour to colour. All the windows were chromatic with the hues of bright costumes, and from many windows and from every roof that had a flagstaff, flags waved heavily against the gorgeous sky.[70]

The English "swarming mass" appears here in the guise of the singularity it projected upon subject peoples of the empire, and the echo of concurrent imperial descriptions is striking. In his narrative of the 1911–12 Imperial Assemblage at Delhi, John Fortescue describes the mass of Indian subjects gathered for George V's coronation as emperor:

> the turbans of the people made a nodding flower-bed of every shade of blue and green and every variety of brown, tawny, yellow and orange. . . . [T]he diversity of colour in the dress of the spectators was even more pleasing against the background of rather unkempt white houses; but it was painful to notice that a few occupants had decorated their balconies with some of the vilest colour produced by Manchester.[71]

In a peculiar imaginative circuit, characteristically English Bursley resembles an imperial Delhi, while the "vilest colour" of India's crowds returns imperial thoughts to the "crude[ness of] tint" in the English provinces.

There is in the passage from *Clayhanger* more than a serendipitous echo of imperial discourse, however, since Edwin's experience at the celebration is marked by violent reverie—a counterpart to *The Old Wives Tale*'s fantasy of colonial suppression—in which the British Empire and the English provinces come to seem two sides of the same imperial map. As the entire Square begins to "chant . . . with gusto" William Cowper's hymn beginning "There is a fountain filled with blood," Edwin suddenly has a vivid hallucination:

With the purple banner waving there a bloody motto, he foresaw each sanguinary detail of the verse ere it came to him from the shrill childish throats. And a phrase from another hymn jumped from somewhere in his mind just as William Cowper's ended and a speech commenced. The phrase was "India's coral strand." In thinking upon it he forgot to listen to the speech. He saw the flags, banners, and pennons floating in the sunshine and in the heavy breeze; he felt the reverberation of the tropic sun on his head; he saw the crowded humanity of the Square attired in its crude primary colours; he saw the great brass serpentine instruments gleaming; he saw the red dais; he saw, bursting with infancy, the immense cars to which were attached the fantastically plaited horses; he saw the venerable zealots on the dais raving lest all the institutions whose centenary they had met to honour should not save these children from hopeless and excruciating torture for ever and ever; he saw those majestic purple folds in the centre embroidered with the legend of the blood of the mystic Paschal Lamb; he saw the meek, stupid, and superstitious faces, all turned one way, all for the moment under the empire of one horrible idea, all convinced that the consequences of sins could be prevented by an act of belief, all gloating over inexhaustible tides of blood. And it seemed to him that he was not in England any longer. It seemed to him that in the dim cellars under the shambles behind the Town Hall, where he had once been, there dwelt, squatting, a strange and savage god who would blast all those who did not enter his presence dripping with gore, be they child or grandfather. It seemed to him that the drums were tom-toms, and Baines's a bazaar. He could fit every detail of the scene to harmonize with a vision of India's coral strand.[72]

Clayhanger's vision suggests that when England slips out of its usual "uncolored" restraint it appears "dripping with gore" before a "savage god," and even the Baineses' prosaic shop appears fabulously exotic. For Edwin, this slippage induces a hallucination in which the provinces appear not to be England any longer. Nor are such impressions Edwin's alone, for he discovers that his friend Hilda "had comprehended without explanation" his observation that "It only wants the Ganges at the bottom of the Square."[73] This shared understanding suggests that when Bursley, "England in little, lost in the midst of England," falls "under the empire of one horrible idea," it seems as "strange and savage" as those under the empire of the English were usually held to be.[74] It also points out that the temporal and cultural distance between exotic reaches and domestic spaces of empire can occasionally collapse within the

English imagination, a sign that the spectacular show of empire intimately shapes perceptions of provincial English cultures.

Edwin's vision in *Clayhanger* gives voice to what Wombwell's Menagerie suggests in *The Old Wives' Tale:* English provincial experience is charged with currents of imperialism, but only through a kind of hallucination, intoxication, or short circuit—an abandonment of what Arnold Bennett calls the "right reason" of objective observation—can one see beyond local instances of Englishness to this larger imperial whole.[75] It is as though only the suspension of this reason—and of the realist practice to which it corresponds—permits the two to be seen together, in the form of fanciful analogy and allegory. The English provinces and the empire's colonial margins form two sides of the same imperial page in Edwin Clayhanger's fantasy and the situation of Englishness at the Bursley wakes in *The Old Wives' Tale* itself becomes confused. Should Englishness be located in the wakes, the trademark excess of which is being turned into commercial channels? In the menagerie, helping to tame the wakes but itself exhibiting imperial excess? In the volunteers, who suppress this excess when it is out of hand, but who engage in overkill? Or in the spectators straining against the police cordon for a glimpse of the spectacle? Where England and empire are fused in the short circuit of fantasy, Bennett's "map of the universe" inscribed in the novel's form situates Englishness within a complex labyrinth of empire.

Mid-Victorian England's Memento Mori

In *The Old Wives' Tale,* the instigating agent of these confusions is not a sanguinary hymn but the frenzied elephant, which has unwittingly come to occupy the place of the baited bear in the wakes. While the elephant may constitute the imaginative stuff from which wakes-time "intoxication" is distilled, it has also the "seductive" power to erase social distinction within Bursley well after its execution. Its pungent presence as a commodity in Bursley endures throughout the wakes-time spectacle, lending a sharp irony to Bennett's commitment to representing the whole of experience, even "what the nose scents":

> The elephant had become a victim to the craze of souvenirs. Already in the night his tusks had been stolen; then his feet disappeared for umbrella-stands, and most of his flesh had departed in little hunks. Everybody in Bursley had resolved to participate in the elephant. One

consequence was that all the chemists' shops in the town were assaulted by strings of boys. "Please a pe[n]north o'alum to tak' smell out o' a bit o' elephant."[76]

The elephant as exotic commodity materially penetrates Bursley, colonizing domestic entry halls in the form of umbrella stands and suffusing the town's air, just as before its death it worked to permeate the provincial fabric of the Staffordshire wakes. The stink of Bursley's elephant is ironic anodyne to the "intoxication of self-importance" of the Volunteers, and the elephant does not simply illustrate or explain Bursley—it assumes an independent agency to shape the contours of daily life at its most local. The elephant, which appears in England as a result of a total imperial system that penetrates wild colonial lands and rules the waves, disappears not only on the train into the night but also in discrete "hunks" into English domestic culture, where it takes up residence as an alien and yet oddly familiar presence.

The elephant's astringent excess helps us "determine the position and relative significance" of a purportedly "finicking and respectable" English provincial culture amidst a burgeoning empire that exceeds the old English forms: the elephant as emblem of empire comes to reside permanently in Bursley in the form of umbrella stands and preserved souvenir bits, and it changes the very constitution of the communal tradition of the wakes. "Such was the greatest sensation that has ever occurred, or perhaps will ever occur, in Bursley," notes the narrator, and "The excitement about the repeal of the Corn Laws, or about Inkerman, was feeble compared to that excitement."[77] It is perhaps the greatest sensation in the narrative as well, and if the elephant persists bodily beyond all reason in the episode, the novel itself insists on the spectacle of elephants to a surprising degree: when Constance's cousin is hanged for strangling his wife, the narrator reports that "Since the execution of the elephant, nothing had so profoundly agitated Bursley"; during the Siege of Paris, Sophia dines at a restaurant whose proprietor announces that his friend the butcher has purchased three elephants from the *Jardin des Plantes* to supply cuts of meat; and on her first return to Bursley since eloping to France, Sophia notices "two camels and an elephant in a field . . . amid manufactories and warehouses and advertisements."[78]

Though the elephant plainly represents an avatar of the alien and the text itself pays unusual attention to the elephant, it is not clear how this exotic excess bears on the central domestic components of the narrative, nor does it explain "the proper level" of provincial Englishness within "the scheme of things." Under the terms Bennett lays out in *The Author's Craft*, the provincial wakes and Wombwell's Menagerie should illuminate Sophia's lapse and her father's death, just as "every street is a mirror, an illustration, an exposition, of the people" in its midst. It is not clear, however, how Wombwell's commercial elephant, emblem of the reaches of empire, explains either Sophia's desire for the commercial traveler or Mr. Baines's "perverse" death. The novel figures the wakes within a whole imperial system and engages the collective desires of Bursley and England for imperial spectacle, whereas Sophia's neglect of her father is an individual lapse. Sophia's desire and its consequences are themselves rendered a matter of apparent "local unimportance." There is thus a fundamental bifurcation in the chapter: in the portion that unfolds in the street, centering on the elephant's violence and execution at the wakes, the primary effect is a sense of "a broad notion" of the social totality; in the section that treats Mr. Baines, the narrative concentrates on Sophia's personal struggle, what Bennett calls the "individual" story of a "domestic creature." These two distinct levels of narration must be reconciled if the narrative is to achieve the cosmopolitan, distanced "perspective" demanded by Bennett's theory. Without the joint exhibition of the typical and the individual from a "true" perspective, Bennett contends, we might as well be "in a vacuum, or in the Sahara, or between Heaven and earth"—that is to say, imprisoned by deserts of the local and cut off from the larger world.[79]

The novel attempts such a reconciliation by resorting to a rhetoric of causality, on one hand, and by introducing a series of linguistic turns that attempt to suture the breach between Mr. Baines and the elephant, on the other hand. The spectacle of the elephant causes the house to empty in the first place, leaving Sophia alone to manage both her father and the shop. This arrangement would be appropriate, had the salesman not scheduled a call on that particular afternoon: "That the elephant should have caused both Mr Povey [the shop manager] and Mrs Baines to forget that the representative of Birkinshaws was due to call was indeed a final victory for the elephant."[80] The elephant is thus charged with both vying for cultural supremacy in Bursley and producing the dilemma by which Sophia must choose to leave her father or neglect the family business (and deny her own desire). Moreover, a neighbor is convinced that the Baineses have colluded with the elephant to kill off Mr. Baines: "with their stupidity, their neglect, their elephants, between them they had done for John Baines."[81] Attributing to the elephant or to the Baineses the agency behind Mr. Baines's death produces a mistaken impression of responsibility, however, and ignores the inexplicability of Sophia's desire for the commercial traveler: "'Why did I forget father?' she asked herself with awe. 'I only meant to tell *him* [the salesman] that they were all out, and run back. Why did I forget father?' She would never be able to persuade anybody that she had literally forgotten her father's existence for quite ten minutes; but it was true enough, though shocking."[82] The narrative of Sophia's lapse is "shocking," not least in its rhetorical inadequacy—its manifest inability "to persuade anybody."

For this reason, the narrator seeks to avoid the conclusion of inexplicability—not a position on which a novel that claims to illustrate and explain can comfortably rest—by placing blame with the salesman, as well as the elephant: "The real murderer was having his dinner in the commercial room up at the Tiger, opposite the Town Hall."[83] Though the inn takes the name of an animal in Wombwell's Menagerie and the commercial traveler represents another branch of the global trade that introduces Wombwell's to the wakes, it is hardly true that the representative can be considered the "real murderer"—after all, his visit was scheduled. Instead, Mr. Baines's death appears highly overdetermined, potentially a consequence of the elephant's "seductions," the traveler's "scorn of everything local," and Sophia's inattentions, as well as his own "invalid's natural perverseness." All these attributions of responsibility serve to defend against the most "shocking" possibility that John Baines's death verges on the meaningless in the narrative, that there can be no simple accounting for his demise, and that we are left only with a profoundly unsettling sense that things in "England in little" have gone wrong in this labyrinth of empire. The rhetoric of causality brought to bear on the dead elephant in particular is logically insufficient to "explain" the death of the invalid, an explanation nevertheless demanded by Bennett's theory of narrative realism. We are therefore left with signs of a loss that exceeds the capacity of the novel's explanatory apparatus.

In the absence of a satisfactory causal relationship, the narrator has recourse to a notion of structural similarity or homology between the elephant and John Baines—perhaps an "illustration" if not an "explanation" of their relation. Both appear "carcasses" in the chapter and both are paid respects by the town, the elephant on the playground and Mr. Baines in the more conventional setting of "the mortuary bedroom" where he is laid out.[84] In this respect, the narrator indulges a rich pun on "wake"—the violence both of the elephant and of the armed Volunteers is awakened at the Bursley wakes, Mr. Baines awakes and asphyxiates, and the family holds his wake—suggested by the shared etymological root for both the mortuary obsequies and the "orgiastic carnival." Such homologous relations do not in this case seem to respond to a shared structure of social relations or a singular circumstance, however, and "a broad notion of the whole" that would situate the consequences of Sophia's individual crime in the large and complex map traced by the elephant and the menagerie appears to elude the novel's explanatory apparatus.

Something like this shared social whole does begin to emerge when Bennett deploys a trope that binds John Baines's death with the revolt and execution of the elephant, and that locates precisely Englishness on the imperial map. In Bennett's manuscript draft of the novel, as a neighbor and Mrs. Baines look upon the corpse of the patriarch, the narrator declares that "They might have been gazing at a vanished era on the bed," in an analogy that would associate John Baines with an age gone by.[85] Yet Bennett canceled this analogy, recasting it instead as allegory:

> They knew not that they *were* gazing at a vanished era. John Baines had belonged to the past, to the age when . . . a gilt-clasped Bible really was the secret of England's greatness. *Mid-Victorian England lay on that mahogany bed.* Ideals had passed away with John Baines. It is thus that ideals die; not in the conventional pageantry of honoured death, but sorrily, ignobly, while one's head is turned.[86]

Making John Baines a representative of mid-Victorian England—a movement that encourages us to read the entire chapter as an elaborate allegory—elevates his corpse to the level of significance assumed by the elephant in its participation in the wakes in the Five Towns, "England in little." The allegory suggests, moreover, that if mid-Victorian England, in establishing its "slow dignity," has displaced its past excesses by consolidating them in avatars of the exotic spaces it has conquered, it nevertheless runs the risk of seeming irrelevant to the larger whole toward which those exotic representations gesture. In this allegory, John Baines and the England for which he stands might be understood to pass away while heads are turned from domestic affairs by the "pageantry" of empire's "spectacular and sensual show." England's "central labyrinth" might, in other words, be a victim of its own imperial greatness, and it figures in the chapter as the superannuated fatherland stretched on an imperial bier of its own fashioning. While Bennett is concerned with recuperating from mid-Victorian fiction a cosmopolitan distance and reserve under the banner of the "modern," the modern England that supplants John Baines's is bound up with empire and with excess. The striking claim that John Baines—in a state of paralysis for fourteen years—*is* mid-Victorian England brings together the collective activities of Bursley's wakes and the private affairs of the Baines household. It also crucially reverses Bennett's narrative prescriptions: the exhibition of the elephant and all it indicates about the broader cultural whole should be "an illustration, an exposition, and explanation" of John Baines's particular circumstances, not vice versa. Bursley during wakes time should illuminate John Baines's place in the social whole, not proclaim his provincial redundancy, as though he were "in a vacuum, or in the Sahara, or between Heaven and earth."[87] As it stands, John Baines as an allegory for mid-Victorian England only reinforces the significance of Bursley's wakes, Wombwell's Menagerie, and imperial modernity. In other words, John Baines is rendered superfluous, his corpse fixed as a mirror for what goes on in the street rather than vice versa in a figuration that overturns Bennett's ideas about the centrality of individual character in the novel.

As a result of this inversion, what Bennett calls "perspective" and the "right reason" of realism is fundamentally disrupted. Though it was a hallmark of circus performances in the nineteenth century, allegory such as the one the English writer offers here is in Georg Lukács's estimation the hallmark of a degenerate modernism because it implies "the negation of any meaning immanent in the world of the life of man."[88] Walter Benjamin similarly argues that "What ruins are in the physical world, allegories are in the world of the mind," a dictum that suggests not only that deep fault lines and rifts underlie the apparently uniform surface of allegory, but also that allegory marks the loss of historical and narrative coherence.[89] In *The Old Wives' Tale*, such lines of fracture rest beneath the allegory of John Baines as mid-Victorian England and are rendered visible in the split narrative focus of the chapter. If, as Benjamin asserts, the world picture inscribed in modern allegory is one characterized by "a process of inevitable decay,"[90] the dissolution of a totalizing perspective within the labyrinth of empire may be allegorized in the rotten bits of elephant that the Bursley boys collect as souvenirs—and which they soon are desperate to sanitize, pleading for something "to tak' smell out o' a bit o' elephant."

The Origin of the Decay of Realism

In asserting that "It is thus that ideals die; not in the conventional pageantry of honoured death, but sorrily, ignobly, while one's head is turned," the narrator suggests the extent to which the elephant is an important diversion in the narrative, a diversion in the sense of both a spectacular entertainment and a deadly distraction. But the narration of the elephant's "dazzling" attraction is also a sort of exhibition in its own right and serves as an important diversion for readers of *The Old Wives' Tale*, constituting one of the most entertaining, lively, and memorable episodes of the novel. The elephant diverts readers' attention also from its proper object, the death of John Baines, just as it diverts the attention of the characters. James G. Hepburn wonders about that "last line: 'while one's head is turned.' Does it refer to Sophia's having gone out of the room? Does it refer to her head being turned by [her lover], to her choosing, implicitly, the code of a younger age? Or does it refer to John Baines's head 'hanging, inverted, near the floor between the bed and the ottoman'?"[91] But the ambiguity of the phrase extends beyond the text, too, for as another critic observes, "We can't accuse Sophia of a sinful neglect because we ourselves had been as forgetful" of John Baines and the "ideals" he represents.[92] The narrative pulls readers along with the Baines family toward the elephant and the commercial traveler at the expense of John Baines, the center of the domestic space that *The Old Wives' Tale* is at such pains to narrate. Here, then, is the triumph of the whole spectacular show of empire and its attendant traveling cultures: the elephant's imperial pageantry has overwhelmed the "conventional pageantry of honoured death," and the diversion of the Baineses' attention from the father and their preoccupation with the elephant reflect the inability of domestic affairs to retain their dominant position at the center of the novel. This sense of lost focus, correlative of the inexplicable loss of John Baines, forms the negative counterpart of the elephant's rancid plenitude—its excess—and if historical processes of restraint and excess are bound together in the midst of England's central labyrinth, the "broad notion of the whole" represented in *The Old Wives' Tale* is one in which a single totalizing vantage fails to turn imperial "grossness" to domestic advantage.

The excesses characteristic of this episode in *The Old Wives' Tale* function also to divert the narrative itself, sending it spinning off to London, to Paris, and to the fantasized circuits of empire. The paths of travel to these metropolitan sites are quite real in the novel, as Sophia's body traverses their routes before settling into a quiet Parisian *arrondissement*. The passages to empire are another matter, however, since they are largely imagined: it is the travel of the menagerie and of Britain's commercial emissaries that activates these circuits. *The Old Wives' Tale*'s diversions put into motion metaphorics of center/periphery, metropole/province, and global/local, thereby transforming each of these sites: where the narrator explicitly situates Bursley in the "central labyrinth of England," the menagerie's exhibitionary cultures would seem to place the various Englands offered in the text—"mid-Victorian" and "modern"—in the midst of a larger labyrinth of empire.[93]

The fragments of elephant collected by the Bursley boys represent one answer to a question posed by a *soi-disant* "cosmopolitan" in Bennett's novel *The Regent*: "Can you tell me what is the origin of the decay of realism?"[94] The space of confusion, excess, and frustrated attempts at restraint that the menagerie represents in *The Old Wives' Tale* situates this origin with a world system that relegates an older version of Englishness to the equivalent of "the Sahara," rendering the mother country itself provincial in its own way. By the time that John Baines and the mid-Victorian England that he allegorizes have been buried, it seems clear that the episode involving the elephant has already—in advance—modified the tenets of realism Bennett describes in *The Author's Craft*: the novel does not maintain an appropriate "perspective" and allows "a broad notion of the whole" signaled by the tableau of Wombwell's and the wakes to overwhelm the individuality of John Baines. In the end, Sophia and her lover are wrong to scorn the wakes, not because they are a "local unimportance" but because their import cannot be calculated precisely—there is no "proper level" because the whole "scheme of things" is untotalizable. In this sense the elephant's revolt—an explicit allegory of colonial insurgency, if John Baines appears in the guise of mid-Victorian England—demonstrates the ways in which Edwardian conventions of realism codified in *The Author's Craft* prove untenable; not, as Virginia Woolf charges, because "human character changed," but because the imperial system has grown to permeate and encompass domestic English life.

The traveling cultures of *The Old Wives' Tale* evoke the "modern" England of the imperial labyrinth that activates both the circuits of the menagerie and Sophia's journeys out of, and back into, the local. But the notion of traveling cultures also resonates with the cosmopolitan passages of international modernists from provincial sites such as Idaho, St. Louis, Dublin, and even, perhaps, Staffordshire to the world cities of London and Paris. The irony of the allegory in which mid-Victorian England is rendered superfluous within a "modern" culture of empire is that Bennett's fiction itself approaches the conclusions of those modernists whose aggressively cosmopolitan products displaced it—paradoxically, because it violates the very observation and restraint he champions under the banner of the modern. As the theoretical standard-bearer for a brand of realism that his own narrative undermines, Bennett comes to occupy the position of John Baines in his novel: the Edwardian ideals of distanced observation and integrated totality in the form of the English novel pass away while our heads are turned by the "whole spectacular and sensual show" of global modernity in the early twentieth century. The seductive violence of the imperial elephant, bound tightly with the localism of the wakes, thus enacts at the diegetic level the toppling of convention that in six short years Wyndham Lewis would seek to effect by "blasting" the mid-Victorian menagerie itself, and that Virginia Woolf was later to register against Bennett most devastatingly as the sound of modernism's "smashing and crashing."[95]

Chapter 4

Monsters on the Verandah of Realism

Virginia Woolf's Empire Exhibition

OF CHAINED BEASTS AND BLOATED CARCASSES

OF ALL EDWARDIAN ENGLISH NOVELISTS, Arnold Bennett perhaps made the fullest transition to modernist practice by the end of his career in novels such as *Riceyman Steps*, for which he won the James Tait Black Prize.[1] Yet his fiction is not usually read in these terms, and in his most significant work, *The Old Wives' Tale*, the modernist element emerges at best fitfully. It appears in narrative moments such as the episode titled "Elephant" in which allegory overruns realistic exposition and narrative focus is divided, both violations of Bennett's theoretical prescriptions in *The Author's Craft*. Even though Bennett's fiction tends not to be read as a part of British literary modernism, his work is frequently perceived through the lens of modernist criticism, and Bennett is best known as the object of Virginia Woolf's denunciation in the several essays titled "Mr. Bennett and Mrs. Brown," published in the early 1920s. In these essays Woolf defines modernist (or "Georgian") literary practice against the anemic realism of her Edwardian predecessors, arguing that "the prevailing sound of the Georgian age" is the violent noise of Joyce's *Ulysses* (1922), Eliot's *The Waste Land* (1922), and, perhaps, her own inchoate *Mrs. Dalloway* (1925) smashing literary convention.[2] In "Mr. Bennett and Mrs. Brown" and "Character in Fiction," Woolf expropriates and elaborates in the context of literary stylistics Bennett's theme in the "Elephant" chapter of *The Old Wives' Tale*, that such "crashing and destruction" are attendant upon the yielding of one generation to the next. Woolf's essays memorably turn Bennett into the object rather than author of such a scene of violence.

Not only does Woolf return to this motif of Bennett's *The Old Wives' Tale* in *The Waves* (1931), the novel that Raymond Williams, among others, treats as Woolf's most representatively modernist text, she takes up the double figuration of the elephant in Bennett's chapter as a violent and dissident force and as a rotten burden.[3] Louis, the son of a colonial businessman, repeatedly gives voice to a menacing elephantine vision throughout the novel: "The beast stamps; the elephant with its foot chained; the great brute on the beach stamps."[4] As a child, the artist-figure Bernard imagines that issuing from the English undergrowth in which he plays are "warm gusts of decomposing leaves, of rotting vegetation. We are in a swamp now; in a malarial jungle. There is an elephant white with maggots, killed by an arrow shot dead in its eye."[5] Bernard's childhood image reappears later in the rhetoric of the grown Rhoda, where, despite its maturity, it remains a partially formed image fashioned within England's domestic spaces. In Rhoda's attempt to express admiration for Percival—"the violent last of the British imperialists"[6]—the rotting elephant serves as an ironic figure that seems to undermine a pretentious imperial rhetoric of enlightenment:[7]

> look—the outermost parts of the earth—pale shadows on the utmost horizon, India for instance, rise into our purview. The world that had been shrivelled, rounds itself; remote provinces are fetched up out of darkness; we see muddy roads, twisted jungle, swarms of men, and the vulture that feeds on some bloated carcass as within our scope, part of our proud and splendid province.[8]

Rhoda gathers "the outermost parts of the earth" under possessive and totalizing rubrics ("our purview," "our scope," "our proud and splendid province") as contemporary writing about imperial administration and display—such as that surrounding the Empire Exhibition of 1924—also did, but instead of conjuring images of integrated wholeness as the latter tended to do, Rhoda's vision lights upon a bloated corpse being dismembered. Rhoda gestures toward a "round" world, one of plenitude and light; yet that world also appears pathologically excessive, twisted, and swarming, harboring within it countervailing impulses toward dismemberment, dissolution, and decomposition.

It is precisely in the volatile space between visions of empire as integrated or "rounded" totality and of its irremediable attenuation or dissolution that I locate Woolf's engagement with the imperial menagerie in this chapter. Though Woolf visited the zoo in Regent's Park and attended a series of colonial and imperial exhibitions, her writing renders exotic animals not in the form she encountered them historically, as actors in imperial pageants, but rather as emblems or symbols, both private (in *The Years* [1937]) and public (in "Thunder at Wembley"). Woolf both distanced herself from historical forms of the imperial menagerie and maintained an intimacy with its symbolic repertoire. Likewise, insofar as we can understand Virginia Woolf to be "against empire," to use Kathy J. Phillips's phrase,[9] she should be located "against" empire in a sense of the word that signifies as much her proximity to and adjunction with empire as it does her well-known opposition, voiced late in her career in *Three Guineas* (1938), to "the desire to impose 'our' civilization or 'our' dominion upon other people."[10] In this chapter I focus especially on her challenges to "Edwardian" realism in 1924, the year of the Empire Exhibition, of Woolf's expansion of her famous essay "Mr. Bennett and Mrs. Brown" as "Character in Fiction," and of the composition of *Mrs. Dalloway*. The first section discusses the figure of a hybridized, elephantine body Woolf introduces at the conclusion of *The Years*, highlighting the complex dynamic of imperial holism and fragmentation this zoological conglomeration signals. A similarly peculiar assemblage of strange beasts and other exotica appeared under the mark of realism at the Empire Exhibition of 1924, which Virginia Woolf and her friend E. M. Forster discussed in a set of critical essays. In her piece on the exhibition, Woolf treats the dominant mode of realism as a kind of praxis that is complicit with the totalizing aims of imperialism, aims openly acknowledged at the 1924 Empire Exhibition at Wembley. Her essay declines to respect the established conventions of Wembley's realism, instead recasting the exhibition as itself a series of resolutely domestic displays that gather creatures of all sorts, but especially the English, for viewing. Woolf in effect turns one kind of exhibition into another, simultaneously reversing the polarity of the logic governing the imperial menagerie.

Woolf's refusal to observe Wembley's limits of realism is couched in prose that deliberately disrupts stylistic continuity in such a way to signal that "The Empire is perishing."[11] Georgian society inherited not only a tradition of large-scale imperial exhibition but also a series of totalizing metaphors that describe the empire. Just as she highlights the arbitrariness of exhibitionary conventions and the unstable character of the elephant, whether it is a menace in chains or a morbid corpse, so also Woolf refigures these metaphors in the geometric emphases of *Mrs. Dalloway*, *The Years*, and *The Waves*, her most overtly "imperialist" novel.[12] In particular, Woolf renders the circle, ring, or chain that signifies holism and integration[13]—and that binds Louis's elephant on the beach—in the end fractured, dissolved, or dispersed in fragments.

Drawing-Room Monsters and Civilization's Ellipses

Woolf's fiction is punctuated by the play between totality and fragmentation or decay, from the leaden circles that expand and dissolve throughout *Mrs. Dalloway* to the gramophone in *Between the Acts* (1941) that spins a record blaring "Unity-Dispersity. It gurgled Un . . . dis . . ."[14] For Woolf, the inevitable falling away from a vision of the whole prepares the ground for art's interventions.[15] From "Character in Fiction," in which Woolf despairs of "catching" the essence of Mrs. Brown in fiction but demands that we "tolerate the spasmodic, the obscure, the fragmentary, the failure" as an approximation of her,[16] to Miss La Trobe's play in *Between the Acts*, which plies its audience with interrogatives about how "civilization [might] be built by . . . orts, scraps, and fragments,"[17] the work of the aesthetic is identified with the partial, the fragmentary, the unfinished sentence that is left to trail off into ellipses. Woolf's fictional assemblages are partial collections, but the fragmentary or the incomplete always emerges against a horizon of the whole. At Delia and Patrick's party at the close of *The Years*, for instance, a curious collection of exotic and domestic figures makes a surprising appearance: "[the partygoers] had been playing a game. Each of them had drawn a different part of a picture. On top there was a woman's head like Queen Alexandra, with a fuzz of little curls; then a bird's neck; the body of a tiger; and stout elephant's legs dressed in child's drawers completed the picture."[18] This collection is presented as a "completed picture" but is plainly absurd by prevailing conventions. This strange party game, which constructs bourgeois amusement around other lands' beasts and another era's queen, can be understood either as simply one more detail in a novel the modus operandi of which is a refusal to be selective in the images it offers, or as an image that might stand even for the novel as a whole. To put this minor crux another way: this monster might be understood as the detritus of civilization, textual ephemera to be disregarded by the reader, or the very stuff—"orts, scraps, and fragments"—from which civilization is built.

The Years itself offers an assemblage of incongruous moments in much the way the partygoers construct the strange beast for their diversion. The parade of figures and historical moments surrounding the Pargiter family in the novel functions not only as a palimpsestic progress, with one era superseding and laying to rest the previous, but also as a kind of national montage, in which England is simultaneously composed of elements Victorian, Edwardian, and Georgian, as the novel draws together moments ranging from 1880 to 1936. With Queen Alexandra perversely at its helm, the simultaneously exotic and domestic animal describes in caricature the Edwardian empire, a peculiar aggregation of discrete geographical and cultural locations. The Bengal tiger is, of course, the animal that stands for India in the official iconography of empire, though the elephant—as in *Household Words* and *All the Year Round*—can just as easily stand in as the unofficial representative of Eastern spaces or empire in its totality. Those "stout elephant legs" seem, moreover, to anticipate the reflections on the Edwardian years offered by George Orwell's narrator George Bowling in *Coming Up for Air* (1939), a novel contemporary with *The Years* and set just before the outbreak of the Second World War. Bowling recalls the opening decade of the twentieth century as a period characterized by "a feeling of continuity.... What [the Edwardians] didn't know was that the order of things could change.... [The Edwardian Era strikes one as] a settled period, a period when civilisation seems to stand on its four legs like an elephant.... They didn't feel the ground they stood on shifting under their feet."[19] Woolf's elephant legs signal a similar sense of false stability on the verge of a second great war, but the legs in children's "drawers" might also encode an anxiety about Mother England's imperial children.

If the diversionary figure at Patrick and Delia's party appears as a metaphor for Woolf's novel, as an emblem of the English state, or even as a symbol of a modernist art that relies in part upon montage for its defamiliarizing effects, it also serves as a figure for the hybrid character of twentieth-century England. A number of moments in "Present Day" suggest that English culture is changing as the circuits of a wider imperial world return to England objects, people, and energies. Before the party in London, Maggie mistakes a conversation about Delia's *fête* for a discussion about Africa.[20] Kitty Lasswade is mistaken for the wife of the viceroy of India.[21] North Pargiter, just returned from Africa, finds himself "falling under their [English] weight.... Could nothing be done about it? he asked himself. Nothing short of revolution, he thought."[22] Yet he complains to Eleanor of a revolution of sorts, accusing the English of having "spoilt England while I've been away."[23] An "Indian in a pink turban"—"One of Eleanor's Indians"—preoccupies the attention of the partygoers.[24] And Eleanor complains, "India's nothing nowadays ... Travel's so easy. You just take a ticket; just get on board ship.... But what I want to see before I die ... is something different.... another kind of civilisation."[25] India, and the empire more generally, have come to seem strangely promixate to England, and England's civilization appears not so different from India's after all. The confusions of England with Africa, the fear that England has been spoiled, the longing for revolution, the desire for "another kind of civilisation" increasingly convey the sense that English identities are now inextricably bound up with the distant spaces England claims as its own. Yet the sheet of paper with the peculiar sketch "of the monster's person," if it does in fact serve as a figure of hybridity in the narrative discourse, is hardly taken for such an emblem by those in the story, for "they all laughed again," "laughed, laughed, laughed."[26] The hilarity of the group seems to overwhelm the beast's symbolic subtleties in *The Years,* and between the careful selectivity of the discourse and the broad laughter of the characters it becomes difficult to determine just what to make of the image.

The difficulty and necessity of reading a figure such as the hybrid animal at Delia's party is Woolf's theme in "The Symbol" (1941), a story whose first glimmerings in Woolf's diary are contemporaneous with the publication of *The Years.* In this late narrative, an anonymous protagonist in the Alps writes a letter to her sister in Birmingham as she watches a string of climbers traverse a mountain. "'The mountain,' the lady wrote, sitting on the balcony of the hotel, 'is a symbol. . . .'"[27] The narrator—as opposed to "the lady"—in a passage Woolf later canceled, observes that the mountain "was a menace: something cleft in the mind like two parts of a broken disk: two numbers: two numbers that cannot be added: a problem that is insoluble."[28] If the mountain is a "problem" for the narrator, it is likewise a problem for the protagonist, who cannot finish her sentence: "She had written the mountain was a symbol. But of what?"[29] This question takes her letter into the realm of free association. The mountain might have a personal resonance by representing an ambition for adventure that probably has a familial origin, as she writes to her sister:

> We come of course of an Anglo Indian family. I can still imagine, from hearing stories told, how people live in other parts of the world. I can see mud huts; and savages; I can see elephants drinking at pools. So many of our uncles and cousins were explorers. I have always had a great desire to explore for myself. But of course, when the time came it seemed more sensible, considering our long engagement, to marry.[30]

The lady writing her letter constructs a tenuous and speculative analogy between the ellipses in her definition of the mountain-symbol—her inability to determine for what the mountain stands—and her decision not to explore "other parts of the world." If the mountain seems to cleave "the mind like two parts of a broken disk," one of those parts represents the reality behind the stories of "mud huts; and savages; [and] elephants drinking at pools," while the other represents marriage and domestic life.[31] The lady's letter is interrupted as the climbers whom she watches while writing disappear into a crevasse in the mountain and perish. When she returns to her letter again later in the evening, she describes their deaths and then ends her letter: "The old clichés will come in very handy. They died trying to climb the mountain ... And the peasants brought spring flowers to lay upon their graves. They died in an attempt to discover . . . ' There seemed no fitting conclusion."[32]

Like the author's initial failure to finish her sentence, "The mountain is a symbol . . . ," and like the ineffable object of the climbers' venture, "The Symbol" itself seems unable to draw any definite conclusions about the meaning of the mountain. This tendency in the story renders the effect sought by Woolf's original design, for she initially titled the story "Inconclusions."[33] The plural construction of the working title indicates not only the protagonist's inability to conclude her inquiries into the symbolic character of the mountain but also the narrative's inconclusiveness as well. In shifting the title away from an emphasis on the referent (which is disappointingly indeterminate in this case) to the sign and its signifying tendencies (the mountain that calls up a split between domestic existence and "other parts of the world"), Woolf suggests that narrative need not supply—or even intend—precise meanings for the symbols it introduces for those symbols to produce significant effects. The significance of the mountain—what the mountain *does* as opposed to what it *means*, or what it is a symbol *of*—unfolds in the "cleft in the mind" the mountain produces between "marriage" and Indian "exploration." The significance of the climbers' doomed efforts toward objectless discovery rests, perhaps, in putting paid to the conviction that "The old clichés will come in very handy" (for they do not). And though "The Symbol" may not draw any conclusions in itself, its significance lies in shifting our critical attention away from "an attempt to discover [something]" in Woolf's symbols and toward an analysis of the effects and energies the symbol as a formal nodal point gathers into its purview.

The symbol in *The Years*—the composite figure of Queen Alexandra, the bird's neck, the tiger's body, and the elephant legs in children's "drawers"—provokes what is false, excessive, and unreal: "[Peggy] stopped laughing; her lips smoothed themselves out. But her laughter had had some strange effect on her. It had relaxed her, enlarged her. She felt, or rather she saw, not a place, but a state of being, in which there was real laughter, real happiness, and this fractured world was whole; whole, vast, and free."[34] In Peggy's eyes, the hybrid figure elicits from the company a laughter that is inauthentic; yet its very inauthenticity contrasts with a glimpse of new order in which the fractured world—a place in which things are cleft and broken, as in "The Symbol"—can be described as an integrated totality, a totality that, though vast, is conceivable in terms of "real laughter," "real happiness," and real liberty. This glimpse provokes her to attempt to describe her vision to the others: "'Look here...' she began. She wanted to express something that she felt to be very important; about a world in which people were whole, in which people were free... But they were laughing; she was serious. 'Look here...' she began again."[35] Peggy's vision is unutterably vague, and she herself discovers that "She had nothing to say when it came to the point, and yet she had to speak." Yet her response to the image of "the monster" and the laughter that image provokes recalls the impact of the mountain on "the lady" in "The Symbol": speech and writing tail off into ellipses; the symbol is cloven from its referent as the mind is riven like the broken halves of a disk; people are not whole; and indeed the world itself appears "fractured." The laughter at the party signifies something apart from "real happiness" or freedom, the proper objects of its reference.

Peggy's desire to discover "not a place, but a state of being" in which the world is "whole, vast, and free" emerges in the context of the manifold confusions of England with the imperial spaces it claims as its own. The party is given at the home of Delia and Patrick, the latter of whom is "the most King-respecting, Empire-admiring of country gentlemen" and who asserts both that "we [Irish a]re savages compared with you [English]" and that the Irish will "be glad enough to join the Empire again, I assure you."[36] Peggy's vision of a "vast" totality might, in this context, be taken as an imperialist one, were it not for the fact that she complains about the cowardice of those friends and family members at the party who live out conventional existences—making small fortunes in the colonies, returning to England, marrying, and writing books—"instead of living... living differently, differently." Because imprecise, Peggy's vision is reduced to a declaration of sheer difference; in its attenuated linguistic form, Peggy's desire can find expression only inadequately. The possibility of a "real" and numinous world beyond language, in which symbol and referent coincide and "fractured world" and subjects are both "whole... and free," appears finally as a horizon beyond language—and, indeed, beyond what the monstrous beast can express without ambiguity.

Given the emphasis on imperialism and the appearance of its zoological traces at the party, it might be tempting to read Peggy's impression of a world that is whole yet free and in which people themselves are whole, as anticipating, say, Frantz Fanon's desire to "help the black man to free himself of the arsenal of complexes that has been developed by the colonial environment" and his theme of "the disalienation of the black man."[37] This surely would be to miss the point, however. Among other failures of her imagination, Peggy does not really engage the colonized, Fanon's "black man," at all; her emphasis is on the English "living differently": hers is a categorically domestic vision. Fanon, moreover, finds the "disalienation" and freedom of the "black man" emerging out of a violent embrace of the cultural fragmentation enjoined upon the Algerians by the manichean world picture of the colonizers: "National liberation, national renaissance, the restoration of nationhood to the people, commonwealth: whatever may be the headings used or the new formulas introduced, decolonization is always a violent phenomenon."[38] Fanon imagines not a fractured world made whole but an Africa disarticulated from an imperial worldview that desires to see the globe made whole in the imperialists' image—from a worldview, in other words, like Peggy's.

In another sense, though, Peggy may glimpse beyond the strategic manicheanism of Fanon to something like what Homi Bhabha describes as an arena "beyond narratives of originary and initial subjectivities," in which "moments or processes . . . are produced in the articulation of cultural differences."[39] In exhorting her contemporaries to live differently, Peggy seems to imagine such a moment: "not a place, but a state of being." Such a "state of being" might perhaps be understood to anticipate what Bhabha calls the "in-between" of culture that constitutes "the terrain for elaborating strategies of selfhood—singular or communal—that initiate new signs of identity, and innovative sites of collaboration, and contestation, in the act of defining the idea of society itself."[40] In this sense, the hybrid, anthropomorphic animal—a laughable figure to the company assembled at Delia and Patrick's party—may *be* such a "new sign of identity," though the referent for the sign (nothing so specific as Fanon's "black man," for example) eludes even Peggy, who intuits but cannot articulate its significance.

The monstrous figure collectively produced at the party can be read to have a significance—as opposed to a meaning—that anticipates a normative social totality in which the promise of hybridity is realized as a free world where "people [are] whole," disalienated. This is Peggy's vision, but it is ineffable, even sublime, and her efforts to articulate the vision result in exhaustion and retreat: "She stopped. There was the vision still, but she had not grasped it. She had broken off only a little fragment of what she meant to say, and she had made her brother angry. Yet there it hung before her, the thing she had seen, the thing she had not said. . . . She had not said it, but she had tried to say it."[41] The impulse toward a "graspable" totality is met by a contrary tendency that results in "only a little fragment." Peggy herself experiences such an antithetical moment, frozen between totalizing vision and fragmentation, as something melancholy, lonely: "Yes, it was over; it was destroyed, she felt. Directly something got together, it broke. She had a feeling of desolation. And then you have to pick up the pieces, and make something new, something different, she thought, and crossed the room, and joined the foreigner."[42] In this case, the antithesis—the visionary whole faced by actual fragmentariness—results for Peggy in action, in the movement toward the foreigner, and it may be that the willing engagement with a representative of the foreign begins to realize the vision of hybridity spawned by the carnivalesque figure of queen, bird, tiger, elephant. In the private rooms of Delia and Patrick, in the intimate movement of Peggy's imagination, the imperial menagerie has been broken down and remade.

Mr. Bennett and Mrs. Brown at Wembley

Woolf undertook a comparable deconstruction of the menagerie in the realm of the historical in "Thunder at Wembley." The occasion of this essay, the Empire Exhibition of 1924, offered up a similar collocation of beasts—including King George V, elephants, monkeys, snakes, and colonial laborers—to a more populist audience than the genteel party in *The Years*. On 29 May 1924 Virginia and Leonard Woolf yielded to the exhibition's insistent invitation to "come and tickle monkeys," as Woolf described it,[43] and to visit "the ancient civilisation of the East" and "the primitive life of the African villages," as advertisements pitched Wembley.[44] The British Empire Exhibition in Wembley, North London, promised to bring home and into view of some 27 million British subjects a realistic picture of imperial landscapes, people, animals, and goods, fetching up out of the margins of empire a simultaneously fabricated and faithful representation of British holdings across the globe. Within the walled bounds of Wembley, one could view real Australian sheep and ostrich farms, tour a model of the Indian jungle, trace the eastward expansion of the empire by following the long procession of elephants across the Wembley Stadium pitch, and learn "What Tanganyika Can Do" by observing a model of an African elephant. In its displays, the British Empire Exhibition sought to round out a view of the world as a whole, laying before the British people the spectacle of an entire empire in miniature. Like the monstrous figure in Delia and Patrick's parlor, this fabrication was designed to amuse and delight, but it also provoked a series of significant meditations on the relation of English experience to life in the empire.

Working within the imaginative arenas of the Wembley exhibition and the periodical press, Woolf exposes the exhibition's realism as a kind of praxis that is complicit with the totalizing aims of imperialism. Her assault on similar realist practices in the novel in "Character in Fiction" figures also as a critique of imperialism, while her essay on the Empire Exhibition titled "Thunder at Wembley" is predicated upon a critique of the exhibition's economy of realism. This economy posits the world as a sociospatial totality that can be observed by a disengaged spectator without either entailing a loss of meaning or entangling the subject with the world as object. Woolf acknowledges that emergent modernisms appear as incomplete projects, but also that they expose the way the "rounding" of the world—representing it as a coherent, spectacular whole—always leaves in the margins a remainder that undermines realist restricted economies. Modernism's exposure of this excess enmeshes the subject with "life itself"[45] and gestures toward the impossibility of a singular totality that might be rendered as a spectacle; instead, its "solidity disappears," "features crumble," and frameworks "topple to the ground."[46] If Wembley sought to enchain the unruly "great brute" of twentieth-century imperial politics in the ring of a spectacular realism, Woolf envisions this orientalist spectacle bursting its bonds and spilling the contents of its bloated carcass into the domestic spaces of Englishness.

Criticism has rarely engaged Woolf's "Mr. Bennett and Mrs. Brown" and "Character in Fiction" in terms other than those laid out in the pages of *The Nation and the Athenaeum*, where Michael Sadleir in February 1924 cast the argument as a "duel between Mrs. Woolf" and her antagonists, "with Mr. Arnold Bennett as injured maiden."[47] Most critics who have subsequently defended Bennett and his mode of realism or upheld Woolf's position that Edwardian conventions of realism are outmoded have assumed that the contention between Bennett and Woolf was motivated chiefly by personal differences: Woolf railed against Bennett because she was a highbrow and he a lowbrow; Bennett invited her attack when he expressed chauvinistically masculinist views in *Our Women: Chapters on the Sex Discord* (1920). What has been missed is the degree to which Woolf's essays engage ongoing elite and popular celebrations and denunciations of realism as a method, particularly as these intensified around the Empire Exhibition of 1924 and occupied the space of the periodical press throughout 1924—especially *The Nation and the Athenaeum*, *Punch*, the *Graphic*, and the *Illustrated London News*.[48]

Woolf's attack upon Bennett's work as representative of the Edwardian novel reflects the fact that he explicitly theorized the objectivity of realism and claimed for the novel all the world as its domain, as we saw in chapter 3.

Woolf sought to dismantle the imaginative circuits through which the novel could appear to "adopt the hue of the British Empire," in Bennett's conception, when she published the article titled "Thunder at Wembley" in *The Nation and the Athenaeum* in June 1924, which concludes with a vision of the British Empire dissolving in a tempest. This relatively neglected essay, which Woolf composed shortly after revising and expanding her attack on Bennett in May, has only recently begun to receive significant critical attention, and just as discussions of the better-known "Mr. Bennett and Mrs. Brown" and "Character in Fiction" have neglected such problems of imperious (and imperial) representation as appear in Bennett's claim, so discussions of "Thunder at Wembley" have left unremarked the critique of economies of exhibitionary realism there.[49] The larger complex of texts from 1924—*Mrs. Dalloway*, "Character in Fiction," and "Thunder at Wembley"—ought to be considered together, since Woolf's notebooks for *Mrs. Dalloway* are interleaved with fragments of the expanded version of "Mr. Bennett and Mrs. Brown" and the complete draft of "Thunder at Wembley," each of which explores the spaces of empire and the modes of representing the real. We get a sense of just how contested this representational terrain is in the modernist period when we consider that at the same time these three documents that seek a new relation to the real were filling out the pages of Woolf's notebooks, models of the British Commonwealth of Nations were rising in the midst of suburban North London as high-fidelity monuments to the empire as a total sociospatial order.

Intense Realism and a Little Tour of the Whole World

The Empire Exhibition sought to rework the themes of an earlier imperialism in order to allay nagging suspicions, raised in *The Nation and the Athenaeum*, that "our fortunes have passed their zenith" and that contemporary global developments would "precipitate our decay."[50] The overarching strategy demanded the representation of the empire as an integrated whole, as a synchronic totality, and Wembley—like the other colonial and imperial exhibitions—"emphasized the notion of Empire as an interlocking economic unit."[51] This monolithic conception of empire appeared also to involve a cultural logic that insisted upon the empire's singular unity despite its great diversity:

> The more exotic the pavilions the more they thrilled . . . in an endless variety of human types, colour of skin and national costume, and in a

profusion of tongues with which the Tower of Babel itself could not have competed—yet all were members of one great empire, united under one king and flag, linked by the English language, financed by sterling, ruled by British justice and protected by the Royal Navy.[52]

This sense of a unitary and unified empire, a complete and variegated circuit in itself, permeated the exhibition's rhetoric,[53] and not only in the spectacles shown but also in the labor that produced the display, as the Prince of Wales highlighted in proclaiming to the King at the opening ceremonies that "The Exhibition is . . . the work of the whole Empire, . . . of all our peoples and all our territories."[54] Against this great labor of all the empire were posed the spectators—"creatures of leisure, civilization, and dignity," Woolf calls them—whom these rhetorics were designed to impress with sentiments auspicious for the future of the empire.[55]

To the end of persuading domestic subjects of the empire's continued significance, the Wembley exhibition that the Woolfs encountered "combined entertainment, education, and trade fair on a spectacular scale."[56] The exhibition included pavilions in which more than twenty-five of the lands under British rule offered "exact reconstructions of native villages, actual living flowers, trees, and beasts of strange countries."[57] The "Olde Englishe Faire" section housed the "Menagerie" exhibit proper, which boasted monkeys, dozens of lions, and more than a hundred snakes.[58] But the most compelling specimens of exotica were mounted in the national pavilions: Ceylon exhibited elephant heads, buffalo, spotted deer, and pigs; Kenya displayed tusks lent by the King for the exhibit; India promised a model jungle with lions, tigers, and elephants; and Sarawak showed a thirty-foot-long stuffed python that had swallowed a whole pig.[59] To a large degree, Wembley reproduced the logic of both the Great Exhibition of 1851 and the zoo in Regent's Park, and it was mentioned in the popular press alongside both of these precedents in the summer of 1924.[60] Unlike these other events and institutions, however, the 1924 exhibition also staged a vast "Pageant of Empire" that promised the largest and grandest historical dramatization ever staged. It included twelve thousand performers and was enacted over three days, portraying the westward, southward, and eastward expansion of the empire and showcasing thousands of actors (among them snake charmers, dervishes, and dancing girls) and native animals—elephants, camels, oxen, llamas, bulls, bears, kangaroos, doves, horses, donkeys, and monkeys—processing across the stadium grounds (fig. 22).[61]

Though the exhibition's displays and pageants—with stuffed or live beasts—were the work of the whole empire, its design and execution were

THE GORGEOUS EAST IN THE GREAT PROCESSION
Passing thousands of enthusiastic spectators in the Stadium.

Figure 22. "The Gorgeous East" at Wembley, *The Graphic*, 23 August 1924. *Permission The British Library (Shelfmark NPL Graphic 24-9-1924 pg.282).*

also characteristically British: the exhibition's enormous pavilions were constructed with the new British-engineered material of steel-reinforced concrete by a crew of British builders. A French visitor lamented in *Living Age* that the British "makers have been content with approximations with which we French, accustomed as we are to more care and more minute perfection, would never have been satisfied,"[62] and Roger Fry, surveying Wembley's architecture in the pages of *The Nation and the Athenaeum*, complained that "It is characteristic of many English artists to be much more concerned with the surface finish of that work than with . . . the design."[63] Nevertheless, it seemed somehow appropriate that this exhibition should bear the telltale marks of what Arnold Bennett had earlier identified as "the English idiosyncrasy"—"a haphazard particularity."[64]

Though the planners surely would have denied the charge of haphazardness, the realism of the exhibition implicitly acknowledged its selectivity in offering portrayals of the empire as a harmonious and profitable unit, and to this extent a distinct economy of realism promoted the interests of a global commercial economy. The logic that the exhibition followed was that of earlier displays—and not only the Great Exhibition of 1851 but also the London Zoological Gardens—where the rule of synecdoche dominated, representing the whole empire through its parts (though at times it resorted to the allegorical, deploying the logic of Astley's Circus and the Lord Mayor's Show). Wembley's planners emphasized the characteristic and the typical in its exhibits, hoping they would, as George V proclaimed during the opening ceremonies, "reveal to us the whole Empire in little, containing within its 220 acres of ground a vivid model of the architecture, art and industry of all the races which come under the British flag."[65] The exhibition was a very deliberate effort to place before domestic English subjects a panoramic scene of the empire in its entirety, as part of an effort to stave off a growing sense of imperial stagnation, decline, and decay through a picturesque display that simultaneously cultivated an awe of empire's sublimity. The novelist G. K. Chesterton promoted this totalizing aspect of the enormous display at Wembley as one of the exhibition's great selling points when he wrote that "It is to be hoped that people will learn to appreciate what is large precisely because they see it when it is little."[66] Indeed, the popular press in the spring of 1924 filled its pages with appreciations, reading the exhibition as a faithful if awesome representation of the empire. The *Illustrated London News*, for instance, described the Hong Kong exhibit in these terms: "There is no 'fake' about Hong Kong at Wembley. Every detail was made in the Colony and shipped to England. The result is most picturesque and attractive—a real view of the real China that salutes the British flag."[67]

In their relentless pursuit of "the real" construed narrowly, the papers tended to hew to the representational strategies of the exhibition, which were designed to offer "a comprehensive survey of the wealth and resources of the British Commonwealth of Nations [and] to reproduce the whole of the Empire in miniature."[68] From January 1924 the *Illustrated London News* offered descriptive maps and special artists' renderings of the entire exhibition; in May it supplied a four-page foldout overview of Wembley; and in July it reproduced aerial photographs of the section of North London, making available the whole of the grounds at one glance. Journalistic realism, like the style of the exhibition, demanded the rendition of Wembley as a whole. A Swedish visitor to Wembley also echoed the official propaganda of Wembley, noting that "Exotica is a large and rich country. Trips to it are both troublesome and expensive, and only a few can hope to see its wonderlands. But this summer a person can make a little tour of the world and have his fill of exoticism at Wembley.... [A]nything is possible in Exotica, and we have the whole world to look at if we like."[69] The exhibition's global extension of synecdochic logic served to render accessible "the whole world" through the "little tour," at the end of which, declared the *Official Guide* to the exhibition, "You may not have put a girdle round the earth in forty minutes, but you will have done something like it."[70]

As something like the world's largest zoo, amusement park, trade show, and "Empire Classroom," the 1924 Empire Exhibition marked its difference from earlier colonial, imperial, and world exhibitions (a few of which Woolf recollects in "Thunder at Wembley") chiefly through its claims to greater comprehensiveness, its sheer overwhelming mass, and the intensity of its imperial "lessons."[71] Wembley's scale and intensity did not, however, make a uniformly positive impression upon those whose aesthetic sensibilities guided their evaluations of the exhibition. In *The Nation and the Athenaeum*, Roger Fry lamented the tasteless bombast of the exhibition's architecture: "An area equal to that of central London has been enclosed, and most of the buildings within it are of abnormal size.... In general, one may say that everything is five times as large as the most exorbitant could demand."[72] If the tour of Wembley was little and manageable, the representations themselves were designed to engross and impress, in an apparent contradiction "between the need to separate oneself from the world and to render it up as an object of representation, and the desire to lose oneself within this object-world and to experience it directly."[73] In part, the "exorbitant," "abnormal" scale of Wembley served to distinguish further the exhibition from the reality it claimed to reproduce: as one visitor pointed out, "all this splendor is after all nothing but a stage-setting, the representation of the moment in which one pushes to its extreme the Empire's dignity and splendor."[74] Even Wembley's enthusiastic contemporaries understood that its selective realism aimed to produce an "allegory of power and wealth, a significant summing-up of infinite resources on a world-wide scale,"[75] and the engulfing scale was important to this allegorical function.

The "summing-up" of empire in these synchronically patterned totalities, however comprehensive, was designed primarily for the British who could both apprehend and remain unencumbered by the alien spaces of the empire or by any competing representations, and it was as if "the rest of Europe did not count."[76] The exhibition's realism appeared, then, as a kind of restricted economy of precise observation bounded in such a way as to conserve and convey meaning in the "schoolroom of the empire," to the exclusion of all competing representations. Official advertisements for the exhibition touted

Figure 23. Ad for the British Empire Exhibition, Wembley, *The Graphic*, 24 May 1924. Permission The British Library (Shelfmark NPL Graphic 24-5-1924 pg.834).

the spectacular yet realistic character of the displays, as in one enthusiastic promotion (fig. 23) which announced that

> The British Empire Exhibition derives its absorbing interest from its intense realism. Stately and picturesque pavilions are constructed of materials brought from the countries they represent; trees and shrubs and flowers are growing around as they grow thousands of miles away. . . . When one has watched the making of Indian carpets by native experts, he may witness an Indian play performed by Indian actors in an Indian theatre, or, spellbound, gaze upon an Indian snake charmer compelling a huge cobra to do his bidding.[77]

English visitors, ostensibly held "spellbound" by the "intense realism" of the spectacle, are nevertheless removed from the more "picturesque" aspects of the exhibition. Their "absorbed interest" is always at a significant remove from the spectacle, apprehending the pavilions and "native experts" as though they were pictures at another sort of exhibition.

The claims of Woolf's contemporary Bror Centerwall that at Wembley we "have the whole world to look at" epitomize modernity's exhibitionary epistemology. If the British Empire Exhibition actively aimed to cement a sense of the empire as unitary and uniform, it also presumed that a global empire could be so described. The representation of the world as spectacle consequently is related to the view of the "real" world outside—and if the spectacle inside the exhibition faltered in its realism, it could mean that indeed "one more doubt [was] cast upon the reality of the external world."[78] The foundation of this modern economy of realism upon the trope of the "world-as-exhibition" is not peculiar to the colonial and imperial exhibitions but directs literary formulae of the era as well: Arnold Bennett had earlier suggested that the obligation of the novelist is "really to see the spectacle of the world (a spectacle surpassing circuses and even street accidents in sustained dramatic interest)."[79] The realist's world-as-spectacle thus became the established way of treating or looking at the world; concomitantly, looking at the world through the lenses of "intense realism" came to be established as an imperial way of treating it.

Realist prescriptions for the novel such as Arnold Bennett's developed during the heyday of colonial and imperial exhibitions, and it is perhaps not coincidental that his conceptions of the novel resemble those strategies of exhibitions designed to foster an intense and engrossing realism, since both the novel and the exhibition share a worldview in which "The so-called real world outside is something experienced and grasped only as a series of further representations, an extended exhibition."[80] Virginia Woolf ironically reverses this perspective as it pertains to the novel, reducing Bennett's work itself to a kind of picture: "we must do as painters do when they wish to reduce the innumerable details of a crowded landscape to simplicity—step back, half shut the eyes, gesticulate a little vaguely with the fingers, and reduce Edwardian fiction to a view."[81] In "Thunder at Wembley," too, Woolf reduces the realism of Wembley to just one kind of picture, challenging the singularity of the totality represented in the exhibition and in the vision of world-as-exhibition, stressing the way in which the real threatens the restricted economies of realism and entangles imperial spectators with "life itself."

Pasteboard Hams and the White Man's Burden

In April 1924, in the pages of the same publication that printed "Mr. Bennett and Mrs. Brown" in December, and in which "Thunder at Wembley" was soon to appear, E. M. Forster cast his eye upon the construction of the muddy pavilions, villages, and streets that would in short order become the British Empire Exhibition. Before the exhibition even opened, he predicted that "Millions will spend money there, hundreds will make money, and a few highbrows will make fun," noting that he himself "belong[ed] to the latter class."[82] This was by no means a small class, since as John MacKenzie points out, "Much contemporary fun was poked at the exhibition by *Punch*, the WGTW (Won't Go To Wembley) Society, by P. G. Wodehouse and Noel Coward."[83] We might add Woolf to this class of "highbrows," for in her *Diary* she associated Wembley with "the enameled Lady Colefax" who was like "a cheap bunch of artificial cherries . . . on a burnished plate of facts," and who, while she could not "sink to the depths," was nevertheless "a superb skimmer of the surface."[84] Woolf was not alone in perceiving a conventional and insubstantial realism surrounding the exhibition: another visitor compared Wembley's displays to "those painted pasteboard hams which give a fraudulent fillip to appetite in the show windows of certain delicatessen stores."[85] The hilarity at the expense of the Empire Exhibition was, like the amusement at Delia and Patrick's party, a result of the sometimes bizarre incongruity and juxtaposition of the imagery, but as in the case of the hybrid creature assembled from queen, bird, tiger, the character of the collection also provoked reflection on the nature of the whole.

The insistence on strict if superficial realism at Wembley rendered it vulnerable to criticism and ridicule of precisely this sort, especially at the borders of its economy of realism. *Punch*'s columnist recorded a tour of the exhibition in which his guide patiently explained that "The whole thing is arranged geographically . . . It's all been planned like an immense map." When the journalist wonders "how . . . the rest of the world [is] filled up? The parts that don't belong to the British Empire, I mean," his guide replies, "Kiosks and restaurants . . . Restaurants in particular."[86] The boundaries of imperial territory consequently appear as the arbitrary circumscribing limit of the exhibition's representation of the world, and *Punch*'s inquiry exposes the underpinnings of the exhibition's "intense realism"—a desire to cultivate imperial consumers and to foster a broader commercial economy by presenting the exhibition itself as "the whole thing." *Punch*'s jokes at the expense of the exhibition's realism frequently treated nonrepresentative features of the exhibition—icicles, the rain, the cold, the restaurants—as part of the exhibition's realistic display, as when the columnist describes scraping thick mud from his boots, "carefully putting a large piece of empire back on the ground," and muttering with disgust about "the White Man's

Burden."[87] While realism in the novel may—as Arnold Bennett claimed—have "poached, colonized, and annexed with [undeniable] success," *Punch* nevertheless probes the boundaries of realism's annexations and denies that its eminent domain extends anywhere near "the whole thing."

While *Punch* managed to exploit the representations at the exhibition for a great many jokes, it also drew attention to the gap between the expectations of audiences who anticipated conventional views of Exotica (those fostered by the imperial romance, for instance) and the actual displays resulting from the exhibition's strategy of calculated realism. After touring the Indian Pavilion, *Punch* directed its sardonic fire at an exhibit of India's representative minerals:

> I can assure you from my own personal knowledge that the popular interest in pirolitic bauxite among ordinary Englishmen has never been at a lower ebb than it is to-day.... [G]ive us instead a life-size working replica of a tiger-shoot on elephants, with a background of Indian Jungle and Indian sky.... A moving elephant, either alive or mechanical, carrying a howdah, should have been provided, and air-guns charged with darts given to the spectators, who thus from a reasonable range might have experienced some of the thrills and glamour of the East.[88]

The rhetorical success of the India exhibit, *Punch* suggests, is imperiled by the unimaginative literalism of the display, which does not conform to a picture of India available through the symbolic lenses of orientalism, lenses through which the English largely understood India. "Let us have more Indian snake-charmers and fakirs," *Punch* demands sarcastically. "Let us have a *pukka suttee* and a car of Juggernaut . . . and above all things, if you can manage it, show us one or two stuffed agitators."[89] What Virginia Woolf calls the "burnished plate of facts" obscures, *Punch* implies, those imaginative and political relations that obtain between England and India that are more significant in themselves than bits of pirolitic bauxite and, indeed, that might suggest cracks in the empire's political foundation. In short, the exhibition has too much of the trade show and too little of the zoo, menagerie, or circus.

In evaluating the architectural specimens housing these exhibits, Roger Fry dismissed "the triviality, the niggling pedantry, and want of invention which . . . every one of these buildings displays,"[90] and in her essay on the Empire Exhibition Woolf, too, complains of the lack of imagination in the exhibition. At previous colonial exhibitions, such as the one she attended in July 1903 at Earls Court,[91] she remembered, "Everything was intoxicated and transformed. But at Wembley nothing is changed and nobody is drunk."[92] The "mediocrity"[93] of the Wembley exhibition, according to Woolf, is owed to its attempted realism: its presentation (like Lady Colefax) as "a burnished plate of facts" and its patent factitiousness ("a cheap bunch of artificial cherries") fail to charm. By contrast with the calculated and ordered realism of the exhibition, Woolf—like *Punch*'s muddy correspondent—relishes the display of what she calls "Nature" in the exhibition grounds, an uncoordinated, unpredictable, and excessive "Nature" that she claims "is the ruin of Wembley."[94]

Like the mud, rain, and restaurants in the view of *Punch*, "Nature" for Woolf exposes the limits of the exhibition's machinery of representation, its carefully circumscribed economy of realism.[95] By "Nature" Woolf means not just the world of birds and trees and sky but also "our contemporaries"—the English "clergymen, schoolchildren, girls, young men, invalids in bath-chairs" who visit Wembley and use the space to their own ends, not necessarily those of the Empire.[96] By contrast with the monumental places of display encased in ferroconcrete, "they reveal themselves simply as human beings, creatures of leisure, civilization, and dignity; a little languid, perhaps, a little attenuated, but a product to be proud of. Indeed they are the ruin of the Exhibition."[97] Woolf's perspective treats the entire exhibition as a display of nature, an alternative collection of creatures that dissolves the artificial boundaries the exhibition depends upon. They destroy the illusion of "intense realism" the exhibition works so hard to establish because they are the observers on whom the illusion depends—to read them as central to the Empire Exhibition is to dissolve the limits of that realism: "As you watch them trailing and flowing, dreaming and speculating . . . the rest of the show becomes insignificant."[98] The boundaries of realism's economy are transgressed by the very spectators that realism was designed to dazzle, and Woolf's vision of the exhibition incorporates the spectator, refusing to acknowledge the comforting distance exhibitionary rhetorics typically fostered. "Nature" for Woolf signals a "dreaming and speculating" excess characteristic of something like what she calls "life itself" in "Character in Fiction," an excess that is incompatible with the "plate of facts" and "niggling pedantry" served up at the exhibition.

Woolf renders the Empire Exhibition a display of Englishness as much as of empire, a spectacle including the ideally disengaged tourists whom *The Graphic* advertisement targets in its emphasis upon "intense realism" as the hallmark of the exhibition's modernity. From this perspective, Wembley chiefly reflects the English character, not that of "a larger world"; "Nature" signals the human experience in the world, instead of that which is amenable to representation in the age of the world-as-exhibition; and the exhibition's spatial strategies appear not as genuinely modern, "Georgian" modes of representation but as testaments to the persistence of Victorian convention. In *Orlando* (1928) she characterizes the nineteenth century in terms of the incongruous assemblages of material that appeared with insistence at the Empire Exhibition—for instance, a stroll over the Old London Bridge delivered the tourist into the Taj Mahal, not far from where one might see a refrigerated Prince of Wales rendered in butter. Orlando perceives the nineteenth century as a similar

> conglomeration ... of the most heterogeneous and ill-assorted objects, piled higgledy-piggledy in a vast mound where the statue of Queen Victoria now stands! Draped about a vast cross of fretted and floriated gold were widow's weeds and bridal veils; hooked on to other excrescences were crystal palaces, bassinettes, military helmets, memorial wreaths, trousers, whiskers, wedding cakes, cannon, Christmas trees, telescopes, extinct monsters, globes, maps, elephants and mathematical-instruments.[99]

Not only the Victorian "crystal palaces," with which the Empire Exhibition liked to compare itself, but the heterogeneity, the military display, the globes, the maps, and the elephants—all appear as key features of the 1924 exhibition. According to *Orlando*, "the British Empire came into existence" along with the accession of Victoria to the throne,[100] and the largest celebration ever of the empire at Wembley marks the belated culmination of nineteenth-century exhibitionary practices, the hallmark of which was Prince Albert's Great Exhibition of 1851 itself.

If the Wembley exhibition seemed Victorian to Woolf in its revival of the old imperial themes—the globes and maps and elephants—so also its brand of realism appears outmoded. Woolf champions "Nature" because it exposes the contingency of, for instance, the "real view of the real China" that the *Illustrated London News* celebrated; and because it exceeds the boundaries of the restricted economy of representation that underpins the vision of empire at Wembley. In Woolf's essay, nature's excessive and disordering tendencies—particularly in the guise of the torrential rains that ruined the first days of the "Pageant of Empire"—overwhelm the bounds of the exhibition's realism, reduce the coherence of the concrete displays to ruins, and herald an imperial apocalypse. As "the Massed Bands of empire are assembling and marching to the Stadium" for the "Pageant of Empire," a wind sweeps in and the sky darkens:

some appalling catastrophe is impending. The sky is livid, lurid, sulphurine. It is in violent commotion. It is whirling water-spouts of cloud into the air; of dust in the Exhibition. Dust swirls down the avenues, hisses and hurries like erected cobras round the corners. Pagodas are dissolving in dust. Ferro-concrete is fallible. Colonies are perishing and dispersing in spray of inconceivable beauty and terror which some malignant power illuminates. Ash and violet are the colours of its decay. ... Cracks like the white roots of trees spread themselves across the firmament. The Empire is perishing; ... the Exhibition is in ruins.[101]

Woolf's vision of imperial destruction here may seem excessively fanciful, but even *Punch* acknowledged that "It was simply an amazing storm."[102] If, as the exhibition organizers maintained, the exhibition was to be understood as a "replica" of the empire in its entirety, then Woolf's reading of the storms at Wembley as foretelling the dissolution of empire is no more outrageous than *Punch*'s curiosity about what at the cartographically arranged exhibition occupied the spaces of the world the English had not colonized. Apprehending the deluge through Wembley's logic of realism undermines both the commercial and the symbolic aims of the exhibition—and, Woolf points out, "*that* is what comes of letting in the sky."[103]

Woolf's critique differs from *Punch*'s in a number of respects, but especially in its deliberately difficult, impressionistic, and fragmentary style: she offers what we might term a modernist explosion of Wembley's logic of realism and its restricted economy of correspondences and exactitudes. The extravagances and difficulties of Woolf's essay match "Nature's" own excess in the storms that washed over the exhibition. It is in these stylistic and symbolic senses—the seemingly irremediable losses of the idea of empire as totality, and of the coherence of exhibitionary rhetorics of realism—that Woolf's imaginative responses to empire open up possibilities of a general (as opposed to restricted) economy of realism, a system of representation in which excess, unaccountable expenditure, and loss are the operative principles. Here that excess figures as the outside of the exhibition that cannot be excluded—human nature, the sky, the weather.

A week before she attended the Wembley exhibition, Woolf had redrafted "Mr. Bennett and Mrs. Brown" as "Character in Fiction," another essay on expenditure, on "smashing and crashing," and on the question of realism. Against the Wembley organizers' assertion that the modern element was apparent in the exhibition's grandeur and enormity, in its ferroconcrete, and in its "intense realism," in "Character in Fiction" and in "Thunder at

Wembley" Woolf insists that the Georgian notion of the real is visible in "the spasmodic, the obscure, the fragmentary, the failure."[104] This position represents a marked break both with the exhibition's emphasis upon "avoiding formlessness... and unrestricted individual effort" and with Arnold Bennett's admonition against "trivial and unco-ordinated details" and his concomitant emphasis upon the coherence of a "broad notion of the whole."[105] The mutual point of interrogation in Woolf's essays, then, is the status of realism's relation to the flux and excess of the real. "What is reality?" Woolf wonders in "Character in Fiction," and despite the impossibility of settling the question, she concludes that the business of the novel that would approach the problem cannot be "to preach doctrines, sing songs, or celebrate the glories of the British Empire"—precisely those things that Wembley's "intense realism" did seek to do. Woolf's interest in the way in which people live out their lives in spaces such as the suburban train on which Mrs. Brown travels and the grounds of the Empire Exhibition—the way in which they turn physical places, "the fabric of things," into special and personal spaces in which narrative unfolds—brings her to concentrate her attention on the question of character.[106]

The distinction between physical place as catalogued by the Edwardians and what Woolf casts as lived space in her essays is perhaps key to understanding her treatment of realism as it appears in Bennett's fiction and in the Wembley exhibition. Woolf concludes that Bennett's fiction—and that of the Victorians and Edwardians more generally—concerns itself too much with ordering and recording the material trappings and environments of people (placing "an enormous stress on the fabric of things") and too little with the ways in which people "reveal themselves" within the spaces they construct.[107] "If you hold that novels are in the first place about people," Woolf writes, "and only in the second about the houses they live in," then the Edwardians, and Bennett in particular, have missed the mark in giving their readers "a house in the hope that [they] may be able to deduce the human beings who live there."[108] In the manuscript of "Thunder at Wembley," Woolf celebrates the exhibition's travelers because "what has happened is simply that they have been lifted out of streets and houses and set down against an enormous background which reveals them for the first time."[109] The incompatibility of human nature with "the fabric of things" in "Character in Fiction" is much the same difficulty that Woolf finds arising within the British Empire Exhibition, which gives the English people replicas of colonial buildings but without a concomitant sense of the ways in which real life might unfold in that space—a result of the resolute separation of the spectator from spectacle.

For Woolf, "against the enormous background of ferro-concrete Britain, of rosy Burma," it becomes clear that the presence of real people living their real lives in the spaces of Wembley must mark "the ruin of the Exhibition"—or at least of its conception of the entire world as an exhibition disengaged from English human nature.[110] Timothy Mitchell understands the exhibition not as dividing spectators directly from the real but rather threading an impression of alienation through the channels of realism: "it creates an effect *called* the real world, in terms of which we can experience what is called alienation."[111] At stake is the logic of empire and of the menagerie—even if the displays were participatory, as Woolf's "Monkey-Teasers" urged,[112] they were designed to demonstrate the dominance of the spectator. For her part, Woolf remakes this aspect of exhibitionary rhetoric so that Wembley becomes not a place with alien pictures of the world on show but the space in which spectators "reveal themselves" in the world. In the process, Woolf relegates what Bennett calls the "whole spectacular and sensual show" of the world to the middle ground, where it becomes just one show among several. In the same way, Woolf makes plain in "Character in Fiction" that human nature "will strike you very differently according to the age and country in which you happen to be born,"[113] posing human nature itself as something that cannot be summed up in what Bennett and exhibition organizers championed as a single, "true perspective."

Unlike the exhibitionary rhetorics that sought to remove the spectator from the enframed totality of the world, Woolf's figures become part of several possible worlds, and in place of Wembley's "summing-up" in an imposing allegory, Woolf offers us at best partial summings-up. As the famous figure Mrs. Brown appears to reveal the Edwardian novelists as having produced merely hollow men rather than characters in "Character in Fiction," so also she appears in Woolf's essay on the exhibition, in the guise of "some woman in the row of red-brick villas outside the grounds [who] comes out and wrings a dish-cloth in the backyard," in a display of everyday waste on the verge of the exhibition.[114] This woman, like Mrs. Brown, shows what the economy of realism must thrust aside in order to establish itself, thereby exposing the exhibition's illusion of realism by the contact with what Woolf calls in "Character in Fiction" "the spirit we live by, life itself."[115] In the latter essay, Woolf foregrounds the sound of conventional boundaries such as those the bounds of the exhibition represent dissolving, particularly through her description of Joyce's "indecency" and "overflowing of superabundant energy" as "smashing and crashing."[116] Woolf notes that *Ulysses* "seems to me the conscious and calculated indecency of a desperate man who feels that in order to breathe he must break the windows," and the "sound of breaking and falling, crashing and destruction" that Woolf remarks as characteristic of modernism more generally heralds the collapse of the edifices of Edwardian literature, in much the way that the storm's ominous thunder reduces the empire to dust and fragments.[117] The destruction of Edwardian literary convention is not effected by crude "Nature," as in "Thunder at Wembley," but rather by a different sort of excess: James Joyce's "savagery" and T. S. Eliot's "obscurity," which approximate "the sound of axes."[118] These, Woolf suggests, have led the avant-garde charge "to outrage [and] to destroy the very foundations and rules of literary society," a destruction visible wherever "grammar is violated" or "syntax disintegrated."[119] The rhetoric of dissolution Woolf deploys in the name of artistic modernism is not hers alone: in a different register, her friend Roger Fry also imagined exploding the exhibition in the name of new aesthetic sensibilities, noting that "if ever a taste for architecture should arise in this country the nation will be asked to foot another large bill for dynamite to blow it all up."[120] In the meantime, Fry harbored hope for the "triumph of intelligent barbarism" represented by West Africans at the exhibition "over the last word in civilized ineptitude," which he takes Wembley to mark.[121]

The woman who wrings her washcloth in "Thunder at Wembley" stands at the very margins of the exhibition, while Mrs. Brown is situated in the transitional space of the moving suburban train. These mediate, transitory positions mark what has escaped Edwardian realism and exhibitionary representation—that which Woolf codes as Georgian or modernist. The liminal positions that "change . . . the shape, shift . . . the accent, of every scene"[122] also bear a striking resemblance to what Bill Ashcroft in a remarkable essay calls "the verandahs of meaning": "In post-colonial discourse the body, place, language, the house of being itself are all 'verandahs.' That is, they are a process in which the marginal, the excess, is becoming the actual. The verandah is not the surplus of the building but the excess which redefines the building itself. The verandah is that penumbral space in which articulation takes form, where representation is contested."[123] West African "triumph[s] of intelligent barbarism," James Joyce's "savagery," and English filth sluicing to the ground at the edge of Wembley's manicured grounds signal the kind of shadowy excess that Ashcroft identifies with the postcolonial, noting that "The hegemony of the absolute always falls short of the continual supplement, the excess, which is the real."[124] Where Bennett's and the Empire Exhibition's representations claim to be absolute, "true," each of Woolf's exemplars of the real appears as a supplement or germ that grounds a particular symbolic economy but exists in a space properly outside it. Inscribing them within a general economy in her essays, Woolf reveals the way in which conventional realisms fall short, and in which life on the verandah reduces to "ruins and splinters . . . this tumbled mansion."[125] What Ashcroft calls "the hegemony of the absolute" fails in Woolf's readings of the Empire Exhibition and of Edwardian realism not only in the face of colonial subjects such as the nameless Indian "native experts" or Ireland's Joyce, but also in the persistence of the English "real," a "product to be proud of"—even as it reveals itself in prosaic "invalids in bath chairs," "clergymen, and children."

Ashcroft enables us to name the space Woolf explores between totality and detotalization, the margin between the exhibition and the display of English nature, and Bhabha's "terrain for . . . new signs of identity" as the "verandah." The monstrous—like the freakish figure at Delia and Patrick's party or the monkeys in the storm—defines the verandah. In short, while "the excess which is the real" is most apparent in the sublime vision of "beauty and terror" that the empire's tempestuous destruction evokes, it also emerges in the quiet activities of human nature unfolding in the avenues and margins of Wembley. Ashcroft suggests that "Post-colonial excess is quintessentially the exuberance of life which is destined to revolt. But the most effective revolt is the one which denies the system its power over representation."[126] This is what "Nature"—especially human nature in Woolf's essays—accomplishes: "the most solemn sights she turns to ridicule; the most ordinary she invests with beauty."[127] At stake for Woolf in denying the Empire Exhibition an unqualified power over representation—even if only in the "highbrow" printed space of *The Nation and the Athenaeum*—is the dominance of a world picture, an epistemological outlook that apprehends the world as exhibition and expresses its force both in imperial sociospatial representation and in the realist novel that presents "the whole spectacular and sensual show" of the world.

Leaden Circles, Jagged Lines, Orts, Scraps, and Fragments

The apocalyptic vision of empire's dissolution Woolf presents in "Thunder at Wembley" as an inversion of the logic of the menagerie unfolded chiefly in the realm of fancy, given that the stormy summer of 1924 in reality only dampened the exhibition, rather than bringing it to ruin. And, indeed, the exhibition reopened in 1925 with a slightly freshened presentation. The provisionality of Woolf's fantastic allegory finds an analogue in the form of modernist style, which, as Woolf suggests in "Character in Fiction," cannot "just at present [offer] a complete and satisfactory presentment" of reality, and Woolf rests at the end of this essay with a view of modernism as "the spasmodic, the fragmentary, the obscure, the failure," between Edwardian and fully realized new conventions.[128] In "Mr. Bennett and Mrs. Brown," "Character in Fiction," and "Thunder at Wembley," though, modernism's force emerges precisely from its "failure" in conventional terms—because it compromises extant representational economies and practices. While Ashcroft helps name the ground between a "rounded," totalized world and its dissolution in the face of the real's excess as the verandah, Woolf herself figures imperial space rather differently. In Woolf's work in general, and in *Mrs. Dalloway* in particular, symbols of dissolving circles mark the imaginative space between imperial totality and fragmentation, realism and its excess.

The manuscript of *Mrs. Dalloway* (still called *The Hours* in the notebooks) is itself broken up by fragments of "Character in Fiction" and by the draft of "Thunder at Wembley," called "Nature at Wembley." It seems only appropriate that in the completed novel Peter Walsh also feels disjointed after his voyage in from India. Like Rhoda's "proud and splendid province" in *The Waves*, and like the menagerie's exotic animals on display at the Empire Exhibition's "Olde Englishe Faire," Peter too seems to be conjured up out of one of the "dark," penumbral spaces of the world. Over the London to which Peter returns, Big Ben's "leaden circles" sound and then "dissolve in the air," binding his experience of the city to his place in the imperial scheme of *Mrs. Dalloway*. As Peter rushes out of the Dalloways' home, having compromised himself to Clarissa in a moment of vulnerability, he "step[s] down the street, speaking to himself rhythmically, in time with the flow of the sound, the direct downright sound of Big Ben striking the half-hour. (The leaden circles dissolved in the air.)"[129] The content of Peter's speech, synchronized with the leaden rings, has to do with his self-aggrandizing imperial work: "All India lay behind him; plains, mountains, epidemics of cholera; a district twice as big as Ireland; decisions he had come to alone—he, Peter Walsh."[130] In this way, London, too, becomes an imperial space for Peter, behind which distant India stands.

Though these leaden circles appear to draw Peter's thoughts back to India, experiencing the space marked out as the center of the rings—Big Ben, Westminster, and London—becomes an estranging encounter for the Anglo-Indian. "Those five years—1918 to 1923—had been," Peter observes, "somehow very important. People looked different. Newspapers seemed different," and Peter finds that London begins to seem incompatible with his Indian experience.[131] As images of containment, the "leaden circles" seem to promise that imperial relations might be described holistically, and yet as they dissolve in the air they announce the radical contingency of such totalizations and allegorize the inevitable dissolution of the bonds holding the notion of empire together. Peter's encounter with the imperial city anticipates that of North Pargiter in *The Years* (1937), the farmer in colonial Africa who returns to London to find himself completely dislocated: "He had a feeling that he was no one and nowhere in particular," and in a moment of utter disorientation he registers not a position in space but rather that "somebody had chalked a circle on the wall with a jagged line in it."[132] Woolf's spreading circles encompass the territory they push across, but as they widen they simultaneously diminish in power, receding back into the "pale shadows on the utmost horizon" that Rhoda seeks to illuminate in *The Waves*. As images of containment, the "leaden circles" seem to offer the possibility that imperial relations might be bound within a totalizing figure, and yet as they dissolve in the air they announce the radical contingency of such totalizations. The imperial center as Woolf draws it—whether in Peter's and North's Londons, or in Wembley's British Empire Exhibition—asserts its force in the world only to have its power dissipate, its ambitions crossed as by some "jagged line," by some sign of excess.

In "Thunder at Wembley" Woolf presents a vision of the empire as a synchronic totality demolished by the storms of 1924; in *Between the Acts* she offers in Miss La Trobe's play a disruption of the kind of diachronic narrative presented in the "Pageant of Empire." The broken circles and ruptured visions of totality that appear throughout Woolf's writing are often accompanied by a pervasive melancholy, a melancholy that responds to a profound sense of loss—of meaning, of imaginative power, and even of the self. This loss is most often figured as a lost center: "the old cronies" complain, after Miss La Trobe's mirrors reveal the spectators as "orts, scraps and fragments," that "What we need is a centre. Something to bring us all together."[133] The Reverend Mr. Streatfield echoes this point of view about Miss La Trobe's pageant: "To me at least it was indicated that we are members one of another. Each is part of the whole. . . . Scraps, orts and fragments! Surely, we should unite?"[134] But such unity around a center is not a real interpretive possibility offered the audience in Miss La Trobe's pageant, nor a narrative luxury afforded the readers of Woolf's last novel. In *The Waves*, in the most striking instance of such a coordinating center, Percival himself is lost. Percival dies in an accident in India, removing from the narrative the imperialist who Rhoda claims "is like a stone fallen into a pond round which minnows swarm. Like minnows, we who had been shooting this way, that way, all shot round him when he came."[135] Such losses do not manifest themselves in the way that, for example, profligate expenditures tend to at the Bursley wakes or at Lord Curzon's Durbar; they are certainly not economic in any simple pecuniary sense. The "expenditures" in Woolf's fiction are imaginative ones, composed as they are of spatial and systemic absences, losses that nevertheless serve to structure a symbolic economy in Woolf's writing. It is in this symbolic sense—of the seemingly irremediable loss of the whole, of the centered self, and even of the symbol's adequacy to mean (though not to have significance)—that Woolf's imaginative responses to the imperial menagerie in particular and imperialism more generally open up considerations of what Georges Bataille calls "general economy," his figuration of a system predicated upon loss.

In the Shadow of the Verandah: Eclipsing the Central Star

In 1941, beyond the bounds of Virginia Woolf's writing career, Carl Sandburg noted that Woolf had remade the places of empire in her work as a kind of festival space: "The British Empire—her special and personal Empire—floats and sways as a bundle of toy balloons."[136] As I hope to have shown in these pages, if Woolf's "personal British Empire" in any way seems a "bundle of toy balloons," these are balloons that round themselves only to burst, like the leaden skies over Wembley in the summer of 1924. If Woolf made "personal" the British Empire, it is equally the case that the empire had a personal claim on her as well. In Leonard Woolf, of course, she married an ambivalent former colonial administrator. But her great-grandfather James Stephen married into the Wilberforce family and worked with the Clapham Sect to abolish the slave trade and to convert "heathens." More notably still, Woolf's grandfather Sir James Stephen has been called a "founder of Victorian imperialism" for his work in the Colonial Office.[137] One of Sir James's most enduring accomplishments is his totalizing characterization of the relation between Britain and its imperial holdings as that between a mother and her children; Sir James Stephen is widely credited with the popularization in colonialist discourse of the phrase "the mother country" to describe England.[138] Consequently, by the time Virginia Woolf matured as a writer, she was conscious of two related sets of tropes entailed upon her by her Victorian ancestors and literary predecessors, tropes that describe the spatial relations within the British Empire as a totality and that were freshly deployed by her contemporaries at the Empire Exhibition. One set describes England as the "mother country" and casts subject imperial spaces in the role of progeny, discrete entities bound to England through filial ties. The other set maps the empire as a space circumscribed by a great circle, the center of whose compass is "the mother country" itself.

The Waves, the novel in which elephants appear both menacing and decaying, offers a double vision in which women desire empire at precisely the moment empire threatens to collapse, highlighting the penumbral space of the verandah between imperial holism and dissolution. "A melodrama for beset imperialists," *The Waves* is set largely at the heart of empire and takes a cyclical frame, following the sun across the sky from dawn to dusk through to the promise of a new dawn.[139] Bernard, perhaps the narrator of the novel, pairs the act of telling stories with acts of totalization. As Bernard, Jinny, Neville, Louis, Rhoda, and Susan dine with Percival before he departs for India, Bernard wonders, "what are stories? Toys I twist, bubbles I blow, one ring passing through another."[140] This act of creation, of producing narratives as fragile wholes, is connected with another totalizing act of creation, for, he observes, "We are creators. . . . We too, as we put on our hats and push open the door, stride not into chaos, but into a world that our own force can subjugate and make part of the illumined and everlasting road."[141] Percival's death in India shatters this illusion, however, and Bernard finds the possibility of holism smashed, concluding that "We have destroyed something by our presence . . . a world perhaps."[142] By the end of Bernard's final section of narrative, darkness has spread over the "illumined and everlasting road," and he wonders, "How then does light return to the world after the eclipse of the sun? Miraculously. Frailly. In thin stripes. . . . It is a hoop to be fractured by a tiny jar."[143] As in *The Years*, in which North finds the circle that should give him his bearings canceled by the jagged line, Bernard finds English light a fragmented, unstable thing. As the book rounds upon itself as a new day begins, Bernard concludes that "The canopy of civilisation is burnt out. . . . There is a sense of the break of day. I will not call it dawn."[144] In rewriting the totalizing Victorian trope in which England appeared as the brilliant center of a solar system,[145] Bernard develops a sense of the fragility and contingency of empire, and Britain's radiance is eclipsed, its luminescence "burnt out." For Bernard, the fragile light of an Englishness under eclipse appears as a blind spot, a dark heart of an imperial existence: "What does the central shadow hold? Something? Nothing? I do not know."[146] The brilliance of Viceroy Curzon's metaphor of the "central star," the cynosure around which the empire revolves, is replaced by the "central shadow" of Englishness in eclipse, in a revision that recalls Marlow's ominous characterization of London as "one of the dark places of the earth" in *Heart of Darkness*.[147]

Yet it is not Bernard but Rhoda and Louis whose identities are most tightly bound up with the British Empire and whose language relies most heavily upon a rhetoric of rings and centers. During a math lesson Rhoda discovers that "The figures mean nothing . . . The clock ticks. The two hands are convoys marching through a desert. . . . The long hand has marched ahead to find water. . . . Look, the loop of the figure is beginning to fill with time; it holds the world in it. I begin to draw a figure and the world is looped in it. . . . The world is entire."[148] Rhoda's loops are literally totalizing figures, enabled by the colonial progress of time, and she conceives of the six "characters" in the novel as circling Percival, the imperialist, as minnows around a stone cast in a pond. Louis, Rhoda's lover, presents a colonial counterpoint to Rhoda's impulses. Because his father is a banker in Brisbane, Louis feels himself outside, though subject to, the machinations of English society. Where Rhoda imagines that she encompasses a world in her chalk figures, Louis contends that her mind merely "steps through those white loops into emptiness."[149] For Louis, the circle of empire that excludes him appears seamless, though he would like to find an aperture through which he might feel himself part of the center. He wonders, "Where then is the break in this continuity? What the fissure through which one sees disaster? The circle is unbroken; the harmony complete. . . . I watch it expand, contract; and then expand again. Yet I am not included."[150] Louis also realizes that his desire for inclusion in the "English Adventure" is a dangerous one, for he discovers in the end that "Life has been a terrible affair for me. I am like some vast sucker, some glutinous, some adhesive, some insatiable mouth. I have tried to draw from the living flesh the stone lodged at the centre."[151] Where Rhoda's desire to be "allowed to spread in wider and wider circles . . . that may at last . . . embrace the entire world"[152] leads to painful longings and her eventual suicide, Louis's desire for the center—for Englishness itself—is presented as equally horrific. As the circles advance yet diminish in an ever-widening sweep, the center itself appears under eclipse.

For Woolf the margins in which these figures expand and retreat is, like the railway carriage in which Mrs. Brown travels or the yard in which the woman wrings a dishcloth at the edge of the Empire Exhibition, the transitional space of the verandah—the arena in which the empire itself is dissipated as an inheritance. This dissipation is precisely to be celebrated alongside the bloated, decomposing elephant and the apocalypse at Wembley, as Peggy suggests in *The Years* in thinking about "living differently," in her incomplete vision of a new, postimperial wholeness. This vision's incompleteness does not trouble Woolf, for she like Peggy is content for the moment with an "in-betweenness," the suspension between empire as dissolving whole and a newly constituted postimperial holism. This "in-betweenness" finds expression in the form of modernist stylistics, which, as Woolf suggests in "Mr. Bennett and Mrs. Brown," cannot "just at present [offer] a complete and satisfactory presentment" of reality.[153] In Woolf's own fiction, symbols of dissolving circles and menacing and decomposing elephants serve to organize energies of imperial detotalization. Such detotalization, as in Bernard's consideration of the "fractured" nature of postimperial light that emerges "in thin stripes," also suggests that the diachronic totality of progressivist narrative is crossed by its other, so that loss and gain appear as complementary aspects of imperial dissolution and are bound up in a kind of general economy. This general economic devolution appears simultaneously as a kind of progress toward a new and whole world, of which the merest glimpses can be seen as in Peggy's vision in *The Years,* and in *Between the Acts* as a return to prehistory, to the primitive, to the "night before roads were made, or houses. It was the night that dwellers in caves had watched from some high place among rocks."[154] Late modernism appears as an era of decomposing elephants and the eclipse of Englishness; yet it also remains haunted by an era before camels, elephants, and monkeys marched across the pitch of Wembley and settled their bloated carcasses on the verandahs of realism for good.

Chapter 5

The "Anglepoised" Novel after Empire

English Creatures and Postcolonial Exhibition

NARRATIVES OF NOSTALGIA AND LOSS

VIRGINIA WOOLF WAS NOT THE only prominent modernist novelist to write about the menagerie's ubiquitous symbolic avatars. In the "Cyclops" episode of Joyce's *Ulysses* (1922), Leopold Bloom recalls the story of Jumbo and his London Zoo companion Alice; in "Nausikaa" he thinks about bears in the zoo; and in "Circe" he contemplates a howdahed, turbaned camel and lewd chimpanzees in the zoo.[1] In "Ithaca," moreover, Bloom imagines a kindergarten with a curriculum emphasizing properties with imperialist overtones: zoological biscuits and globemap playing balls. But in "Calypso" he scans his wife's sensational novel of circus life, *Ruby: The Pride of the Ring,* lamenting the "Cruelty behind it all. Doped animals," and again in "Circe"—an episode dominated by references to animals like gazelles, hyenas, and lions—he concludes that "All tales of circus life are highly demoralising."[2] Bloom's general ambivalence about the zoological collection—his indulgence in imagining the exotic beast on one hand, and his abhorrence of the material forms and practices of their exhibition on the other—anticipates a decline in the fortunes of nearly all forms of the menagerie in the twentieth century. Indeed, by the time of Djuna Barnes's *Nightwood* (1937), the circus appears not as a popular entertainment featuring animals drawn from exotic landscapes but as a repository for the aberrant forms of the human in Western Europe's domestic spaces; the version of the circus upon which Barnes draws operates largely outside the menagerie's imperial frames of reference.[3]

These developments in the modernist novel's treatment of the forms of the menagerie reflect the larger condition of English zoological displays in the postwar years. With the new dominance of foreign forms of showmanship, the rise of the cinema and mass-mediated attractions, and the revolt of public opinion against the most spectacular of animal displays, the exotic beast's profitability declined in the era of late modernism. By the late 1930s the traveling menagerie had all but vanished, and with a few exceptions the circus in England was dominated by American enterprise and rendered subordinate to the more genteel, metropolitan displays of zoos. The overhunting of animals and the destruction of habitat in Africa and Asia, homelands of the most attractive beasts on show in the nineteenth century, meant that British zoos themselves evolved in their missions away from displays that evoked far-flung spaces of empire and toward the conservation of rare and endangered species. Though the zoo remains fundamentally a collection of remarkable beasts—"like sentient plants, laid out as in flower-beds, objects of study, contemplation, surmise and fantasy," writes Angela Carter[4]—it no longer suggests in the first place that the wild animal's exotic environment is an imagined adjunct to domestic English life.

Instead, the zoo furnishes a substitute for it, an alternative total environment for the endangered animal. In *Minima Moralia* (1951) Theodor Adorno declared, "The whole is the false,"[5] and observed that only under the special dispensation of modernity,

> in the nooks and crannies of the cities, to which the walls, towers and bastions of the zoos wedged among them are merely an addition, can nature be conserved. The rationalization of culture, in opening its doors to nature, thereby completely absorbs it, and eliminates [along] with difference the principle of culture, the possibility of reconciliation.[6]

For Adorno, zoo animals in the second half of the twentieth century do not appear as avatars of the alien any more, but rather serve to mark an "abolished . . . exotic." Even as the British empire embarked upon its major programs of decolonization, Adorno suggested that modernity as a totalizing regime had already eliminated heterogeneity and difference. Where once zoos reflected the "nineteenth-century colonial imperialism . . . which paid symbolic tribute in the shape of animals" whose "value . . . was measured by their exoticism, their inaccessibility,"[7] zoological collections now represent the total triumph of a Western capitalism that has overwhelmed rather than come to terms with the alien.

To the extent that zoos continue to foster a sense of exoticism, they consign it to the past, evoke it in the form of nostalgia, and cultivate a sense of melancholy for what has been lost. As Adorno wittily puts it, "Zoological gardens . . . are laid out on the pattern of Noah's Ark [as] allegories of the specimen or the pair who defy the disaster that befalls the species *qua* species. This is why the over-richly stocked zoos of large European cities seem like forms of decadence: more than two elephants, two giraffes, one hippopotamus, are a bad sign."[8] The zoo as ark or heritage park consequently becomes part of "the history of aesthetic styles [that] displaces 'real' history" in Fredric Jameson's formulation, a way of cultural appearing that evokes an imperial past but without the material work of forging a cultural whole that the menagerie performed in late Victorian England.[9] Where the nineteenth century zoo, menagerie, and circus fostered a sense of the exotic as a descriptive or normative component of a larger whole, in the late twentieth century the surviving forms of zoological display appear as spaces of melancholic pastiche or remembrance of an "abolished exotic"—and, I want to argue, of nostalgia for the old forms of imperial totalization (even in Adorno's essays)—in the face of a new global environment that represents not the triumph of imperialism but the final abolition of the global unevenness upon which imperialism—and Englishness—depended.

In this environment, the collection of "wonder-fauna" does not appear any longer in the guise of picturesque ambition, delineating and materializing a burgeoning imperial whole, but instead functions to monumentalize the constriction of the world's "waste" space as the machinations of globalization deterritorialize national cultural life. Eleanor Pargiter's complaint in *The Years*, that "India's nothing nowadays . . . Travel's so easy," records this shrinkage of the globe in virtually the terms laid out by Thomas Cook himself: "This going round the world is a very easy and almost imperceptible business; there is no difficulty about it."[10] Instead, Eleanor's desire for "something different . . . another kind of civilisation" expresses a nostalgic longing for the spaces outside global history and beyond the range of Thomas Cook's package tours.[11] Likewise, the menagerie once celebrated England's expansion into novel, unbounded arenas, but in the late twentieth century it marked the "ero[sion] by infinite divisibility" (in Sartre's terms)[12] of the imperial landscape—memorializing the political idea of empire, the imaginative topography of the whole, and the enabling difference of jungle, savannah, and desert. Victoria called up these ideas when she ordered the many caravans of beasts in Wombwell's Menagerie and Sanger's Circus to Windsor Castle for viewings of "The British Lion Queen" and for feedings of the elephants. By contrast, the jubilee celebrations of Elizabeth II featured only "Pete White's Suitcase Circus," a one-man show that stripped the notion of "circus" of all vestiges of the bestial and the exotic, confining its performances to clowning and displays of balance. The difference between Sanger's and White's performances is telling for the corresponding worldviews they represent, and the last gifts of animals to the Queen occurred in 1976 (an armadillo and anteater from Brazil).

Yet the absence of animals from "Pete White's Suitcase Circus" and from royal tribute should not suggest that traces of zoological exoticism and imperial nostalgia do not continue to mark British culture in important ways—indeed, this concluding chapter is devoted to an exploration of the ways in which three novels of the last two decades of the twentieth century engage the logic and traditions of the menagerie—but it does highlight a sea change in the configurations of British popular culture in decades that witnessed a dramatic shift in British imperial policies as well as the assimilation of postmodernism in the British novel. The circus or menagerie comes to appear as a formal space of remembrance, of anxious conservation rather than ambitious totalization, and of nostalgia for a totality from which Englishness can be distilled. This reimagining of the menagerie as a space of remembrance—especially as a space commemorating loss—accompanies a similar shift in the novel. At the end of the twentieth century, loss comes to be inscribed in the English novel as a governing formal and thematic principle. Novels in this period seem to take for granted the efficacy of Bataille's "general economic" principles, as postimperial hybridity, excess, contingency, and provisionality stand in place of totality as imaginative horizons, while a decentered global capitalism appears as the inheritor of English imperialism, in an entailment that simultaneously provincializes Englishness. The exhibition, once the space in which imperial totality was asserted, becomes a space of negotiating a postimperial Englishness.

The World at One's Feet: Rushdie and Postcolonial Exhibition

In the last decade of the century in which Britain's global sweep reached its limits and receded, what can it mean for an Irish showman to have exhibited an Indian on a stage in London, the spectacular center of what was once the world's most extensive empire? Moreover, how can we make sense of the fact that this exhibition in the early 1990s itself formed part of a larger display that represented itself as a zoo? Given the long colonial history of the *zoo humain* and of imperial exhibition, we ought to think carefully about what such a display can tell us about the politics of postcolonial representation. Here, for instance, is Salman Rushdie writing in 1982 about the way in which the zoo is a site marking the persistence of imperial frames of reference:

> Recently, on a radio programme, a professional humorist asked me, in all seriousness, why I objected to being called a wog. He said he had always thought it a rather charming word, a term of endearment. "I was at the zoo the other day," he revealed, "and a zoo keeper told me that the wogs were best with the animals; they stuck their fingers in their ears and wiggled them about and the animals felt at home."[13]

The comedian's unhappy anecdote resonates with a neocolonial logic: the British zoo is the site in which expatriate and exiled Indians, on one hand, and imported, traded, and bred animals, on the other, can feel "at home" together under the mark of the exotic. These terms dictate that the British institution can never *be* a proper home for the exhibited animal (or for the transplanted Indian, for that matter), and the zoo remains a site pervaded by a sense of coerced displacement. According to the humorist's narrative, the performance of the Indian naturalizes the zoo, makes the exhibition itself complete, and charms the captive animals into a sense of being "at home."

Such a formulation as Rushdie rejects here makes it all the more uncanny, *unheimlich* to find that ten years after his essay "Imaginary Homelands," the Indian on display in Britain's premier space of exhibition is none other than Rushdie himself, produced by U2 from the wings of the stage at Wembley during the band's *Zooropa* tour (1993). At the time of Rushdie's appearance on stage, the stadium at Wembley was itself notable as the sole surviving building from the Empire Exhibitions of 1924 and 1925, a structure built to the special demands of the exhibition: to stage the opening and closing ceremonies over which the King and the Royal Family presided, as well as the three-day-long Pageant of Empire. The scene at Wembley in 1924 was, as we saw in chapter 4, one of elephants lumbering toward the stadium along streets bearing names chosen by Rudyard Kipling, processing in step to Elgar marches, and of Indians—transplanted from the subcontinent—on view as they wove baskets in the "native villages" meant to convey the breadth and diversity of Britain's empire. If in the humorist's version of the zoo the Indian serves to make the exotic animals at home as part of an exhibitionary whole, at the Empire Exhibition of 1924 Indians and other exotic people were exhibited to make British subjects feel at home with the idea of empire as a global project.

The picture at Wembley almost seventy years later was, of course, superficially quite different: gone were the ferroconcrete models of the Old London Bridge and the Taj Mahal, Kipling's lanes and Elgar's strains, the elephants and the weavers. Nevertheless, in the 1990s Rushdie, like so many Indians in 1924 and 1925, "*found himself,* for a few minutes, up on the Wembley stage," apparently through no agency of his own, on view in the "cage of light" that fronted the stage and divided the spectators from the show.[14] The impresario of this exhibition was U2's Bono, in his "white-faced, gold-lamé-suited, red-velvet-horned MacPhisto incarnation."[15] In Rushdie's account of his experience in the Wembley arena, this diabolic Bono also figures as one of the animals on show: "when I looked into [Bono's] face on the Wembley stage I saw a stranger there, and understood that this was the Star-creature that normally lay hidden in him, a creature as powerful as the big beastie it sang to, so overwhelming that it could be let out only in this cage of light."[16] The performer Bono, we might say, makes both the "Star-creature" aspect of himself and "the big beastie it sang to" (the crowd of thousands) feel at home, while his exhibition of a vulnerable Rushdie produces a broad sense of daring, of (counter)cultural unity, and of aesthetic solidarity: the ostensible reason for the presentation of Rushdie to the "big beastie" is that "U2 wanted to make a gesture of solidarity," in a time in which Rushdie was threatened both by the fatwa issued against him and by the British media.[17]

Where is Rushdie's place here, and on what terms is such solidarity established? Can any performance make him feel "at home" in Wembley's cage of light? It turns out that the author's appearance was volitional after all, since "Bono called to ask if I'd like to come out onstage."[18] Yet in offering himself up to the band to be exhibited, Rushdie submits not only to be framed within what was once a prime symbolic space of the British Empire but also to be conscripted into the service of a new dynamic of power remapping the world. Recalling his travels in Nicaragua in the late 1980s, Rushdie writes about a woman who does not recognize Bono's name: "Tell me, who is Bono?" she asks. Rather than understanding the woman's question to signal the relatively circumscribed province of English-language pop music, Rushdie instead presses the woman and her society into the margins of the globe: "the question was as vivid a demonstration of her country's beleaguered isolation as anything I heard or saw in the front-line villages, the destitute Atlantic Coast bayous, or the quake-ravaged city streets."[19] The Irish rock band becomes the very touchstone by means of which connectedness or globality—and its counterparts, backwardness and isolation—should be measured: do we recognize the interpellative challenge of *Achtung Baby* (U2's 1991 album) or don't we? Do we feel "at home" within the confines of *Zooropa* (1993), comforted by its promises that each of us can "be a winner" and "be all that [we] can be,"[20] or will we find ourselves consigned to "destitut[ion]" and "beleaguered isolation"?

In framing these questions so absolutely, I do not mean to suggest that by appearing at Wembley Rushdie suddenly and unthinkingly acquiesced in a kind of global neoimperialism (he is not quite the unregenerate "Businessist" described by one of his novel's narrators,[21] for instance), or that he has abandoned altogether the searching, skeptical politics outlined in earlier essays such as "Commonwealth Literature Does Not Exist" and "The New Empire Within Britain." Despite his recent writing in support of the U.S. "war on terrorism" and his blanket criticism of Islamist politics, plenty of evidence remains of Rushdie's suspicion of easy pieties when it comes to international and global politics. Likewise, the heavy ironies of U2's vision of *Zooropa* or the graphic kitsch of *Achtung Baby* should not be understood in the mode of the earlier *War*, as a kind of high earnestness: the playfully juxtaposed fragments of cliché and Western military and consumer advertisement ("be all that you can be"; "eat to get slimmer") constitute this sardonically dystopic "Zooropa." The politics of exhibition, of showmanship, of display, in popular as well as traditionally "literary" registers, persist as central problems here, and the echoes of the imperialist pageants of the 1920s invite me to ask what difference postcoloniality makes to the ways in which we represent the world as a whole. Salman Rushdie and U2 alike are bound up with this politics just as surely as they are with the history of Wembley when they mount the boards of its stage and stand in the "cage of light."

Exhibitionary rhetorics of empire have, as these chapters have shown, tended to be totalizing, and the space of Wembley's Empire Exhibition was conspicuously marked by gestures toward totality, as Virginia Woolf and her colleagues recognized. The empire's great human and geographic diversity required a significant investment of imaginative energy to render it in a mode of solidarity, of holism, and the spectacle of the Empire Exhibition represented perhaps the last large-scale totalizing cultural project of the imperium. Three-quarters of a century later, Rushdie notes emphatically that the project has failed in the end, since "Europe's empires are long gone,"[22] and we can state definitively that the totality that the Empire Exhibition sought to conjure up has dissolved, if it was ever really constituted at all. At the end of the twentieth century, the 220 acres of Wembley's exhibition space were reduced to a stadium that hosted domestic football cups and served as the ground for Mick Jagger and the Rolling Stones to commemorate both the heyday of the "British Invasion" and the inauguration of the pop "world tour" (Rushdie writes about the Stones at Wembley, too, concluding that they hardly seem "dangerous" and are "no longer . . . a threat to decent, civilized society"[23]). The recession of this imaginative or performative power that rendered Britain's global aspirations whole means that the British must abandon the notion of world empire as "a kind of transcendence," for "in empire's aftermath, [the British] have been pushed back into their box, their frontier has closed in on them like a prison."[24] Totalizing exhibitions in the imperial mode can no longer adequately represent such a world of contractions and devolutions.

No less an exhibitionary instrument than the palimpsestic space of Wembley, the novel and its own totalizing aspirations have at times appeared to follow a similar trajectory of dissolution and decline. In the decade following the Empire Exhibition at Wembley, George Orwell expressed his conviction that the novel, if not utterly doomed, was at least destined "to survive in some perfunctory, despised, and hopelessly degenerate form, like . . . the Punch and Judy Show," a reified vestige of an earlier, living, plastic exhibit.[25] More recently, Rushdie has argued against this narrative of decline, pointing out that "the half century whose literary output [in Europe ostensibly] proves . . . the novel's decline is also the first half century of the post-colonial period."[26] The novel, Rushdie suggests, may now properly be the province not of "the old imperial powers," which have a "new, diminished status in the post-colonial world,"[27] but of that postcolonial world that rises into view even as those older powers recede.

This formulation in which "Zooropa"—the collection of erstwhile colonial powers—shifts into the background, consigned to play on "the cramped boards of home,"[28] while postcolonial writing moves toward front and center of what the Empire Exhibition called "the great stage of the world" might begin to answer the question of what it means to exhibit the Indian at Wembley in the 1990s: postcolonial cultural production, in the form of an Irish rock band and an Indian novelist, overwhelms the attenuated symbolic spaces of a contracted empire. It is nevertheless worth pressing our inquiries further to ask about the difference that such a protrusion of the postcolonial makes to narrating the global and—since Rushdie is in the first place a novelist—more particularly to the novel as exhibitionary vehicle. The exhibitionary mode survives richly in Rushdie's own fiction: *The Ground Beneath Her Feet* (1999), the words of which U2 set to music, is about the self-display of a globe-trotting pop star; *The Satanic Verses* (1988) features a set of television and film personalities and performers at its center; and a recent Rushdie protagonist (Malik Solanka in *Fury* [2001]) designs puppets that dominate global pop culture.

Before these, though, there was *Midnight's Children* (1981), which Rushdie has himself characterized as "the stuff of showmanship and myth."[29] Rushdie's first blockbuster book enacts its pageant of India in the lingering light of English novels such as Thackeray's *Vanity Fair,* whose narrator also sets himself up as a showman—"the Manager of the Performance"—and whose characters appear as "puppets." Rushdie's self-anatomizing narrator Saleem Sinai acknowledges the persistence of what we might call the Anglo literary twilight, paying homage to its traditions through his own "Anglepoise-lit writing."[30] Saleem's characterization of his postcolonial narrative in these terms simultaneously signals that British cultural authority lingers in a newly born India and acknowledges the peculiarly skewed perspective (poised at an angle) of the show he mounts on "the great stage of the world." Unlike Thackeray's Manager or Bono's MacPhisto, however, Saleem as Anglepoised impresario exercises only a compromised authority over his performance: he can hardly hold himself together, much less maintain the integrity of his narrative. Saleem nevertheless persists in offering up the showman as the essential type of the storyteller. While he sometimes acknowledges that "entertainers would [repeatedly] orchestrate my life," unwittingly describing the passive role that Rushdie himself seems to assume on the Wembley stage, Saleem also recalls that he himself once "performed the function of barker. 'Roll up roll up—once in a life-time an opportunity such as this—ladees, ladahs, come see come see come see!'"[31]

Saleem's role as barker calls up not only custom for his friend Picture Singh, the snake charmer, but also the memory of the peepshow man Lifafa Das, whose cries beckon, "See the whole world, come see everything!" while he attempts to cram everything into his peepshow.[32] Here is Saleem's nearest approximation of the 1924 Empire Exhibition: Lifafa Das's peepshow, like Wembley, promises to deliver the whole world in one space, but unlike the exhibition the peepshow's expansive vision is cobbled together out of an arbitrary selection of mass-produced picture postcards. As a totalizing strategy, it is contingent upon the availability of images produced elsewhere and encountered by chance; it reflects the serendipity of the world's networks, rather than the determinism of the systematic all-red routes mapped out in Wembley displays, and as Timothy Brennan points out, *Midnight's Children* is preoccupied with such new networks and "communications."³³ That Lifafa Das's exhibition might be understood to form one of the symbolic centers of the novel is suggested by the script for a planned British television film of *Midnight's Children* that never came to pass; in the script Lifafa Das rather than Saleem introduces each of the episodes of Saleem's life through his peepshow.³⁴ The efforts of the novelized Lifafa Das to collect and display the whole world through postcards reminds Saleem of a similar model of encapsulating the world in another, higher cultural register: he describes "a painter whose paintings had grown larger and larger as he tried to get the whole of life into his art. 'Look at me,' he said before he killed himself, 'I wanted to be a miniaturist and I've got elephantiasis instead!'"³⁵ Although Saleem's narrative presents the painter's story as a fantastic episode, the miniaturist's compulsion to include everything merely offers another version of G. K. Chesterton's rationale for the Empire Exhibition: "It seems to me that man has made things almost too great for his own imagination to measure. . . . It is to be hoped that people will learn to appreciate what is large precisely because they see it when it is little."³⁶ While the English Chesterton celebrates miniaturization, however, the Indian painter despairs of his "elephantiasis."

Although Saleem can be found in the role of coordinating showman or barker near the end of his Anglepoised story, more frequently he offers himself up as just the sort of miniature, peepshow, or exhibition that Lifafa Das and the painter struggle to orchestrate: "to know me, just the one of me, you'll have to swallow the lot as well. Consumed multitudes are jostling and shoving inside me."³⁷ Saleem would have us believe that he is himself a *zoo humain:* not merely a metaphorical exhibition of typical humanity but a single human being containing within him a comprehensive collection of global types. "To understand me," Saleem insists again near the end of his narrative, "you'll have to swallow a world."³⁸ Yet Saleem himself does not swallow a world—rather, he buries it. He recalls having "a world of [my] own," made up of

> Two cheap metal hemispheres, clamped together by a plastic stand. . . . It was a world full of labels: *Atlantic Ocean* and *Amazon* and *Tropic of Capricorn*. And, at the North Pole, it bore the legend: MADE AS ENGLAND. . . . [T]his tin world had lost its stand; I found Scotch Tape and stuck the earth together at the Equator, and then, my urge for play overcoming my respect, began to use it as a football . . . , secure in the knowledge that the world was still in one piece (although held together by adhesive tape) and also at my feet.³⁹

Saleem soon inters this globe in the yard as a time capsule devoted to remembering his own historical role, offering up another, material version of his autobiographical narrative as a whole. Years later, upon his return to his childhood home, he digs it up with great nostalgia.[40] As allegory, this "world" realizes what Saleem describes as the Indian "national longing for form"—an "obsess[ion] with correspondences" and a conviction "that forms lie hidden within reality; that meaning reveals itself only in flashes."[41] The form of Saleem's world is itself imperfectly Anglepoised: it is a globe made in England's image, but this resemblance is acknowledged in a compromised, or at least improvised, language ("MADE AS ENGLAND"): this is an English world scored by difference. In another sense, though, it is a world no longer "poised" at all, since it has nothing to stand on, nothing coordinated—like a global empire or a world system—to clamp it together. Instead, its integrity is improvised, bound together with whatever is at hand; the world once "MADE AS ENGLAND" is—like Lifafa Das's peepshow—rendered whole only serendipitously, articulated by and contingent upon whatever binding agent is available. The form of this globe is uneven and battered, but it nevertheless conveys the impression of being "in one piece" through Saleem's active work of binding it together. Finally, it rests comfortably at Saleem's feet, characterized by the promise of the future rewards of global "play."

As a metaphor extending across hundreds of pages, Saleem's globe assumes its special significance only when it is recuperated after being buried and forgotten. That old, battered world of dubious integrity becomes a repository of memory, a way of remembering the initial promise of the postcolonial—the sense of having "the world at one's feet" after decolonization—in a less happy time of neocolonial oppression. The "postcolonial world" that Rushdie champions in his defense of the novel is, of course, not one thing, much less one world, and the incongruity of the globe "MADE AS ENGLAND" with the world as it appears in the time of Indira Gandhi's emergency measures signals the temporal and spatial discontinuities of "the" postcolonial itself. Saleem's "Anglepoised" writing appears to be complicit with this older order of the globe, and he struggles to come to terms with the contemporary world, a world that resists the sort of exhibition typified by Saleem's globe or the Empire Exhibition. Saleem's attempt to comprehend his contemporary world therefore draws upon the older totalizing tropes: he wonders, "is this an Indian disease, this urge to encapsulate the whole of reality? Worse, am I infected, too?"[42] But this is not a specifically Indian disease, communicable as it is through residual exhibitionary rhetorics of empire: Saleem's affliction is, at least in part, a function of his identity as an Anglepoised writer, made as England. Brennan notes that Saleem casts himself in the role of Ganesh, who "provides the culmination of national style. . . . [Saleem's] style is from Ganesh, Rushdie implies, simply because it represents *Midnight's Children's* and India's *elephantiasis* of style."[43] For Brennan, Ganesh's "style amounts to the chaotic 'sum total of everything'—an appropriate paradigm for diversity, but . . . 'everything' means not just India. If neither Saleem nor [his companion] Padma create[s] 'true' national images, it is because the truth of postwar nationalism is international."[44] Under Brennan's reading, Saleem as elephant-headed writer is authentically Indian, suffering from elephantiasis, the "Indian disease," and—in attempting to represent his world—offering the elephant-god as an image of globality. I would suggest, though, that Ganesh as Indian style, India as elephant(iasis), is at least in part an illusory image cast by the Anglepoised light of Saleem's narrative itself: Saleem notes that "January 26th, Republic Day, is a good time for illusionists. When the huge crowds gather to watch elephants and fireworks, the city's tricksters go out to earn their living."[45] The spectacle of the elephant becomes a diversion from, and alibi for, more significant things happening elsewhere: while "the colorful, touristic elephant-taxi India . . . is presently being sold to the world," Rushdie notes in a recent essay, entire states are suffering from drought and disease.[46] The author hopes that such Anglepoised diversions will cease, that the "fake glamorizing is coming to an end, and the India of elephants, tigers, peacocks, emeralds, and dancing girls is being laid to rest."[47] This is the exotic India of the menageries, circuses, and imperial exhibitions, which can never appear to be at home in Britain and Europe *except* in the extraordinary space of display. We ought consequently to be wary of the way in which Saleem's assumption of Ganesh's mantle also functions as an illusion, a diversion.

From what is such an Anglepoised discourse of postcolonial exhibition diverting us? Is it possible to lay to rest—indeed, to bury—the zoological, exhibitionary India and still feel, with confidence and optimism, that the world is whole and at one's feet? Ian Baucom argues that "the challenge of the global is that of rethinking the form of the globe—rethinking the globe not . . . as a sort of Wallersteinian world system . . . but as something closer to a route work."[48] Saleem's narrative does not necessarily perform this "route work," invested as it still is in that older globe, "MADE AS ENGLAND." It does, though, investigate what Baucom calls the "hauntological": while global expansion concentrates political, financial, and cultural power in discrete nodes (global cities such as London and New York, for instance), the enrichment of these global nodes also renders them "the scenes of the haunting return of difference."[49] The "great stage of the world" in this aspect of globality will be haunted by the differential performances not only of the past but also of the present—perhaps in the way that Saleem is haunted by the vision of his still-alive sister's slowly decaying face, which superimposes itself upon that of his lover Parvati in moments of intimacy. Under the machinations of the "hauntological," Bono's exhibition of Rushdie at Wembley must inevitably bear traces of those earlier Wembley exhibitions: "Zooropa" will continue to be marked by the vestiges of its past performances on the global stage, as well as by the consequences of its current acts on the cramped boards of home. It should perhaps also be haunted by another kind of difference, the "beleaguered isolation" from globalization's chief "route work" that pointedly asks, "Who is Bono?" Avoiding the hauntological altogether in an era of increasing globality is perhaps impossible, although several tropes present themselves as routes of avoidance. There is the Romantic drive to escape and to forget global geometries—and zoogeographies—of power altogether: "I want to run / I want to hide / ... / Where the streets have no name," sang Bono on 1987's album *The Joshua Tree*.[50] There is also the fatalism that understands such geographies of power to be fixed, inevitable: *Midnight's Children's* Mary Pereira insists that it is "No good worrying. . . . Better you drink your Coke; nothing is going to change."[51] Such impulses to forget or concede the form of the networks continually battering and binding our globe (no longer "MADE AS ENGLAND") work despite themselves to secure what Rushdie in a meditation on globalization calls "the metamorphosis of Planet Earth into McWorld,"[52] a world in which all of us run the haunting risk of being permanently out of place in the *zoo humain*, and in which no mere performance or conventional story can make us feel "at home."

Circus Animals' Desertions: Carter's *Nights at the Circus*

"I'm here to write a story," says the journalist Jack Walser to the aerialist named "Fevvers" at the center of Angela Carter's *Nights at the Circus* (1984). "Story about the circus. About you and the circus."[53] In critics' hands, *Nights at the Circus* has been read almost exclusively as a story about gender and the performance of individual identity—that is, about Fevvers rather than about the circus, or about the "Britannic Angel" (as she is also called) in relation to the circus. This is hardly surprising, since the novel's female protagonist, named for the extraordinary feathered wings that spread from her back, emphasizes the theatricality of her femininity in her exchanges with Walser, who follows her from the London stage (part I) to Colonel Kearney's circus in St. Petersburg (part II) and on to the wastes of Siberia (part III). Such readings tend not to consider a whole range of other cultural phenomena littered across the landscape of the novel, however: for instance, the espionage of Lizzie, Fevvers's surrogate mother, on behalf of British Marxists; the exploration of the spread of "white history" across the globe; and the arrangement of zoological exotica at the heart of the novel. Critical attention has tended to overlook the fact that *Nights at the Circus* explicitly identifies the circus as a material arena for the staging of all kinds of stories and performances about Englishness, about empire and global capitalism, and indeed about storytelling itself.[54]

This is especially curious since the narrative audience of *Nights at the Circus* must sign on to the story about the circus in order to get the other story—about gender and performance—in much the same way that Jack Walser must join Colonel Kearney's outfit to get closer to Fevvers and her history (though at one point he removes Fevvers altogether from his list of motives, concluding that he joined up only "to delight my reading public with accounts of a few nights at the circus").[55] Kearney's circus features elephants, a tiger, chimpanzees, and a sapient pig among the most important of its acts, along with a large contingent of clowns and a number of novelty acts like the strongman, Fevvers's aerialism, and the Ape-Man. It appears on the grand scale of "Lord" George Sanger's historical operation at the end of the nineteenth century, though with a Kentuckian rather than an Englishman for a proprietor, and with the para-imperial ambition of going Hannibal one better and sending elephants across the tundra of Asia. Despite its spectacular presence in the novel, and despite Carter's claim that the heart of the novel "is very elaborately plotted, like a huge circus with the ring in the middle," Kearney's circus, its para-imperialist echoes, and its place at the intersection of several master narratives have attracted relatively little attention in a growing body of criticism on the novel.[56]

This is, I think, because *Nights at the Circus* itself resists totalization in the conventional terms in which Dickens's, Bennett's, or even Woolf's novels might be read. That it does not present itself as a simple totality follows not only from its mode as an exuberantly picaresque tale "that . . . moves inexorably onward, ever onward, generating stories out of stories,"[57] but from something more fundamental to Angela Carter's notion of the genre itself. Carter's conception of the novel strips it of much of its usual definition as a comprehensive whole constructed from a single perspective or series of perspectives, even as it expands possibilities beyond limits. By contrast with the work of Arnold Bennett, Henry James, and E. M. Forster to consolidate a definition of the novelist's craft, Carter insists that "anything that wants to call itself a novel is a novel, by definition," and "so fiction can do anything it wants to do. I think it can do more things than we tend to think it can."[58] In Carter's formulation, the novel has no defining signature except for the author's imprimatur—if that. To the extent that the novel might be said to constitute a totality, it is a consequence of an interpretive effort to meet the expectation that a given narrative appear as a total aesthetic object that offers up a whole world in its content. When Carter says that the novel "can do more things than we tend to think it can," she should be understood to outline a reading strategy as well: an approach to *Nights at the Circus* that would do justice to the possibility that the novel "can do more things" than its traditional theory accounts for might have to be able to hold two or more mutually exclusive ways of reading in mind at once.

Under such a dispensation, *Nights at the Circus* appears as a total work of art only to the extent that we can understand it to demand a complementarity of critical perspective, in which two mutually exclusive possibilities are entertained, *both of which* are necessary for the novel to fulfill its "role and responsibility in helping to explain experience and making the world comprehensible," as Carter says.[59] Put otherwise, Walser's ambition to write the "story of you and the circus" might be understood to engender two divergent critical strands, one exploring Fevvers and gender performativity (the "story of you") and one concentrating on the broad historical dynamics that the circus constellates (the "story of the circus"). While such a theory necessarily implies a certain loss of meaning in the reading process (to the extent that it is impossible to bring into concert two ways of reading simultaneously, rather than serially), nevertheless it also has the merit of doing justice to Carter's frequent identification of herself as both a feminist and a materialist.

Sally Robinson's persuasive argument that "*Nights at the Circus* plays fast and loose with mythologies of difference, pushing official narratives of gender to their limits in order to dismantle them"[60] might stand for one of these perspectives. The chief emblem for these official narratives (or technologies) of gender in the novel is the panopticon, which a Russian countess constructs for the rehabilitation of women who have killed their husbands:

> It was a *panopticon* she forced them to build, a hollow circle of cells shaped like a doughnut, the inward-facing wall of which was composed

of grids of steel and, in the middle of the roofed, central courtyard, there was a round room surrounded by windows. In that room [the Countess would] sit all day and stare and stare and stare at her murderesses and they, in turn, sat all day and stared at her.[61]

Carter claims that her work offered a series of "straightforwardly intellectual arguments,"[62] and the panopticon in *Nights at the Circus* constitutes a figure deliberately lifted from Foucault's *Discipline and Punish* and dropped into Siberia in order to illustrate the way in which the dominant forms of femininity work to discipline wayward subjects through the spectacularization of gender. In other words, Carter adapts to feminist analysis what Foucault terms the "carceral complex." The panopticon is "official," in Robinson's terms, as a technology of the state, while the imprisoned women's deepening love for one another offers an analogy of the way in which female-centered communities might "dismantle" the imprisoning disciplinary complexes of gender.

The possibility of a second perspective, complementary to the one ranged around panoptical femininity, is laid out by Mary Russo, who suggests that *Nights at the Circus* "seems to have gone beyond the more individualistic psychic model of spectacularity . . . to map an historical and even global notion of spectacle."[63] Such an alternative map unfolds along a geopolitical axis of cultural formation, rather than in the terms of individual gender performances and the psychological processes of identity formation that dominate Robinson's reading. A striking contrast to the panopticon in Siberia, the chief emblem for this form of spectacularity is the circus itself, the totalizing exhibition of human and zoological exotica. "A circus is always a microcosm" of the world, Carter contends in an interview, and within the bounds of the narrative Lizzie makes the same point: she proposes that the circus represents "a microcosm of humanity" and notes that "we were an emblematic company, each signifying a different proposition in the great syllogism of life."[64]

At the center of the circus that, like Saleem in *Midnight's Children*, contains emblematic multitudes is the totalizing figure of the ring itself, the "magic circle" that the novel's narrator describes as

> a cheap, convenient, expressionist device, this sawdust ring, this little O! Round like an eye, with a still vortex in the centre; but give it a little rub as if it were Aladdin's wishing lamp and, instantly, the circus ring turns into that durably metaphoric, uroboric snake with its tail in its mouth, wheel that turns full circle, the wheel whose end is its beginning, the

wheel of fortune, the potter's wheel on which our clay is formed, the wheel of life on which we all are broken.⁶⁵

Against the Foucauldian resonances of the panopticon, which epitomizes the novel's concern about the pervasive regulation of individual gender performances, the circus ring evokes Tony Bennett's exhibitionary complex, complementary to carceral regimes but describing the spectacularization of totality rather than of individuality. As in her deployment of the panopticon, Carter's description of the ring offers a series of "straightforwardly intellectual arguments": it emphasizes the way in which the circus commands spectatorial focus (it is "round like an eye"); it appropriates the language of early modernists like Wyndham Lewis's Vorticists, who condemned the circus's Victorian associations, and redeploys it in service of the exhibition (the circus has "a still vortex at the centre"); and it evokes a climate of orientalism when it alludes to "Alladin's wishing-lamp," in an echo of late Victorian exoticism such as that of taxidermist Rowland Ward, who described his assemblages as a kind of zoological "wishing-carpet of the East." The circus ring in *Nights at the Circus*, Brian H. Finney notes, "constitutes a figurative representation of the world at large,"⁶⁶ and Carter's novel deserves to be read in the company of Victorian and modernist narratives that also engage the totalizing dynamics of the imperial menagerie as well as in relation to the individual politics of gender performance. After all, she says, "my fiction is very often a kind of literary criticism."⁶⁷

How, then, does *Nights at the Circus* deal with the circus as a material fact, the world as a totality, and the novel as a form of literary criticism? While Carter observes that "All fictional animals are imaginary animals,"⁶⁸ her practice as a materialist is to render the imaginary—including the imagined animal—as concrete as possible, in a reversal of Dickens's strategy of dematerializing the Asiatic elephant in *Hard Times*. As Fevvers insists, the trajectory of her story moves insistently toward a perspective from which the idea will be "no longer an imagined fiction but a plain fact."⁶⁹ To concretize the "imagined fiction" is a strategy she deploys particularly in the mode of literary pastiche, which she honed in her earlier *The Bloody Chamber* (1979) by focusing on the materiality of animals in fairy tales. Consequently, where Woolf's *The Waves* opens with an elephant in chains stamping on the beach, a simultaneously menacing and pathetic figure that finds currency only through Louis's distinctive focalization, in *Nights at the Circus* Carter renders substantive Woolf's emblematic elephant, making it and its kind both material and public once again—not as an individually imagined fiction or a deeply coded symbol but as a plain diegetic fact. The narrator reports

> the faint jingling of Colonel Kearney's elephants of flesh and blood as they rattled the chains on their legs as they did continually, all their waking hours, since in their millennial and long-lived patience they knew quite well how, in a hundred years, or a thousand years' time, or else, perhaps, tomorrow, in an hour's time, for it was all a gamble, a million to one chance, but all the same there *was* a chance that if they kept on shaking their chains, one day, some day, the clasps upon the shackles would part.[70]

The insistence upon "flesh and blood" in Carter's circus distinguishes it from the figurative work of Woolf and of Dickens: where, as Leavis notes, Dickens strips the circus of grossness and vulgarity in his narrative, Carter restores them at the very heart of hers, putting on display among other things gluttony, alcoholic excess, selfishness, libertinism, and—what Joyce's Bloom laments—displays of deliberate cruelty.

One way to trace the trajectory of the geopolitics of the exhibitionary collection in the novel, then, is through the concrete, "flesh and blood" figures of the circus. In St. Petersburg, Colonel Kearney's "flesh and blood" circus animals straining against their shackles come to displace the less impressive animals in the menagerie of the Russian Imperial Circus, the entrance to whose building is

> flanked on either side by ten-foot stone caryatids, splashed with pigeon droppings, in the shape of caparisoned elephants, squatting on their hind legs and holding their front legs up in the air. Such were the guardian spirits of the place, the elephants, the pillars of the circus itself who uphold the show upon the princely domes of their foreheads as they do the Hindu cosmos.[71]

Around the figures of the elephants, Carter's narrator concretizes the tropical (making "the pillars of the circus" the literal columns upholding the circus building) and renders tropical what is in the first instance concrete (the "ten-foot stone caryatids" symbolically appear to sustain both the circus's performative work and a worldview or cosmos).

The relation between the two forms of the elephant appears simultaneously monumentalizing and phantasmatic. Buried deep beneath these stone monuments or simulacra, "[u]nder the ring, in the cellarage" rest Colonel Kearney's "flesh and blood" elephants, interred in a kind of mausoleum that is the "menagerie [of] imperial beasts."[72] The stone elephants serve as memorials to the "flesh and blood" animals resting beneath them in this "forlorn place."[73] Yet as the "guardian spirits" of the circus, the beasts buried deep within the Imperial Circus haunt the place with a "perpetual, soft jangle as the elephants within the building agitate their chains."[74] In his reminiscences of his life as a showman, George Sanger made much of the fact that in December 1850 he unknowingly staged a series of pantomimes, lion tamings, mock bearbaitings, and a masquerade ball in an old charnel house, in the silent company of "over a hundred barrels of human bones and remains, and, as a sort of grim joke, the coffin of the minister himself [which], instead of being removed, had been cemented up in the floor."[75] Carter's narrative appears to invert Sanger's grim circus story, burying the living while elevating the inanimate above them, and rendering both oddly spectral or phantasmatic.

This method produces a kind of vacillation in the space of the circus between what W. B. Yeats posed in "Byzantium" (1933) as "death-in-life" and "life-in-death," between monumental and accomplished art and "all complexities of mire or blood."[76] This space is occupied not just by Colonel Kearney's elephants in the cellarage of the Imperial Circus but also by the British troupe of clowns, whose leader is Buffo, "the Clown of Clowns" and "a great patriot, British to the bone, even if as widely travelled as the British Empire in the service of fun."[77] Buffo specializes in the "Dance of disintegration; and of regression; celebration of the primal slime," and particularly in the art of "convulsive self-dismemberment."[78] In short, says the narrator, invoking Yeats's "The Second Coming" (1921), "Things fall apart at the very shiver of his tread on the ground. He is himself the centre that does not hold."[79] The clowns' specialty is "The Clown's Funeral," a version of the ballad of "Finnegan's Wake," in which Buffo with great difficulty is fit to "an exceedingly large coffin draped with the Union Jack" and processed around the ring by clown pallbearers. All at once, however, Buffo bursts through the coffin lid: "Here he is again, large as life and white and black and red all over! 'Thunder and lightning, did yuz think I was dead?'"[80] The "Tumultuous resurrection of the clown" nevertheless leaves Buffo in a kind of ghostly liminal space, for underneath his greasepaint and despite "his immense form," the king of clowns "is merely not-Buffo. An absence. A vacancy."[81]

In the context of the other performances at Kearney's circus, it is hard not to read Buffo's performance as an allegory of imperial masculinity. Clown

Alley is exclusively male, but the clowns are distinctly overshadowed by the performances of Fevvers, the aerialist; the Princess of Abyssinia, the tiger tamer; and Mignon, the vocalist. If the elephants and the clowns alike inhabit liminal spaces, caught between "flesh and blood" and stone, between "immense form" and "vacancy," between "life-in-death" and "death-in-life," between "convulsive self-dismemberment" and "tumultuous resurrection," between a "customary mask-like inhumanity" and the "hideously partly human,"[82] this in part has to do not only with challenges to their masculine authority within the circus but also with their inextricable entanglement with empire. Virginia Woolf's abstract figures of detotalization—bloated elephants and dissolving circles—provide an imagistic guide to the space between imperial holism and its dissolution, but Buffo the Great's person and performance *embody* these contradictory and countervailing impulses, as he tries to hold himself together amidst an overwhelming compulsion to shiver himself to bits.

Fevvers celebrates a sexual triumph over Colonel Kearney, who "Couldn't get 'is star-spangled banner up," in terms that look back in history to the end of the first British empire, describing Kearney's humiliation as "Britannia's revenge for the War of 1812."[83] At nearly the same moment, the emasculation of the British patriot Buffo the Great culminates in a final breakdown, which consigns him to "the coffin of . . . madness [from which] there is no escape."[84] The British clown whose steps have marked out an empire of fun has no future; the elephants are already in a kind of living death, buried in the sepulcher of the Russian Imperial Circus; and the British Empire to the extent that it appears itself takes the form of a "fugue of hallucinations" like Walser's, "in which birds, witches, mothers and elephants mixed up with sights and smells of Fisherman's Wharf, the Alhambra Theatre, London, the Imperial Circus, Petersburg, and many other places." In this shadowy place on the verge of oblivion, totality and narrative alike appear impossibilities to Buffo and Walser, however solid the world around them seems; for Walser, "all his life coursed through his head in concrete but discrete fragments and he could not make head nor tail of any of it."[85] In Buffo's madness and Walser's hallucinations, imperialism and masculinity, respectively, face a situation in which totality and narrative—or narrative *as* totality—are opposed to the "microcosmic" holism of the circus; where the circus ring represents the "uroboric snake, with tail in its mouth," Walser cannot "make head nor tail of any of it."

These dissolutions and hallucinations of masculinity appear under the banner of the British Union flag and suggest the price of Fevvers's vision of a "new era," "the new dawn," in which woman "will tear off her mind forg'd manacles, will rise up and fly away. The dolls' house doors will open, the brothels will spill forth their prisoners, the cages, gilded or otherwise, all over the world, in every land, will let forth their inmates singing together the dawn chorus of the new, the transformed."[86] This liberation—not only of women but of people globally and, perhaps, the shackled elephants—demands that "things fall apart" and that "the centre" no longer hold. It requires, in short, the shivering to pieces of traditional forms of masculinity, the eclipse of Englishness as imperial cynosure, and the burial of the Union flag along with Buffo. Fevvers's dream reflects what Linda Hutcheon describes as Carter's essential "politics of representation," those moments in which Carter's narrator appropriates and elaborates masculine poetic figures, especially those modernists and protomodernists like Blake, Ibsen, Wyndham Lewis, and especially Yeats, as "ironic feminizations of traditional or canonic male representations of the so-called generic human."[87]

Hutcheon illustrates one such "ironic feminization" by pointing to another borrowing from Yeats, when Fevvers describes a perverse brothel as "this lumber room of femininity, this rag-and-bone shop of the heart."[88] Yet neither Hutcheon nor any other commentator seems to have made much of the poem that Carter subjects to pastiche in the passage, Yeats's final poem, "The Circus Animals' Desertion" (1939). The poem laments the writer's failure to find a theme—indeed, the failure of the literary imagination generally—and waxes nostalgic for "those masterful images" which "because complete / grew in pure mind." The poem resolves to make do with life's detritus, the incomplete, unmastered impurities that remain after the beasts of the imagination disappear. Yeats casts the poetic work in the role of circus animal, and the poem's title alludes to the abandonment of poetry itself.

At the beginning of the third part of *Nights at the Circus*, in a moment in which Fevvers assumes the narration, she returns to Yeats's metaphorics of "The Circus Animals' Desertion" to ask, "But what shall the tamer do when the beasts are gone?"[89] This question becomes quite pointed at the diegetic level—concrete at the level of narrative in a way it is not for Yeats's poemstory—in the third section of the novel, since the learned chimpanzees pack their bags and depart as a result of a contractual dispute, the tiger has revolted against the Princess of Abyssinia and been shot dead, the elephants perish in the aftermath of a train accident in Siberia, and the remaining performers are compelled to eat the circus dog. While Yeats's poem laments that "Players and painted stage took all my love / And not those things that they were emblems of," no such distinction is available in *Nights at the Circus*: Buffo's fundamental vacancy suggests that the circus performance *produces* those things they are emblems of, and indeed the novel renders moot the question posed by Colonel Kearney's marketing, of whether Fevvers "is fact or fiction," a player or the thing she emblematizes. To the extent that Yeats's "circus animals" emblematize the literary performance itself, Carter's appropriation, "ironization," and concretization of Yeats's circus animals means that the answer to the question of what happens when the elephant, for instance, is gone holds consequences not just for the circus (which the elephant upholds like the universe), nor even for Englishness and empire (with which it is historically entangled), but ultimately for the novel itself.

Carter offers a narrative of the circus in 1899—by that point an amalgam of British imperial sensibilities and American entrepreneurial principles—that subjects the exhibition to a literal train wreck in Siberia. The circus animals, performers, and proprietor—those responsible for offering views of geopolitical and temporal elsewheres—find themselves in a literal desert space, populated only by a primitive nomadic tribe. The intermingling of exhibitionary exotica and the real thing, circus folk and beasts with the native people and animals, disables the circus's performative power, even before the circus animals desert. This might suggest the failure of the geopolitical movement the English circus emblematizes—the totalizing grasp of imperialism, which in Siberia appears as "the bubbling samovar of the Empire on which the sun never sets."[90] Yet

> even in these remote regions, in those days, those last bewildering days before history, that is, history as we know it, that is white history, that is, European history, that is, Yanqui history—in that final little breathing space before history *as such* extended its tentacles to grasp the entire globe, the tribespeople ... knew more than they said. The future was more present to them than they were prepared to admit; every day they drank it and they handled it [in the form of tea and rifles].[91]

Even as the distinction collapses between those who render up performances or delineations of exotic people and the tribespeople themselves, white-European-Yanqui history has begun to claim this Siberian wasteland as its own in a last vanishing instant before elsewhere itself is folded into the narrative of "white history." While the view *of* elsewhere fostered by the circus finds itself foreclosed upon by the train wreck that destroys the circus, the view *from* elsewhere—the vision of, for instance, the nomadic shaman—appears for a fleeting moment "in that final little breathing space" before it ceases to be elsewhere and becomes fully part of "white" history in the twentieth century.

What is "white history"? For Carter it seems to be something like the saturation of the globe with an imperious—rather than strictly imperial—capitalism and its antagonists, that is, the pincerlike movement of the Colonel's "free enterprise" on one hand, and Lizzie's revolutionary socialism, on the other, to encompass the globe.[92] Like Adorno, Carter's narrator identifies the twentieth century as a time in which geopolitical unevenness—that which underpinned both the Victorian collection of zoological exotica and the imperialism it emblematized—is leveled by the tentacle-like grasp of European-Yanqui whiteness. But in the early part of the century the residue of this unevenness generated new representational possibilities, even as it witnessed the redundancy of older exhibitionary modes. I would argue that, as in the breakup of the circus in the Siberian train wreck of *Nights at the Circus*, the era of aesthetic modernism (the period of Ibsen's influence, Lewis's Vorticism, and Yeats's poetry) is the field over which the novel's view *of* elsewhere breaks up. Simultaneously, the free play of narrative perspective in Carter's novel, usually termed postmodernist but essentially evincing a modernist sensibility, enables views *from* elsewhere, inviting the narrative audience to assume vantage of the tribal shaman or the circus's monkeys. Yet, Carter's narrator ultimately argues, this is an evanescent view from elsewhere, always already drawn within the constricting horizons of white history's narrative—the telltale sign of which, according to Adorno, is the abolition of the elsewhere itself—and dependent upon the residues of modernity's exhibitions and delineations of elsewhere.

What then does the tamer do when the "flesh and blood" circus animals depart, or in Rushdie's terms, when "the India of elephants, tigers, peacocks, emeralds, and dancing girls is . . . laid to rest," along with Buffo the imperialist clown? Carter poses at least two answers to the question. The first is quite cynical. Colonel Kearney, the pragmatic American circus proprietor, simply resolves to buy more animals: "I shall return! Out of the ashes of my enterprise I shall arise renewed! Colonel Kearney . . . will return again, with more and bigger elephants; larger and more ferocious tigers; an en-tire army of infinitely more hilarious clowns! Yes! The Old Glory will wave once again across the tundra!"[93] For the British figures—Buffo the clown and Fevvers the aerialist—things are not so simple, however: Buffo's fragmentation, the madness of his brand of patriotism, is irremediable. Buffo's case demonstrates that Britain and its Union are diminished, the empire superannuated, before the encroaching "white history" embodied by Kearney himself, the decentered multipolar triumph of Western modernity.

Yet Fevvers's case offers new possibilities: having smashed her wings upon the cold wastes of Russia, the prospect of Walser "not as a lover, but as a scribe, as an amanuensis" suggests to Fevvers that "the Britannic Angel"—if not Britannia herself—might "once again . . . become whole."⁹⁴ At the end of *Nights at the Circus,* with the abolition of the exotic before the inexorable encroachment of "white history," the exhibition space is stripped of its performative power; it is no longer the circus that stages the possibility of holism, but narrative itself—which can "do more things than we tend to think it can," especially in the form of the novel, a form of narrative that announces itself as novel. What the tamer does when the beast is gone is to tell the histories of the "nameless and forgotten, [those] erased from history" by "white history's" abolition of heterogeneity, to narrate the stories "of all those whose tales we've yet to tell," and to "help to give the world a little turn into the new era that begins tomorrow," at the cusp of the twentieth century.⁹⁵ If narrative retains the ability to articulate a kind of holism, it must be able to "do more things than we tend to think it can"; indeed, it must abandon the notion that English experience in the world can be described in its totality without some sort of loss in another register.

The Novel and the Menagerie After the Flood: Barnes's Island Arks

Rushdie pleads for the burial of the old zoological India, the elephant-taxi East being "sold to the world," while Carter abandons the circus ring as totalizing microcosm in favor of narrative's promise when "flesh and blood" circus animals depart. What, however, remains of the imperial menagerie in England's home spaces? What happens to the English exhibitionary collection when animals have bolted it or been buried beneath it, along with the exotic it emblematized? If, as I have argued throughout this book, the display of zoological exotica has shaped narratives of Englishness over the course of the past two centuries—particularly in the quintessentially English form of the novel—the circus animals' desertion and the prospect of an East independent of the zoological at the end of the twentieth century should entail a refiguration of the relationship among English exhibitionary cultures, narratives of Englishness, and the novel. Ian Baucom has noted a relationship between the "imaginative return to the glories of imperial dominance [in so-called Raj revivalism] and the mournful wanderings through the lapsing architectures of the English past [as in the televised serial of Evelyn Waugh's *Brideshead Revisited*]" in the 1980s, but what unfolds in the wake of this phenomenon that Baucom terms "postimperial melancholy"?[96] What cultural whole remains to shape and be totalized by English exhibitionary cultures, including the novel?

The work of Julian Barnes, "one of the writers who have earned England its international reputation for contemporary literature,"[97] might pose one answer to these questions: Barnes's writing proposes that the task of English narrative is to take seriously the forging of a new cultural identity in the domain formerly occupied by imperial Englishness, and while such a charge might invite a return to older scenes of exhibition, nevertheless what is important is the form of the new imaginings of Englishness. While Barnes concedes that his work bears the marks of a "pervasive melancholy,"[98] he simultaneously describes himself as "totally postcolonial, if you can apply that to an Englishman,"[99] and he even professes an interest in watching "over the next thirty or forty years whether the United Kingdom breaks up." His curious detachment as a "postcolonial Englishman" and writer—or as he describes himself in *Letters from London*, "a foreign correspondent in my own country"[100]—holds important consequences for his understanding of the contemporary novel as well. He argues that "British writers of one or two generations ago would have thought the English novel was the real novel in English and the American novel was a sort of an upstart." But "partly because of our imperial and colonial and Commonwealth history," he notes, "now British writers would say that the British novel is just one of the forms of the novels in English around the world."[101] The new position of the British novel also challenges Barnes's notion of the novel as "an extended piece of prose, largely fictional, which is planned and executed as a whole piece" and leads him to fight a rearguard battle on behalf of "the continental idea—which used to be the English idea as well—that the novel is a very broad and generous enclosing form."[102] If the prospective loss of a sense of the "English idea" of the novel as a "whole piece" that encloses the broadest of materials troubles Barnes, one encouraging consequence of the decentering of the British novel is that British "novels are traveling" in translation to an extent they had not previously, and "this is an example of *good* globalization."[103] Barnes's work on the menagerie and the shape of Englishness ultimately apprehends both—England and the spectacular collection—from the perspective of a "postcolonial Englishman," sometimes even from what might be termed a global perspective, and he concludes by championing the notion of "serious" storytelling over retrenchment behind an "authentic" notion of English culture.

Barnes's writing demonstrates an understanding of the fundamental questions and problems of the collection of zoological exotica. In *A His-*

tory of the World in 10½ Chapters (1989) Barnes approaches the menagerie in the opening episode, "The Stowaway," as both a foundational form and myth of traveling culture in the Western imaginary and as an always already globalized form. "The Stowaway" retells the story of Noah's ark through the focalization of a woodworm, whose hiding place affords a view of the ark as incorporating "the whole of the animal kingdom on board."[104] Through the woodworm, the narrative interrogates the most important problems of assembling a floating zoo: its commercial underpinnings, the relation of part to whole, how the animals ought to be ordered, and their management within the collection. Although the dominant narrative of the flood asserts that "when the waters receded and the world was new-born, he gave Man dominion over the animals," the narrator notes that Noah had already arrogated to himself this authority. Noah assembles his collection by advertising a competition to choose the most eligible bestial pairs, "a sort of beauty contest cum brains trust cum Darby-and-Joan event," an arrangement likely to attract "only the grabbiest" of animals. What is more, those species hibernating, too lazy, or too slow to make it to the contest are necessarily disqualified, even before taking into consideration that "Some creatures were simply Not Wanted on Voyage," or that the nobler of the beasts find the terms of Noah's proposal insulting and stalk off in a huff to certain extinction.[105] Despite the ark's claim to represent the whole of the antediluvial animal kingdom, in practice it appears a selective and ideologically interested vehicle for representing and, indeed, for forging a new order after the flood. Moreover, Noah arranges the animals into a hierarchy of clean and unclean beasts, purebred and hybrid species, an organization fundamentally aesthetic in character (one literally based on taste, since Noah and his family eat certain of the animals on the voyage) and one that privileges the pure and clean over the mongrel and the unclean, the classic over the decadent.

The logic of the ark that the woodworm uncovers is essentially that of the menagerie in the nineteenth century, and indeed Barnes notes that he "go[es] back to the 19th century a lot" in his own reading.[106] Yet Barnes's ark appears as a menagerie narrated in the sociopolitical terms of the late twentieth century, an era of quiz competitions, reality television, cruise ships, and "*good* globalization." The late twentieth century also boasted a certain carnivalesque strain, in which the British prime minister's parentage included a "music-hall and circus artiste" and in which his government ministers sought to pay colonies to embark upon programs of decolonization.[107] The woodworm, in other words, reads the ark as a floating zoo from a historical perspective in which the circus has begotten England's most powerful political figure, and yet at a moment in which the imperial landscape underpinning the exotic collection has vanished from view. What is more, like the old world over which the floodwaters closed, late twentieth-century England was awash in prophetic narratives of decline, cultural deracination, and even national atavism. As Barnes put it, "Pious moralists and historical depressives like to comfort themselves with the notion that Britain is downwardly mobile. This is abundantly true in the geopolitical sense: Dean Acheson's 1962 remark that 'Great Britain has lost an empire and not yet found a role' continues to sting, because it continues to be accurate."[108] Like Rushdie, who argues that frontiers have closed and the English have been pressed back into their "box," Barnes envisions the island unhappily adrift between past and future: "Britain is a medium-ranked trading nation with memories of great wealth and fear of future poverty."[109] A history of the contemporary English world in a single chapter comparable to "The Stowaway" might find in the flood a metaphor for the sea change of the postcolonial, in which the long deluge of decolonization uproots England from its empire and sets it afloat on a global sea. Put otherwise, Rushdie's "box" of an island into which the English are obliged to retreat in the aftermath of decolonization appears just a smaller version of Barnes's global ark.

Barnes's 1998 novel *England, England* offers itself up as his most sustained meditation on Englishness, narrative, and the collection. It should be read, Barnes argues, as "an idea-of-England novel, rather than a state-of-England novel,"[110] and as Matthew Pateman observes, the novel constitutes itself as "an island world of Barnes's other books," a composite of self-parody and broad intellectual pastiche.[111] Even as the novel takes as its subject matter the reconstitution of Englishness (or of a simulacrum of Englishness) on the Isle of Wight, Barnes in this reading reconstitutes his own literary corpus in the form of *England, England*: "Barnes . . . is himself deploying the strategies of simulacra, inauthenticity, and fake in order to tell a story of simulacra, inauthenticity, and fake."[112] *England, England,* an island or ark in its own right, launches in effect two English arks in its story: one is a corporate response to a conviction that "patriotism should be pro-active,"[113] in which Englishness is reinvented in the space of England, England; the other represents an imagined return to a preindustrial Anglia on the grounds of the old England. Each experiment represents a salvage effort in the face of a postimperial deluge: as one corporate consultant in the narrative puts it, "There are some people out there—classical historical depressives in my book—who think it's our job, our particular geopolitical function, to act as an emblem of decline, a moral and economic scarecrow."[114] The novel's two versions of the ark—England, England, and Anglia—aim to reconceive that "geopolitical function" by serving as island zoos designed to convey into the future the essential remainders of the past—though featuring only "heritage animals," not exotic specimens, among its collections. In a postimperial climate, England finds itself engaged in a massive rescue effort that entails collecting its cultural past and selling it "to other nations as their future" (in the case of England, England) or collecting the past and reinvesting it with meaning and belief as England's future (in the case of Anglia).

In advance reviews of the novel, *England, England* was understood as "a book about England's relationship with the past and especially with the process of creative and selective remembering that has been dubbed [by Eric Hobsbawm and Terence Ranger] 'the invention of tradition.'"[115] In an enthusiastic review in the *Sunday Times*, John Carey added that *England, England* is "a philosophical novel about authenticity and the idea of the replica."[116] But beyond elaborations upon these notions—that English traditions are invented and inauthentic, but no less real and significant for being artificial or replicas—criticism of the novel has not traveled very far. It is certainly the case that the novel raises the questions of simulation, simulacra, and cultural heritage (Barnes himself notes that one chapter comprises a satire on the work of Jean Baudrillard[117]), but these are not new themes for Barnes. In an essay titled simply "Fake!" (1990) Barnes introduces what might be understood as the *donée* of *England, England* almost a decade in advance of the novel's appearance:

> The British are good at tradition; they're also good at the invention of tradition (from plowman's lunch to the clan tartan). And like any other nation, they aren't too keen on having those invented traditions exposed as bogus: . . . If we can't believe *that,* what can we believe? And since individual identity depends in part upon national identity, what happens when those symbolic props to national identity turn out to be no more authentic or probable than a furbearing trout?[118]

Barnes goes on to point out that "in the old imperial days, the British looted the treasure houses of their dominions (sometimes in the nicest possible way, of course, but sometimes not); now that the British are less dominant, their prizes are up for grabs."[119] As a "philosophical novel" or a book that "provides highly self-conscious reflections upon the process that has come to be known as the invention of traditions,"[120] then, *England, England* does no more than recapitulate arguments that Baudrillard, Hobsbawm and Ranger, and Barnes himself had already advanced.

The distinguishing feature of Barnes's novel, what sets it apart from these theoretical discussions, is its work to imagine the collections themselves, the arks (Anglia and England, England), as societies in the making and to treat the English creatures and cultures harbored in these cultural menageries in a mode of seriousness that does not insist upon their authenticity. That is, while John Carey is doubtless correct that *England, England* frequently operates in a philosophical mode, and while it would be hard to fault criticism for finding in the narrative an investigation of the processes of "inventing tradition," these features do not distinguish *England, England* from, say, "Fake!" or Baudrillard's *Simulacra and Simulation*. Rather, I want to argue by way of conclusion, what distinguishes Barnes's novel *qua* novel from his essays or the historical inquiries of Hobsbawm and Ranger appears in excess of its philosophical point and has to do with figuring the content of these cultural arks: Barnes's own narrative work of collecting, ordering, exhibiting, and managing representative cultural materials that imagine future forms of Englishness in the moment of constituting themselves as novel wholes. That is, Barnes plays the part of a George Wombwell, William Batty, or George Sanger but without the grounding of the imperial whole; instead, he puts Englishness afloat on a postcolonial sea, a contemporary Noah.

By contrast with the imperial menagerie, Barnes's collections do not insist upon the authenticity of the exhibited materials and bodies that underpin English identity. Barnes's menageries and heritage parks are imagined whole, but as wholly inauthentic, which enables a series of reversals of field in thinking about Englishness in a global environment. In the first instance, Barnes's version of "Britannia's menagerie" collapses the crucial distinction between the overseer and the collection, as Britannia herself becomes part of her collection. Consequently, the English as a traveling culture find themselves the objects rather than the subjects of travel and spectacular display. The content of the display is no longer "all the wonder-fauna of the world" but rather the detritus of the already known, the cultural flotsam that gets the English to swallow an island rather than the whole world, as Rushdie's Saleem proposes for India. Most importantly, however, Barnes's collections invite us to abandon the distinction between the authentic and the simulated, in favor first of a distinction between the cynical and the serious and then between a cultural seriousness driven and ordered by the market or by an organic condition of storytelling.

Anglia, the novel makes clear in its third section, is no less a collection of invented traditions than England, England, nor is it any more serious than the patriotic, recuperative, regenerative efforts on the Isle of Wight. Instead it appears organic and popular; it reflects a refusal after the deluge to concede that Carter's "White History" can only proceed on the terms established by the likes of Colonel Kearney and Sir Jack Pitman. Anglia refuses the central planning of England, England's commercial endeavors, which totalize that version of Englishness: the flow of capital through the boardroom of Pitco Industries charts the course of Englishness on the Isle of Wight as a whole. England, England, in other words, reproduces the old imperial model of center and periphery, replacing London as the central star in an imperial universe with Pitco as capitalist cynosure. By contrast, Barnes's Anglia—for all its "willed antiquarianism,"[121] its sense of morbidity in inhabiting the past—remains open and provisional in its essential character, reflecting perhaps Sartre's "totalisation" (a *developing* activity) rather than Sir Jack's totality ("an inert ensemble").[122] The stories of "Old England" (as Anglia is also known) reflect this openness and provisionality: whenever a schoolmaster in the exemplary village followed by Barnes's narrative suggests "that folklore, and especially invented folklore, should not be the subject of monetary exchange or barter," the village storyteller "would decline the reprimand, and with various winks and scalp-scratchings draw Mr Mullin into his own narrative."[123] Barnes's novel, a kind of island, ark, or menagerie in its own right, ultimately rests with this kind of serious, ongoing, and provisional storytelling. After the flood, this is the work of the "postcolonial Englishman" as menagerist, the novelist as new Noah.

Epilogue

Small Islands, Frozen Arks

The foregoing chapters have argued that in the nineteenth and twentieth centuries the novel and the menagerie appear homologous cultural forms, collections of materials bound to a notion of empire through their efforts to imagine geopolitical totality. What is more, the collection of zoological exotica over these centuries constitutes a significant line of mediation between the evolving form of the domestic English novel and the shifting configurations of empire in the English imagination. These two key English cultural formations—the novel and the menagerie—have accommodated themselves to one another through their shared capacities to exhibit, reflect, and model imperial totality. At the center of this rich relationship, both the novel and the menagerie have traditionally depended upon the wild beast's authenticity, its strong association with localities exotic to England, and its assimilability to national-imperial frameworks. At the opening of the twenty-first century, however, the menagerie's underpinnings appear more contingent than at any point in the past two hundred years. Imagining the collection as fundamentally inauthentic, as Julian Barnes does in the body of writing discussed in the last chapter, profoundly changes the relation of the novel and the menagerie, while the increasing globalization of the zoological collection disembeds fauna and environment from traditional imperial frameworks and locales.

In the new century the zoo remains a powerful vestige of the most recognizable and influential forms of the totalizing exhibition of wild beasts, far more robust than the circus or taxonomic display. Yet the zoo's dependence on live zoological exhibits, its capacity to evoke exotic locality, and its tendency to express geopolitical authority have all diminished in recent decades. In England, indeed, the logic of the menagerie seemed to be turned inside out in August 2005, when the London Zoo displayed a collection

Figure 24. English creatures at the London Zoo, August 2005. *Photograph by Gareth Cattermole/Getty Images.*

of eight white Britons in the Bear Mountain exhibit (fig. 24).[1] Though just two months earlier there had been widespread outcry against the Augsburg Zoo's prominent display of black Africans in its African Village exhibit for its echoes of nineteenth-century colonialist ethnographic displays,[2] the naïve claims made for the English exhibit—that it constituted "the world's first 'human zoo'"[3]—similarly overlooked the colonial histories of the zoological exhibition. When, for instance, a Nigerian spectator looked upon the British subjects in the zoo and complained, "They're not doing much, are they?" it significantly reversed the old imperial strategies in which the exotic is framed as a whole and spectacularized for a domestic audience.[4] In 2005 the London Zoo's totalizing efforts—to complete its collection by adding the last specimen, the white Briton—rendered Englishness itself a kind of primitive spectacle. It would seem that Johnnie Bull no longer runs Britannia's global menagerie, as he does in the nineteenth-century music-hall standard; rather, he appears on show to the world as a curiosity in his own right.

The zoo's composition has undergone other sweeping changes. Most notably, zoos have moved away from the authentic animal as guarantor of their spectacles. They have, for instance, substituted artificial animals for live specimens;[5] divested themselves of keynote animals, including elephants;[6] exhibited fantastic, artificial megafauna such as animatronic dinosaurs; and foregrounded theme-park environments at the expense of the animals themselves.

On one hand, these environments are often simulacral, offering up misleading or confused conjunctions of past landscapes—Disney's Maharajah Jungle Trek® in its Animal Kingdom, for instance, appears nostalgic for both Asian and South African sites of British imperialism. On the other hand, the menagerie's exotic stock has increasingly drifted from its exclusive association with "native" localities: crocodiles now inhabit the marshes of East London, wallabies plague England's motorways,[7] and estates of England's landed nobility have become "safari parks" that house giraffes, zebras, rhinos, and monkeys.[8] Further afield, herds of elephants wander the hills of Tennessee,[9] and a series of evolutionary biologists have gone so far as to suggest the large-scale relocation of African megafauna to North America to "restore" large vertebrates comparable to those that vanished thirteen thousand years ago.[10] In a few years, if zoos retain their commitment to the display of live animals, it might well prove difficult to distinguish "exotic" from "native" species in anything except a historical sense.

Indeed, the exotic animal no longer seems the primary means by which to foster imaginative travel to the world's far-flung reaches. Instead, this function is increasingly borne by simulated environments in the zoo's spaces. In general, the zoo has in recent years separated exhibition from its totalizing ambitions, isolating zoological totality as that which must be conserved on one hand, and turning exhibitionary technologies and frames—rather than the exotic beast—into the primary objects of display. At one end of things is the Frozen Ark project, a collaboration among the London Zoo, the London Museum of Natural History, and the University of Nottingham, and others, which freezes samples of endangered animals in order to establish a comprehensive DNA collection for the long-term preservation of species, and simultaneously maintains a database of these specimens as well as "a global list of animals needing to be sampled."[11] The Frozen Ark represents the epitome of the menagerie's emphasis on totality as conservation, striving after a complete zoological catalogue but removing specimens altogether from the scene of display. On the other hand, Microsoft's *Zoo Tycoon 2*® (2004), a game in which players build zoo exhibits and maintain virtual animals, represents the extreme version of menagerie as exhibition. "Zoo Guest Mode" and "Photo Safari Mode" permit forms of spectatorship that bypass the authenticity of the animal or locale, and instead the simulacrum—and the technologies through which it is constructed—is exhibited as the primary exotic novelty. A "Dinosaur Digs" expansion pack permits players to house dinosaurs and Ice Age animals in their zoos as well, echoing zoos' own turn toward the display of mechanical, extinct beasts.[12] In the wake of these divergences from the traditional roles of the zoo, totalizing geopolitical associations still attach themselves to exhibitions of animals, but primarily in nostalgic, historical senses. The Combe Martin Wildlife and Dinosaur Park in southwest England expresses a longing for lost worlds in its emphasis upon extinct megafauna,[13] while the West Midlands Safari Park's promise to patrons that they can "track down the African Big Five in the UK"[14] suggests African megafauna as similarly lost from their native continent—and might also harbor a longing for an imperial Africa lost in the previous century. For the zoo, zoological totality has become a relic or vestige of the past to be conserved in databases and "frozen arks" away from the world's view, while the scene of exhibition is increasingly dominated by the simulacra of exoticism rather than by the beast itself.

Andrea Levy's novel *Small Island* (2004) might be understood to represent a kind of analogue to these inversions and revisions effected in the English menagerie. Levy's narrative contemplates the reconfiguration of the empire during and after the Second World War, particularly the influx of black colonial subjects. Her prefatory section, set in the African pavilions at the Wembley Empire Exhibition of 1924, exposes the simulacral origin of English notions that a multiracial Britain emerged only with postwar immigration from the colonies some two decades later. The exhibition reveals both imperial savagery and English civilization to be factitious. The scene at Wembley also highlights the discrepancies that dominate the novel: between imperial ideals and English parochialism, between English global ambitions and local inabilities to manage domestic affairs, and ultimately between black Britain's new expansiveness and England's "smallness" in the midst of its empire's postwar homecoming. As it seeks to rewrite the history of postwar black Britishness, the novel simultaneously looks backward to a moment prior to the landmark immigration wave of the late 1940s and 1950s, and longs for a new integrity, both in its content and in its form. Levy's two "small" islands of Jamaica and Great Britain, no less than Julian Barnes's England, England and Anglia in *England, England*, represent cultural wholes adrift in a postimperial world, and the novel poses as a kind of totalizing exhibition in its own right—the novel's title might be understood to allude to the novel itself, suggesting the strategies of miniaturization that were hallmarks of the Empire Exhibition and reversing the gaze of Wembley and the zoological collection by miniaturizing England, rather than its empire. At the very least, *Small Island*—as a characterization of the novel itself and as a description of postwar England—like recent zoological collections suggests totality as the object rather than objective of display.

In the instances of Barnes and Levy, the totalizing form of the collection—whether Barnes's display of English creatures or Levy's constricted island as a counter-exhibition to Wembley—attaches to the notion of geopolitical *survival* rather than *expansion*. That is, Barnes and Levy—like Jeanette Winterson's revision of Noah's story in *Boating for Beginners* (1985)—offer up ark stories about reimagining the contemporary cultural situation as a new kind of whole, rather than conventional zoo stories about the extensiveness and integrity of an expanding empire. These stories are certainly about the varieties of English creatures and their strategies for survival—whether Barnes's postimperial Anglians at the end of the century or Levy's black Britons disembarking from ships like the *Empire Windrush* in 1948. Yet I wish to suggest by way of conclusion that we might understand this ark to be as much like the biblical Ark of the Covenant—the essential totalizing form that harbors narrative authority as its kernel—as it is like Noah's ark or the *Windrush,* the totality built up from the representative, synecdochic materials it incorporates ("two of every kind" of animal or colonial subject). The totalizing form of the contemporary zoo has floated free of the authenticity of exotic beast, of the animal's association with localizable elsewheres, and the collection's amenability to current national-imperial frameworks. So, too, narrative as ark or zoo has been weaned from its dependence upon the typicality of its materials and its English frames of reference, as Winterson's novel, which incorporates deliberate anachronisms and allusions from across the Anglophone world, illustrates. In place of the collection's authentic specimens that gesture toward imperial referents, the ark as totalizing form might be understood to drive contemporary narrative independent of its content. The novel displays itself as a curiosity of totality, rather than as a totalizing instrument, and empire at best exerts a spectral power in these narratives, like the dusty contents of the Ark of the Covenant smuggled from Africa in *Raiders of the Lost Ark* (1981). Despite the film's evocation of Rider Haggard and Rudyard Kipling's visions of empire,[15] the famous closing scene of that film in which the ark is crated and warehoused makes a case that in *form*—from ark, to crate, and ultimately to warehouse, in a sublime *mise-en-abŷme*—the new law is inscribed, rather than in its dusty contents or desert homelands.

The focus of this book has been totality as a powerful regulative principle for the menagerie, for the novel, and for the empire in Britain over the past two hundred years. The conclusions of these final pages both represent the logical culmination of the idea of totality as imparting essential form and mark a historic divorce of the alliances among these terms. While the novel and the zoo remain homologous responses to a contemporary geopolitical situation, the menagerie has steadily drifted from its emphasis upon geopolitical specificity and its strategies of affiliation to the real, and the novel no longer takes as its aim the contemplation of empire from the vantage of the domestic English subject. Though the exotic beast is disappearing from the zoological collection and the imperial whole that underpinned the novel over the past two centuries has dissipated, nevertheless totalizing form itself—that of the zoological park or garden, and that of the novel—appears to have *become* the exotic animal. "We are by no means finished with totalities," wrote Arkady Plotnitsky in the last decade of the twentieth century. "They are powerful beasts . . . and we can never quite escape them."[16] Likewise, though the past century stripped the British empire of pretensions to global totality, and even of the fiction that the empire could be understood as an integrated whole, in the opening decade of a new century we are hardly finished with the idioms of totality entailed upon us by the discourses of imperial totality and its cultural affiliates—at least, we have yet to learn to do without the imaginative work enabled by the zoological display and by the novel. Indeed, well beyond the limits of the empire, we can observe that the exotic animal is no longer captured and managed by the Western subject as an exercise in empire-modeling. Rather, the "powerful beast"—the totality itself—claims postimperial English subjects as its own and, like the human zoo in Regent's Park, offers them up for forms of exhibition and narration yet to come.

Notes

Preface

1. George, *Animals and Maps*, 25.
2. Ellis, "Introduction," 23.
3. Friedman, *Mappings*, 109.
4. Said, *Culture and Imperialism*, 6.
5. Renan, "What Is a Nation?" 19.
6. Bhabha, "DissemiNation," 297.

Introduction

1. Davies, "East End."
2. Hamilton, "East End Passion."
3. Freud, "'Uncanny,'" 220, 241.
4. In his 1920 essay "Notes on the English Character," E. M. Forster holds responsible the English middle classes—characterized by "solidity, caution, integrity, [and] efficiency" (3) as well as by coldness and emotional restraint (7)—for both "the rise and organization of the British Empire" and "the literature of the nineteenth century" (3).
5. Jameson, "Modernism and Imperialism," 51.
6. Hamilton, "East End Passion," 3.
7. Seeley, *Expansion of England*, 87.
8. Viswanathan, *Masks of Conquest*, 3.
9. Seeley, *Expansion of England*, 307.
10. As a definition of "exhibit" (5), the *Oxford English Dictionary* offers "A showing, producing in evidence, display," while the word's etymology suggests a "holding out" or showing forth. *To narrate*, by contrast, is "to give an account of" (1a). In popular cultural practices, however, the distinction between display and storytelling is hardly observed: exhibitions of exotica almost always furnish accounts of distant reaches of the empire, while accounts of England's elsewheres often narrate stories precisely *as* a showing forth or "producing in evidence" local details of, say, Indian daily life.
11. Henry James, "Art of Fiction," 13, 18, 17.
12. Chaudhuri, "Forms of Renewal."

13. Gunning, "World as Object Lesson," 426.
14. de Certeau, *Practice of Everyday Life*, 78.
15. On the important shifts in the menagerie as a symbolic register, see Veltre, "Menageries, Metaphors, and Meanings." On the imperial exhibition, see Hoffenberg, *Empire on Display*; Timothy Mitchell, *Colonising Egypt*; Auerbach, *Great Exhibition of 1851*; and Hobhouse, *The Crystal Palace and the Great Exhibition*. On displays of exotic animals, see Ritvo, *The Animal Estate*. On the circus, see Stoddart, *Rings of Desire*. On the development of the zoo and its representations, see Malamud, *Reading Zoos*; Baratay and Hardouin-Fugier, *Zoo*; and Rothfels, *Savages and Beasts*.
16. Stallybrass and White, *Politics and Poetics of Transgression*, 2–3.
17. Berger, *About Looking*, 21.
18. "Traveling culture" is James Clifford's phrase to describe the ways in which culture "comes to resemble as much a site of travel encounters as of residence" (*Routes*, 25).
19. E. M. Forster, *Passage to India*, 153.
20. West, *Harriet Hume*, 125. While West's vision has no historical basis, Cook's did open a branch office devoted to the transport of Indian princes, sacred bulls, Bengal tigers, and elephants to Britain (Swinglehurst, *Cook's Tours*, 82).
21. See Ritvo, *Animal Estate*, especially the chapter titled "Exotic Captives" (205–42); and Altick, *Shows of London*, 288–331, and *Presence of the Present*, 493–532.
22. On the "exhibitionary complex" see Tony Bennett, *Birth of the Museum*, 62. On the Victorian novel as a reflection of—and opening onto—a world that itself appeared increasingly like a display window, see Andrew Miller, *Novels Behind Glass*.
23. Foucault, *Order of Things*, 129–31.
24. At times these miscellanies drew explicitly on the institutions of the menagerie, as for instance in *Jumbo's Picture Book of Natural History* (1883) or Camden's *Travelling Menagerie* (1873). The text of the former is mostly descriptive, while that of the latter is shaped as narrative.
25. Benedict, *Curiosity*, 12.
26. In British Library Playbills 171 (dated 21 October 1839).
27. *Zoological Cabinet*, 5–6.
28. Seeley, *Expansion of England*, 56.
29. On the history of the elephant's figurations, see Scigliano, *Love, War, and Circuses*.
30. See the Queen's "Jubilee Journal" for 9 May 2002 at http://www.royal.gov.uk/output/Page1174.asp.
31. See Nairn, *Break-Up of Britain*, 13; and Porter, *Britain, Europe and the World*, 56–57.
32. Paxman, *English*, 15.
33. Ibid., 13.
34. Jonathan Miller, "Devolution Revolution."
35. Norfolk, "Who's Out."
36. Terry Eagleton attributes the decline in "indigenous English writing" to an "inability . . . to 'totalise' the significant movements of its own culture" (*Exiles and*

Émigrés, 15). Cf., however, Joshua D. Esty's argument in "Amnesia in the Fields" that Eliot, Woolf, and Forster were able to do just this via the pageant play.

37. Huggan, "Postcolonial Exotic," 25.
38. Showalter, "Coming to Blows."
39. Martel, *Life of Pi*, 302, 317.
40. Kaveney, "Guess Who's for Dinner."
41. J. C., "NB."
42. Wood, "Credulity."
43. Martel, *Life of Pi*, 47.
44. Ibid., 18.
45. Wood, "Credulity."
46. British Library Playbills 172 (11 October 1844).
47. "The British Empire: Imperial Amnesia."
48. Martel, *Life of Pi*, viii.
49. Owen, "Where We Went Right." Owen registers a strong dissent from the "declinist" point of view he summarizes.
50. Hamilton, "East End Passion."
51. See, for instance, Rushdie, "The New Empire within Britain." In *Buddha of Suburbia*, Kureishi decries the lingering imperialist obsessions in Britain in exploring the experiences of his mixed-race protagonist: one character notes that "Everyone looks at [him], I'm sure, and thinks: an Indian boy, how exotic, how interesting, what stories of aunties and elephants we'll hear now from him. And [he's] from Orpington" (141).
52. Kenner, *Sinking Island*, 3, 5, 9.
53. Ibid., 9.
54. The only lion associated with the memorial was removed from William Theed's design for Africa in the conceptual stage and replaced by the camel (Bayley, *Albert Memorial*, 106).
55. Paxman, *English*, 1.
56. Seeley, *Expansion of England*, 190.
57. Ellmann, *James Joyce*, 131.
58. Orwell, *English People*, 11–12.
59. Ibid., 12.
60. Paxman, *English*, 3.
61. E. M. Forster, "Notes on the English Character," 15, 14.
62. On totality and the modern novel, see Caserio, *Novel in England*.
63. Lidell, "My Zigzag British Empire Tour."
64. James, "Art of Fiction," 3.
65. Virginia Woolf, "Character in Fiction," 427.
66. Tony Bennett, *Birth of the Museum*, 63.
67. E. M. Forster, "Notes on the English Character," 6.
68. Orwell, *English People*, 12.
69. Kipling, *Beast and Man in India*, 1.
70. In "Surgery for the Novel," Lawrence wondered what would happen if "a bomb were put under the whole scheme of things," and desired "some convulsion or

cataclysm" to wrench the novel from its contemporary forms (116, 115). Wyndham Lewis's *Blast 1* (1914) hoped to be just such a bomb, while Virginia Woolf identified Joyce's *Ulysses* with an attempt "to outrage [and] to destroy the very foundations and rules of literary society" ("Character in Fiction," 3:434).

71. Seeley, *Expansion of England*, 304.

72. For a discussion of imperial discourses of surplus and empire, see Bivona, *Desire and Contradiction*, 113–27. For an outline of the theory of "the ethnological unity of the whole" empire, see Seeley, *Expansion of England*, 47–50.

73. Jameson, "Modernism and Imperialism," 50.

74. Ashcroft, "Excess," 34, 42.

75. Bataille, *Accursed Share*, 22, emphasis in original.

76. See, for instance, Jameson, "Modernism and Imperialism"; Crawford, *Devolving English Literature*; North, *Dialect of Modernism*; Torgovnick, *Gone Primitive*; and a number of essays in Booth and Rigby, *Modernism and Empire*.

77. "Zoo stories" is Randy Malamud's label for "a wide range of cultural descriptions (and often reactions against) [zoos'] existence" (*Reading Zoos*, 12). Harriet Ritvo calls the animals in Victorian menageries "exotic captives" (*Animal Estate*, 205).

78. Jameson, "Modernism and Imperialism," 51, emphasis added.

79. E. M. Forster, *Aspects of the Novel*, 34.

80. Ibid., 220.

81. Edward Said characterizes "the Napoleonic expedition (1798–1801) as a sort of first enabling experience for modern Orientalism" in *Orientalism*, 122. C. C. Eldridge describes the move away from the seventeenth- and eighteenth-century mercantilist imperialism in the first decades of the nineteenth century in *Victorian Imperialism*, 10–17. Hegel's *Phenomenology of Spirit* first appeared in 1807. The Romantic emphasis on holism and totality is the theme of Abrams's *Natural Supernaturalism*.

82. Chesterton, "Our Notebook," 19 July 1924.

Chapter One

1. Sketchley, *Mrs. Brown at the International Exhibition*, 5.
2. Ibid., 63–64.
3. Sketchley, *Mrs. Brown and King Cetewayo*, 89. For a comprehensive bibliography of the *Mrs. Brown* books, see Topp, *Victorian Yellowbacks and Paperbacks*.
4. Stallybrass and White, *Politics and Poetics of Transgression*, 39, 41.
5. Sketchley, *Mrs. Brown at the Crystal Palace*, 53.
6. Wilson, *Acclimatisation*, 6.
7. Carter, "At the Zoo," 295.
8. Edward Bennett, *Tower Menagerie*, 174.
9. Foucault, *Order of Things*, 131.
10. See Hobsbawm, "Introduction," and Ranger, "The Invention of Tradition," 211.

11. Tony Bennett, *Birth of the Museum*, 65–66.
12. E. Mitchell, Foreword, v–vi.
13. British Library Playbills 171, 16 September 1845.
14. British Library Playbills 172, 11 June 1849; Playbills 173, 26 December 1854.
15. Coleridge, "Lay Sermons," 661.
16. Nat Clifford, "Britannia's Menagerie," stanza 1.
17. *Embellished History*, 14.
18. Timothy Mitchell, "The World as Exhibition," 220.
19. Ibid., 222.
20. Ibid., 229.
21. Stein, "Street Figures," 244–45.
22. Sanger, *Seventy Years a Showman*, 201.
23. "Wombwell's Menagerie at Windsor Castle."
24. Wiener, *English Culture*, 56.
25. Ritvo, *Animal Estate*, 209.
26. Salisbury letter to Lytton.
27. See, for instance, Val C. Prinsep's characterization of it as "a gigantic circus" in *Imperial India*, 29. *Punch* concluded that the lavish dress and elephants' elaborate trappings belonged in a Christmas pantomime ("Manager Beaconsfield's Transformation Scene," 12).
28. Hobson, *The Psychology of Jingoism*, 12.
29. Stallybrass and White, *Politics and Poetics of Transgression*, 193.
30. Chesterton, "Our Notebook," 21 May 1924, emphasis added.
31. Seeley, *Expansion of England*, 304.
32. Henry I established a Royal Menagerie at Woodstock to house his lions, leopards, and camels—"animals which England does not produce," as William of Malmesbury described them—but it did not endure even so long as to form the core of his grandson Henry III's collections. See Edward Bennett, *Tower Menagerie*, xiii, and Hahn, *Tower Menagerie*, 13.
33. Hahn, *Tower Menagerie*, 7–35; Frost, *Old Showmen*, 88–89.
34. Frost, *Old Showmen*, 91–92.
35. Ritvo, *Animal Estate*, 206.
36. Cross, *Companion to the Royal Menagerie*, 3.
37. Altick, *Shows of London*, 308; Hahn, *Tower Menagerie*, 118–20.
38. Middlemiss, *Zoo on Wheels*, 11.
39. Letters to Edward Cross (undated; 29 July 1833; and 7 June 1833), British Library Surrey Zoological Garden Collection (Th.Cts.51), Vol. 1.
40. Bostock, *Menageries, Circuses and Theatres*, 11.
41. Ritvo, *Animal Estate*, 244.
42. Disher, *Greatest Show on Earth*, 276–77. Sanger bought Astley's Amphitheatre at Westminster Bridge in 1871 and managed it simultaneously with his other traveling shows until 1893 (*Seventy Years a Showman*, 197, 230).
43. The Tower Menagerie reflected interests of the state, while the Exeter 'Change Menagerie was a commercial enterprise. Yet animal keepers moved easily

between the Exeter 'Change Menagerie and the Tower Menagerie, and though the Tower Menagerie was a Royal institution, nevertheless Edward Cross termed his Exeter 'Change collection "The Royal Menagerie."

44. Quoted in *Picturesque Guide*, 42.
45. Ritvo, *Animal Estate*, 211.
46. Blunt, *Ark in the Park*, 191.
47. Ritvo, *Animal Estate*, 213.
48. Quoted in *Picturesque Guide*, 42. The phrase "the mere exhibition of animals" does not appear in the prospectus itself but is the *Guide*'s gloss of the prospectus.
49. *Picturesque Guide*, 18.
50. Prospectus quoted in ibid., 42.
51. Ibid.
52. *Catalogue of the Animals*, 1.
53. "Surrey Zoological Gardens," 2.
54. Handbill, British Library Surrey Zoological Garden Collection (Th.Cts.51), Vol. 1.
55. "Surrey Zoological Gardens," 2.
56. Manuscript notes, British Library Surrey Zoological Garden Collection (Th. Cts.51), Vol. 1.
57. Unidentified newspaper clippings of October 1839 and 2 September 1842 in the British Library Surrey Zoological Garden Collection (Th.Cts. 53, 54), Vol. 3, 4.
58. Baratay and Hardouin-Fugier, *Zoo*, 73.
59. Unidentified newspaper clipping of 16 September 1831, British Library Surrey Zoological Garden Collection (Th.Cts.51), Vol. 1.
60. Baratay and Hardouin-Fugier, *Zoo*, 80.
61. Bostock, *Menageries, Circuses and Theatres*, 149.
62. See, e.g., Middlemiss, *Zoo on Wheels*.
63. *Scotsman*, 10 April 1872, quoted in Bostock, *Menageries, Circuses and Theatres*, 7.
64. Steedman, *African Glen*, 4, 7–8, 11.
65. *Illustrated Description*, 3; see also *Grand Moving Diorama [of] Hindostan*.
66. Astley's playbill for 27 March 1826 also promises a representation of "The Royal Rath or Carriage Drawn by Elephants," alongside a "PROCESSION OF THE SACRED WHITE ELEPHANT" (British Library Playbills 171). Whether the Rath's proprietors hired the display out to Astley's or the circus sought to compete with the Egyptian Hall is unclear, but both appearances of the carriage depend upon the zoological exhibition to certify that the representation of the carriage is "correct, authentic and costly," as Astley's advertised it.
67. *The Rath*, 4, 9.
68. Ibid., 4.
69. Broadside handbill, *Now Exhibiting*, 1, 4.
70. Quoted in ibid., 1.
71. Undated handbill, British Library Collection of Handbills Relating to Leicester Square (shelfmark b.25.1880).
72. Weaver, *Exhibitions and the Arts of Display*, 2.

73. "The Colonial Exhibition—India." Peter Hoffenberg argues that the essential work of the long-run exhibition was to "create the ideas and forms of 'Great Britain, India, and our Colonies,' as well as binding together these polities" (*An Empire on Display*, 20).
74. *Colonial and Indian Exhibition, 1886*, lix.
75. Cundall, *Reminiscences of the Colonial and Indian Exhibition*, 24.
76. *Colonial and Indian Exhibition, 1886*, 248.
77. Sketchley, *Mrs. Brown at the International Exhibition*, 74.
78. Knight, *The Exhibitions, Great White City*, 37.
79. Thomas, "Preface," 3.
80. Cross, *Companion to the Royal Menagerie*, 2.
81. *Empire of India Exhibition 1895*, 5–6.
82. These are typical descriptions of the circuses' assemblages, in this case taken from Astley's playbills in British Library Playbills 173 (26 December 1854), Playbills 172 (13 October 1845), and Humphreys, *The Memoirs of J. Decastro*, 55.
83. *Picturesque Guide*, 18.
84. "Surrey Zoological Gardens," 2.
85. Qtd. in Knight and Sabey, *The Lion Roars at Wembley*, 12.
86. Gilpin, *Three Essays*, 19, 14.
87. H. P. Robinson, *Pictorial Effect in Photography*, 35.
88. Ibid., 21.
89. Saville, "Imperialism and the Victorians," 167.
90. Fortescue, *Narrative of the Visit to India*, 2.
91. Newman, *Indian Peepshow*, 291.
92. Price, *Essay on the Picturesque*, 81.
93. British Library Playbills 171 (29 August 1825).
94. Seeley, *Expansion of England*, 9.
95. Sketchley, *Mrs. Brown on the Prince's Visit to India*, 22.
96. Ibid., 104.
97. Burt, *Delineation of Curious Foreign Beasts*; Edward Bennett, *Gardens and Menagerie of the Zoological Society Delineated*.
98. British Library Playbills 172 (24 June 1844).
99. Stein, "Street Figures," 241.
100. Quoted in Bayley, *Albert Memorial*, 100.
101. *The Minute Book of the Prince Consort Memorial*, quoted in Bayley, *Albert Memorial*, 17.
102. Seeley, *Expansion of England*, 202.
103. Berger, *About Looking*, 23.
104. Stallybrass and White, *Politics and Poetics of Transgression*, 39, 41, 42.
105. H. P. Robinson, *Pictorial Effect in Photography*, 29.
106. Reed, *King and Queen in India*, 87.
107. Tyrwhitt-Drake, *English Circus and Fair Ground*, 153.
108. Frost, *Old Showmen*, 305
109. These are associations exploited in, for instance, the title of Judd's *The Lion and the Tiger*.
110. Samuel Johnson gives "Ivory; the teeth of elephants" as his second definition

of "Elephant" in his *Dictionary*.
111. Speaight, *History of the Circus*, 85.
112. Saxe, *Clever Stories of Many Nations*, 61.
113. Ibid., 64.
114. "The Blind Men and the Elephant" was set to music and published in 1906 in the Novello School Song series, which also included a preponderance of songs celebrating Britain as an imperial power.
115. Ritvo, *Animal Estate*, 220.
116. These lines form the epigraph to "The Irish Avatar."
117. "Freaks of Mr. Wombwell's Elephant."
118. "Elephants and Their Keepers."
119. The phrase derived from the attraction of the lions in the Tower Menagerie. By 1832 *Kidd's New Guide to the "Lions" of London* included among the chief metaphorical "lions" Astley's Circus, the Regent's Park Zoo, the Surrey Zoological Gardens, and the Zoological Society Museum.
120. Palmatier, *Speaking of Animals*, 337.
121. Kipling, *Beast and Man in India*, 334–35.
122. Ibid., 335–36.
123. Parks, *Wanderings of a Pilgrim*, 2.frontispiece and 2.121.
124. Altick, *Shows of London*, 310–12, quotation on 312.
125. See, for instance, *Correct Detail of the Destruction* and John Taylor, *Life, Death, and Dissection*.
126. Anonymous account, quoted in Frost, *Circus Life and Circus Celebrities*, 75–76.
127. "The 'Zoo' Elephant Who Will Not Go to America."
128. Haley, "The Colossus of His Kind," 63, also quoting *Harper's Weekly*.
129. Saxon, *P. T. Barnum*, 292.
130. *Daily Telegraph*, quoted in James, "World went mad," 138.
131. Fitzsimons, *Barnum in London*, 1.
132. James, "World went mad," 138. See also Fitzsimons, *Barnum in London*, 168; and Barnum, *Barnum's Own Story*, 430.
133. "Jumbo."
134. Sketchley, *Mrs. Brown on Jumbo*, 7.
135. Ibid., 3, 75.
136. Orwell, "Shooting an Elephant," 4.
137. Ibid., 8.

Chapter Two

1. Disher, *Greatest Show on Earth*, 157. Tyrwhitt-Drake notes that "the heyday of the travelling circus may be said to have been from 1850 to 1900," and he calls this period "the good old days" (*English Circus and Fair Ground*, 17).
2. Dickens letter to Edwin Landseer, 13 June 1847, in *Letters*, 5:89.
3. Thackeray, *Vanity Fair*, 158–59.

NOTES TO CHAPTER 2   227

4. Ibid., 160.
5. Ibid., 160–62.
6. Ibid., 39.
7. Deborah Thomas, *Thackeray and Slavery*, 54.
8. D. J. Taylor, *Thackeray*, 25.
9. Bristed, "Vanity Fair," 69, 73.
10. Thackeray, *Vanity Fair*, 34–35.
11. Ibid., 263. These jokes are not merely the property of the wag at the auction, Old Sedley, and Osborne: the narrative itself makes a joke of the fact that Jos makes inquiry "at the door of the Elephant Hotel" (630).
12. Ibid., 418.
13. Ibid., 28. Astley's advertised its dramatization of "Blue Beard, or Female Curiosity!" on several occasions, including 1 September 1828, when it promoted the spectacular arrival of "BLUE BEARD seated on a Real Elephant." See the British Library Playbills 171.
14. Brantlinger, *Rule of Darkness*, 75.
15. Ibid., 93.
16. John Forster, review of *Vanity Fair* in the *Examiner*, 22 July 1848, 57.
17. Thackeray, *Vanity Fair*, 5.
18. Forster review of *Vanity Fair*, 54.
19. Charlotte Brontë letter to W. S. Williams, 14 August 1848.
20. Rintoul review of *Vanity Fair* in the *Spectator*, 22 July 1848, 59.
21. Rigby, "*Vanity Fair—and Jane Eyre*," 79.
22. Gaskell, *Cranford*, 112.
23. Ibid.
24. Tyrwhitt-Drake, *English Circus and Fair Ground*, 17.
25. Gaskell, *Cranford*, 112. When Peter returns to Cranford from India, he plays upon just such desires: "I don't think the ladies in Cranford would have considered him such a wonderful traveller if they had only heard him talk in the quiet way he did to [the Rector]. They liked him the better, indeed, for being what they called 'so very Oriental'" (154). Patrick Brantlinger reads the discrepancy between Peter's exotic tales and the "tame, monotonous realm of domestic routines and responsibilities" as illustrative of a fundamental "antithesis" between the imperial and the domestic (*Rule of Darkness*, 12). Yet, I would argue, from the point of view of domestic Cranford, Peter's tales ("so very Oriental"), like the elephant and Jos Sedley's stories of tiger hunting, seem to establish an imaginative bridge from the one realm to the other, however inaccurate.
26. Gaskell, *Cranford*, 81.
27. Thackeray, *Vanity Fair*, 28.
28. Ibid., 30.
29. Dickens letter to Elizabeth Gaskell, 18 February 1854, in *Letters*, 7:278.
30. Dickens letter to Miss Marguerite Power, 13 July 1847, in *Letters*, 5:128.
31. Dickens, "Greenwich Fair," 117.
32. Dickens, *Old Curiosity Shop*, 122–23.
33. In "Astley's" Dickens applauds the "scenes in the circle," defying "any one

who has been to Astley's two or three times not to be amused" by its performances (106–7). The repertoire of "scenes in the circle" at the time of *Sketches by Boz* included the "SURPRISING and SAGACIOUS TRICKS" of the elephant arranged by Edward Cross of Exeter 'Change (1 September 1828), and by the middle of his career promised "monkeys on coursers" (7 February 1848); among its other offerings, Astley's featured regular "SIMULACRE of . . . the FINAL TRIUMPH of BRITISH POWER in INDIA!" (27 April 1829) and other British military campaigns. See British Library Playbills 171 and 172.

34. Dickens, "Some Particulars Concerning a Lion," 677, 680, 676.
35. Saxon, "Circus as Theatre," 304–5.
36. British Library Playbills 171, 23 July 1827.
37. British Library Playbills 171, 14 October 1839.
38. Dickens, *Our Mutual Friend*, 563.
39. See, for instance, "Elephants, Fossil and Musical," which concludes that "Droves of elephants, then, have lived where we live."
40. Dickens, *Mystery of Edwin Drood*, 1.
41. Dickens, *Our Mutual Friend*, 749.
42. Horne, "Elephants. Wholesale and Retail," 229, 234, 229.
43. Tyrwhitt-Drake in 1946 noted that "Only once, back in the 'eighties, has an elephant been born in this country," and that elephant either was stillborn or died immediately after birth (*English Circus and Fair Ground*, 145).
44. Horne, "Elephants. Wholesale and Retail," 229.
45. Dickens, "Mr. Booley's View," 217.
46. *Illustrated London News*, 9 November 1850.
47. Dickens, "Mr. Booley's View," 217.
48. Hack, "'Sublimation Strange,'" 130.
49. Dickens, "Mr. Booley's View," 217.
50. Dickens, "Mr. Booley's View," 219.
51. Ibid.
52. Hack, "'Sublimation Strange,'" 130.
53. Quoted in John Forster, *Life of Charles Dickens*, 1:121.
54. Dickens, letter to Mark Lemon, 20 February 1854, in *Letters* 7:279.
55. Dickens, *Hard Times*, 1990 ed., 15n7. *Hard Times*, 2003 ed., 305–6n11.
56. British Library Playbills 173 (Astley's, 5 December 1853). Paul Schlicke describes the "Wise Elephants of the East" as "the most celebrated novelty of the 1853–54 circus season" (*Dickens and Popular Entertainment*, 163).
57. Dickens, *Hard Times*, 1990 ed., 15, 27. Unless otherwise noted, all subsequent references are to this edition.
58. Schlicke, *Dickens and Popular Entertainment*, 163. Simpson's "Hard Times and Circus Times" traces analogues between Sleary's Circus and Astley's.
59. Schlicke, *Dickens and Popular Entertainment*, 163, 148, 7.
60. Tyrwhitt-Drake, *English Circus and Fair Ground*, 144.
61. Stoddart, *Rings of Desire*, 97.
62. Dickens, *Hard Times*, 206.
63. Ibid., 51. See also Dickens's letter to Charles Knight of 17 March 1854

(*Letters*, 7:294), which reveals that the narrator's voice is indistinguishable from that of Dickens on this point.

64. Coles, "Politics of *Hard Times*," 150.
65. Dickens, *Hard Times*, 47.
66. Dickens, letter to John Forster, February 1854, in *Letters* 7:282. See also Butt and Tillotson, *Dickens at Work*, 203.
67. Dickens, "Preface" to *Memoirs of Joseph Grimaldi*, xviii.
68. Stoddart, *Rings of Desire*, 134, 136.
69. "The Elephant at Home," 131.
70. Leavis, *Great Tradition*, 230–31.
71. Dickens, *Hard Times*, 9.
72. Leavis, *Great Tradition*, 231; Dickens, *Hard Times*, 89.
73. Williams, *Culture and Society*, 93.
74. Dickens, *Hard Times*, 149, 215.
75. Williams, *Culture and Society*, 95.
76. Brough, "Hard Times (Refinished)," 309n1.
77. Ibid., 312–13.
78. Dickens, *Hard Times*, 114, 215.
79. "More Trifles from Ceylon," 250.
80. Dickens, *Hard Times*, 11.
81. Ibid., 218, 208.
82. Compare Pleasant Riderhood's "vaporous visions of far-off islands in the southern seas or elsewhere (not being geographically particular)" (*Our Mutual Friend*, 407). Like Rogue Riderhood's daughter, Dickens's narrators often seem to evoke far-off places without "being geographically particular."
83. Dickens, *Hard Times*, 95.
84. Ibid., 174.
85. Ibid., 90.
86. Ibid., 218.
87. Nunokawa, "For Your Eyes Only," 152.
88. Dickens, *Hard Times*, 37, 139.
89. Horne and Dickens, "Great Exhibition and the Little One," 257, 260.
90. Dickens, "Chinese Junk," 72. It is perhaps worth remarking that Dickens's conclusions about the junk do not differ substantially from those provided in the official guide, which concludes above all that the Chinese "unconquerable prejudice, the innate and utter contempt for everything foreign, is a hindrance to all improvement." See *Description of the Royal Chinese Junk*, 12.
91. Dickens, *Hard Times*, 204.
92. Bivona, *Desire and Contradiction*, 114.
93. Ibid., 115.
94. Nayder, "Class Consciousness and the Indian Mutiny," 692.
95. Hobson, *Imperialism*, 201.
96. Ibid., 202.
97. See "Chinese Junk," in which Dickens asserts that "It is pleasant, coming back from China by the Blackwall Railway, to think that . . . in our civilization, we sacrifice

absurd forms to substantial facts" (74). The asserted superiority of fact over fancy here suggests that in *Hard Times* Dickens chiefly objects to facts that have no fanciful forms sacrificed to them. In other words, facts can only seem "substantial" as a result of an encounter with fancy. This is the conclusion Martha Nussbaum draws about the novel as a whole, understanding the opposition between fact and fancy to be resolved dialectically in the form of the novel itself. In *Poetic Justice* she argues that "The novel speaks not of dismissing reason, but of coming upon it in a way illuminated by fancy" (44).

98. Dickens, letter to Charles Knight, 30 December 1854, in *Letters* 7:492.
99. Dickens, *Hard Times*, 36.
100. Leavis, *Great Tradition*, 233.
101. Schlicke, *Dickens and Popular Entertainment*, 156.
102. Dickens, "Some Particulars Concerning a Lion," 677.
103. In *Dickens and Popular Entertainment*, Schlicke notes that at Astley's "during the week of 12 December 1853 characters from *Oliver Twist* were impersonated on horseback, and for two weeks in February roles from *Pickwick* were enacted" (154). Dickens seems to have been quite enthusiastic about the show ring that kept his stories in circulation.
104. Stoddart, *Rings of Desire*, 86.
105. Dickens, *Hard Times*, 19.
106. Ibid., 14.
107. Ibid., 204.
108. Ibid., 207.
109. Ibid., 209.
110. Ibid., 208, 209.
111. Transportation to penal colonies is threatened elsewhere in the novel (112–14), so it is not clear that Tom's escape differs so dramatically from the alternative.
112. Dickens, *Hard Times*, 209.
113. Ibid.
114. Ibid., 212.
115. Dickens, "Some Particulars Concerning a Lion," 676.
116. Dickens, *Hard Times*, 22.
117. Ibid., 22.
118. Dickens, "Noble Savage," 198, 201. As Jeff Nunokawa observes, "The African is not only the object of occidental surveillance . . . but also a character whose native aspect is an exhibition" ("For Your Eyes Only," 147). It is just this "native aspect" of the circus's exhibition that Dickens elides.
119. Dickens, "Noble Savage," 201.
120. Ibid., 197, 202.
121. Ibid., 202.
122. Catherine Gallagher glosses the description of Coketown as a savage in these terms: "These separate metaphors and similes coalesce into a single image of Coketown as a jungle, an image that was used by advocates of 'internal missions'" (*Industrial Reformation of English Fiction*, 160).
123. Stoddart, *Rings of Desire*, 126.
124. Schlicke, *Dickens and Popular Entertainment*, 180.

125. Dickens, "Gin-Shops," 182.
126. Dickens, "Scotland Yard."
127. Buckland, "Zoological Auction."
128. Dickens, *Sketches by Boz*, xiii.
129. Wills, "Forty Years in London," 257.
130. Dickens, *Hard Times*, 11.
131. Kearns, "Tropology of Realism, 857, 859.
132. Dickens, *Hard Times*, 10.
133. Dickens, letter to Peter Cunningham, 11 March 1854, in *Letters* 7:291.
134. Gallagher, *Industrial Reformation of English Fiction*, 159.
135. Dickens, *Hard Times*, 114, 78.
136. Ibid., 47.
137. Cf. John Kucich's claim "that Dickens replaces what Bataille would call a restricted economy . . . with a general economy" ("Repression and Representation," 68). Kucich is concerned primarily with the circulation of individual psychic energies, while the focus here is on the totality of social energies that Dickens binds in the service of a commercial-industrial mode of production.
138. Dickens, *Hard Times*, 219.
139. Nunokawa, "For Your Eyes Only," 138.
140. Bataille, *Accursed Share*, 22.

Chapter Three

1. R. M. Ballantyne's *The Gorilla Hunters* (1861), for instance, offers a humorous piece of dialogue in the middle of Africa: "I'm a student of nature myself, and I have picked up a little useful knowledge in the course of my travels. Did you ever travel so far as the Zoological Gardens in London?" (48). In *The Island of Doctor Moreau* (1896), H. G. Wells's narrator presumes familiarity with the zoo in noting that Moreau's "creatures did not decline into such beasts as the reader has seen in zoological gardens" (198).
2. Darwin, letter to Caroline Darwin, 28 April 1831, in *Letters* 1:131.
3. Browne, *Charles Darwin*, 378.
4. Arnold Bennett, "Elixir of Youth," 26.
5. Ibid.
6. Ibid., 28.
7. Ibid., 26, 28.
8. Ibid., 27.
9. Ibid., 29.
10. Ibid., 36–37.
11. Ibid., 37.
12. Esty, "Amnesia in the Fields," 251.
13. Virginia Woolf, "Character in Fiction," 3:421, 430; Woolf, "Mr. Bennett and Mrs. Brown," 3:387.
14. Quoted in Warrillow, *Arnold Bennett and Stoke-on-Trent*, 53.
15. Arnold Bennett, *Old Wives' Tale*, 1983 ed., 344. All subsequent references to

the novel are to this edition, unless otherwise noted.
16. Ibid., 342.
17. Arnold Bennett, *Author's Craft*, 23.
18. Arnold discusses the "note of provinciality" in literature as indicating a "remoteness from . . . a centre of correct taste" in "The Literary Influence of the Academies," 245. In the preface to *Culture and Anarchy*, he identifies "provincialism" with "loss of totality" and "culture" with the process of "disinterestedly trying . . . to see things as they really are" (36, 30).
19. Lewis et al., "Manifesto—I," 18, 19–20.
20. Virginia Woolf, "Character in Fiction," 3:434.
21. See Hynes, "Whole Contention." For a reading of the exchange between Bennett and Woolf that emphasizes the role of gender rather than class in the debate, see Daugherty, "Whole Contention, Revisited."
22. Arnold Bennett, review of *Room of One's Own*, 225.
23. Wain, *Arnold Bennett*, 8–9.
24. Lucas, "The Idea of the Provincial," 14.
25. Lewis et al., "Manifesto—II," 38.
26. Arnold Bennett, "Desire for France," 51.
27. Trotter, *English Novel in History*, 135.
28. Leonard Woolf, *Imperialism and Civilization*, 15–16.
29. See Pechell, "Paradise of Women," and "Adventurous Woman Traveller."
30. "D'you Know?"
31. Pound, *Arnold Bennett*, 20.
32. Arnold Bennett, *Old Wives' Tale*, 37.
33. Ibid.
34. Ibid. The description of Constance appears in Bennett's *Journal* (245). A character in *The Regent* (1913) describes the Five Towns as "the most English place I've ever seen" (38).
35. Arnold Bennett, *Old Wives' Tale*, 38.
36. Arnold Bennett, *Regent*, 51.
37. "Uncolored" is Rebecca West's characterization of the Five Towns in "Arnold Bennett Himself." She finds Bennett's writing marked by a "preference for the uncolored stuff that lasts over the colored stuff which wears into holes, which is characteristic of English provincial life."
38. Arnold Bennett, *Old Wives' Tale*, 107.
39. Ibid., 109.
40. Arnold Bennett, *Author's Craft*, 19.
41. Robbins, *Feeling Global*, 5.
42. Quoted in Pound, *Arnold Bennett*, 126.
43. Arnold Bennett, *Author's Craft*, 23–24.
44. See Stendhal, *The Red and the Black*, 446–47.
45. Arnold Bennett, *Author's Craft*, 39–40.
46. Lukács, *Meaning of Contemporary Realism*, 34; Arnold Bennett, *Author's Craft*, 27.
47. Warrillow, *Arnold Bennett and Stoke-on-Trent*, 12.

48. Arnold Bennett, *Old Wives' Tale*, 103.
49. Ibid., 104.
50. Ibid., 102.
51. Quoted in Reid, "Interpreting the Festival Calendar," 126–27. In *Borough of Stoke-upon-Trent* (1843), John Ward observed that "A custom formerly prevailed [in Burslem], of adorning the church on the Wake Sunday with branches of trees and shrubs, and was understood as having reference to the dwelling of the Patron Saint, John the Baptist, 'in the Wilderness'" (269–70). For excellent discussions of the wakes traditions in Lancashire and in the area surrounding Birmingham, see Reid, "Interpreting the Festival Calendar"; Poole, "Lancashire Wakes Week" and "Oldham Wakes"; and Walton and Poole, "Lancashire Wakes."
52. Scarratt, *Old Times in the Potteries*, 76.
53. Ward, *Borough of Stoke-upon-Trent*, 269.
54. Walton and Poole, "Lancashire Wakes," 117.
55. For instance, Ebenezer Hunt's *The Rush-Bearing* complains that the wakes "are bad in their institution and hurtful in their consequences to Morality" (6); and *Conversation Between William and James at a Country Wake* indicts "the abominable wickedness of a Wake" (8).
56. Burton, *Rush-Bearing*, 158.
57. Ibid., 157. The list of attractions comes from the *Staffordshire Daily Sentinel* of 23 July 1875, quoted in Edwards, *Potters at Play*, 9.
58. Warrillow, *Arnold Bennett and Stoke-on-Trent*, 53.
59. "A Fight Between Zulu Chiefs."
60. *Embellished History*, 47.
61. *To Mr. Wombwell*.
62. *Embellished History*, 14.
63. "Wombwell's Menagerie" (1849).
64. In *Studies in the Sources of Arnold Bennett's Novels*, Louis Tillier suggests that "The episode [involving the elephant] can probably be traced to a small fact of local history. On April 13, 1872, when Bostock and Wombwell's circus was at Hanley for the Wakes, an elephant ran amok without warning, lifted a boy in his trunk and crushed him against a wall with his head and tusks" (49). This incident could not have occurred at the wakes, however, since the season ran from June to November, and the Stoke wakes were held in the first week of August (Edwards, *Potters* 8), so the carnivalesque setting for the scene is Bennett's invention. Moreover, as both the *Staffordshire Sentinel* and *Staffordshire Advertiser* from 1872 make clear, the elephant was aggravated by the boy, who was throwing stones in the elephant's mouth. Bennett's narrative therefore also strips all provocation from the incident of the elephant's madness. See "Boy Killed by an Elephant at Hanley" and "Killed by an Elephant."
65. When Bennett's literary estate was auctioned in 1936, Sotheby listed among his "Notes for Plots" a cutting of "the original of the dead elephant episode used in 'The Old Wives' Tale,'" which appears to have had to do with the difficulty of disposing of an elephant's corpse, rather than with the violent behavior of the elephant or its execution (*Catalogue of Manuscripts*, 18). The clipping likely recorded the death

of Wombwell's elephant Abdellah, who died after eating a yew tree in September 1898 in Hanley (Middlemiss, *Zoo on Wheels*, 53 plate 76).

66. Arnold Bennett, *Old Wives' Tale*, 102.
67. Ibid., 103.
68. Arnold Bennett, *Regent*, 119.
69. Arnold Bennett, *Clayhanger*, 226.
70. Ibid., 228.
71. Fortescue, *Narrative of the Visit to India*, 120–21.
72. Arnold Bennett, *Clayhanger*, 230.
73. Ibid., 231.
74. Edwin's vision of a host of people "under the empire of one horrible idea" bowing before "a strange and savage god" recalls Conrad's Marlow in *Heart of Darkness* (1899), who famously asserts that "What redeems [imperial conquest] is the idea only. An idea at the back of it, not a sentimental pretence but an idea; and an unselfish belief in the idea—something you can set up, and bow down before, and offer a sacrifice to" (10).
75. Arnold Bennett, *Author's Craft*, 27.
76. Arnold Bennett, *Old Wives' Tale*, 117.
77. Ibid., 103.
78. Ibid., 271, 436. Constance explains to Sophia that the elephant and camels are there because of "Barnum's, you know. They have what they called a central depôt here, because it's the middle of England" (500).
79. Arnold Bennett, *Author's Craft*, 24.
80. Arnold Bennett, *Old Wives' Tale*, 108.
81. Ibid., 112.
82. Ibid., 110.
83. Ibid., 113.
84. Ibid., 116.
85. Arnold Bennett, *Old Wives' Tale: Facsimile Edition*, 90.
86. Arnold Bennett, *Old Wives' Tale*, 113, emphases added.
87. Arnold Bennett, *Author's Craft*, 24.
88. Lukács, *Meaning of Contemporary Realism*, 40.
89. Quoted in ibid., 41.
90. Quoted in ibid.
91. Hepburn, *Art of Arnold Bennett*, 146.
92. J. E. Dearlove, "Artistic Control," 86.
93. In *Politics and Poetics of Transgression* Stallybrass and White cite *The Old Wives' Tale* as an example of a text in which an increasingly capitalist society "locat[es] its most powerful *symbolic* repertoires at borders, margins and edges, rather than at the accepted centres, of the social body" (20–21).
94. Arnold Bennett, *Regent*, 186.
95. Virginia Woolf, "Character in Fiction," 3:434.

Chapter Four

1. Squillace, *Modernism, Modernity, and Arnold Bennett*, 17.
2. Virginia Woolf, "Character in Fiction," 3:434.
3. Williams, *Long Revolution*, 306.
4. Virginia Woolf, *Waves*, 10.
5. Ibid., 22.
6. Marcus, "Britannia Rules *The Waves*," 144.
7. The rhetoric that represented imperialism as a way to reclaim remote provinces from their darkness also ensured that those remote provinces appeared dark in the first place. For a detailed account of the progressive "darkening" of Africa, for instance, see Brantlinger, *Rule of Darkness*, 173–97.
8. Virginia Woolf, *Waves*, 137.
9. See Phillips, *Virginia Woolf Against Empire*.
10. Virginia Woolf, *Three Guineas*, 109.
11. Virginia Woolf, "Thunder at Wembley," 3:412.
12. In *The Voyage Out* (1915), Woolf curiously introduces tigers and elephants into South America: as night falls on the travelers in Santa Marina, the narrator observes that "here in the darkness . . . the houseless animals were abroad, the tigers and the stags, and the elephants coming down in the darkness to drink at pools" (100). The incongruity of these animals in South America suggests Woolf's general desire to evoke colonial space, and perhaps the influence of Leonard Woolf's *The Village in the Jungle* (1913), set in Ceylon.
13. Hegel, for example, emphasizes the "circle rounded and complete in itself" as "a real totality" in *The Logic of Hegel* (quoted in Abrams, *Natural Supernaturalism*, 226).
14. Virginia Woolf, *Between the Acts*, 201.
15. As Caserio asserts in *Novel in England*, Woolf "identifies novelistic art with the separation" of holistic aspirations from their achievement, and her work chronicles "missed encounters of all kinds—political, historical, social, personal" (76).
16. Virginia Woolf, "Character in Fiction," 3:436.
17. Virginia Woolf, *Between the Acts*, 188.
18. Virginia Woolf, *Years*, 389.
19. Orwell, *Coming Up for Air*, 126.
20. Virginia Woolf, *Years*, 348.
21. Ibid., 393.
22. Ibid., 375.
23. Ibid., 376.
24. Ibid., 354.
25. Ibid., 335.
26. Ibid., 389.
27. Virginia Woolf, "The Symbol," 288.
28. Ibid., 312n1.
29. Ibid., 288.
30. Ibid., 289.

31. The vision of elephants drinking at pools is a recurrent one in Woolf's writing. In addition to those noted above, see "Nurse Lugton's Curtain" (1924), in which a whole host of animals is loosed from the print of Nurse Lugton's curtain fabric while she sleeps, and wanders off to a lake. There "the elephants drank; and the giraffes snipped off the leaves on the highest tulip trees" (161).
32. Virginia Woolf, "Symbol," 290.
33. Ibid., 312n.
34. Virginia Woolf, *Years*, 390.
35. Ibid., 390.
36. Ibid., 398, 399, 401.
37. Fanon, *Black Skin, White Masks*, 30, 38.
38. Fanon, *Wretched of the Earth*, 35.
39. Bhabha, *Location of Culture*, 1.
40. Ibid., 1–2.
41. Virginia Woolf, *Years*, 391.
42. Ibid., 392–93.
43. Virginia Woolf, "Thunder at Wembley," 3:412.
44. Empire Exhibition advertisement, 12 April 1924.
45. Virginia Woolf, "Character in Fiction," 3:436.
46. Virginia Woolf, "Mr. Bennett and Mrs. Brown," 3:387.
47. Sadleir, "Why Only Dickens?" If a duel, Bennett nevertheless offered no counterblast to Woolf's assault.
48. On 21 May 1924, eight days before attending the Empire Exhibition, Woolf delivered "Character in Fiction" to T. S. Eliot for his consideration for publication in *The Criterion*. The exhibition clearly did not determine the shape of "Mr. Bennett and Mrs. Brown" or "Character in Fiction"; there are, however, discernible logics linking Woolf's separate critiques of realism in "Character in Fiction" and "Thunder at Wembley," and this connection—rather than any possible causal relation—concerns me here.
49. See, for instance, Phillips, *Virginia Woolf Against Empire*, xxix; Mark Wollaeger, "Woolf, Postcards, and the Elision of Race," 48–51; and Cohen, "Empire from the Street."
50. "Outlook for Great Britain," 38.
51. MacKenzie, *Propaganda and Empire*, 107.
52. Eric Pasold quoted in ibid., 112.
53. A column in the *Graphic*, titled "As an Australian Sees Wembley," noted that the exorbitant cost of the exhibition would be worthwhile "if Wembley served no other purpose than to foster this sense of unity among the British race throughout our scattered Empire."
54. Quoted in Knight and Sabey, *Lion Roars at Wembley*, 12.
55. Virginia Woolf, "Thunder at Wembley," 3:412.
56. MacKenzie, *Propaganda and Empire*, 97.
57. "As Others See the Exhibition."
58. Knight and Sabey, *Lion Roars at Wembley*, 93, 95.
59. Ibid., 52, 55, 57, 59, 67.

60. The term "Great Exhibition" was often used casually in describing Wembley, and handbooks traced the history of the 1924 and 1925 Empire Exhibitions back to the Hyde Park Exhibition of 1851. In the spring the *Graphic* offered an article on three summer "Exhibitions in the Making": the Empire Exhibition, the zoo aquarium, and the Royal Academy. In August the same paper noted that Wembley's competing attractions had left "the popularity of London's Zoo . . . undiminished" ("Familiar Faces at the Zoo").

61. Knight and Sabey, *Lion Roars at Wembley*, 102, 103. The portion of the three-day pageant that depicted the conquest of India seems to have been the most exotic. It "include[d] a state procession of Jehangir, the Great Mogul, in which is seen a group of elephants," in an oriental scene that reprised a typical tableau from the Romantic theater and the Victorian pantomime ("£100,000 Pageant of Empire").

62. Naudeau, "British Empire at Wembley," 33.

63. Fry, "Architecture at Wembley," 242.

64. Arnold Bennett, *Author's Craft*, 23, 27. Sir Lawrence Weaver, director of the UK Exhibits at the Empire Exhibition, noted that "Exhibitions were an English invention" and argued that "their development should be studied with care by a commercial community which owes so much to them" (*Exhibitions and the Arts of Display*, v).

65. "Wembley and Its Millions," 106.

66. Chesterton, "Our Notebook," 19 July 1924.

67. "Wanderer at Wembley," 932.

68. "The British Empire in Microcosm."

69. Centerwall, "Men and Beasts at Wembley," 221–22.

70. *Official Guide: British Empire Exhibition*, 30.

71. Starr, *Lies and Hate in Education*, 31. In this book Starr repeatedly notes the extraordinary impact of the Wembley exhibition on British curricula and textbooks in the 1920s.

72. Fry, "Architecture at Wembley," 242.

73. Timothy Mitchell, "World as Exhibition," 231.

74. Naudeau, "British Empire at Wembley," 30.

75. Ibid., 28.

76. Ibid., 33.

77. Empire Exhibition advertisement, 24 May 1924.

78. Naudeau, "British Empire at Wembley," 32.

79. Arnold Bennett, *Author's Craft*, 11.

80. Timothy Mitchell, "World as Exhibition," 233.

81. Virginia Woolf, "Mr. Bennett and Mrs. Brown," 3:385.

82. E. M. Forster, "Birth of an Empire," 111.

83. MacKenzie, *Propaganda and Empire*, 111.

84. Virginia Woolf, *Diary* 2:305. In criticizing the Edwardians in "Mr. Bennett and Mrs. Brown," Woolf makes a similar complaint about "how feeble a voice and how flimsy a body" their characters exhibit (3:385). In "Character in Fiction" she laments, "The literary convention of the time is so artificial" (3:434).

85. Naudeau, "British Empire at Wembley," 32.

86. "Pioneers of Empire XX," 62.
87. "Pioneers of Empire I," 238.
88. "Pioneers of Empire XIII," 574–75.
89. Ibid., 574.
90. Fry, "Architecture at Wembley," 242.
91. Virginia Woolf, *Passionate Apprentice*, 179–81.
92. Virginia Woolf, "Thunder at Wembley," 3:411.
93. Ibid.
94. Ibid., 3:410.
95. Though Woolf here appears in accord with *Punch* in criticizing Wembley's organization and marketing, it would be a mistake to see Woolf, Roger Fry, *Punch*, and E. M. Forster as a unified front of "modernists" opposing Arnold Bennett, George V, G. K. Chesterton, and the *Illustrated London News* as champions of retrograde, jingoistic methods. The Empire Exhibition of 1924 is a particularly visible site (though not the only one) in the modernist period over which a broad range of figures and institutions struggled to define new relations between contemporary modes of representation and the politics of empire.
96. Virginia Woolf, "Thunder at Wembley," 3:411. In "Nature at Wembley," the manuscript of the essay, Woolf makes this point clearer: "Not nature of wind & forest, but . . . human nature" (34).
97. Virginia Woolf, "Thunder at Wembley," 3:412.
98. Ibid.
99. Virginia Woolf, *Orlando*, 232.
100. Ibid., 229.
101. Virginia Woolf, "Thunder at Wembley," 3:413.
102. "Pioneers of Empire XXI," 118.
103. Virginia Woolf, "Thunder at Wembley," 3:413, emphasis added.
104. Ibid., 3:436.
105. Weaver, "'The Palace of Industry'"; Bennett, *Author's Craft*, 14.
106. Virginia Woolf, "Character in Fiction," 3:426, 425, 432. I invoke here Michel de Certeau's distinction between place and space: "In short, *space is a practiced place*. Thus the street geometrically defined by urban planning is transformed into a space by walkers" (*Practice of Everyday Life*, 117).
107. Virginia Woolf, "Character in Fiction," 3:432.
108. Ibid., 3:432.
109. Virginia Woolf, "Nature at Wembley," 35. In opening the 1925 version of the Wembley exhibition, the King declared, "It was a happy inspiration to make housing and home building a central feature of the Exhibition. For the foundation of the Empire is in the home" (quoted in Knight and Sabey, *Lion Roars at Wembley*, 114). In figuring the Edwardian novel as house and proclaiming its destruction, Woolf might also be acknowledging "home" as the foundation of empire, fully a year before George V's speech.
110. Virginia Woolf, "Thunder at Wembley," 3:412.
111. Timothy Mitchell, "World as Exhibition," 225.
112. Virginia Woolf, "Thunder at Wembley," 3:412.

113. Virginia Woolf, "Character in Fiction," 3:425.
114. Virginia Woolf, "Thunder at Wembley," 3:412.
115. Virginia Woolf, "Character in Fiction," 3:436.
116. Ibid., 3:434.
117. Ibid.
118. Ibid., 3:435.
119. Ibid., 3:434.
120. Fry, "Architecture at Wembley," 242.
121. Ibid., 243.
122. Virginia Woolf, "Mr. Bennett and Mrs. Brown," 3:387.
123. Ashcroft, "Excess," 42.
124. Ibid., 35.
125. Virginia Woolf, "Mr. Bennett and Mrs. Brown," 3:388.
126. Ashcroft, "Excess," 38.
127. Virginia Woolf, "Mr. Bennett and Mrs. Brown," 3:387.
128. Virginia Woolf, "Character in Fiction," 3:436.
129. Virginia Woolf, *Mrs. Dalloway*, 48.
130. Ibid.
131. Ibid., 71.
132. Virginia Woolf, *Years*, 311, 310.
133. Virginia Woolf, *Between the Acts*, 198.
134. Ibid., 192.
135. Virginia Woolf, *Waves*, 136.
136. Sandburg, *Home Front Memo*, 54.
137. Noel Annan quoted in Hussey, *Virginia Woolf A to Z*, 265.
138. See, e.g., Marcus, "Britannia Rules *The Waves*," 148; Hussey, *Virginia Woolf A to Z*, 265. Marcus overstates what she calls Stephen's "brilliant invention of the phrase." It had already appeared in Johnson's *Dictionary* and in the thirty-first chapter of Marx's *Capital*.
139. Marcus, "Britannia Rules *The Waves*," 143.
140. Virginia Woolf, *Waves*, 144.
141. Ibid., 146.
142. Ibid., 232.
143. Ibid., 286.
144. Ibid., 296.
145. See, for instance, former viceroy of India Lord Curzon's speech at Birmingham on 11 December 1907, in which he argued against those anti-imperialists who desired "the strengthening of the centre of the Empire, instead of wasting our force upon its outskirts." Instead he advocated shoring up "the economy of the imperial household" so that "the concentric rings shall continue to revolve round the central star," England. In unapologetically mixing these metaphors, Curzon weds the economic metaphor of domestic space to the systemic imagery of Copernican solarity. See Curzon of Kedleston, "Speech at Birmingham," 354, 355.
146. Virginia Woolf, *Waves*, 292.
147. Conrad, *Heart of Darkness*, 9.

148. Virginia Woolf, *Waves*, 21.
149. Ibid., 22.
150. Ibid., 94.
151. Ibid., 201.
152. Ibid., 223–24.
153. Virginia Woolf, "Character in Fiction," 436.
154. Virginia Woolf, *Between the Acts*, 219.

Chapter Five

1. Joyce, *Ulysses*, 333, 379, 439, 471.
2. Ibid., 64, 444, 454.
3. Djuna Barnes wrote about the Hippodrome in New York City, which did feature zoological exotica, as Laura Winkiel notes, but she treated it primarily as a form of American entrepreneurship ("Circuses and Spectacles").
4. Carter, "At the Zoo," 295.
5. Adorno, *Minima Moralia*, 50.
6. Ibid., 116.
7. Ibid.
8. Ibid., 115.
9. Jameson, *Postmodernism*, 20.
10. Quoted in Rae, *Business of Travel*, 135.
11. Woolf, *Years*, 335.
12. Sartre, *Critique of Dialectical Reason*, 46.
13. Rushdie, "Imaginary Homelands," 18–19.
14. Rushdie, "In the Voodoo Lounge," 87, 88, emphasis added.
15. Rushdie, "U2," 97.
16. Rushdie, "In the Voodoo Lounge," 88.
17. Rushdie, "U2," 95.
18. Ibid., 95.
19. Ibid., 94.
20. U2, "Zooropa."
21. Rushdie, *Midnight's Children*, 474.
22. Rushdie, "In Defense of the Novel," 51.
23. Rushdie, "In the Voodoo Lounge," 91.
24. Rushdie, "Step Across This Line," 364–65.
25. Quoted in Rushdie, "In Defense of the Novel," 50.
26. Ibid., 51.
27. Rushdie, "Step Across This Line," 364.
28. Ibid., 365.
29. Rushdie, "Influence," 69.
30. Rushdie, *Midnight's Children*, 38.
31. Ibid., 116, 537.
32. Ibid., 83–84.

Notes to Chapter 5

33. Brennan, *Salman Rushdie and the Third World*, 96
34. Rushdie, "Adapting *Midnight's Children*," 76.
35. Rushdie, *Midnight's Children*, 50.
36. Chesterton, "Our Notebook," 19 July 1924, 104.
37. Rushdie, *Midnight's Children*, 4.
38. Ibid., 458.
39. Ibid., 319.
40. Ibid., 546.
41. Ibid., 359.
44. Ibid., 84.
43. Brennan, *Salman Rushdie and the Third World*, 116.
44. Ibid., 117.
45. Rushdie, *Midnight's Children*, 494.
46. Rushdie, "A Dream of Glorious Return," 196.
47. Rushdie, "Step Across This Line," 375.
48. Baucom, "Globalit, Inc.," 170.
49. Ibid, 162.
50. U2, "Where the Streets Have No Name."
51. Rushdie, *Midnight's Children*, 355.
52. Rushdie, "Globalization," 267.
53. Carter, *Nights at the Circus*, 114.
54. This is true even of Stoddart's *Rings of Desire*, which mentions Carter's novel only in passing and as part of a discussion of how female aerialists have been represented in the twentieth century.
55. Carter, *Nights at the Circus*, 293.
56. Carter, interview with John Haffenden, 89.
57. Sage, *Angela Carter*, 50.
58. Carter, interview with Haffenden, 79.
59. Ibid.
60. Sally Robinson, *Engendering the Subject*, 131.
61. Carter, *Nights at the Circus*, 210.
62. Carter, interview with Haffenden, 79.
63. Russo, *The Female Grotesque*, 160.
64. Carter, interview with Haffenden, 89; Carter, *Nights at the Circus*, 279.
65. Carter, *Nights at the Circus*, 107.
66. Finney, "Tall Tales and Brief Lives," 170.
67. Carter, interview with Haffenden, 79.
68. Carter, "Animals in the Nursery," 300.
69. Carter, *Nights at the Circus*, 286.
70. Ibid., 106.
71. Ibid., 105.
72. Ibid.
73. Ibid., 106.
74. Ibid., 146.
75. Sanger, *Seventy Years a Showman*, 159.

76. Yeats, "Byzantium," 11.16, 24.
77. Carter, *Nights at the Circus*, 117, 118.
78. Ibid., 125, 117.
79. Ibid., 117.
80. Ibid., 117–18.
81. Ibid., 118, 178, 122.
82. Ibid., 173.
83. Ibid., 171.
84. Ibid., 178.
85. Ibid., 238.
86. Ibid., 285.
87. Hutcheon, *Politics of Postmodernism*, 98.
88. Carter, *Nights at the Circus*, 69.
89. Ibid., 206.
90. Ibid., 231.
91. Ibid., 265.
92. Ibid., 278.
93. Ibid., 273–74.
94. Ibid., 285.
95. Ibid.
96. Baucom, *Out of Place*, 166, 189.
97. Lanchester, "Vision of England."
98. Julian Barnes, interview with Freiburg, 51.
98. Julian Barnes, interview with Birnbaum.
100. Julian Barnes, *Letters from London*, x.
101. Julian Barnes, interview with Birnbaum.
102. Quoted in Moseley, *Understanding Julian Barnes*, 9, 10.
103. Julian Barnes, interview with Birnbaum.
104. Julian Barnes, *A History of the World*, 4.
105. Ibid., 75, 6, 7, 8.
106. Julian Barnes, interview with Birnbaum.
107. Julian Barnes, *Letters from London*, 69, 44–45. John Major's father, Barnes notes, was a circus performer before going into business selling garden gnomes. Nicholas Ridley, Secretary of State for Trade and Industry, sought without success to pay the Turks and Caicos Islands so they would be independent of the UK.
108. Ibid., 160.
109. Ibid., 269.
110. Quoted in Lanchester, "Vision of England."
111. Pateman, *Julian Barnes*, 73.
112. Ibid., 75.
113. Julian Barnes, *England, England*, 39.
114. Ibid., 40–41.
115. Lanchester, "Vision of England."
116. Carey, "Land of Make-Believe."
117. Julian Barnes, interview with Freiburg, 64.

118. Julian Barnes, *Letters from London*, 27.
119. Ibid., 28.
120. Nunning, "Invention of Cultural Traditions," 59.
121. Julian Barnes, *England, England*, 266.
122. Sartre, *Critique of Dialectical Reason*, 47, 46. Sartre offers as an instance of totalization activity fostering imperial expansion (720). On Sartre's distinction between totality and totalization, see Jay, *Marxism and Totality*, 351.
123. Ibid., 252.

Epilogue

1. Mangan, "Homo Exhibitionist Takes Over."
2. "Row Over German Zoo's Africa Show."
3. Mangan, "Homo Exhibitionist Takes Over."
4. Szalwinska, "Don't Feed the Humans."
5. See, e.g., "Houston Zoo Admits a Snake Was a Fake."
6. Phil Milford, "Philadelphia Zoo."
7. Alderson, "Rector on Wild Wallaby Watch."
8. For instance, Lord Bath's home, Longleat, claims to host the first safari park outside Africa and was opened to the public in 1966. See http://www.longleat.co.uk.
9. In the Elephant Sanctuary of Hohenwald, Tennessee. See http://www.elephants.com.
10. Donlan et al., "Re-wilding North America."
11. See http://www.frozenark.org/organization.html.
12. See http://zootycoon.com/default.htm.
13. See http://www.dinosaur-park.com.
14. See http://www.wmsp.co.uk.
15. Brantlinger, *Rule of Darkness*, 239.
16. Plotnitsky, *Reconfigurations*, 288.

Bibliography

"The £100,000 Pageant of Empire: Acting History." *Illustrated London News*, 2 August 1924.
Abrams, M. H. *Natural Supernaturalism: Tradition and Revolution in Romantic Literature*. New York: Norton, 1971.
Adorno, Theodor W. *Minima Moralia: Reflections from Damaged Life*. 1951. Translated by E. F. N. Jephcott. London: Verso, 1974.
"An Adventurous Woman Traveller." *Woman*, 27 January 1897.
Alderson, Andrew. "Rector on Wild Wallaby Watch After 70mph Collision on M1." *Daily Telegraph*, 21 August 2005.
Altick, Richard D. *The Presence of the Present*. Columbus: The Ohio State University Press, 1991.
——. *The Shows of London*. Cambridge, MA: Harvard University Press, 1978.
Arnold, Matthew. *Culture and Anarchy*. 1869. Edited by J. Dover Wilson. Cambridge: Cambridge University Press, 1960.
——. "The Literary Influence of the Academies." 1865. In *Lectures and Essays in Criticism*, edited by R. H. Super, 232–57. Ann Arbor: University of Michigan Press, 1962.
"As an Australian Sees Wembley." *The Graphic*, 6 September 1924.
"As Others See the Exhibition: The American Point of View." *The Graphic*, 10 May 1924.
Ashcroft, Bill. "Excess: Post-colonialism and the Verandahs of Meaning." In *Describing Empire: Post-colonialism and Textuality*, edited by Chris Tiffin and Alan Lawson, 33–44. New York: Routledge, 1994.
Auerbach, Jeffrey A. *The Great Exhibition of 1851: A Nation on Display*. New Haven, CT: Yale University Press, 1999.
Ballantyne, R. M. *The Gorilla Hunters*. 1861. Philadelphia: Porter & Coates, 1876.
Baratay, Eric, and Elisabeth Hardouin-Fugier. *Zoo: A History of Zoological Gardens in the West*. Translated by Oliver Welsh. London: Reaktion, 2002.
Barnes, Djuna. *Nightwood*. New York: Harcourt, Brace, 1937.
Barnes, Julian. *England, England*. 1998. New York: Knopf, 1999.
——. *A History of the World in 10½ Chapters*. 1989. New York: Vintage, 1990.
——. Interview with Robert Birnbaum. http://www.julianbarnes.com/birnbaum-ee.html.
——. Interview with Rudolf Freiburg. In "*Do You Consider Yourself a Postmodern*

Author?" *Interviews with Contemporary English Writers*, edited by Rudolf Freiburg and Jan Schnitker, 39–66. Muenster: LIT, 1999.

———. *Letters from London.* New York: Vintage, 1995.

Barnum, P. T. *Barnum's Own Story.* Edited by Waldo R. Browne. New York: Viking, 1927.

Bataille, Georges. *The Accursed Share. Vol. 1: Consumption.* Translated by Robert Hurley. New York: Zone Books, 1991.

Baucom, Ian. "Globalit, Inc.; or, The Cultural Logic of Global Literary Studies." *PMLA* 116.1 (January 2001): 158–72.

———. *Out of Place: Englishness, Empire, and the Locations of Identity.* Princeton, NJ: Princeton University Press, 1999.

Baudrillard, Jean. *Simulacra and Simulation.* Translated by Sheila Faria Glaser. Ann Arbor: University of Michigan Press, 1994.

Bayley, Stephen. *The Albert Memorial: The Monument in Its Social and Architectural Context.* London: Scolar Press, 1981.

Benedict, Barbara M. *Curiosity: A Cultural History of Early Modern Inquiry.* Chicago: University of Chicago Press, 2001.

Bennett, Arnold. *The Author's Craft.* 1913. London: Hodder and Stoughton, 1914.

———. *Clayhanger.* 1910. Harmondsworth, UK: Penguin, 1989.

———. "The Desire for France." 1913. In *Sketches for Autobiography,* edited by James Hepburn, 49–52. London: Allen and Unwin, 1979.

———. "The Elixir of Youth." 1907. In *The Matador of the Five Towns,* 26–37. New York: Doran, 1912.

———. *The Journal of Arnold Bennett.* New York: Viking, 1933.

———. *The Old Wives' Tale.* 1908. Harmondsworth, UK: Penguin, 1983.

———. *The Old Wives' Tale: Facsimile Edition of the Author's Manuscript.* New York: Doran, 1927.

———. *The Regent.* 1913. London: Methuen, 1929.

———. Review of *A Room of One's Own.* 1929. In *"The Author's Craft" and Other Critical Writings,* edited by Samuel Hynes, 225–27. Lincoln: University of Nebraska Press, 1968.

———. *Riceyman Steps.* New York: Doran, 1923.

Bennett, Edward Turner. *The Gardens and Menagerie of the Zoological Society Delineated.* 2 vols. Volume 1, London: John Sharpe, 1830; volume 2, London: Charles Tilt, 1831.

———. *The Tower Menagerie.* London: Robert Jennings, 1829.

Bennett, Tony. *The Birth of the Museum.* New York: Routledge, 1995.

Berger, John. *About Looking.* 1980. New York: Vintage, 1991.

Bhabha, Homi. "DissemiNation." In *Nation and Narration,* edited by Homi Bhabha, 291–322. New York: Routledge, 1990.

———. *The Location of Culture.* London: Routledge, 1994.

Bivona, Daniel. *Desire and Contradiction: Imperial Visions and Domestic Debates in Victorian Literature.* New York: Manchester University Press, 1990.

"The Blind Men and the Elephant." *Novello's School Songs No. 657.* London: Novello, 1906.

Blunt, Wilfrid. *The Ark in the Park: The Zoo in the Nineteenth Century.* London: Hamish Hamilton, 1976.
Booth, Howard J., and Nigel Rigby, eds. *Modernism and Empire.* Manchester, UK: Manchester University Press, 2000.
Bostock, E. H. *Menageries, Circuses and Theatres.* New York: Frederick A. Stokes, 1928.
"A Boy Killed by an Elephant at Hanley." *Staffordshire Sentinel,* 20 April 1872.
Brantlinger, Patrick. *Rule of Darkness: British Literature and Imperialism, 1830–1914.* Ithaca, NY: Cornell University Press, 1988.
Brennan, Timothy. *Salman Rushdie and the Third World.* New York: St. Martin's Press, 1989.
Bristed, Charles Astor. "Vanity Fair." *American Review,* October 1848. Reprinted in *Thackeray: The Critical Heritage,* edited by Geoffrey Tillotson and Donald Hawes, 68–76. London: Routledge and Kegan Paul, 1968.
"The British Empire: Imperial Amnesia." *The Economist,* 28 March 1998: 52.
"The British Empire in Microcosm: The Largest Exhibition Ever Planned, as It Will Appear." *Illustrated London News,* 19 January 1924.
Brontë, Charlotte. Letter to W. S. Williams, 14 August 1848. Reprinted in *Thackeray: The Critical Heritage,* edited by Geoffrey Tillotson and Donald Hawes, 51–52. London: Routledge and Kegan Paul, 1968.
Brough, Robert. "Hard Times (Refinished)." 1857. In *Dickens: The Critical Heritage,* edited by Philip Collins, 309–13. New York: Barnes and Noble, 1971.
Browne, Janet. *Charles Darwin: The Power of Place.* New York: Knopf, 2002.
Buckland, Francis Trevelyan. "A Zoological Auction." *Household Words* 12.303 (12 January 1856): 570–72.
Burt, N. *Delineation of Curious Foreign Beasts and Birds, in Their Natural Colours.* London: N. Burt, 1791.
Burton, Alfred. *Rush-Bearing.* Manchester, UK: Brook and Chrystal, 1891.
Butt, John, and Kathleen Tillotson. *Dickens at Work.* London: Methuen, 1957.
Byron, George Gordon Lord. "The Irish Avatar." 1821. *Complete Poetical Works,* Vol. 6. Edited by Jerome McGann and Barry Weller. Oxford: Clarendon Press, 1991.
C., J. "NB." *Times Literary Supplement,* 1 November 2002.
Camden, Charles. *The Travelling Menagerie.* London: Henry S. King & Co., 1873.
Carey, John. "Land of Make-Believe." *Sunday Times* (London), 23 August 1998.
Carter, Angela. "Animals in the Nursery." 1976. In *Shaking a Leg: Collected Writings,* 298–301. New York: Penguin, 1998.
———. "At the Zoo." 1976. In *Shaking a Leg: Collected Writings,* 294–98. New York: Penguin, 1998.
———. Interview with John Haffenden. 1984. In *Novelists in Interview,* edited by John Haffenden, 76–96. New York: Methuen, 1985.
———. *Nights at the Circus.* 1984. New York: Penguin, 1986.
Caserio, Robert L. *The Novel in England, 1900–1950.* New York: Twayne, 1999.
Catalogue of the Animals Preserved in the Museum of the Zoological Society. London: Richard Taylor, 1829.
Catalogue of the Manuscripts and Correspondence of Arnold Bennett. London: Sotheby & Co., 1936.

Centerwall, Bror. "Men and Beasts at Wembley." *Living Age* 322 (2 August 1924): 221–24.
Chaudhuri, Amit. "Forms of Renewal." *Times Literary Supplement*, 6 February 2004.
Chesterton, G. K. "Our Notebook." *Illustrated London News*, 21 May 1924.
———. "Our Notebook." *Illustrated London News*, 19 July 1924.
Clifford, James. *Routes: Travel and Translation in the Late Twentieth Century*. Cambridge, MA: Harvard University Press, 1997.
Clifford, Nat. "Britannia's Menagerie." London: Francis, Day, and Hunter, [1900].
Cohen, Scott. "The Empire from the Street: Virginia Woolf, Wembley, and Imperial Monuments." *MFS* 50.1 (Spring 2004): 85–109.
Coleridge, Samuel Taylor. "Lay Sermons." 1816. In *Samuel Taylor Coleridge*, edited by H. J. Jackson, 660–65. Oxford: Oxford University Press, 1985.
Coles, Nicholas. "The Politics of *Hard Times*: Dickens the Novelist versus Dickens the Reformer." *Dickens Studies Annual* 15 (1986): 145–79.
Colonial and Indian Exhibition, 1886. Official Catalogue. London: William Clowes and Sons, 1886.
"The Colonial Exhibition—India." *The Graphic*, 15 May 1886.
Conrad, Joseph. *Heart of Darkness*. 1899. Edited by Robert Kimbrough. New York: W. W. Norton, 1988.
A Conversation Between William and James at a Country Wake. London: J. Evans and Sons, [1800].
A Correct Detail of the Destruction of the Furious Elephant at Exeter Change. London: J. Harrison, 1826.
Crawford, Robert. *Devolving English Literature*. Oxford: Clarendon Press, 1992.
Cross, Edward. *Companion to the Royal Menagerie, Exeter 'Change*. London: Tyler & Honeyman, 1820.
Cundall, Frank, ed. *Reminiscences of the Colonial and Indian Exhibition*. London: William Clowes, 1886.
Curzon of Kedleston, George, Lord. "Speech at Birmingham, 11 December 1907." In *The Concept of Empire*, edited by George Bennett, 354–57. London: Adam and Charles Black, 1953.
Darwin, Charles. *The Correspondence of Charles Darwin*. 2 vols. Cambridge: Cambridge University Press, 1985.
Daugherty, Beth Rigel. "The Whole Contention Between Mr. Bennett and Mrs. Woolf, Revisited." In *Virginia Woolf: Centennial Essays*, edited by Elaine K. Ginsberg and Laura Moss Gottlieb, 269–94. Troy, NY: Whitston Publishing, 1983.
Davies, Caroline. "East End Gives the Queen a Cosmopolitan Festival Welcome." *Daily Telegraph*, 10 May 2002.
Dearlove, J. E. "Artistic Control and an All-Embracing Compassion in *The Old Wives' Tale*." *Arnold Bennett Newsletter* 2.1 (Winter–Spring 1976): 76–89.
de Certeau, Michel. *The Practice of Everyday Life*. Translated by Steven Rendall. Berkeley: University of California Press, 1988.
A Description of the Royal Chinese Junk, "Keying." 5th edition. London: The Proprietors, 1848.
Dickens, Charles. "Astley's." In *Sketches by Boz*, 104–10.

———. "The Chinese Junk." 1848. In *Old Lamps for New Ones*, edited by Frederick G. Kitton, 70–74. New York: New Amsterdam Book Company, 1897.
———. "Gin-Shops," In *Sketches by Boz*, 182–87.
———. "Greenwich Fair." In *Sketches by Boz*, 111–18.
———. *Hard Times*. 1853–54. Edited by George Ford and Sylvère Monod. 2nd edition. New York: W. W. Norton, 1990.
———. *Hard Times*. 1853–54. Edited by Kate Flint. New York: Penguin, 2003.
———. *Letters of Charles Dickens*. 12 vols. Edited by Madeline House, Graham Storey, and Kathleen Tillotson. Oxford: Clarendon Press, 1965–2002.
———. "Mr. Booley's View of the Last Lord Mayor's Show." *Household Words* 36 (30 November 1850): 217–19.
———. *The Mystery of Edwin Drood*. 1870. London: Oxford University Press, 1963.
———. "The Noble Savage." 1853. In *Reprinted Pieces*, 197–202. New York: Macmillan, 1896.
———. *The Old Curiosity Shop*. 1840–41. Edited by Elizabeth M. Brennan. Oxford: Clarendon Press, 1997.
———. *Our Mutual Friend*. 1864–65. Edited by Stephen Gill. Harmondsworth, UK: Penguin, 1985.
———. "Preface." In *Memoirs of Joseph Grimaldi*. Edited by "Boz" (Charles Dickens). 2 vols. London: Richard Bentley, 1838.
———. "Scotland Yard." *Morning Chronicle*, 4 October 1836.
———. *Sketches by Boz*. 1836. London: Oxford University Press, 1963.
———. "Some Particulars Concerning a Lion." In *Sketches by Boz*, 676–80.
Disher, M. Willson. *Greatest Show on Earth*. London: G. Bell, 1937.
Donlan, Josh et al. "Re-wilding North America." *Nature* 436 (18 August 2005): 913–14.
"D'you Know?" *Woman*, 7 July 1897.
Eagleton, Terry. *Exiles and Émigrés: Studies in Modern Literature*. New York: Shocken Books, 1970.
Edwards, Mervyn. *Potters at Play: A Look at Popular Entertainment in the Six Towns*. Leek, Staffs.: Churnet Valley Books, 1996.
Eldridge, C. C. *Victorian Imperialism*. Atlantic Highlands, NJ: Humanities Press, 1978.
"The Elephant at Home." *All the Year Round* 2.32 (3 December 1859): 129–32.
"Elephants and Their Keepers." *Times* (London), 20 April 1855.
"Elephants, Fossil and Musical." *All the Year Round* 5.120 (10 August 1861): 473–75.
Ellis, Havelock. "Introduction." 1922. In J. K. Huysmans, *Against the Grain (A Rebours)*. 1889. New York: Hartsdale House, 1931.
Ellmann, Richard. *James Joyce*. New York: Oxford University Press, 1959.
Embellished History of the Extensive and Superb Caravan of Animals. New York: Raymond, Ogden, & Co. [1850].
Empire Exhibition advertisement. *The Graphic*, 12 April 1924.
Empire Exhibition advertisement. *The Graphic*, 24 May 1924.
Empire of India Exhibition 1895. Illustrated Guide to The Jungle. London: Rowland Ward & Co., 1895.

Esty, Joshua D. "Amnesia in the Fields: Late Modernism, Late Imperialism, and the English Pageant Play." *ELH* 69 (2002): 245-76.

Esty, Jed. *A Shrinking Island: Modernism and National Culture in England.* Princeton, NJ: Princeton University Press, 2004.

"Exhibitions in the Making." *The Graphic,* 5 April 1924.

"Familiar Faces at the Zoo." *The Graphic,* 23 August 1924.

Fanon, Frantz. *Black Skin, White Masks.* Translated by Charles Lam Markmann. New York: Grove, 1967.

———. *The Wretched of the Earth.* Translated by Constance Farrington. New York: Grove, 1963.

The Festival of Empire and the Pageant of London. May, June, July 1910. At the Crystal Palace. Bristol: Edward Everard, 1910.

"A Fight Between Zulu Chiefs." *Times* (London), 25 October 1890.

Finney, Brian H. "Tall Tales and Brief Lives: Angela Carter's *Nights at the Circus.*" *Journal of Narrative Technique* 28.2 (Spring 1998): 161-85.

Fitzsimons, Raymund. *Barnum in London.* New York: St. Martin's Press, 1970.

Forster, E. M. *Aspects of the Novel.* London: Edward Arnold, 1927.

———. "The Birth of an Empire." *The Nation and the Athenaeum,* 26 April 1924, 110-11.

———. "Notes on the English Character." 1920. In *Abinger Harvest,* 3-15. New York: Harcourt, Brace & World, 1964.

———. *A Passage to India.* New York: Harcourt, Brace, 1924.

Forster, John. *The Life of Charles Dickens.* 1872-74. 2 vols. London: J. M. Dent, 1966.

———. Review of *Vanity Fair* in the *Examiner,* 22 July 1848. Reprinted in *Thackeray: The Critical Heritage,* edited by Geoffrey Tillotson and Donald Hawes, 53-58. London: Routledge and Kegan Paul, 1968.

Fortescue, John. *Narrative of the Visit to India of Their Majesties King George V and Queen Mary.* London: Macmillan, 1912.

Foucault, Michel. *Discipline and Punish.* Translated by Alan Sheridan. New York: Vintage, 1979.

———. *The Order of Things: An Archaeology of the Human Sciences.* 1970. New York: Vintage, 1990.

"Freaks of Mr. Wombwell's Elephant." *Times* (London), 3 May 1850.

Freud, Sigmund. "The 'Uncanny.'" 1919. In *The Standard Edition of the Complete Psychological Works of Sigmund Freud,* edited by James Strachey, vol. 17, 219-56. London: Hogarth Press, 1964.

Friedman, Susan Stanford. *Mappings: Feminism and the Cultural Geographies of Encounter.* Princeton, NJ: Princeton University Press, 1998.

Frost, Thomas. *Circus Life and Circus Celebrities.* London: Tinsley Brothers, 1875.

———. *The Old Showmen and the Old London Fairs.* London: Chatto & Windus, 1881.

Fry, Roger. "Architecture at Wembley." *The Nation and the Athenaeum,* 24 May 1924, 242-43.

Gallagher, Catherine. *The Industrial Reformation of English Fiction.* Chicago: University of Chicago Press, 1985.

Gaskell, Elizabeth. *Cranford.* 1853. Edited by Elizabeth Porges Watson. London: Oxford University Press, 1972.
George, Wilma. *Animals and Maps.* Berkeley and Los Angeles: University of California Press, 1969.
Gilpin, William. *Three Essays: On Picturesque Beauty; On Picturesque Travel; and on Sketching Landscape.* 2nd edition. London: R. Blamire, 1794.
Grand Moving Diorama [of] Hindostan. London: Asiatic Gallery, 1851.
Gunning, Tom. "The World as Object Lesson." *Film History* 6 (1994): 422–44.
Hack, Daniel. "'Sublimation Strange': Allegory and Authority in *Bleak House.*" *ELH* 66.1 (Spring 1999): 129–56.
Hahn, Daniel. *The Tower Menagerie.* London: Simon & Schuster, 2003.
Haley, James L. "The Colossus of His Kind: Jumbo." *American Heritage* 24.5 (August 1973): 62–68, 82–85.
Hamilton, Alan. "East End Passion Puts the Pearl in Jubilee Crown." *Times* (London), 10 May 2002.
Hepburn, James. *The Art of Arnold Bennett.* Bloomington: Indiana University Press, 1963.
Hobhouse, Hermione. *The Crystal Palace and the Great Exhibition.* London: Athlone Press, 2002.
Hobsbawm, Eric. "Introduction: Inventing Traditions." In *The Invention of Tradition*, edited by Eric Hobsbawm and Terence Ranger, 1–14. Cambridge: Cambridge University Press, 1983.
Hobson, J. A. *Imperialism: A Study.* 1902. Ann Arbor: University of Michigan Press, 1965.
———. *The Psychology of Jingoism.* London: Grant Richards, 1901.
Hoffenberg, Peter H. *An Empire on Display: English, Indian, and Australian Exhibitions from the Crystal Palace to the Great War.* Berkeley: University of California Press, 2001.
Horne, R. H. "Elephants. Wholesale and Retail." *Household Words* 3.62 (31 May 1851): 229–35.
Horne, R. H., and Charles Dickens. "The Great Exhibition and the Little One." *Household Words* 3.67 (5 July 1851): 356–60.
"Houston Zoo Admits a Snake Was a Fake." *New York Times*, 20 September 1984.
Huggan, Graham. "The Postcolonial Exotic." *Transition* 64 (1994): 22–29.
Humphreys, R., ed. *The Memoirs of J. Decastro.* London: Sherwood, Jones, & Co., 1824.
Hunt, Ebenezer. *The Rush-Bearing: A Poem, With a Probable Account of the Rise of Wakes.* Huddersfield: Joseph Brook, 1784.
Hussey, Mark. *Virginia Woolf A to Z.* New York: Oxford University Press, 1996.
Hutcheon, Linda. *The Politics of Postmodernism.* New York: Routledge, 1989.
Hynes, Samuel. "The Whole Contention Between Mr. Bennett and Mrs. Woolf." In *Edwardian Occasions*, 24–38. New York: Oxford University Press, 1972.
An Illustrated Description of the Diorama of the Ganges. London: Portland Gallery, 1850.
James, Henry. "The Art of Fiction." 1888. In *The Art of Fiction and Other Essays*, edited by Morris Roberts, 3–23. New York: Oxford University Press, 1948.

James, Theodore, Jr. "World Went Mad When Mighty Jumbo Came to America." *Smithsonian* 13.2 (1982): 134–52.
Jameson, Fredric. "Modernism and Imperialism." In *Nationalism, Colonialism, and Literature*, edited by Terry Eagleton, Fredric Jameson, and Edward W. Said, 43–66. Minneapolis: University of Minnesota Press, 1990.
———. *Postmodernism or, The Cultural Logic of Late Capitalism*. Durham, NC: Duke University Press, 1991.
Jay, Martin. *Marxism and Totality: The Adventures of a Concept from Lukács to Habermas*. Berkeley and Los Angeles: University of California Press, 1984.
Johnson, Samuel. *A Dictionary of the English Language*. 1755. 2 vols. New York: AMS Press, 1967.
Joyce, James. *Ulysses*. 1922. New York: Vintage, 1990.
Judd, Denis. *The Lion and the Tiger: The Rise and Fall of the British Raj, 1600–1947*. New York: Oxford University Press, 2004.
"Jumbo." *New York Times*, 11 April 1882.
Jumbo's Picture Book of Natural History. London: George Routledge, 1883.
Kaveney, Roz. "Guess Who's for Dinner." *Times Literary Supplement*, 19 July 2002.
Kearns, Katherine. "A Tropology of Realism in *Hard Times*." *ELH* 59 (1992): 857–81.
Kenner, Hugh. *A Sinking Island: The Modern English Writers*. New York: Knopf, 1988.
Kidd's New Guide to the "Lions" of London. London: W. Kidd, 1832.
"Killed by an Elephant." *Staffordshire Advertiser*, 20 April 1872.
Kipling, John Lockwood. *Beast and Man in India: A Popular Sketch of Indian Animals in Their Relations with the People*. 2nd edition. London: Macmillan, 1892.
Knight, Donald R. *The Exhibitions, Great White City, Shepherds Bush, London*. London: Barnard & Westwood, 1978.
Knight, Donald R., and Alan D. Sabey. *The Lion Roars at Wembley: British Empire 60th Anniversary 1924–25*. London: Barnard & Westwood, 1984.
Kucich, John. "Repression and Representation: Dickens's General Economy." *Nineteenth-Century Fiction* 38 (1983): 62–77.
Kureishi, Hanif. *The Buddha of Suburbia*. New York: Penguin, 1990.
Lanchester, John. "A Vision of England." *Electronic Telegraph*, 29 August 1998 (www.telegraph.co.uk).
Lawrence, D. H. "Surgery for the Novel—Or a Bomb." 1923. In *Selected Literary Criticism*, edited by Anthony Beal, 114–18. London: Heinemann, 1967.
Leavis, F. R. *The Great Tradition: George Eliot, Henry James, and Joseph Conrad*. New York: George W. Stewart, 1948.
Levy, Andrea. *Small Island*. 2004. New York: Picador, 2005.
Lewis, Wyndham. "Manifesto—I." In *Blast 1*, 11–28. 1914. Santa Rosa, CA: Black Sparrow Press, 1992.
———. "Manifesto—II." In *Blast 1*, 30–43. 1914. Santa Rosa, CA: Black Sparrow Press, 1992.
Lidell, Scotland. "My Zigzag British Empire Tour." *The Graphic*, 9 August 1924.
Lucas, John. "The Idea of the Provincial." In *Romantic to Modern Literature:*

Essays and Ideas of Culture, 1750–1900, 7–29. Brighton, UK: Harvester Press, 1982.

Lukács, Georg. *The Meaning of Contemporary Realism.* Translated by John and Necke Mander. London: Merlin Press, 1963.

MacKenzie, John M. *Propaganda and Empire.* Manchester, UK: Manchester University Press, 1986.

Malamud, Randy. *Reading Zoos: Representations of Animals and Captivity.* New York: New York University Press, 1998.

"Manager Beaconsfield's Transformation Scene." *Punch,* 13 January 1877.

Mangan, Lucy. "Homo Exhibitionist Takes Over Zoo's Bear Mountain." *The Guardian,* 26 August 2005.

Marcus, Jane. "Britannia Rules *The Waves.*" In *Decolonizing Tradition,* edited by Karen R. Lawrence, 136–62. Urbana and Chicago: University of Illinois Press, 1992.

Martel, Yann. *Life of Pi.* New York: Harcourt, 2001.

Middlemiss, J. L. *A Zoo on Wheels: Bostock and Wombwell's Menagerie.* Burton-on-Trent, UK: Dalebrook Publications, 1987.

Milford, Phil. "Philadelphia Zoo May Move Elephants as Costs Rise." *Plain Dealer* (Cleveland), 19 November 2005.

Miller, Andrew H. *Novels Behind Glass: Commodity Culture and Victorian Narrative.* Cambridge: Cambridge University Press, 1995.

Miller, Jonathan. "Devolution Revolution: Are Swells of Politics and Pride Breaking Up the United Kingdom?" *Washington Post,* 18 October 1998.

Mitchell, E. Rosslyn. Foreword to E. H. Bostock, *Menageries, Circuses and Theatres.* New York: Frederick A. Stokes, 1928.

Mitchell, Timothy. *Colonising Egypt.* Cambridge: Cambridge University Press, 1988.

———. "The World as Exhibition." *Comparative Studies in Society and History* 31.2 (April 1989): 217–36.

"More Trifles from Ceylon." *All the Year Round,* 11.261 (23 April 1864): 249–53.

Moseley, Merritt. *Understanding Julian Barnes.* Columbia: University of South Carolina Press, 1997.

Nairn, Tom. *The Break-Up of Britain: Crisis and Neo-Nationalism.* London: NLB, 1977.

Naudeau, Ludovic. "The British Empire at Wembley." *Living Age* 322 (5 July 1924): 28–33.

Nayder, Lillian. "Class Consciousness and the Indian Mutiny in Dickens' 'The Perils of Certain English Prisoners.'" *SEL* 32 (1992): 689–705.

Newman, Henry. *Indian Peepshow.* London: G. Bell, 1937.

Norfolk, Lawrence. "Who's Out." *Times Literary Supplement,* 11 April 2003.

North, Michael. *The Dialect of Modernism: Race, Language, and Twentieth-Century Literature.* Oxford: Oxford University Press, 1994.

Now Exhibiting, at the Egyptian Hall, Piccadilly The Bosjesmans, Or Bush People. London: Egyptian Hall, 1847.

Nunning, Vera. "The Invention of Cultural Traditions: The Construction and Deconstruction of Englishness and Authenticity in Julian Barnes' *England,*

England." Anglia 119 (2001): 58–76.

Nunokawa, Jeff. "For Your Eyes Only: Private Property and the Oriental Body in *Dombey and Son*." In *The Macropolitics of Nineteenth-Century Literature*, edited by Jonathan Arac and Harriet Ritvo, 138–58. Philadelphia: University of Pennsylvania Press, 1991.

Nussbaum, Martha. *Poetic Justice: The Literary Imagination and Public Life*. Boston: Beacon Press, 1995.

Official Guide: British Empire Exhibition 1925. London: Fleetway, 1925.

Orwell, George. *Coming Up for Air*. 1939. New York: Harcourt, Brace, 1950.

———. *The English People*. London: Collins, 1947.

———. "Shooting an Elephant." In *Shooting an Elephant and Other Essays*, 3–12. New York: Harcourt, Brace, 1950.

"The Outlook for Great Britain." *The Nation and the Athenaeum*, 12 April 1924, 38–39.

Owen, Geoffrey. "Where We Went Right." *Times Literary Supplement*, 2 April 2004.

Palmatier, Robert A. *Speaking of Animals: A Dictionary of Animal Metaphors*. Westport, CT: Greenwood Press, 1995.

Parks, Fanny. *Wanderings of a Pilgrim in Search of the Picturesque, During Four-and-Twenty Years in the East*. 2 volumes. London: Pelham Richardson, 1850.

Pateman, Matthew. *Julian Barnes*. London: Northcote House, 2002.

Paxman, Jeremy. *The English: A Portrait of a People*. London: Michael Joseph, 1998.

Pechell, M. "The Paradise of Women." *Woman*, 13 January 1897.

Phillips, Kathy J. *Virginia Woolf Against Empire*. Knoxville: University of Tennessee Press, 1994.

A Picturesque Guide to The Regent's Park. London: John Limbird, 1829.

"Pioneers of Empire I." *Punch*, 5 March 1924, 238–39.

"Pioneers of Empire XIII.—India." *Punch*, 28 May 1924, 574–75.

"Pioneers of Empire XX.—Forty Winks." *Punch*, 16 July 1924, 62–63.

"Pioneers of Empire XXI.—The Pageant is Delayed." *Punch*, 30 July 1924, 118–19.

Plotnitsky, Arkady. *Reconfigurations: Critical Theory and General Economy*. Gainesville: University Press of Florida, 1993.

Poole, Robert. "Lancashire Wakes Week." *History Today* 34 (August 1984): 22–29.

———. "Oldham Wakes." In *Leisure in Britain, 1780–1939*, edited by John K. Walton and James Walvin, 71–98. Manchester, UK: Manchester University Press, 1983.

Porter, Bernard. *Britain, Europe and the World, 1850–1986: Delusions of Grandeur*. 2nd edition. London: Allen & Unwin, 1987.

Pound, Reginald. *Arnold Bennett: A Biography*. London: Heinemann, 1952.

Price, Uvedale. *An Essay on the Picturesque, as Compared with the Sublime and the Beautiful*. London: J. Robson, 1794.

Prinsep, Val C. *Imperial India. An Artist's Journal*. London: Chapman and Hall, 1879.

Rae, W. Fraser. *The Business of Travel: A Fifty Years' Record of Progress*. London: Thomas Cook and Son, 1891.

Ranger, Terence. "The Invention of Tradition in Colonial Africa." In *The Invention of Tradition,* edited by Eric Hobsbawm and Terence Ranger, 211–62. Cambridge: Cambridge University Press, 1983.

The Rath; or, Burmese Imperial State Carriage and Throne, Studded with 20,000 Precious Stones. 5th edition. London: The Egyptian Hall, 1826.

Reed, Stanley. *The King and Queen in India: A Record of the Visit of Their Imperial Majesties the King Emperor and Queen Empress to India.* Bombay: Bennett, Coleman, & Co., 1912.

Reid, Douglas A. "Interpreting the Festival Calendar: Wakes and Fairs as Carnivals." In *Popular Culture and Custom in Nineteenth-Century England,* edited by Robert D. Storch, 125–53. New York: St. Martin's Press, 1982.

Renan, Ernest. "What Is a Nation?" 1882. Trans. Martin Thom. In *Nation and Narration,* edited by Homi Bhabha, 8–22. New York: Routledge, 1990

Rigby, Elizabeth. "*Vanity Fair*—and *Jane Eyre.*" *Quarterly Review,* December 1848. Reprinted in *Thackeray: The Critical Heritage,* edited by Geoffrey Tillotson and Donald Hawes, 77–86. London: Routledge and Kegan Paul, 1968.

Rintoul, Robert Stephen. Review of *Vanity Fair* in the *Spectator,* 22 July 1848. Reprinted in *Thackeray: The Critical Heritage,* edited by Geoffrey Tillotson and Donald Hawes, 58–61. London: Routledge and Kegan Paul, 1968.

Ritvo, Harriet. *The Animal Estate: The English and Other Creatures in the Victorian Age.* Cambridge, MA: Harvard University Press, 1987.

Robbins, Bruce. *Feeling Global: Internationalism in Distress.* New York: New York University Press, 1999.

Robinson, H. P. *Pictorial Effect in Photography.* London: Piper & Carter, 1869.

Robinson, Sally. *Engendering the Subject: Gender and Self-Representation in Contemporary Women's Fiction.* Albany: SUNY Press, 1991.

Rothfels, Nigel. *Savages and Beasts: The Birth of the Modern Zoo.* Baltimore, MD: The Johns Hopkins University Press, 2002.

"Row Over German Zoo's Africa Show." *BBC News,* 8 June 2005. http://news.bbc.co.uk/go/pr/fr/-/2/hi/africa/4070816.stm.

Rushdie, Salman. "Adapting *Midnight's Children.*" 1999. In *Step Across This Line,* 70–79.

———. "A Dream of Glorious Return." 2000. In *Step Across This Line,* 180–209.

———. "Globalization." 1999. In *Step Across This Line,* 267–69.

———. "Imaginary Homelands." 1981. In *Imaginary Homelands,* 9–21. New York: Penguin, 1991.

———. "In Defense of the Novel, Yet Again." 2000. In *Step Across This Line,* 49–57.

———. "In the Voodoo Lounge." 1995. In *Step Across This Line,* 87–91.

———. "Influence." 1999. In *Step Across This Line,* 62–69.

———. *Midnight's Children.* 1981. 9th impression. New York: Penguin, 1991.

———. "The New Empire within Britain." 1982. In *Imaginary Homelands,* 129–38. New York: Penguin, 1991.

———. "Step Across This Line." In *Step Across This Line,* 347–81.

———. *Step Across This Line.* New York: Random House, 2002.

———. "U2." 2001. In *Step Across This Line,* 94–98.

Russo, Mary. *The Female Grotesque: Risk, Excess, and Modernity.* New York: Routledge, 1994.

Sadleir, Michael. "Why Only Dickens?" *The Nation and the Athenaeum*, 9 February 1924, 667.
Sage, Lorna. *Angela Carter*. London: Northcote House, 1994.
Said, Edward W. *Culture and Imperialism*. New York: Vintage, 1994.
———. *Orientalism*. New York: Vintage, 1979.
Salisbury, Marquess of (Robert Gascoyne-Cecil). Lord Salisbury to Robert Earl of Lytton, 29 November 1876. In *Personal & Literary Letters of Robert First Earl of Lytton*, ed. Lady Betty Balfour, 2:41. London: Longmans, Green, & Co., 1906.
Sandburg, Carl. *Home Front Memo*. New York: Harcourt, Brace, 1943.
Sanger, Lord George. *Seventy Years a Showman*. New York: Dutton, 1926.
Sartre, Jean-Paul. *Critique of Dialectical Reason I: Theory of Practical Ensembles*. Trans. Alan Sheridan-Smith. Ed. Jonathan Rée. London: NLB, 1976.
Saville, John. "Imperialism and the Victorians." In *In Search of Victorian Values*, edited by Eric M. Sigsworth, 162–78. Manchester, UK: Manchester University Press, 1988.
Saxe, John Godfrey. *Clever Stories of Many Nations*. Boston: Ticknor & Fields, 1865.
Saxon, A. H. "The Circus as Theatre: Astley's and Its Actors in the Age of Romanticism." *ETJ* 19 (October 1975): 299–312.
———. *P. T. Barnum: The Legend and the Man*. New York: Columbia University Press, 1989.
Scarratt, William. *Old Times in the Potteries*. 1906. East Ardsley, Yorks.: S. R. Publishers, 1969.
Schlicke, Paul. *Dickens and Popular Entertainment*. London: Allen & Unwin, 1985.
Scigliano, Eric. *Love, War, and Circuses: The Age-Old Relationship Between Elephants and Humans*. Boston: Houghton Mifflin, 2002.
Seeley, J. R. *The Expansion of England*. 1883. Boston: Little, Brown and Co., 1909.
Showalter, Elaine. "Coming to Blows Over the Booker Prize." *Chronicle of Higher Education*, 28 June 2002.
Simpson, Margaret. "*Hard Times* and Circus Times." *Dickens Quarterly* 10.3 (September 1993): 131–46.
Sketchley, Arthur. *Mrs. Brown and King Cetewayo*. London: George Routledge, [1882].
———. *Mrs. Brown at the Crystal Palace*. London: George Routledge, [1875].
———. *Mrs. Brown at the International Exhibition and South Kensington*. London: George Routledge, [1871].
———. *Mrs. Brown on Jumbo*. London: George Routledge, [1882].
———. *Mrs. Brown on the Prince's Visit to India*. London: George Routledge, [1875].
Speaight, George. *A History of the Circus*. London: Tantivy Press, 1980.
Squillace, Robert. *Modernism, Modernity, and Arnold Bennett*. Lewisburg, PA: Bucknell University Press, 1997.
Stallybrass, Peter, and Allon White. *Politics and Poetics of Transgression*. London: Methuen, 1986.
Starr, Mark. *Lies and Hate in Education*. London: Hogarth Press, 1929.
Steedman, A. *The African Glen, Colosseum, Regent's Park*. 12th edition. London: W.

Clowes, 1836.

Stein, Richard L. "Street Figures: Victorian Urban Iconography." In *Victorian Literature and the Victorian Visual Imagination*, edited by Carol T. Christ and John O. Jordan, 233–63. Berkeley: University of California Press, 1995.

Stendhal. *The Red and the Black.* 1830. Translated by C. K. Scott-Moncrieff. New York: Modern Library, 1984.

Stoddart, Helen. *Rings of Desire: Circus History and Representation.* Manchester, UK: Manchester University Press, 2000.

"Surrey Zoological Gardens." *Mirror of Literature, Amusement, and Instruction*, 7 January 1832.

Swinglehurst, Edward. *Cook's Tours: The Story of Popular Travel.* Poole, UK: Blandford Press, 1982.

Szalwinska, Maxie. "Don't Feed the Humans." *The Guardian*, 31 August 2005.

Taylor, D. J. *Thackeray: The Life of a Literary Man.* New York: Carroll & Graf, 2001.

Taylor, John. *The Life, Death, and Dissection, of the Largest Elephant Ever Known in This Country.* London: W. Watling, 1826.

Thackeray, William Makepeace. *Vanity Fair: A Novel Without a Hero.* 1847–48. Edited by Geoffrey and Kathleen Tillotson. Boston: Houghton Mifflin, 1963.

Thomas, Deborah. *Thackeray and Slavery.* Athens: Ohio University Press, 1993.

Thomas, J. H. "Preface." In *The Pageant of Empire Souvenir Volume*, edited by Martin Hardie. London: Fleetway, 1924.

Tillier, Louis. *Studies in the Sources of Arnold Bennett's Novels.* Paris: Didier, 1969.

To Mr. Wombwell, The Celebrated Menagerist (Addressed to him while exhibiting at Maldon Fair, in 1838). N.p.: [1838].

Topp, Chester W. *Victorian Yellowbacks and Paperbacks, 1849–1905. Vol. 1: George Routledge.* Denver: Hermitage Antiquarian Bookshop, 1993.

Torgovnick, Marianna. *Gone Primitive: Savage Intellects, Modern Lives.* Chicago: University of Chicago Press, 1990.

Trotter, David. *The English Novel in History, 1895–1920.* London: Routledge, 1993.

Tyrwhitt-Drake, Sir Garrard. *The English Circus and Fair Ground.* London: Methuen, 1946.

U2. "Where the Streets Have No Name." *The Joshua Tree.* Island Records, 1987.

———. "Zooropa." *Zooropa.* Polygram, 1993.

Veltre, Thomas. "Menageries, Metaphors, and Meanings." In *New Worlds, New Animals: From Menagerie to Zoological Park in the Nineteenth Century*, edited by R. J. Hoage and William A. Deiss, 19–29. Baltimore, MD: The Johns Hopkins University Press, 1996.

Viswanathan, Gauri. *Masks of Conquest: Literary Study and British Rule in India.* 1989. Oxford: Oxford University Press, 1998.

Wain, John. *Arnold Bennett.* New York: Columbia University Press, 1967.

Walton, John K., and Robert Poole. "The Lancashire Wakes in the Nineteenth Century." In *Popular Culture and Custom in Nineteenth-Century England*, edited by Robert D. Storch, 100–124. New York: St. Martin's Press, 1982.

"A Wanderer at Wembley." *Illustrated London News*, 21 May 1924.

Ward, John. *The Borough of Stoke-upon-Trent.* London: W. Lewis and Son,

1843.

Warrillow, E. J. D. *Arnold Bennett and Stoke-on-Trent*. 1963. Hanley, UK: Etruscan, 1993.

Weaver, Lawrence. *Exhibitions and the Arts of Display*. London: Country Life, 1925.

——. "'The Palace of Industry': A Note on the Arrangement of Exhibits." In *The Empire Exhibition 1924 Official Catalogue*, n.p. London: Fleetway Press, 1924.

Wells, H. G. *The Island of Doctor Moreau*. 1896. Edited by Leon Stover. Jefferson, NC: McFarland, 1996.

"Wembley and Its Millions of Visitors." *Illustrated London News*, 19 July 1924.

West, Rebecca. "Arnold Bennett Himself." *Wings* 7.6 (June 1933): 10.

——. *Harriet Hume: A London Fantasy*. New York: Doubleday, Doran & Co., 1929.

Wiener, Martin J. *English Culture and the Decline of the Industrial Spirit, 1850–1980*. Cambridge: Cambridge University Press, 1981.

Williams, Raymond. *Culture and Society, 1780–1950*. 1958. New York: Columbia University Press, 1983.

——. *The Long Revolution*. London: Chatto & Windus, 1961.

Wills, William Henry. "Forty Years in London." *All the Year Round* 13.311 (8 April 1865): 253–57.

Wilson, Edward. *Acclimatisation*. London: Unwin, 1875.

Winkiel, Laura. "Circuses and Spectacles: Public Culture in *Nightwood*." *Journal of Modern Literature* 21.1 (Fall 1997): 7–28.

Winterson, Jeanette. *Boating for Beginners*. London: Methuen, 1985.

Wollaeger, Mark. "Woolf, Postcards, and the Elision of Race." *Modernism/Modernity* 8.1 (January 2001): 43–75.

"Wombwell's Menagerie." *Times* (London),15 June 1849.

"Wombwell's Menagerie at Windsor Castle." *Pictorial Times*, 6 November 1847.

Wood, James. "Credulity." *London Review of Books*, 14 November 2002.

Woolf, Leonard. *Imperialism and Civilization*. London: Hogarth, 1928.

——. *The Village in the Jungle*. 1913. London: Hogarth, 1961.

Woolf, Virginia. *Between the Acts*. New York: Harcourt Brace, 1941.

——. "Character in Fiction." 1924. In *The Essays of Virginia Woolf*, 3:420–38.

——. *The Diary of Virginia Woolf*. Vol. 2. Edited by Anne Olivier Bell and Andrew McNeillie. London: Hogarth Press, 1978.

——. *The Essays of Virginia Woolf*. 3 vols. Edited by Andrew McNeillie. New York: Harcourt Brace Jovanovich, 1986–88.

——. "Mr. Bennett and Mrs. Brown." 1923. In *The Essays of Virginia Woolf*, 3:384–89.

——. *Mrs. Dalloway*. New York: Harcourt Brace Jovanovich, 1925.

——. "Nature at Wembley." 1924 Notebooks, Volume 2. British Library shelfmark Add. 51044–51046, 33–38.

——. "Nurse Lugton's Curtain." In *The Complete Shorter Fiction of Virginia Woolf*, edited by Susan Dick, 160–61. 2nd edition. New York: Harcourt Brace, 1989.

——. *Orlando: A Biography*. New York: Harcourt Brace Jovanovich, 1928.

——. *A Passionate Apprentice*. Edited by Mitchell Leaska. London: Hogarth, 1990.

———. "The Symbol." In *The Complete Shorter Fiction of Virginia Woolf*, edited by Susan Dick, 288–90. 2nd edition. New York: Harcourt, Brace, 1989.

———. *Three Guineas.* New York: Harcourt Brace Jovanovich, 1938.

———. "Thunder at Wembley." In *The Essays of Virginia Woolf,* 3:410–14.

———. *The Voyage Out.* 1915. Harmondsworth, UK: Penguin, 1992.

———. *The Waves.* New York: Harcourt, Brace, 1931.

———. *The Years.* New York: Harcourt, Brace, 1937.

Yeats, W. B. "Byzantium." 1933. In *The Collected Poems of W. B. Yeats,* 248–49.

———. "The Circus Animals' Desertion." 1939. In *The Collected Poems of W. B. Yeats,* 346–48.

———. *The Collected Poems of W. B. Yeats.* Edited by Richard J. Finneran. New York: Collier, 1989.

———. "The Second Coming." 1921. In *The Collected Poems of W. B. Yeats,* 187.

"The 'Zoo' Elephant Who Will Not Go to America." *Illustrated London News,* 25 February 1882.

The Zoological Cabinet; or, Menagerie of Living Characters. London: Thomas McLean, 1832.

Index

Note: Italicized page numbers refer to illustrations.

Acheson, Dean, 208
Achtung Baby (U2 recording), 188
Adelphi Theatre (London), 69
Adorno, Theodor, 183–84, 204
Aesop, 39
aesthetic modernism. *See* modernist era
aesthetics. *See* picturesque
Afghanistan, 51
Africa, 62, 63, 92, 126, 174; animals from, 55, 78, 215; British imperialism in, 118, 177; camels as representing, 19; elephant as representing, 13, 66–68, 92, 94; endangered species in, 183; people from, on display, 55, 56, 134, 135, 213, 215; in Woolf's works, 153. *See also* South Africa
Albert (prince consort of England), 18, 19, *45*, 45. *See also* Albert Memorial; Great Exhibition of Works of Industry of All Nations
Albert Hall (London), 32
Albert Memorial (London), 18–20, 32, 42, 45, 63–64, *65*
Alexandra (queen of England), 152, 155
Algeria, 124, 157
alien. *See* aliens (foreigners); exotic (alien)
aliens (foreigners): English people as joining with, 158; English projection of excess onto, 22–23, 47–49, 83, 87, 95, 96–106, 110–17, 134–37; English reserve measured against, 120. *See also* exotic
allegory: of circuses, 42, 43, 163; Coleridge on, 68–70; in exhibitions, 164, 176; of globes, 191–92; in menageries, 28, 38–39, 61–62, 163; in novels, 82, 87, 92, 94–95, 140, 144–45, 147, 149–50; theologic, 68–70; of zoos as Noah's ark, 184
All the Year Round (Dickens), 91, 96, 101, 153
Altick, Richard, 10, 50, 77
America. *See* United States
analogies, 110, 113, 140–41
"Anglepoise," 31, 190–93
animals (exotic). *See* exotic animals; *specific exotic animals*
anteaters, 55, 185
antelopes, 55
Arabian Nights, 82
A Rebours (Huysmans), xi
armadillos, 185
Arnold, Matthew, 123
Ashcroft, Bill, 24, 174–76
Asia, 19, 62, 63, *64*, 68, 92, 214; endangered species in, 183. *See also* Ceylon; China; India; Orientalism
Asiatic Gallery (London), 55
Astley's Circus: Dickens and, 96, 101, 223n42, 230n103; imperial connections of, 9, 65, 163; London

location of, 4, 51, 60, 90, 91, 95; playbills of, 11, 16, 38, 61–62, *97, 98*; processions by, 92; royal connections of, 43
Atkins' Menagerie, 9, 50, 77
auction houses, 83–89, 101
Augsburg Zoo, 213
The Author's Craft (Bennett), 122, 129, 141–43, 147, 149, 166

The Bad Child's Book of Beasts (Belloc), 11
Ballantyne, R. M., 231n1
Barnes, Djuna, 182
Barnes, Julian, 6, 7, 12, 24, 31, 205–12, 215–16
Barnum, P. T., 78–80, 134
Bartholomew Fair, 49–51, 77, 90
Bataille, Georges: on "restricted" and "general" economies, xi–xii, 24–25, 116, 132, 178, 185
Batty, William, 92, 94, 95. See also Batty's Circus
Batty's Circus, 113–14
Baucom, Ian, xiii, 193, 205–6
Baudrillard, Jean, 209, 210
Beagle voyage, 118
bear-baiting. *See* brutality
bears, 49, 56, 161, 182
beast fables, 39. *See also* exotic animals
Belloc, Hilaire, 11
Benedict, Barbara, 11
Benjamin, Walter, 145
Bennett, Arnold, 7, 12, 118–50, 162, 195, 196; *Author's Craft*, 122, 129, 141–43, 147, 149, 166; *Clayhanger*, 126, 137–40; "Elixir of Youth," 119–20, 123; *Old Wives' Tale*, 6, 30, 119, 121–23, 125, 127–32, 135–36, 140–47, 149–50; *Our Women*, 159; realism of, 29, 121–23, 127, 130, 140, 145–47, 149, 159–60, 166, 168, 172, 173, 175, 176; *Regent*, 147;

Riceyman Steps, 121, 149
Bennett, Tony, 198
Berger, John, 9, 64
bestiaries, 39
Between the Acts (Woolf), 152, 177, 181, 221n36
Bhabha, Homi, xiii, 157, 175
"Billy Button's Journey to Brentford" (Astley's Circus performance), 96, *98*, 101
Birmingham (England), 54
bisons, 19
Bivona, Daniel, 106, 116
black subjects: from Africa, 55, 56, 134, 135, 213, 215; as Britons, 18, 215, 216; Dickens on, 94–95, 110–11, 113, 115; Fanon on, 156–57
Blair, Tony, 16
Blake, William, 202
Blast (Lewis), 123, 125, 222n70
Bleak House (Dickens), 107
"The Blind Men and the Elephant" (Saxe), 68–70, *69*, 71, 72, 76, 123
Bloody Chamber (Carter), 198
boa-constrictors, 88, 89, 112. *See also* serpents
boars, 56, 60. *See also* pigs
Boating for Beginners (Winterson), 216
Bodleian Library, 73, *76*
Bono. *See* U2 (musical group)
Booker Prize. *See* Man Booker Prize
Bostock, E. H., 50, 65. *See also* Bostock and Wombwell's traveling menagerie
Bostock and Wombwell's traveling menagerie, 37–38, 50, 51
Brantlinger, Patrick, 87, 227n25
Brennan, Timothy, 190–91, 193
Brideshead Revisited (Waugh), 205
Bristol (England), 54
Britannia, 4, 43, 61, 63, *63*, 92
"Britannia's Menagerie" (song), ix, 39–40
British Commonwealth of Nations, 160

British Empire: amnesia about, 16–18;
break-up of, 14–15, 17, 20–21, 24,
80, 151, 156–57, 160, 163, 170–71,
188–89, 192, 202, 205–11, 217;
demands placed on, by colonies,
xi; distance between England and,
23, 40–41, 48, 96–112, 116–17,
122; elephant as synecdoche for,
13, 66–68, 72–81, 135–36, 141,
149–50; England as centerpiece
of, 17, 27, 32–35, 55, 63, 116,
178–79, 239n145; exotic animals
as linking Englishness to, xiii,
1–4, *8*, 9–10, 82–117; growth of, in
Victorian era, xi, 19, 61, 118; India
as representing, 10, 61, 96–106; as
informing Englishness, xiii, 1, 4–5,
12, 27–29, 42, 43, 63–64, 124–27,
130–40, 145–47, 195–205; nostalgia
for, 18, 31, 183–85, 191–94, 205–6,
214; revolts against, 24, 70, 71,
136, 137, 147; "spoils" of, 25; as a
totality, ix, xii, xiii, 5–6, 12–14, 17,
21, 23, 25, 27–29, 38–49, 55, 59–76,
81–83, 123, 151, 158–66, 175, 178–
79, 184, 216; wars of, 25, 38, 51, 61,
80, 228; Woolf on, 151, 238n109.
See also Britannia; decolonization;
distance; England; Englishness;
exotic animals; fragmentation;
imperial exhibitions; novel;
processions; traveling culture;
specific countries of
British Empire Exhibition (Wembley,
1924), 57, 150, *162, 165;* Chesterton
on, 48, 163, 191; elephants at, 76,
161; humans exhibited at, 55, 56,
186–87, 215; later uses of site of,
186–89, 194; menagerie at, 161,
176; Pageant of Empire at, 57–58,
161, 170–71, 177, 186; Prince of
Wales on, 60, 161, 170; Rushdie's
approximation of, 190–92;
totalizing aims of, 151, 158–66, 179,
188–89; Woolf on, 30, 151, 158–60,
166–75
British Empire Exhibition (Wembley,
1925), 57, 186
British Museum, 36
Brontë, Charlotte, 87
Brough, Robert, 103–4, 113
brutality (bear-baiting; bull-baiting;
violence): early English character
associated with, 4, 20, 22–23, 65,
119, 132–40; in modernist novels,
23, 148–50, 173–74, 221n70; in
postimperial writing, 199, 215;
projection of, onto foreigners, 95,
136, 137; and unpredictability of
exotic animals, 21–22, 35, 40, 57,
64, 65–66, 71, 76–79, *78*, 89, 90,
96–104, 111–17, 119–20, 122–23,
129, 131–36, 140–45, 149–50. *See
also* excess; executions
Buckingham Palace, 79, 126
buffalo, 161
bull-baiting. *See* brutality
bulls, 19, 119–20, 123, 161
Burma: England's war with, 51, 80;
Orwell on, 137; state carriage from,
55, *57*
Burslem (England), 133
Burton, Alfred, 133
Bush People, 56
Butt, John, 100
Butterworth, Edwin, 133
Byron, Lord (George Gordon), 7, 71
"Byzantium" (Yeats), 200

"cabinets," 11–12, 22. *See also*
collections and collecting
camels, 114, 115, 182, 223n32; on
Albert Memorial, 19; in England,
91; in London processions, 55, 92,
161
Canada, 17
Cape Colony, 107
capitalism: and commercial
culture, 133–34; Dickens on,
96–106; global, 183, 185, 204;

and imperialism, 23, 27, 65, 81, 129; as overwhelming the exotic, 183–94. *See also* circuses: a part of commercial world; globalization; trade
Carey, John, 209, 210
the carnivalesque, 81; in Bennett's works, 119, 132–33, 143; in Elizabeth II's Golden Jubilee procession, 4; of the late twentieth century, 207–8; in Sketchley's *Mrs. Brown* books, 32–35, 65; and totality, xii, 29, 30; unpredictable exotic animals as embodying, 64–66, 71, 76, 79. *See also* picturesque
Caroline (queen of England), 45
Carter, Angela, 7, 12, 24, 36, 183, 194–205, 211
Caserio, Robert L., 235n15
Catalogue of Animals Preserved in the Museum of the Zoological Society, 53
Centerwall, Bror, 166
Certeau, Michel de, 6
Ceylon, 96, 161
Champney, W. L., *69,* 69, 70
Chapman, Ellen, 90, 99
Chapman, G. B., 51
"Character in Fiction" (Woolf), 30, 149, 151, 152, 159, 160, 169, 171–73, 176
Chaudhuri, Amit, 6, 28
Chesterton, G. K., 27, 48, 163, 191
Childers, E. W. B., 96
chimpanzees. *See* monkeys
China, 96, 106, 163. *See also* Orientalism
Chunee (elephant), 76, 77, *78,* 113–14, 117, 123
circle (chain; ring) imagery: in Carter's works, 197–98, 205; in Woolf's works, 30, 151, 152, 175–80
"The Circus Animals' Desertion" (Yeats), 202–3
circuses: animals for, 51–52, 66, 99, 185; in Carter's *Nights at the Circus,* 194–205; decline of, 30, 54, 182, 185, 212; in Dickens's *Hard Times,* 30, 83, 96–111, 114–17; humans exhibited in, 182, 195; imperial connections to, xiii, 4, 7, 10, 46, 194–205; in Joyce's *Ulysses,* 182; in *Life of Pi,* 16; as "low" culture, 7, 108–9, 116–17, 119; nostalgia for, in postmodern works, 185; as part of commercial world, 100, 102, 108–9, 115, 116, 133–34, 136, 140–41; as part of display culture, ix, 4, 7, 10, 12, 23; totalizing aims of, 197–98, 205; travel by, 9, 43, 44, 45, 51, 78, 184, 226n1. *See also* exotic animals; menageries; wakes festivals; *specific circuses and animals*
Clapham Sect, 178
"classic style," xi
class issues: Bennett's concern with, 124, 133, 140–45; and English "character," 82; between zoo and menagerie, 52–54. *See also* Englishness; "high" vs. "low" culture; middle class
Clayhanger (Bennett), 126, 137–40
Cleopatra's Needle, 34
Clifford, James, 220n18
Colefax, Lady, 167, 169
Coleridge, Samuel Taylor, 38–39, 68, 69–70
Colindian Exhibition. *See* Colonial and Indian Exhibition
collections and collecting: auction houses compared to, 83; composite drawings of elephants as, 72–76; delineation as activity of, 62–63; in Dickens's *Hard Times,* 109; novels as form of, 212; Woolf on, 172; zoos', menageries', and circuses' involvement with, x, 11–12, 33, 35, 36–49, 52, 65. *See also* "cabinets"; circuses; exotic animals;

menageries; Noah's ark; zoos
Colonial and Indian Exhibition (South Kensington, 1886), 57, 62–63, *63*, 76
colonial exhibitions. *See* imperial exhibitions
Colosseum (Regent's Park, London), 55, 57
Coming Up for Air (Orwell), 153
"Commonwealth Literature Does Not Exist" (Rushdie), 188
completeness. *See* totality
composite drawings, 72–76, *73–76*
Conrad, Joseph, 180, 234n74
Cook, Thomas, ix, 9–10, 184, 220n20
Cooke, William, 96
cosmopolitanism: in Bennett's life, 124–27, 147; in Bennett's work, 118–23, 142, 147; ethos of, 129–30. *See also* exotic; provincialism
Covent Garden (London), 77
Coward, Noel, 167
Cowper, William, 138–39
cranes, 56
Cranford (Gaskell), 13, 30, 83, 88–90, 94, 102, 108, 115
crocodiles, 214
Cross, Edward: and Chunee, 77; and the Exeter 'Change Menagerie, 50–54, 58–59, 77, 86, 87, 227n33; imperial connections of, 65
Cross, Mrs. Edward, 113
Cross, William, 51
Crystal Palace. *See* Great Exhibition of Works of Industry of All Nations
culture of display. *See* exhibitionary culture
Cunningham, Peter, 115
Curzon, Lord, 178, 179–80, 239n145

Daily Telegraph (London), 1, 2, *2*, 4, 17
Darwin, Charles, 118
"decadent style," xi
decay. *See* fragmentation
decline. *See* decolonization; fragmentation
decolonization, 183; England's marginal global role following, 14–15, 17, 20, 205–11; as opportunity for colonial and oppressed peoples, 156–57, 192, 202; and postimperial writing, 24, 182–211, 215–16. *See also* British Empire; fragmentation
deer, 92, 161
"delineation," 62–63
detotalization. *See* fragmentation
Diary of Virginia Woolf, 167
Dickens, Charles, 12, 90, 131, 195, 227n33, 229n82; *All the Year Round*, 91, 96, 101, 153; Bennett on, 130, 132, 136; *Bleak House*, 107; circus renditions of works by, 7, 230n103; *Dombey and Son*, 116; "Gin-Shops," 113; *Hard Times*, 30, 82–83, 96–117, 119, 198–99; *Household Words*, 91–92, 102–3, 112–13, 116, 153; James on, 21; "Mr. Booley's View of the Last Lord Mayor's Show," 92, 94–95, 107, 113; *Mystery of Edwin Drood*, 91–92, 116; "Noble Savage," 112; *Oliver Twist*, 230n103; *Our Mutual Friend*, 91, 229n82; *Pickwick Papers*, 230n103; "Scotland Yard," 113–14; *Sketches by Boz*, 114; "Some Particulars Concerning a Lion," 111
Dictionary of the English Language (Johnson), 68, 124
Discipline and Punish (Foucault), 197
disintegration. *See* decolonization; fragmentation
Disney's Animal Kingdom, 214
display culture. *See* exhibitionary culture
Disraeli, Benjamin (Lord Beaconsfield), 78–79
dissolution. *See* decolonization; fragmentation
distance: collapse of, 48, 62, 139–40, 166, 169, 203, 205; between

empire and England, 23, 40–41, 48, 96–112, 116–17, 122; between restraint and excess, 46–49, 96–117, 119–20, 130–40, 144–47; between spectators and spectacle, 66, 122, 130, 133–34, 161, 165, 169, 172–73; between zoo and menagerie, 52–53. *See also* aliens (foreigners); reserved nature
divorce, 102–3, 115
dogs, 39, 57, 78, 90, 103, 113, 132, 202
Dombey and Son (Dickens), 116
donkeys, 161
doves, 161
Ducrow, Andrew, 91
Durbars, 9, 12, 46–47, 66, 138, 178

eagles, 49, 57
Eagleton, Terry, 15, 21, 220n36
East. *See* Asia; Ceylon; China; India
Economist, 16
economy: Bataille on "restricted" and "general," xi–xii, 24–25, 116, 132, 178, 181, 185; British Empire Exhibition as example of "restricted," 164, 166, 170, 171; of England and empire, 23, 48; political, in Dickens's *Hard Times*, 102, 103–11, 115, 116; of realism, 159, 160, 163, 173; symbolic, 174–75, 178. *See also* capitalism; trade; traveling culture
Edwardian era, xii, 30, 118–50, 159–60, 166, 168, 172, 173, 175, 176
Edward VII (king of England), 9
Egyptian Hall (London), 55, 56, 57
"The Elephant at Home," 101
elephantiasis, 191, 193
The Elephant of Siam (play), 68
elephants: on Albert Memorial, 19, 20; in Bennett's *Old Wives' Tale*, 30, 122–23, 131–32, 135–36, 140–47; in Carter's *Nights at the Circus*, 195, 198–205; in circuses, 66, 68, 90, 91, 96, *97*, *98*, 227n33; composite drawings of, 72–76, *73–76*; dead, 30, 76–81, 113–14, 117, 122–23, 129, 131–36, 140–45, 150; in Dickens's *Hard Times*, 83, 96–103, 106, 111, 112–17, 198–99; in Durbars, 9, 46–47, 66; exhibiting of, 55, 57, 161, *162*; in fairs, 50, 77; in Forster's *Passage to India*, 9; in Gaskell's *Cranford*, 13, 88–90, 94, 102, 112; in Joyce's *Ulysses*, 182; as keynote animal, 12–13, 29, 35, 66–76, 99, 135–36, 213; on maps, 63, *63*; mechanical, in Elizabeth II's Golden Jubilee procession, 1–2, *2*, 13, 15, 17, 18, 26; in menageries, 38, 43, *44*, 49, 52, 135; in North America, 214; real, in London processions, 55, 158, 161, 186; as representing Africa, 13, 66–68, 92, 94; as representing India, 9, 13, 19, 62, 66–67, 82, 84–87, 89, 96–106, 112, 153, *162*, 168, 193, 204; as representing multiculturalism in postimperial Britain, 1, 4, 13; as representing totality, 33, 68–76, 88–90, 123, 141; as synecdoche for British Empire, 13, 66–68, 72–81, 135–36, 141, 149–50; as synecdoche for menageries, 13, 72–74; in Thackeray's *Vanity Fair*, 84–88, *85*, 94, 101; traffic in, 91–92, 95; violent, 71, 77–79, *79*, 96–104, 111, 113–14, 117, 122–23, 129, 131–36, 140–45, 149–50; in West's *Harriet Hume*, 9–10; in the wild, 59; in Woolf's works, 149–58, 179, 181, 198, 235n12, 236n31; in zoos, 53–54, 68
Elgar, Edward, 186, 187
Eliot, T. S., 121, 124, 149, 174, 221n36
"The Elixir of Youth" (Bennett), 119–20, 123
Elizabeth II (queen of England): Golden Jubilee procession of, 1–2, *2*, 4, 13–15, 17, 18, 26–27, 185

elk, 63
Ellis, Havelock, xi–xii
Ellmann, Richard, 20
Empire Exhibition. *See* British Empire Exhibition
Empire of India Exhibition (1895), 57, 62
Empire Windrush (ship), 216
endangered species, 183–84, 214, 217
England: as centerpiece of British Empire, 17, 27, 32–35, 55, 63, 116, 178–79, 239n145; distance between empire and, 23, 40–41, 48, 96–112, 116–17, 122; imperial wars of, 25, 38, 51, 61, 80, 228; as irrelevant when compared to exotic spaces, 144–45, 147; lions as symbol of, 32, 43, 45, 62, 68; as "mother country," 178–79; as much like India, 153, 156; as multiethnic in late twentieth century, 1, 4–5, 13–14, 18, 215–16; as postimperial nation, 13, 14–15, 17–18, 20, 31, 185, 215–16; provinces of, as synecdoche for, 127–31, 136, 139–40, 146–48. *See also* Britannia; British Empire; distance; Englishness; London; national; provincialism; traveling culture
England, England (Barnes), 31, 208–11, 215–16
Englishness (identity): after decolonization, 14–15, 17, 30, 205–11, 215–16; amnesia about British Empire in contemporary, 16–18; British Empire as informing, xiii, 1, 4–5, 12, 27–29, 42, 43, 63–65, 124–27, 130–40, 145–47, 195–205; at British Empire Exhibition, 169–70, 172–75; characterizations of, 4, 20, 22–23, 46–48, 79, 82, 120–21, 130–36, 144–45, 147, 169–70, 219n4; in early twentieth century, 153–54; elephant as synecdoche for, 13–14, 123, 131–36, 181; during empire-

building, 19–20; exhibition of, as a curiosity, 212–14; menagerie as mediating novel's relation to, x, xii–xiii, 4, 7, 20, 26, 29, 118–48; as a totality in itself, xiii, 19; zoological representations of, 32–49, 82–117
Ervine, St. John, 121
Esty, Jed, xiii, 220n36
Europe, 25, 50, 62, 63, 92. *See also* France
evolution, 118
excess: Bennett on, 119–20, 130–40, 144–47; Carter on, 199; of circuses, 108–9, 111–17; English projection of, onto foreigners, 22–23, 47–49, 83, 87, 95, 96–106, 110–17, 134–37; in marriage, 102–3, 106; postcolonial, 174–75; vs. restraint in English character and culture, 21–25, 37–38, 46–49, 96–117, 119–20, 130–40, 144–47; vs. restraint in menageries, 21–23, 30, 57; Woolf on, 171, 173–74. *See also* brutality; distance; "high" vs. "low" culture; reserved nature (of English character)
executions, 120, 122, 137, 140, 141, 144, 202. *See also* elephants: dead
Exeter 'Change Menagerie, 50, 52, 53, 58, 86, 87, 90, 223n43, 227n33; Chunee in, 76, 77, *78*, 113–14, 117, 123
exhibitionary culture, ix–x, 5, 6–7, 20–21; amnesia about former, 17; circuses as part of, ix, 4, 7, 10, 12, 23; excess vs. restraint in, 21–25, 37–38; exotic's role in, 193; homogenization by, 135–36; humans as spectacles in, 55, 56, 134, 135, 182, 185–89, 195, 199, 213, *213*, 215; inauthenticity of contemporary, 213–17; menageries as part of, ix, 6–7, 10–11, 23, 29, 32–49; novels as part of, 10–11, 25, 29; picturesque vs. carnivalesque in

Victorian, 33–35; in postimperial novels, 31, 183–217; realism of, 166; and storytelling, 219n10; technologies of, 27–28, 214; in Thackeray's *Vanity Fair,* 86–87; Woolf on, 151; zoos as part of, ix, 7, 10–12, 23, 32–33, 52–53. *See also* circuses; exotic animals; fairs; imperial exhibitions; menageries; spectators; theaters; traveling culture; zoos

the exotic (alien), 2; capitalism and homogeneity as overwhelming the, 183–94, 205; as distraction, 193; imagining, through the known, 68–69; imperial connection to, 9, 141; London as, 123, 127, 128, 176–77; menageries as emphasizing, 29; narratives about, 11, 15–16, 58, 59–62, 65–66; vs. provincial in Bennett's work, 118–31, 136, 139–48. *See also* exotic animals

exotic animals (zoological collections): Dickens's familiarity with, 90–92; as endangered species, 183–84, 214, 217; exhibits' emphasis on separation of, from domestic, 53; imperial connection of, ix, 9–10, 28, 32–79, 135, 158, 186; imperial connection of, in English novels, x–xiii, 7, 15–17, 28–29, 82–117, 135, 140–42, 212; mastery over, 16, 40, 57, 70–71, 80, 83, 90, 91, 202; in postimperial England, 208–11, 213–16; practical uselessness of, in England, 36; royal connections with, 1–4, *2, 3, 8,* 9, 13–15, 17, 18, 23, 26–27, 32–34, 43, *44,* 45, *45,* 46, 47, 49, 52, 66, *67,* 78–80, 138, 178, 184–85; as symbol for conquered peoples, 39–40, 70–71, 80–81, 102–3, 136–37, 147; as symbols in Woolf's works, 151; Thackeray's uses of, in his novels, 84–85; in theaters, 32, 41, *42,* 51, 68, 77, 90, 91; traffic in, 26, 37, 50–51, 53, 61, 65, 91–92, 95; unpredictability of, 21–22, 35, 40, 57, 65–66, 71, 76–79, *78,* 89, 90, 96–104, 111–17, 119–20, 122–23, 129, 131–36, 140–45, 149–50. *See also* circuses; exhibitionary culture; menageries; "Nature"; zoos; *specific species*

The Expansion of England (Seeley), 5, 64
expositions. *See* exhibitionary culture
Eyre, Edward John, 137

fairs: carnivalesque associated with, 34, 35, 64–65; commercialization of, 133; dead elephants at, 77; menageries at, 49–51, 90; and Victoria's coronation, 43. *See also* wakes festivals; *specific fairs*
"Fake!" (Barnes), 209, 210
Fanon, Frantz, 156–57
fatalism, 194
Fiji Islands, 136
Finney, Brian H., 198
Flint, Kate, 96
Ford, George, 96
Forster, E. M., 12, 100, 125, 151, 196, 221n36; on British Empire Exhibition, 167; on imperial influence on fiction, 26; "Notes on the English Character," 20, 22, 219n4; *Passage to India,* 9, 125
Forster, John, 87
Fortescue, John, 138
Foucault, Michel, 10, 36, 197, 198
fragmentation (breakup; decay; decline; detotalization; dissipation; dissolution; dying; incompletion; incongruity; loss; rupture), xii; of the British Empire, 14–15, 17, 20–21, 80, 151, 156–57, 160, 163, 170–71, 188–89, 192, 205–11, 217; of novelistic discourse since the modernist era, 24–25, 30, 152–58, 171, 176, 181, 190–205; of totalizing perspective, 143–45,

150–58, 160, 170–71, 173–75, 177–81, 188–96. *See also* decolonization
France: in Bennett's *Old Wives' Tale*, 121–22, 127–31, 141, 146; Bennett's residence in, 124–25, 147; exhibitions in, 34, 40; visitors from, to British Empire Exhibition, 162. *See also* Franco-British Exhibition
Franco-British Exhibition (Shepherd's Bush, 1908), 57
Freud, Sigmund, 2, 13
Friedman, Susan Stanford, xii
Frost, Thomas, 77
Frozen Ark project, 214, 215
Fry, Roger, 162, 164, 168, 174
Fury (Rushdie), 190

Gallagher, Catherine, 115, 230n122
Gandhi, Indira, 192
Gaskell, Elizabeth, 12, 82, 83; *Cranford*, 13, 30, 83, 88–90, 94, 102, 108, 115
gazelles, 55, 182
gender: and Bennett's *Our Women*, 159; in Carter's *Nights at the Circus*, 194–98, 200–202; in Woolf's "Mr. Bennett and Mrs. Brown," 232n21
"general economies": Bataille on, xi–xii, 24–25, 178, 185; in Woolf's works, 181
George, Wilma, xi
George IV (king of England), 45, 119
George V (king of England), 21, 23–24; at British Empire Exhibition, 158, 161, 163; coronation Durbars for, 9, 66, 138
Georgian era, xii, 149–81
Germinal (Zola), 130
Gilpin, William, 60, 61
"Gin-Shops" (Dickens), 113
giraffes, 54, 56, 63, 214
Gladstone, William, 80
Glasgow (Scotland), 54
globalization, 184–85, 187, 190–94, 204–12; British Empire Exhibition's promotion of, 163, 164, 168

globe imagery, 191–94
The Gorilla Hunters (Ballantyne), 231n1
The Graphic (magazine), 159, 169
"Great Britain," 20. *See also* British Empire; England
Great Exhibition of Works of Industry of All Nations (Crystal Palace, 1851), 4, 9, 19, 34, 57, 161, 163, 170; catalog of, 18; Dickens on, 106
Greenwich Fair, 51, 90, 99
Grimaldi, Joseph, 101
The Ground Beneath Her Feet (Rushdie), 189–90

Hack, Daniel, 94, 95
Hagenbeck, Carl, 51
Haggard, Rider, 216
Hamlyn, J. D., 51
Hannibal, 195
Hard Times (Dickens), 30, 82–83, 96–117, 119, 198–99
Harper's Weekly, 78
Harriet Hume (West), 9–10
the "hauntological," 193–94
Heart of Darkness (Conrad), 180, 234n74
Hegel, G. W. F., 27
Heidegger, Martin, 40
Henry I (king of England), 223n32
Henry III (king of England), 49, 223n32
Hepburn, James G., 146
"high" vs. "low" culture: Bennett and Woolf on, 124, 159; and British Empire Exhibition, 167, 175; and circus vulgarity, 7, 108–9, 116–17, 119; modernist era's gap between, 7; in wakes celebrations, 119; zoos vs. menageries' claims to, 52–53
Hilton's Menagerie, 50
History of the World in 10-1/2 Chapters (Barnes), 207
Hobsbawm, Eric, 36, 209, 210
Hobson, J. A., 47, 48, 107, 125

Hoffenberg, Peter, 225n73
holism. *See* totality
homogeneity, 35, 135–36, 183–94, 205
Hong Kong, 163
horses, 39, 66, 72, 92, 98, 100, 102, 103, 161, 230n103
"Hottentots," 55
Household Words (Dickens), 91, 92, 102, 103, 112, 113, 116, 153
Huggan, Graham, 15
Hunt, Ebenezer, 233n55
Hutcheon, Linda, 202
Hutton, William, 132
Huysmans, J-K, xi
hyenas, 55, 182
Hynes, Samuel, 124

Ibsen, Henrik, 202, 204
identity. *See* Englishness; gender; national
Illustrated London News, 43, *44*, 45, 92, *93*; on the British Empire Exhibition, 159, 163, 170
"Imaginary Homelands" (Rushdie), 186
"imperial amnesia," 16–18
Imperial Assemblage (Delhi, 1877), 9, 46–47, 66, 138
imperial exhibitions (colonial exhibitions): in England, ix, 9, 13, 19, 30, 32–34, 40–41, 56–58, 62, 63, 163, 168; Woolf attends, 150, 160–75. *See also* British Empire Exhibition; Colonial and Indian Exhibition; exhibitionary culture
Imperial Institute (London), 19
Imperialism: A Study (Hobson), 107
Imperialism and Civilization (L. Woolf), 125
imperialist agents, 51, 80–81, 176–77. *See also* Orwell, George; Woolf, Leonard
incompletion. *See* fragmentation
India: Bennett's articles about, 125; in British Empire Exhibition, 161, 168; elephant as representing, 9, 13, 19, 62, 66–67, 82, 84–87, 89, 96–106, 112, 153, *162*, 168, 193, 204; England as much like, 153, 156; England's construction of, 64; English literature studied in, 5; English traveling menageries in, 50; English wars in, 51, 228; exhibiting of people from, 185–89, 194; imperial revolts in, 24, 70, 137, 147; in international exhibitions, 57–58, 62; in *Life of Pi*, 16, 17, 26; practical uselessness of exotic animals from, 36; as representing British Empire, 10, 61, 96–106; in Rushdie's *Midnight's Children*, 190–94; tigers as representing, 153, 193, 204; Victoria crowned Empress of, 9, 19, 46, 66, 78–79; in Woolf's works, 176–78. *See also* Orientalism
Indian Mutiny, 70, 137
Indians (American), 96
Industrial Revolution, 82–83, 133
International Exhibition (1862), 19, 32–34
International Exhibition (1871), 57
Ireland, 14, 62, 71, 80, 156, 175; revolts in, 24; showman from, 185–89
"The Irish Avatar" (Byron), 71
Isaac Van Amburgh and His Animals (Landseer), 32, 41, *41*
Islam, 187, 188
Island of Doctor Moreau (Wells), 119, 231n1
Isle of Wight, 208–11
ivory, 68

Jagger, Mick, 189
Jamaica, 137, 215
James, Henry, x, 5–6, 21, 28, 196
Jameson, Fredric, 4, 24, 184
James Tait Black Prize, 149
Jamrach, W. and C., 51
jingoism, 47
Jocko (monkey), 2, 54

John Bull. *See* Englishness: characterizations of
Johnson, Samuel, 68, 124
The Joshua Tree (U2 recording), 194
"Journey to Brentford" (Astley's Circus performance). *See* "Billy Button's Journey to Brentford"
Joyce, James, xi, 23, 149, 173–74, 182, 199, 222n70
Jumbo (elephant), 34, 78–80, 182

kangaroos, 57, 60, 161
Kaveney, Roz, 15–16
Kearns, Katherine, 115
Kenner, Hugh, 18, 21
Kenya, 161
Kingsley, Mary, 125–26
Kipling, John Lockwood, 23, 72, 73, *73*, 74
Kipling, Rudyard, 186, 187, 216
Knight, Charles, 107, 229n63
Kucich, John, 231n137
Kureishi, Hanif, 18

The Lady of Lyons (performance), 34
Landseer, Edwin, 19, 32, 33, 41, *41*, 42, *42*, 83, 90
Lawrence, D. H., 23, 221n70
"Lay Sermons" (Coleridge), 38
Leavis, F. R., 101–2, 108, 109, 115, 119, 199
Leeds (England), 54
Lemon, Mark, 98
leopards, 49, 90, 223n32
Letters from London (Barnes), 206
Levy, Andrea, 215–16
Lewis, Wyndham, 23, 123, 148, 198, 202, 204, 222n70
Life of Pi (Martel), 15–17, 26
lions: on Albert Memorial, 18–19; as British symbol, 32, 43, 45, 62, 68; Dickens on, 111; on maps, 63, *63*; in menageries and circuses, 43, 90, 91, 161, 182, 223n32; and the picturesque, 60; skins of, 56; unpredictability of, 89, 90, 102; in the wild, 68
Living Age, 162
llamas, 161
London (England): as alien to British imperial agents, 176–77; as alien to residents of English provinces, 123, 127, 128; Bennett's life in, 124; Conrad on, 180; Elizabeth II's Golden Jubilee procession in, 1–2, *2*, 4, 13–15, 17, 18, 26–27, 185; Thomas Cook's procession in, 9–10. *See also* imperial exhibitions; Lord Mayor's Shows; *specific places and institutions in*
London Museum of Natural History, 214
London Zoological Gardens. *See* Regent's Park Zoological Gardens (London)
Lord Mayor's Shows, 43, 55, 90, 92, *93*, 94–95, 107, 163
loss. *See* decolonization; fragmentation; nostalgia
"low" culture. *See* "high" vs. "low" culture
Lowes Dickinson, Goldsworthy, 125
Lucas, John, 124
Lukács, Georg, 131, 145
Lytton, Robert, First Earl of, 46–47

MacKenzie, John, 167
Major, John, 207–8, 242n107
Man Booker Prize, 15–17, 26
Manchester (England), 54
marriage, 99–103, 106, 107–8. *See also* divorce
Martel, Yann, 15–17
Marway, Sukhdev, 4, 14
menageries: decline of, 30, 50, 54, 182–83, 212, 217; elephant as synecdoche for, 13, 72–74; as English institution, 23, 26; excess vs. restraint in, 21–23, 30, 57; history of, in England, 49–59; as

homologous to the novel, x, 27–29, 81, 212, 217; imperial connections of, xiii, 6–7, 10, 25–27, 32–49, 59–66, 78–79, 82–83; in Julian Barnes's works, 206–7; as mediating novel's relation to Englishness, x, xii–xiii, 4, 7, 20, 26, 29, 118–48; as part of display culture, ix, 6–7, 10–11, 23, 29, 32–49; as symbolically breaking and being remade, 152–58; as totalizing effort, 27–29, 36–49, 216; traveling, 4, 9, 30, 37–38, 44, 43–46, 50–51, 54, 88–89, 123, 128, 131–36, 146, 147, 183, 207; word origins of, 21, 37. *See also* Atkins' Menagerie; circuses; Exeter 'Change Menagerie; exotic animals; Tower Menagerie; Wombwell's Menagerie; *specific animals*

middle class: Dickens's appeal to, 108–11, 114, 115, 117; mores of, as essence of Englishness, 82, 131–36, 219n4

Middle East, 66–67

Midnight's Children (Rushdie), 31, 190–94, 197

Miller, Jonathan, 14

Minima Moralia (Adorno), 183–84

Mitchell, Timothy, 40, 173

modernist era: and Bennett, 121–25, 132, 144–45, 149–50; English character in, 22; homogeneity of, 183; language of, 198; "low" vs. "high" culture in, 7, 124, 159; novel's form and imperial themes under, x–xi, xii, 6, 12, 15, 21, 23–26, 30, 149–82, 202–4

monkeys (chimpanzees), 114, 115, 182; black subjects analogized to, 110, 113; in British Empire Exhibition, 161; in Carter's *Nights at the Circus*, 195, 202, 204; in circuses, 90, 227n33; on English estates, 214; at fairs, 49; royal connections with, 2, 54

Monod, Sylvére, 96

More Beasts for Worse Children (Belloc), 11

Morning Post (London), 56

Morrell, Ottoline, 124

"Mr. Bennett and Mrs. Brown" (Woolf), 30, 124, 149, 151, 159–60, 166, 171, 176, 181

"Mr. Booley's View of the Last Lord Mayor's Show" (Dickens), 92, 94–95, 107, 113

Mrs. Brown at the International Exhibition and South Kensington (Sketchley), 32–35, 49, 57, 65, 71

Mrs. Brown on Jumbo (Sketchley), 80

Mrs. Brown on the Prince's Visit to India (Sketchley), 34, 62, 65

Mrs. Dalloway (Woolf), 30, 149, 151, 152, 176–78

The Mystery of Edwin Drood (Dickens), 91–92, 116

Nairn, Tom, 14

Napoleonic Wars, 19

the national, xii–xiii, 43–45, 54, 64, 100. *See also* England; Englishness

The Nation and the Athenaeum, 159, 160, 162, 164, 175

natural history, 10–11, 36, 58–59; zoo's emphasis on, 52–55. *See also* collections and collecting; evolution

naturalism: in art, 84, 86, 87; in menageries, 28; in novels, 82

"Nature" (Woolf on), 169–71, 174, 175

Nelson, Horatio, 19

Nelson's Column (Trafalgar Square, London), 19

"The New Empire Within Britain" (Rushdie), 188

Newham (England). *See* London

New York Times, 78–79

Nicaragua, 187

Nights at the Circus (Carter), 31, 194–205

Nightwood (Barnes), 182
Noah's ark, 34, 184, 207–11, 216. *See also* Frozen Ark project
"The Noble Savage" (Dickens), 112
nostalgia, xi; in English novels in twentieth century, x, 16, 18, 31, 185, 191–94, 205–6; zoo and theme parks' evocation of, 184–85, 214, 215
"Notes on the English Character" (Forster), 20, 22, 219n4
novel (English): as curiosity of totality, 216; as English form of narrative, x, xi, 23; fragmentation of discourse in, since modernist era, 24–25, 30, 152–58, 171, 176, 181, 190–205; as "high" culture, 7; menagerie as mediating relationship of, to Englishness, x, xii–xiii, 4, 7, 20, 26, 29, 118–48; menageries as homologous to, x, 27–29, 81, 212, 217; as part of display culture, 10–11, 25, 29; as part of traveling culture, 206; postimperial, 24, 182–211, 215–17; study of, as begun in India, 5; as totalizing instrument, x–xii, 5–6, 12, 27–29, 115–17, 130–31, 159–60, 166, 168, 172, 175, 206, 216; treatment of empire and exotic animals in, ix, xi, 2, 4–7, 9–11, 15–21. *See also* realism; *specific novels and novelists*
Nunokawa, Jeff, 230n118
"Nurse Lugton's Curtain" (Woolf), 236n31
Nussbaum, Martha, 230n97

Oak, George, 134
ocelots, 54
Old Wives' Tale (Bennett), 6, 30, 119, 121–23, 125, 127–32, 135–36, 140–47, 149–50
Oliver Twist (Dickens), 230n103
opossums, 49
Orientalism: advent of modern, 27; in Carter's *Nights at the Circus*, 198; character associated with, 22, 46–47, 55, 138–39; in circuses, 51, 66–67; of composite drawings, 72–76, *73–76*; in menageries, 69; vs. realism, 168; in theaters, 51, 68. *See also* aliens (foreigners); China; exotic; India
Orlando (Woolf), 170
Orwell, George, 12, 20, 22–23, 80–81, 137, 153, 189
Oscar, William, 134
ostriches, 49
"otherness," xii. *See* aliens (foreigners); exotic (alien)
Our Mutual Friend (Dickens), 91, 229n82
Our Women (Bennett), 159
Out of Place (Baucom), xiii
oxen, 161

Pageant of Empire (at British Empire Exhibition), 57–58, 161, 170–71, 177, 186
pageant plays, 26, 54, 56–58, 177, 220n36. *See also* tableaus
pageants (imperial), 9, 47–48, 54, 56. *See also* Durbars; Pageant of Empire; pageant plays; processions
Palmatier, Robert A., 72
panopticon, 196–98
Paris Exhibitions, 34, 40
Parks, Fanny, 72, *75*
A Passage to India (Forster), 9, 125
Pateman, Matthew, 208
Paxman, Jeremy, 14, 19
peacocks, 193, 204
peepshow, 190–92
Pepys, Samuel, 50
Pete White's Suitcase Circus, 185
Phenomenology of Spirit (Hegel), 27
Phillips, Kathy J., 151
Pickwick Papers (Dickens), 230n103
Pictorial Times, 43, 45
the picturesque, 81; at the British

Empire Exhibition, 165; vs. carnivalesque, 33–35; defined, 60; and exotic animals' unpredictability, 65–66, 71; vs. sublime, 61; and totality, xii, 29, 40–42, 43, 60–61, 72–76, 184
Pidcock, Gilbert, 50–51
pigs, 161, 195. *See also* boars
platypuses, 57
Plotnitsky, Arkady, 217
political economy: in Dickens's *Hard Times*, 102, 103–11, 115, 116
Polito, S., 50
Porter, Bernard, 14
Portland Gallery (London), 55
Portrait of Mr. Van Amburgh as He Appeared with His Animals at the London Theatre (Landseer), 32, 41, 42
postmodernist era, xii, 24, 185–211, 215–17
Price, Uvedale, 61
Prinsep, Val C., 223n27
print culture, 7, 10–12, 45, 65–66, 77. *See also* novel
processions: in Bennett's *Clayhanger*, 138; at British Empire Exhibition, 57–58, 161, *162*, 170–71, 177, 186; by circuses, 4, 43, 61; in Dickens's *Mystery of Edwin Drood*, 91, 102; of Elizabeth II's Golden Jubilee in London, 1–2, *2*, 4, 13–15, 17, 18, 26–27, 185; of exotic animals in London, 9–10, 55, 158, 161, 186; of recently purchased elephants being led to their English destinations, 92–95. *See also* Durbars; pageants
provincialism: in Bennett's work, 118–31, 136, 139–48. *See also* England: provinces of, as synecdoche for
Punch, 2, *3*, 4, *8*, 9, 66, 67, 96; and the British Empire Exhibition, 159, 167–69, 171
pyramids (Egypt), 105

Raffles, Stamford, 52, 53
Raiders of the Lost Ark (film), 216
Raj revivalism, 205
Ranger, Terence, 36, 209, 210
realism: in Bennett's works, 29, 30, 121–23, 127, 130, 140, 145–47, 149, 159–60, 166, 168, 172, 173, 175, 176; of British Empire Exhibition, 160–75; in Dickens's work, 83, 109, 115, 117; in *Life of Pi*, 16; as suppressing excess, 23; and totality, xi, 6, 12, 127; Woolf's challenges to, 30, 149–51, 158–60, 166–75
Reed, Stanley, 66
Regent (Bennett), 147
Regent's Park Zoological Gardens (London), 90, 92, 150, 161, 163, 182; Darwin on, 118; dead elephants at, 77–80; humans exhibited in, 212–13, *213*, 214, 217; as picturesque, 60; rise of, 9, 52–55
Renan, Ernest, xiii
reserved nature (of English character), 4, 20, 22, 46–48, 79, 82, 120–21, 130, 144, 219n4
"restricted economies": Bataille on, xi–xii, 24–25, 116; British Empire Exhibition as example of, 164, 166, 170, 171
rhinos, 214
Rhodes, Cecil, 107
Riceyman Steps (Bennett), 121, 149
Rigby, Elizabeth, 88
ring imagery. *See* circle imagery; circuses
Rintoul, Robert Stephen, 88
Ritvo, Harriet, 10, 46, 51, 52, 70
Robbins, Bruce, 129
Robinson, H. P., 60
Robinson, Sally, 196–97
Rolling Stones (musical group), 189
Romanticism, 27, 194
A Room of One's Own (Woolf), 124
Rose, George. *See* Sketchley, Arthur
Le Rouge et le Noir (Stendhal), 130

Royal Academy (London), 32
Royal Covent Garden Theatre, 51
Royal Menagerie, Exeter 'Change. *See* Exeter 'Change Menagerie
Royal Zoological Gardens (Surrey). *See* Surrey Zoological Gardens
Runga-Rung elephant. *See* elephants: mechanical
The Rush-Bearing (Hunt), 233n55
Rushdie, Salman, 7, 12, 18, 24, 30, 204, 205, 208, 210; exhibiting of, 185–89, 194; *Midnight's Children*, 31, 190–94, 197
Russian Imperial Circus, 199–201
Russo, Mary, 197

Sadleir, Michael, 159
Said, Edward, xii
St. Catherine's Docks, 54
St. Petersburg (Russia), 195
Salisbury, Lord, 46–47, 49
Sandburg, Carl, 178
Sanger, George, 200, 210, 223n42. *See also* Sanger's Circus
Sanger's Circus, 4, 43, 51, 184–85, 195
Sarawak, 161
Sartre, Jean Paul, 184, 211
The Satanic Verses (Rushdie), 190
savagery. *See* brutality
savages: Dickens on, 112–13, 115; Zulus depicted as, 134, 135. *See also* aliens (foreigners); black subjects
Saville House (London), 55
Saxe, John Godfrey, 68–72
Schlicke, Paul, 97–98, 108, 113, 115, 230n103
Scotland, 14–15, 62
"Scotland Yard" (Dickens), 113–14
Scotsman, 54
Scott, George Gilbert, 63
"The Second Coming" (Yeats), 200
Seeley, J. R.: on empire, 5, 12, 20, 23, 27, 48, 62, 122; on English construction of India, 64
"see the elephant" (phrase), 71–72

separation. *See* distance
serpents, 62; in British Empire Exhibition, 161; in Carter's *Nights at the Circus*, 201; in Dickens's *Hard Times*, 103, 104, 111–12, 114, 115. *See also* boa-constrictors
sexuality. *See* marriage
"Shooting an Elephant" (Orwell), 80, 137
Showalter, Elaine, 15
A Shrinking Island (Esty), xiii
Siberia, 195, 197, 202–4
Sikh War, 38
Simulacra and Simulation (Baudrillard), 210
Singapore, 50, 52
A Sinking Island (Kenner), 18
Sketches by Boz (Dickens), 114
Sketchley, Arthur: Mrs. Brown novels of, 32–35, 49, 57, 62, 65, 71, 80
slavery, 110, 134, 178. *See also* black subjects
Sloane, Hans, 36
Small Island (Levy), 215–16
solidity. *See* totality
"Some Particulars Concerning a Lion" (Dickens), 111
South Africa, 25, 50, 214
Southport (England), 54
spectators: distance between spectacle and, 66, 122, 130, 133–34, 161, 165, 169, 172–73. *See also specific spectators and spectacles*
Stallybrass, Peter, 7, 34, 35, 47, 234n93; on transgression, 29, 65
Stein, Richard L., 41, 63
Stendhal, 130
Stephen, James, 178
Stoddart, Helen, 101, 113, 241n54
Stoke-on-Trent (England), 121
Sturt, George, 130
the sublime, 61, 69, 71–72
Sunday Times (London), 209
Surrey Zoological Gardens, 2, 9, 53–55, 60, 65, 113

"The Symbol" (Woolf), 154–56
symbols, 38–39, 68, 71; in Dickens's *Hard Times*, 101-2; exotic animals as, for conquered peoples, 39–40, 70–71, 80, 102–3, 136–37, 147; lion as, of England, 32, 43, 45, 62, 68; Woolf's use of, 151. *See also* economy: symbolic

tableaus, 60–62, 92, 134. *See also* pageants; picturesque
Thackeray, William Makepeace, 6, 12, 82–90; Bennett on, 130, 132, 136; James on, 21; *Vanity Fair*, 30, 83–90, 94, 101, 115, 190
theaters: exotic animals in, 32, 41, *42*, 51, 68, 77, 90, 91
Three Guineas (Woolf), 151
Thumb, Tom, 78
"Thunder at Wembley" (Woolf), 30, 151, 158–60, 166–77, 188
tigers: in Carter's *Nights at the Circus*, 195, 202; India as home of, 62, 68, 168; in *Life of Pi*, 16, 26; in menageries, 43, 90, 91, 135; as representing India, 153, 193, 204; in Thackeray's *Vanity Fair*, 84, 87, 88; in the wild, 59, 68; in Woolf's works, 235n12
Tillier, Louis, 233n64
Tillotson, Kathleen, 100
Times (London), 1, 13, 17, 56
Times Literary Supplement (*TLS*), 15–16
totality (completeness; holism; solidity; whole): British empire conceived as, ix, xii, xiii, 5–6, 12–14, 17, 21, 23, 25, 27–29, 38–49, 55, 59–76, 81–83, 123, 151, 158–66, 175, 178–79, 184, 216; and British Empire's fragmentation, 143–45, 150–58, 160, 170–71, 173–75, 177–81, 188–96; circuses' aims regarding, 197–98, 205; conservation as, 214, 215; elephants as representing, 33, 68–76, 88–90, 123, 141; English writers' depiction of breakdown of, xi, 24–25, 123, 143–81, 188–89, 194–205, 215–17, 220n36; English writers' depiction of imperial, in nineteenth century, x, xi, 82–118; English writers' nostalgia for, in late twentieth century, x, xi, 183–94, 205–6; evolution as, 118; global, and English difference, 53; as homogeneity, 35, 183, 194, 205; menagerie's efforts at, 27–29, 36–49, 216; novel as instrument of, x–xii, 5–6, 12, 25–29, 115–17, 130–31, 159–60, 166, 168, 172, 175, 206, 216; and the picturesque, xii, 29, 40–42, 43, 60–61, 72–76, 184; and realism, xi, 6, 12, 127; shift in attitudes toward, xii, 5–6, 20–21, 24–25, 29–31, 212, 216–17. *See also* economy; fragmentation
Tower Menagerie (London), 36, 49, 50, 52, 90, 223n43
trade, 68; British Empire Exhibition's promotion of, 163, 164, 168; in elephants, 91–92, 95
traveling culture, 220n18; actual, in England, 9, 72; allegory in, 42, 43; in Bennett's *Old Wives' Tale*, 121–22, 127–31, 141–43, 146, 147; circuses as part of, 9, 43, *44*, 45, 51, 78, 184, 226n1; as easy in twentieth century, 153, 184; imaginative, 9–10, 23, 34, 214, 219n10, 227n25; menagerie's involvement in, 4, 9, 37–38, 43, *44*, 45, *45*, 50–51, 54, 65, 134, 135, 184; of modernist writers, 147; novels as part of, 206. *See also* circuses; globalization; menageries; processions; trade
Trotter, David, 125
twentieth-century novels. *See* Edwardian era; Georgian era; modernist era; postmodernist era
Tyrwhitt-Drake, Garrard, 66, 226n1, 228n43

U2 (musical group), 185–90, 194
Ulysses (Joyce), xi, 23, 149, 173–74, 182, 199, 222n70
United Kingdom, 14–15, 20, 206
United States, 62, 63, 92; Bennett as visitor to, 124; elephants in, 214; English circuses owned by, 183, 203; Jumbo purchased for circus in, 78–80; novels from, 15, 206

Van Amburgh, Isaac, 32, 33, 35, 38, 41, *41*, 91, 113; Dickens as, 83, 95, 117
Vanity Fair (Thackeray), 30, 83–90, 94, 101, 115, 190
"verandah" trope, 174–76, 179, 180
Victoria (queen of England), 41, 53, 170; and Albert Memorial, 18; coronation fair of, 43; Diamond Jubilee of, 126; as Empress of India, 9, 19, 46, 66, 78–79; and exotic animals, 2, 3, 4, 32–34, 54, *67*, 78–80, 184
Victorian era, 32–49; imperial totality under, 32–81, 170, 178–79; nostalgia for, 18–19, 184–85, 205–6; novel's form and imperial themes under, x–xii, 2, 12, 16–17, 21, 23, 29–30, 82–148. *See also* British Empire; collections and collecting; natural history; realism
The Village in the Jungle (L. Woolf), 235n12
violence. *See* brutality; fragmentation
Viswanathan, Gauri, 5
Vorticists, 198, 204
The Voyage Out (Woolf), 235n12

Wain, John, 124
wakes festivals, 50, 65, 233n51; Bennett on, 119, 128–29, 131–47, 178
Wales, 14–15
wallabies, 57, 214

War (U2 recording), 188
Ward, John, 133, 233n51
Ward, Rowland, 58–59, 62, 76, 198
Warrillow, Ernest, 131
The Waste Land (Eliot), 149
Waugh, Evelyn, 205
The Waves (Woolf), 30, 150, 151, 176, 177–80, 198–99
Weaver, Lawrence, 237n64
Wells, H. G., 119, 231n1
Wembley Stadium: exhibiting of Rushdie at, 185–89, 194. *See also* British Empire Exhibition
West, Rebecca, 9–10, 232n37
West Midlands Safari Park (England), 215
Westminster Bridge. *See* Astley's Circus
WGTW Society, 167
"What Is a Nation?" (Renan), xiii
White, Allon, 7, 34, 35, 47, 234n93; on transgression, 29, 65
White, Pete, 185
"white history," 195, 203–5, 211
whole. *See* totality
Wiener, Martin, 46
William of Malmesbury, 223n32
Williams, Raymond, 102, 150
Windsor Castle: circus visits to, 43, *44*, 45, 78, 184; zoological displays in, 4, 43, *44*
Winkiel, Laura, 240n3
Winterson, Jeanette, 216
"The Wise Elephants of the East" (Astley's circus performance), 96, 101, 106
Wodehouse, P. G., 167
Woman (magazine), 125–26
Wombwell, George, 50–51, 77, 135, 210
Wombwell's Menagerie: in Bennett's *Old Wives' Tale*, 123, 129, 131–36, 140–45, 147; Dickens's visit to, 90, 102; elephants in, 68, 71, 76, 77, 129, 131–36; in Gaskell's *Cranford*,

88–90, 108, 112; picturesque exhibits of, 60; as traveling exhibit in England, 4, 9, 37–38, 43, *44*, 45, *45*, 50–51, 54, 65, 134, 135, 184

Wood, James, 16

Woolf, Leonard, 125, 178, 235n12

Woolf, Virginia, 12, 147, 149–82, 195, 201, 221n36, 222n70; *Between the Acts*, 152, 177, 181, 221n36; "Character in Fiction," 30, 149, 151, 152, 159, 160, 169, 171–73, 176; *Diary of Virginia Woolf*, 167; on exotic animals, 7, 235n12; "Mr. Bennett and Mrs. Brown," 30, 124, 149, 151, 159–60, 166, 171, 176, 181; *Mrs. Dalloway*, 30, 149, 151, 152, 176–78; "Nurse Lugton's Curtain," 236n31; *Orlando*, 170; *A Room of One's Own*, 124; "Symbol," 154–56; *Three Guineas*, 151; "Thunder at Wembley," 30, 151, 158–60, 166–77, 188; *Voyage Out*, 235n12; *The Waves*, 30, 150, 151, 176, 177–80, 198–99; *The Years*, 30, 151, 152–58, 177, 179, 181, 184

"world exhibition," 40

The Years (Woolf), 30, 151, 152–58, 177, 179, 181, 184

Yeats, W. B., 200–204

zebras, 56, 214

Zola, Émile, 130

"zoogeography," xi, xii

The Zoological Cabinet; or Menagerie of Living Characters, 11–12

zoological exotica. *See* exotic animals

Zoological Society (London), 52–53, 78, 90, 118

Zooropa tour (U2), 186, 188, 189

zoos: elephants as central symbol of, 68; imperial connections to, xiii, 7, 9–12, 46, 186; in *Life of Pi*, 16; metaphors of England as, 209; original purposes of, 52–55; as part of display culture, ix, 7, 10–12, 23, 32–33, 52–53; shifts in purpose and practices of, 30–31, 54, 183–84, 212–16; spread of, 54. *See also* exotic animals; menageries; spectators; *specific zoos*

Zoo Tycoon 2 (game), 214

Zulus, 134, 135

www.ingramcontent.com/pod-product-compliance
Lightning Source LLC
Chambersburg PA
CBHW020943230426
43666CB00005B/144